Creating Interactive Websites *with* PHP *and* Web Services

Creating Interactive Websites *with* PHP *and* Web Services

Eric Rosebrock

SYBEX

San Francisco · London

Associate Publisher: Joel Fugazzotto
Acquisitions Editor: Tom Cirtin
Developmental Editor: Brianne Agatep
Production Editor: Susan Berge
Technical Editor: Grant K. Rauscher
Copyeditor: Kim Wimpsett
Compositor/Graphic Illustrator: Happenstance Type-O-Rama
Proofreaders: Emily Hsuan, Laurie O'Connell, Nancy Riddiough
Indexer: Lynnzee Elze
Cover Designer: Caryl Gorska, Gorska Design
Cover Photographer: Jon Morgan, Photo Japan

Library of Congress Card Number: 2003114161

ISBN: 0-7821-4279-6

Manufactured in the United States of America

10 9 8 7 6 5 4 3 2 1

This book is dedicated in memory of my father who passed away shortly before I completed the last chapters of my writing. My father was a hard-working, dedicated man who believed in God, family, friends, and his country. He raised me well and taught me that the important things in life are not the things we want, but the true happiness of everyone you affect in your own special way. I will always miss him, and I will always carry with me the memories we had together. I dedicate this book in memory of John Dennis Rosebrock, my father, and to Marilyn Rosebrock, my mother, to whom I wish strength, courage, and happiness along her path.

Acknowledgments

I want to acknowledge the people who came together and helped me write this book. Without them, it would not have been possible. I want to thank Dan Del Pino, Bradley Beard, Tim McKinzey, Cody William Brocious, Brian Swan, George Derek Ford, Rick Blundell, Joel Bondorowsky, Eric Gach, Alex Beauclair, Jeraimee Hughes, and my friends known as the *Blue Tails* for all of their encouragement.

I also want to thank all of the staff at Sybex involved with this book. Every person I have worked with at Sybex has shown me outstanding courtesy, commitment, and professionalism that is unparalleled by any other company in the industry.

The next group of people I want to acknowledge is the large community of supporters at `www.phpfreaks.com`. If it were not for them, this book would not have been written. I gathered their input and created a book that they all wanted. I thank them for their ongoing support, and I look forward to working with them.

Finally, and most important, I would like to thank my wife and kids who put up with me as I pulled my hair out every step of the way during the writing of my first book. They were supportive, forgiving me for the sacrifices I had to make, and they gave me the space I needed to accomplish this major task. Thanks to Tracy, Summer, and Gage for loving me and providing support when I needed it the most.

Contents at a Glance

Contents

Introduction

If you are a webmaster, web developer, or just a web junky, you may have noticed the rapidly growing scripting language known as PHP. It's no joke; PHP is becoming the top web developing language of choice, and many webmasters are dropping their old scripting languages to pick up PHP. The reasoning is simple: PHP was written with ease of use in mind, but at the same time, the developers did not sacrifice functionality.

By using PHP in your website, you will have a large realm of options with which to work. You can store information in databases, write files on the fly, manage content, alter the website's appearance, process credit cards, interact with remote servers, and do so much more. The features and capabilities with PHP are endless!

If the *PHP fairy* gave me one wish a year ago, I would have asked for a book that was written by an author who takes the time to explain every step of the learning process instead of listing lines of code with no explanation. I would have asked for a book in which the author did not assume the reader was an experienced developer. With those needs in mind and the practical input and requests from a community of more than 10,000 PHP developers, I have written the book that eluded me a year ago.

This book helps you enhance your website using PHP. You will learn about the language—from the basics to some of the more intermediate levels of web design. This book is packed with many useful code examples and routines that took more than a year to compile into my bag of tricks.

You will also learn about the powerful database server known as MySQL. Using PHP, you will learn how to manage your MySQL databases and information on the fly without using command line tools. Additionally, you will learn the methodology that I have used to successfully plan and implement websites on the Internet.

If you are interested in learning PHP, have already dabbled with it, or would like to have a reference library of practical code examples with explanations handy, this book is for you.

Conventions Used in This Book

This book uses certain typographic styles to help you quickly identify important information and to avoid confusion over the meaning of words such as onscreen prompts:

- *Italicized text* indicates technical terms that are introduced for the first time in a chapter. (Italics are also used for emphasis.)

- A `monospaced` font indicates the contents of configuration files, messages displayed at a text-mode Linux shell prompt, filenames, and Internet addresses.

- *`Italicized monospaced text`* indicates a variable—information that differs from one system or command run to another, such as the name of a client computer or a process ID number.

- **`Bold monospaced text`** is information you need to type into the computer, usually at a Linux shell prompt. This text can also be italicized to indicate that you should substitute an appropriate value for your system.

In addition to these text conventions, which can apply to individual words or entire paragraphs, a few conventions are used to highlight segments of text.

NOTE   A Note indicates information that's useful or interesting but that's somewhat peripheral to the main discussion. A Note might be relevant to a small number of networks, for instance, or refer to an outdated feature.

TIP   A Tip provides information that can save you time or frustration and that may not be entirely obvious. A Tip might describe how to get around a limitation or how to use a feature to perform an unusual task.

WARNING   Warnings describe potential pitfalls or dangers. If you fail to heed a Warning, you may end up spending a lot of time recovering from a bug or even restoring your entire system from scratch.

Help Us Help You

The goal of this book is to help you learn and understand PHP. Additionally, this book is widely supported by the community at www.phpfreaks.com. If you have any trouble or need assistance, please feel free to stop by; the community there will be glad to help.

Furthermore, please stay up-to-date! PHP is a rapidly evolving language. If you find that information in this book has changed and will no longer work, you can submit errata reports at the Sybex website: www.sybex.com. To easily find the errata for this book, search for *4279*.

Additionally, the source codes for this book will be available on the book's page at the Sybex website. On the book's web page, you will find a download section for the code.

CHAPTER 1

Introducing PHP

P HP, which stands for *PHP: Hypertext Processor*, is a widely used, general-purpose scripting language that is especially suited for Web development and can be embedded into Hypertext Markup Language (HTML). PHP is rapidly spreading through the Internet and is soon to be the leading development language on the Internet. It gives you the ability to interact with users on your website similarly to what you could do on a website using Perl (CGI) and Active Server Pages (ASP).

Because PHP is an *open-source* project (which means that the source code is available to developers to enhance and expand its functionality and features), the possibilities are limitless. Virtually anyone can contribute to the expansion of the project, unlike commercial products with source code that is updated only by the people who own it. With PHP, you can create membership systems, process credit card transactions, view system statistics, store data in databases, and much, much more. Throughout this book, I cover what you need to know to build your own dynamic website with PHP.

In this chapter, you'll learn all about the history of PHP and how to start using it.

Getting a History Lesson in PHP

In 1994, Rasmus Lerdorf set out on a project called *Personal Homepage Tools* for tracking access to his online resume. He wrote Personal Homepage Tools in C with a small part of it utilizing Perl. As Personal Homepage Tools grew in popularity and more functionality was needed of it, Rasmus rewrote Personal Homepage Tools utilizing a much larger C implementation that could communicate to databases, which in turn allowed a more dynamic capability. Eventually, Rasmus released a version called *Personal Home Page Forms Interpreter* (PHP/FI).

Eventually, Rasmus decided to release the source code of PHP/FI so everybody could use it, expand upon it, and fix bugs in it. Even though the project was in the early stages—much more limited than Perl and somewhat inconsistent—PHP/FI was growing in popularity quite rapidly. By 1997, PHP/FI 2.0, the second version, was known to have several thousand users around the world. Some 50,000 domains were reported to have PHP/FI installed, which accounted for one percent of the domains on the Internet. Even though there were several contributions to the project, Rasmus continued to carry the weight and led PHP to the next phase. Shortly after he officially released PHP/FI 2.0 in November of 1997, the initial stages of the popular PHP 3.0 were underway.

PHP 3.0 was the first version of the project that resembles the PHP you see on the Internet today. Andi Gutmans and Zeev Suraski decided to rewrite the PHP/FI parser after they found it did not have enough functionality and power for their requirements. Andi, Rasmus, and Zeev teamed up to continue the project with a much stronger work force than previous versions.

PHP 3.0 was a significant phase in the evolution of this project. It was released under the new name of *PHP*, which is a recursive acronym for *PHP: Hypertext Processor*. The new name was derived from a desire to remove the implications of limited personal use from the old name, *Personal Home Page Tools*. Other significances of this release were the introduction of object-oriented programming (OOP) and a much more powerful and consistent language syntax.

PHP 3.0 was officially released in June 1998 after nine months of public beta testing. By the winter of 1998, PHP was installed on approximately 10 percent of the web servers on the Internet.

The next major release of PHP was version 4.0. In May 2000, the development team officially released 4.0 and introduced more significant changes to the core of PHP. For example, the Zend engine, a complete rewrite of the version 3 core, was implemented as the new PHP engine. Zend (the name composed of the developers' first names, Zeev and Andi) and PHP 4.0 implemented support for many more web servers, HTTP sessions, output buffering, enhanced security, and a wide range of new language constructs.

Currently, PHP is being used by hundreds of thousands of developers and is estimated to be installed on several million web servers, which accounts for more than 30 percent of the web servers on the Internet. At the time of writing this book, PHP has just entered the 4.3.*x* version.

If you are interested in more accurate and up-to-date statistics for how many domains are using PHP, you can visit these links:

PHP Usage Report	`www.php.net/usage.php`
SecuritySpace's Web Survey	`www.securityspace.com/s_survey`
Programming Community Index	`www.tiobe.com/tpci.htm`

Understanding the Requirements for PHP

Depending on the intentions and design of your scripts, PHP can run on virtually any hardware because of its compact design and system resource requirements. If you are installing on a Unix-based system, then basic Unix skills, including knowledge of make, to build installation binaries and a web server are required. If you are installing on Windows-based systems, administrator privileges and a web server are required.

Operating System Support

You can install PHP on HP-UX, Linux, MacOS, OpenBSD, Solaris, Unix, and Windows operating systems. Complete operating system installation instructions are available in the PHP manual on the PHP website located at `www.php.net`.

Web Server Support

You can install PHP on a wide range of web servers including Apache, Netscape, iPlanet, Caudium, fhttpd, OmniHTTPd, Oreilly Website Pro, Sambar, and Xitami. PHP can also be custom built for other web servers if needed.

Exploring PHP-Related Software

PHP supports a wide range of other software. There are many key elements to any successful PHP-driven website; the following are the ones I think are the most important:

Apache web server   Apache is the most widely used web server on the Internet today. PHP and Apache integrate smoothly to provide you with a free, powerful, and easy-to-use combination to run your website reliably. Apache is supported by a wide range of operating systems including Unix/Linux and Windows. Approximately 12MB of disk space is required to install the Apache web server. You can learn more about the Apache web server at `httpd.apache.org`.

MySQL database server   Combined with PHP, MySQL gives you the ability to store, edit, delete, and format information using a database with the PHP MySQL functions. You can download a free copy of the MySQL database server at `www.mysql.org`.

MySQL Database Management Tools

There are many great tools for managing your MySQL databases. Here are a few I use every day:

phpMyAdmin   phpMyAdmin is a free complete set of PHP scripts you can download from the project's website and install on your web server to manage virtually every aspect of your MySQL server. With phpMyAdmin, you can do the following:

- Create databases, tables, and users
- Search, browse, insert, and delete data
- Export and import data files
- View MySQL usage statistics
- Reload/flush your MySQL server

You can download phpMyAdmin for free at `www.phpmyadmin.net`.

SQLyog   SQLyog is a Windows-based application that allows full control over your MySQL server. Its features are similar to phpMyAdmin, except you access it as an application rather than through your web browser. You can download a trial version at `www.webyog.com/sqlyog/download.html`.

PHP Editors

More than a handful of editors can handle PHP editing. PHP is a text-based scripting language that does not require any special compiling or building to create a script. You may use an editor as basic as Notepad (for Windows) or VI (for Linux), or you may use advanced text editors such as UltraEdit-32 or jEdit. Let's discuss a few of those editors now:

Notepad   Notepad is as simple as it gets and comes preinstalled on Windows operating systems. I do not recommend editing your PHP scripts with Notepad because it does not come with any special features to make your code easier to understand.

UltraEdit-32   UltraEdit-32 is an advanced text editor, which includes PHP and HTML syntax highlighting. With UtraEdit-32, you have the ability to create templates to use over and over again, the ability to perform advanced search and replace functions, and the ability to search and replace criteria on entire directories at the same time. The latter is very useful! User contributed add-ons are available. A trial version of UltraEdit-32 is available at www.ultraedit.com.

jEdit   jEdit is an advanced text editor. It includes PHP and HTML syntax highlighting. It has the ability to "skin" or create custom themes for the editor. Because jEdit is Java based, you must have Java Runtime Environment (JRE) installed. Another useful feature of jEdit is that it gives you the ability to collapse function brackets to condense the view of your code in the editor. User contributed add-ons are available, and jEdit itself is free software. See www.jedit.org for more information.

Dreamweaver MX   Dreamweaver MX is an advanced HTML WYSIWYG (What-You-See-Is-What-You-Get) editor and has the ability to generate record set MySQL queries. Dreamweaver MX supports various database formats. It is commercial software and is quite expensive, around $399. You can get more information at www.macromedia.com.

There are many editors out there, and I have given you some information about the editors I have used. The bottom line is if you can type directly into the PHP script as if it were a text document, then your editing application is serving its purpose. The syntax highlighting, function collapsing, templates, and so on are just bonuses. Find something you feel comfortable using and stick with it.

Once you have found a good editor, you are ready to begin coding. Let's begin your first PHP script.

Working with PHP

To begin working with PHP, you'll need to ensure you have a web server installed and configured to use PHP. The PHP manual has complete installation instructions to set up PHP for the most popular web servers available.

For developmental purposes, I prefer to install Apache web server and PHP on either Linux or Windows, depending on where I am developing. At home, I use a dedicated Linux server that is similar to the production environment I use. This method ensures maximum compatibility between the development server and the production server and dramatically reduces headaches when it is time to push a project onto the live production server. If I am traveling, I configure Apache with PHP on a laptop and use Windows. Either way, if you use good developing habits, you should not have any issues when going live with your project.

Writing Your First PHP Script

The first script you will work with shows you how to identify if PHP is installed properly on your system. This is an important script to use because it tells you virtually everything about your PHP installation and your web server.

In your web server's document root (where the web page files are stored for access to the public), create a new file and call it info.php. Next, open the file with your editor of choice and type the following:

```php
<?php
phpinfo();
?>
```

Next, save the file and open it in your web browser from your web server—for example, http://localhost/info.php. You should see a web page like that shown in Figure 1.1.

FIGURE 1.1:
phpinfo script

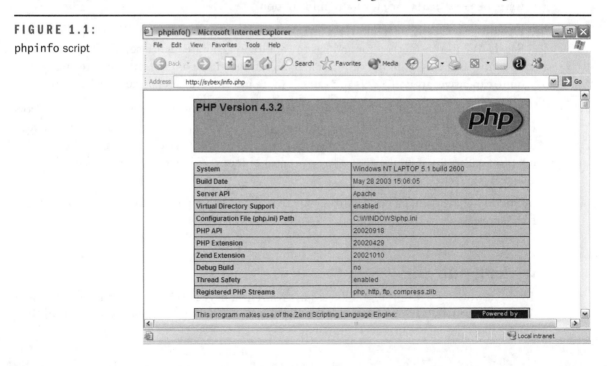

NOTE   If you are prompted to download a file attachment, or you see your code exactly as it is in the script when you access this script in your web browser, then you do not have your Apache web server configured properly. You should edit your `httpd.conf` file to add **AddType application/x-httpd-php .php**. Please check the PHP documentation located in your PHP directory regarding the installation of PHP on Apache web server. You will find complete instructions on configuring your `httpd.conf` file for using Apache with PHP.

If you see the PHP information page similar to Figure 1.1, then congratulations to you! You have created your first useful PHP script! Don't get too exited, the `phpinfo` function is a freebie; the formatting of your next PHP script is up to you!

Let's take a moment to break down those three lines of code you just used. This will help you understand the structure of a PHP script a little more. The first line is considered the *open tag*:

```
<?php
```

This simply starts processing any subsequent code through the PHP engine. Otherwise, the PHP engine is not processing the code, and the web server is simply transmitting the text. From the open tag, everything until the close tag will be processed by PHP.

NOTE   If you edit your `php.ini` settings file and change `short_open_tags` to the On value, you can eliminate the longer `<?php` and just use `<?` instead.

On the second line of this code, you used a PHP function. PHP has a large supply of functions, quite a few of which are covered in this book. This particular function is called `phpinfo` and does just that—it gives you the PHP info:

```
phpinfo();
```

You may also notice that you use parentheses () after the function name. This allows you to pass arguments to the function. To determine which arguments you may pass to this function, you should look the function up in the PHP documentation. Don't worry; I am going to cover PHP functions later in this chapter.

One more thing to note about the second line of code: You may notice that the last thing on the line is a semicolon. This terminates the line and tells the PHP engine that there is no further code to the line, and the engine may go to the next line to process the code. If you do not terminate the line, PHP will give you a nasty error, and your script will exit without giving you the output you originally intended.

Let's stop the PHP engine from processing any further code by adding the close tag:

```
?>
```

From this point on, the PHP engine will not process anything further in the script as PHP code until it reaches another open tag. This is extremely useful for you because you can create an HTML outline and simply insert the PHP code when you need it into the HTML. You will see some examples of this shortly.

Now that you have seen a basic PHP script, let's discuss the next important key element to PHP, working with strings and variables.

Working with Strings and Variables

When developing your PHP code, you will be dealing with strings and variables every day. They partially make up the PHP scripts you write.

A *string* is a group of characters that make up code. In PHP, a character is the same as a byte. There are 256 different characters available in PHP. Do not be fooled: There is no limit on how long a string can be. You can have a string that is five characters long or 5,000 characters long. There are no major performance concerns for really long strings.

A *variable* is a simple identifier for strings and other data. In PHP, a variable is represented by a dollar sign ($), followed by the variable name. A simple example is $MyVariable. Without strings and variables, the PHP script is an empty shell.

Building Strings

There are a few different methods for building a string; you may decide you like to use single quotes, or you may determine that double quotes are better for you. Let's look at the differences.

Using Single-Quoted Strings

A single-quoted string uses single quotes to contain the contents. They will appear like this in your code:

```
echo 'This is an example of a single-quoted string';
```

There are major advantages of using single-quoted strings; some of them may be the ability to simply paste HTML into a string without escaping each double quote in the HTML tags. (I go into more depth on this in the "Using Double-Quoted Strings" section.) A simple way to explain a single-quoted string is that you get exactly what you type into a single quoted string, nothing more.

NOTE   You complete a string by issuing a closing single quote and terminate the line with a semicolon.

Escaping Single-Quoted Strings

If you are using a character such as the single quote or apostrophe (') character, you need to escape that character by a backslash (\) in the string itself; otherwise, PHP will exit the script and give you a Parse Error because it will think you have already closed the string where you used your apostrophe. Everything after that code will cause PHP to error because it is not valid PHP code.

For example, the following example will cause PHP to exit because everything after the apostrophe in I'm will be treated as code:

```
echo 'Hi, I'm using PHP!';
```

A simple way to fix this problem when using single-quoted strings is to use a backslash (\) to escape the apostrophe from terminating the string. Here is an example:

```
echo 'Hi, I\'m using PHP!';
```

Do not be fooled—you do not have to escape a double quote in a single-quoted string. Here is an example of what I am talking about:

```
echo 'He said, "PHP is awesome!"';
```

There is nothing wrong with this string because it was not enclosed between double quotes; therefore, you do not need to escape the quotes.

Another important concern when using a single-quoted string is that you cannot display another string inside it without concatenation. *Concatenation* is the arrangement (in this case, of strings of characters) into a chained list.

Let's look at a few examples of embedding a string variable within a single-quoted string. It might be illustrative to first look at an example of a common mistake:

```
$string1 = 'String 1 Example';
echo 'This is an incorrect example of embedding $string1 into this string';
```

This will display the following:

```
This is an incorrect example of embedding $string1 into this string
```

Through the usage of string concatenation, you can still display the contents of another string imbedded into the current string. Let's see how this works.

```
$string1 = 'String 1 Example';
$string2 = 'This is a correct way to embed '.$string1.' into  this string!';
```

If you were to display $string2 using the echo function, you will see the following:

```
This is a correct way to embed String 1 Example into this string!
```

As you can see, by closing the current string, adding a single quote and a period, the variable name you want to embed, and then another period and a single quote, you can concatenate the strings together. Do not forget to close out the rest of the string with a single quote and terminate the line with a semicolon.

The echo function is a built-in PHP function that allows you to display the contents of a string to your web browser. I discuss echo in the "Working with PHP Functions" section later in this chapter.

Using Double-Quoted Strings

A double-quoted string uses double quotes to enclose the contents of a string. They will appear in your code similar to this example:

```
"This is a double quoted string."
```

As with single-quoted strings, the double-quoted string has advantages and disadvantages. The major disadvantage is that you have to escape double quotes with a backslash. The only time this would be a problem is if you are using double-quoted strings with a large portion HTML code. However, I discuss when to use HTML with strings throughout this book, and you will learn methods of getting around this disadvantage.

One great advantage of using double-quoted strings is that you can embed strings together much more easily using the double-quoted method. Let's see how:

```
$string1 = "String 1 Example";
$string2 = "This is an example of embedding $string1 into the current string";
```

You do not have to concatenate this method, and you could save yourself a lot of time and characters by using the double-quoted method. The output of this string through the echo function is as follows:

```
This is an example of embedding String 1 Example into the current string.
```

The results are the same as the single-quoted method but with fewer characters in your code.

Escaping Double-Quoted Strings

Let's look at escaping double quotes. First, you will explore an error in escaping a double-quoted string:

```
echo "<a href="http://www.phpfreaks.com">Visit PHP Freaks.com!</a>";
```

This example would produce a nasty parse error, and your script would exit. Here is the proper way to escape this string:

```
echo "<a href=\"http://www.phpfreaks.com\">Visit PHP Freaks.com!</a>";
```

This correctly formatted example would produce a hyperlink that says "Visit PHP Freaks.com!"

Second, a great advantage of using double-quoted strings is the ability to utilize escape sequences for special characters such as linefeeds, tabs, carriage returns, and so on. For example:

```
echo "Line 1: This string is an example of a carriage return.\n
      Line 2: As you see, this is the second line!";
```

This example, if output to a text document or viewed through special HTML tags such as `<pre></pre>`, will display the following:

```
Line1: This string is an example of a carriage return.
Line2: As you see, this is the second line!
```

If you viewed this code using the echo function, you would see one continuous line and no new lines because HTML does not display carriage returns without the use of `<br />` tags.

Table 1.1 shows more examples of the special escape sequences.

TABLE 1.1: Special Escape Sequences

Sequence	Meaning
\n	Linefeed
\r	Carriage return
\t	Horizontal tab
\\	Backslash
\$	Dollar sign
\"	Double quote
\'	Single quote

Throughout this book, you will use strings quite extensively. I will give you examples of common string usage as you view other code examples. If you want to learn more about string usage, please refer to the "Strings" section in the PHP documentation at www.php.net/docs.php.

Using Variables

In the previous section, you learned about strings, which contain information. Now you will see how to identify a string with a name by using variables. For example:

```
$MyVariable = "This is my string assigned to a variable";
```

With this example, you made a new variable called MyVariable and assigned it a value using a string.

There are many uses for variables. You do not always have to assign a string to a variable; you can assign numeric values and Boolean values to them as well. Let's see how to do some math with a variable:

```
$a = 5;
$b = 15;
$c = $a + $b;
echo $c;
```

Output: 20

With this example, you assigned to each variable a numerical value, which does not need quotes. Then, you added the values of variables $a and $b together and stored the result in the variable $c. When you echo $c to the browser, you will see the total of $a and $b combined, which in this case equals 20. This is not practical for everyday use, but you see now that you can add the values of variables together.

NOTE   *Boolean* is a data type or variable in a programming language that can have one of two values, true or false.

A Boolean allows you to assign true or false values to a variable. A simple example of a Boolean usage is as follows:

```
$A = true;
$B = false;
if($A){
    echo "A is true";
}
if(!$B){
    echo " and B is false";
}
```

In this example, you defined the $A variable as true and the $B variable as false. Next, you used a control structure called IF to verify the conditions of the variables and take the applicable action. In this example, the output to the web browser is "A is true and B is false."

Using a Boolean will give you simple methods of validating logic and allowing the output of your PHP script based on that logic. I will go more in depth using the IF ELSE control structures throughout this book.

Naming Variables

You should be aware of a few limitations to naming variables:

Numbered naming   You cannot start a variable name with a number. For example, $6Pack is an invalid variable name. However, you may use a number in the variable name after the first alphabetic character. For example, $My6Pack is a valid variable name.

Underscore naming   You cannot start a variable name with an underscore. For example, $_MyVariable is an invalid variable name. But you may use an underscore in the variable name after the first alphabetic character. So, $My_Variable is a valid variable name.

Altering and Referencing Variables

Now you're ready for something a little more fun, but it can be confusing. PHP allows you to reference and alter variables within your code. A good example is assigning a name to a variable and referencing that same variable within another variable using the & operator. Let's see how this works:

```php
<?php
$var1 = 'Blue';
echo "1.) $var1<br />";

$var2 = &$var1;

echo "2.) var2 = $var2<br />";

$var2 = "3.) The color of the sky is $var2 <br />";

echo $var2;
?>
```

The output to the web browser looks like this:

```
1.) Blue
2.) var2 = Blue
3.) The color of the sky is Blue
```

Let's start from the beginning on this code example. First, you use your "open tag" and define $var1 as Blue and then echo the value of $var1 followed by an HTML line break:

```php
<?php
$var1 = 'Blue';
echo "1.) $var1<br />";
```

Next, you reference $var1 from $var2, which makes $var2 have the same value of $var1, and then echo the contents of $var2:

```php
$var2 = &$var1;

echo "2.) var2 = $var2<br />";
```

After you display the contents of $var2, you modify the value of it and echo the new value:

```php
$var2 = "3.) The color of the sky is $var2 <br />";

echo $var2;
?>
```

Variable referencing is not very popular, but it may be useful if you can figure out ways to implement this feature. For example, using variable references can be helpful if you are developing your code and you know that you need to fill in a blank later. Specifically, you can use a reference, and during a global definition file you can fill in that blank later without going back to modify all of the code on which you previously worked.

Variable and String Appending, or Concatenating

A method that works well is to *concatenate*, or append, to a string using your variables. Using this method, you will have the ability to append to a string using loops and IF statements, or you can use them just to keep your code more legible. Let's see how this works:

```php
<?php
$var1 = "This is a test";
$var1 .= " for appending strings.";
$var1 .= " You can append information to strings";
$var1 .= " on multiple lines.";
echo $var1;
?>
```

And the output is as follows:

```
This is a test for appending strings. You can append information to strings on
multiple lines.
```

Through the usage of the string concatenating assignment operator .=, you can append values to an existent string. Let's take one more look at a useful method to append strings:

```php
<?php
$message = "Welcome ";
if($first_name == "Eric"){
    $message .= "Eric";
} elseif($first_name == "Jeff"){
    $message .= "Jeff";
} else {
    $message .= "Stranger";
}
$message .= " to our website!";
echo $message;
?>
```

With this script, you have initiated a string and assigned it to a variable named $message. Using some control structures on a variable called $first_name, you are able to customize the message for anyone named Eric or Jeff. If this name is not found, you append the Stranger name to your $message variable. After completing the control structure, you append the rest of the sentence, and you now have something that would look like this if your name is not Eric or Jeff:

```
Welcome Stranger to our website!
```

Throughout this section, I have discussed variables, Booleans, variable naming, referencing and altering, and string appending. If you have never used PHP before, you may be curious about using control structures and functions by now. Let's move on to the next section where you learn how to use functions in PHP.

Working with PHP Functions

A function is simply a group of operations or information assigned to a name and is waiting to be used. PHP has thousands of functions readily available to use. Additionally, you can compile or enable more functions through installing PHP. Functions have many uses—from text formatting to database querying and so on. One of the greatest features of PHP is the ability to create a custom function. In the following sections, I will show you how to echo text, format text, query a database, include files, and create a custom function.

Using the *echo* Function

In the previous few sections of this chapter, I have mentioned and used the echo function a few times. The echo function is actually a language construct, but it is still listed under the "Functions" section of the PHP manual. So, for now, I will refer to it as a function.

According to the PHP manual, the echo function will output one or more strings. However, echo, defined as a function, also has a shortcut syntax that allows you to echo a string much more simply. Let's look at both of the methods of echoing information. The normal echo function usage looks like this:

```php
<?php
echo "This is an example for the echo function.<br />";

$var1 = "This is a method to echo a single string<br />";
echo $var1;
?>
```

Whereas the echo function shortcut syntax usage looks like this:

```php
<?="This is an example for the echo function shortcut
syntax.<br />";?>
```

Both of these examples will display the contents to the web browser.

Text Formatting Functions

PHP has some great text formatting functions. You can convert the carriage returns to the HTML <br /> characters, convert the first letter of a string to upper case, and much more. Let's review some examples of these functions.

nl2br() Function

The nl2br or New Line to br function is simple and will automatically insert the HTML equivalent of a carriage return (<br />) before the \n or \r\n special characters. This function is especially useful for converting user input from form posts so that it will display properly in HTML. The same goes for data that was posted and stored into MySQL and then extracted and displayed in your page.

Let's view a usage of the nl2br function now:

```php
<?php
// Information posted from the user
$user_post = "This is an example of nl2br.\n
              This function translates carriage returns to the HTML
              equivalent.";

echo nl2br($user_post);
?>
```

The nl2br raw HTML output is as follows:

```
This is an example of nl2br.<br />
This function translates carriage returns to the HTML equivalent.
```

This is displayed in a web browser as follows:

```
This is an example of nl2br.
This function converts carriage returns to the HTML equivalent.
```

Anytime the user hits the Enter key on the keyboard, a \n on Unix\Linux or a \r\n on Windows-based systems will be generated in the raw data. The nl2br function allows you to translate the carriage returns much more simply.

ucwords() Function

One of the most annoying things as a data manager is when users use all lower-case letters to enter content on a website. The bottom line is that it makes things look unprofessional, and you have to fix it if it bothers you. With PHP, a function called ucwords will convert the first letter to upper case of each word and leave the rest of the characters in the string the way they are:

```php
Let's take a look at the ucwords function usage: <?php
$data = "eric";
$data = ucwords ($data);
echo $data;
?>
```

The output looks like this:

```
Eric
```

Pretty simple, eh? You convert the first letter of each word in the string, and things look much better already. But wait! What if someone uses all upper-case letters in the posted data? This is much more annoying, and you have to fix this! This example is great because now you get to compound two functions together and use them both at the same time. Let's see how:

```php
<?php
// Compounded Example
```

```
$data = "ERIC";
$data = ucwords(strtolower($data));
echo $data;
?>
```

The ouput looks like this:

```
Eric
```

You can also achieve the same results from the previous example without compounding the functions:

```
<?php
// Non-Compounded Example
$data = "ERIC";
$data = strtolower($data);
$data = ucwords($data);
echo $data;
?>
```

As you would expect, the output looks like this:

```
Eric
```

In the previous example, I gave you two methods of achieving the same result. The first way is the shorter way and reduces the code and file size of your script, and the second method is the longer version of the first example. Either way, both examples produce the same result—the results desired. The beauty of PHP is there are at least five different ways to achieve the same result for nearly everything you do. You will discover this more as you become proficient as a developer.

Also in the previous example, I utilized the function strtolower, which simply converts all characters in a string to lower-case characters. Let's look at some of the other text formatting functions.

strtoupper   Converts all characters in a string to upper case.

strtolower   Converts all characters in a string to lower case.

ucwords   Converts the first character of each word to upper case in a string.

ucfirst   Converts only the first character in a string to upper case.

Database Querying Functions

PHP would not be complete without methods of querying a database. For this chapter, I will list the most commonly used MySQL functions and their definitions. As you move through this book, I will show you how to use these functions when you build your website.

NOTE   A *resource link identifier* is a name assigned to a resource such as `mysql_query`. An example is `$sql = mysql_query("query_here")`. `$sql` becomes your resource identifier.

The following are the most commonly used MySQL functions:

`mysql_connect [string server [, string username [, string password [, bool new_link [, int client_flags]]]]])`   Opens a connection to a MySQL server.

`mysql_pconnect ( [string server [, string username [, string password [, int client_flags]]]])`   Opens a persistent connection to a server. A persistent connection allows a single connection to be used by multiple users asynchronously instead of opening and closing new connections; a persistent connection remains open and will be assigned to a user upon request.

`mysql_select_db ( string database_name [, resource link_identifier])`   Selects a specific database by name with the resource identifier from one of the previous functions, `mysql_connect` or `mysql_pconnect`.

`mysql_query ( string query [, resource link_identifier [, int result_mode]])`   Sends a MySQL query to the server.

`mysql_fetch_array ( resource result [, int result_type])`   Fetches the results of the resource identifier from `mysql_query` and returns the results as an array.

`mysql_result ( resource result, int row [, mixed field])`   Gets the result data of a `mysql_query` resource identifier.

`mysql_fetch_assoc ( resource result)`   Fetches a result row as an associative array.

`mysql_num_rows ( resource result)`   Gets the number of rows in the result for a `mysql_query` resource identifier.

`mysql_error ( [resource link_identifier])`   Returns the text of the error message from the previous MySQL operation.

`mysql_affected_rows ( [resource link_identifier])`   Gets the number of affected rows in the previous MySQL operation.

`mysql_insert_id ( [resource link_identifier])`   Gets the ID generated from the previous INSERT operation from an AUTO_INCREMENT column.

The functions listed here are used in nearly every website using PHP with MySQL. You will find in-depth examples of these functions as you move along and get deeper into the code.

File Include Functions

Many functions are for including files into your PHP scripts. The great advantage of including files is that you can reuse code in many different files and keep your scripts looking cleaner without having the same code over and over again. Let's look at a few of the functions:

require   Same as the `include` function except failure will result in a fatal error.

require_once   This function will evaluate the code being executed before including the code again. If the code has already been included in the current script, `require_once` will skip the inclusion and avoid duplicate code. Failure will result in a fatal error.

include   Same as the `require` function except failure will result in a warning message.

include_once   Same as `require_once` except failure will result in a warning message.

With the functions listed here, you will have the ability to include files within another file. Let's see how `include` works:

```
File name: test.php

<?php
$var1 = "This string is part of the \"test.php\" file.";
?>


File name: current.php

<?php
include 'test.php';
echo $var1;
?>
```

This is the output from `current.php`:

```
This string is part of the "test.php" file.
```

When I build a website, I create a directory called `includes` on my server's document root. Inside that directory, I create files for sending e-mails, connecting to databases, and just about any common routine that my scripts would require. Using these functions, I have now reduced my code dramatically, and I don't have to research or retype the code in the included scripts any longer.

Creating Custom Functions

If you desire to create custom functions, you are in luck! PHP allows you to create custom functions as long as they do not use a reserved function's name. Let's say you want the ability to create a function that will allow you to calculate what day is 100 days after a specific date and then display that date in a particular format, such as "June 5, 2004." Each time you want to perform this operation, you would have to type the date and mktime function code together and then format the date as well. If you create your own function, you can create a method for you to call this function much more easily. Let's look at this code:

```php
<?php

function date_add ($hour, $minute, $day) {
    $newdate = date("r", mktime(date('h') + $hour,
            date('i') + $minute, 0,
            date('m'), date('d') +$day,
            date('y')));
    return $newdate;
}
echo "Today's Date: ".date('r');
echo "<br />";
echo "New Date: ".date_add(0, 0, -9);

?>
```

The output displays today's date and the date nine days ago:

```
Today's Date: Wed, 9 Apr 2003 20:58:59 +0200
New Date: Mon, 31 Mar 2003 08:58:00 +0200
```

In this code example, you created a custom function called date_add and then defined three arguments that you will pass to this function: $hour, $minute, and $day. You enclose the function's content with the curly braces ({ }) and then entered the code.

This custom function example is comprised of prebuilt PHP functions such as date, which formats and displays a date, and mktime, which can be used for arithmetic operations on dates. Take a close look; each time you want to add a date in your PHP script, you would have to type everything between those curly braces. That would be a waste of time if you used this in many places throughout your website, so instead you make your own function that is suitable for your needs.

Consider the return $newdate section of the last line inside the custom function. The return simply returns the value created by the date math you used in the $newdate string. By using return, you can simply tell PHP all that you want is a value, and you will choose what to do with it. You could have simply used echo $newdate, and then when the function executed, PHP would have displayed the value in the web browser immediately. With return, you can do whatever you desire with this value, including insertion into a database, echo to the user's browser, and so on.

If you were to save this custom function and include the file into the PHP script you want to use it in, you could call up the function using date_add(5, 0, 0); and simply add five hours, zero minutes, and zero days to the current date. Now you can start building a custom code library of functions each time you find something useful that required a lot of research to make happen.

I will expand on the usage of custom functions throughout this book. Along with custom functions, you can also create a container system for similar functions called a *class*. Starting in Chapter 3, "Building a Database Schema with MySQL," I will start demonstrating classes and introduce them thoroughly.

Now that you have a better understanding of PHP functions, you will move on to error handling and trapping. Do not worry if you do not know how to use functions just yet—you will revisit using functions throughout this book.

Error Handling and Trapping

One of the most important considerations on a production server and website is handling errors properly. You want to hide the errors from an end user as much as possible while, at the same time, log those errors and fix them behind the scenes. PHP has many methods for you to use such practices.

The following sections cover error handling and trapping and show you the best methods to hide errors and log them. I refer to this process as *error handling and trapping*.

Error Reporting Levels

PHP has different levels of error reporting in its engine. Through a setting called `error_reporting` in your `php.ini` file, you will be able to manage those error levels and turn the error reporting on or off with various settings. For a complete list of the error reporting levels, please refer to the "Error Reporting" section of the PHP manual.

In your `php.ini` file, you will find a section called "Error Reporting." There you will find a brief explanation of a few of the settings listed in this section. You can change the levels of error reporting that you desire. I do not recommend disabling the error reporting during your development phase. I recommend you use a setting on your development server such as:

```
error_reporting = E_ALL & ~E_NOTICE
```

This setting will ensure that all errors are reported to you at the time of development and will allow you to fix them before you get too deep into your code and realize there were errors that could have been fixed in the early stages. If you can code your PHP scripts without displaying errors with these settings, you are definitely on the right track.

On a production server, I also recommend you keep the same levels of reporting; however, you have the option to use a setting in your `php.ini` file called `display_errors`. Simply change this setting to `off` and restart your web server. You should no longer see any errors on your website; however, you'll probably get a blank white screen if an error occurs. This could be confusing to some people, even you. I will describe how to log these errors in the "Error Trapping" section shortly.

You should take special note that if you edit your php.ini file on a web server that runs multiple virtual hosted websites, you will be making these changes for every virtual host, not just one. If you need to change only one website, I recommend using the virtual host configuration files or a .htaccess file in the Apache web server.

You can also change the error reporting of a specific PHP script only. You can do this with the error_reporting function that is compiled into PHP by default. Let's look at an example:

```
<?php
error_reporting('E_ALL');
// rest of script here.
?>
```

Using the error_reporting function, you will be able to change error_reporting levels without affecting your entire website. This is great for debugging a script if you choose not to log errors to a file. Let's look at error logging or error trapping now.

Error Trapping

Every webmaster should view log files on a regular basis. Log files are an important factor in maintaining a smooth-running website. PHP allows you to log the errors into a file of your choice.

Here is how you do it: In your php.ini file, you will find the settings log_errors and error_log. You will want to set the log_errors to On and define a filename and path to the file you want to log your errors for the error_log setting.

Here is an example of a Linux production server php.ini with error handling and error logging:

```
error_reporting = E_ALL & ~E_NOTICE
display_errors = Off
log_errors = On
error_log = /var/log/phpfreaks.com/php_error.log
```

Whenever a PHP error occurs with these settings, the error is directly entered into the log, and the user is presented with a blank page that does not display the errors directly to them.

Using Output Buffering

Output buffering allows you to control the output of a script and put that output into a buffer for later use. This is useful for building a buffer of information in one part of your script and displaying it later. Using some built-in functions that PHP has to offer, you can accomplish this.

To find a complete list of output buffering functions, please refer to the "Output Buffering" section of the PHP manual.

When using output buffering to capture information, you will more than likely use more than one of the associated output buffering functions at a time. Here is an example of how to build an output buffer:

```php
<?php
ob_start();
echo "This is an output_buffering example";
$mybuffer = ob_get_contents();
ob_end_clean();

// HTML or PHP code here

echo $mybuffer;
?>
```

In this example, you build a buffer that contains the echo statement and that will not be displayed by the script until you tell it to be displayed. This method allows you to build more of your script, set cookies, and even start sessions before displaying the original buffer that you built.

What's Next?

This chapter introduced PHP, gave a history lesson in PHP, and introduced strings, variables, functions, error handling, error trapping, and output buffering.

Now that you have looked at the beginning of coding PHP and where it can take you, let's discuss methods of planning your projects. The next chapter covers some basic concepts involved with coming up with an idea and planning to develop a project.

CHAPTER 2

Planning Your Project

Once you have an idea for a website, you want it to be up and running as soon as possible. However, for a website to be successful, it has to be well planned. If you want to take chances by using a shotgun method of building a large-scale project, it will more than likely fail.

For example, if I came up with an idea to sell funnel cakes on the Internet and offer free delivery worldwide without researching and planning this kind of idea, I would definitely be in for a big surprise. Say I built the website from this idea without researching how to actually ship a funnel cake to a person without it becoming rotten—not only would my customers be irritated at me, but I would lose a lot of money. I think you can figure out where I am going with this: Planning is essential.

Furthermore, investing some time for planning in the early stages of a project can save a lot of time on the back end. In this chapter, I walk you through the methods used to plan a full-scale project. It is well worth the time and effort to do this right.

Getting the Most from Your Idea

When an idea for a website pops into your head or someone brings you an idea and wants you to design a website, the possibilities may seem endless. You should allow your mind to wander into as many depths of creative thinking as you can. Creative thinking is the key to a great start with the website.

Do not approach your website idea with a single focus or a narrow mind. You should take into account your development skills, budget, hardware, target audience, and the time involved to implement your idea. When you have considered all of these variables, the idea turns into a project.

Usually, when I come up with an idea, I try to make every effort to mull over the idea before taking it seriously. If I can keep my mind focused on this idea for more than a day or two, then I begin the next phase, brainstorming.

Let's look at an example: Around Christmas time a few years ago, I decided I would try to get my wife a dog. I looked up all of the phone numbers for dog kennels or veterinarians in our local phone directory. Unfortunately, the phone directory was not organized very well, so I became frustrated. I had the impression that the phone directory had a website, so I called the publisher and asked if they had a website where a person could search for phone numbers. The reply I received was not too promising. The previous webmaster had moved on to other things, and the website was built with Macromedia Flash and was no longer updated because nobody had the source files. Unfortunately, this website was two years old, and most of the information was incorrect anyway.

After I hung up the phone from talking to the publisher of the phone directory, I started thinking. I came up with the idea to use PHP and MySQL to create a dynamic website that would allow users to search for the phone numbers they desired as well as a method for the company that owns the phone directory to allow people in their office to easily manage and maintain it through web-based administration pages. After thinking for a few more days of how useful it would be to have a website such as this, I started to brainstorm some details for this idea.

Brainstorming Details for an Idea

When you start brainstorming details for an idea, you should consider every variable possible for all types of audiences. Think of every detail you can for your project and then write them down. It does not matter how crazy the details you think of for your idea, you should make a record of them. You will start the process of eliminating the bad ideas later; for now, just write them down while they are still fresh in your head. Try to give this phase of the process at least a day or two to get your initial ideas documented; when it is time to move on, you will start the process of elimination.

Expanding on the example I started in the previous section, the following list contains the ideas I came up with for the user-accessible pages:

- Phone number listings
  - Which data fields need to be collected?
    - Business name
    - Voice phone number
    - Fax number
    - E-mail address
    - Website address
    - Office hours
    - Other information (products for sale, special contact information, and so on)
- Phone directory index with categories for phone numbers to be assigned to based on their genre
  - Yahoo-style link index?
  - Subcategories under parent category
    - How many subcategories before displaying a More link?
    - Only show one subcategory depth to the main category?
    - How to sort the subcategories under each parent category: alphabetical, sort order, or number of listings assigned to the category?

- Drop-down menu category list?
  - Which method to sort the parent categories: alphabetical, sort order, or number of listings assigned to a category?
- Search engine
  - Which fields to search?
  - Advanced search options
  - Limit search result options
- Custom telephone list
  - Allow users to create a custom telephone list via the MySQL database
  - Use cookies or sessions?
  - Allow users to print their custom telephone lists with a printer-friendly page

This example shows a small portion of my brainstorming ideas for the project. The list could go on for quite awhile. As you can see, I simply started writing down my ideas and kept them flowing. Even though they may not be fully suited to the project and may not be used, I still wrote them down.

After I have a complete list of ideas on paper, so to speak, I start researching them to every extent possible.

Researching Concepts

Once you have your idea and brainstorming phases completed, you can start researching the details. Researching can be simple, or it can be hair pulling. As valuable as the Internet is these days, it is still difficult to find the information you need. PHP has only been around for a few years. This makes researching ideas for using a PHP-based development platform somewhat complicated. However, there are still some great places to find the information you need. Here are some I use every day:

Google search engine   A priceless asset for finding virtually anything you need on the Internet. See www.google.com.

Google Groups   Millions of newsgroup messages have been indexed in the Google Groups section for nearly all of the newsgroups in existence. Google Groups is a great source for finding questions and answers from newsgroups for nearly the last five to 10 years. See groups.google.com.

PHP manual   The PHP manual, although not always the most comprehensive material for everyone, has some great information that may directly involve your project. Also, the online version of the manual and the Windows Help (CFM) version also have helpful user comments. See the "Documentation" section at `www.php.net`.

PHP information sites   Another great source of PHP information are the sites that fellow developers have set up for you to find tutorials, code examples, and user forums. Here are a few:

PHP Freaks.com   This is my personal site, and nearly 15,000 visitors a day interact to help each other with various PHP topics. The site is complete with forums, tutorials, code examples, live chat, and more. See `www.phpfreaks.com`.

OxyScripts.com   A fellow PHP developer has his own site with a small community similar to PHP Freaks.com. See `www.oxyscripts.com`.

Zend Technologies   This is another great source for tutorials, tips, and much more. Zend Technologies is also the home of Zend PHP accelerators and other add-on software. See `www.zend.com`.

HotScripts.com   This is a great script directory with links to scripts and tutorials. See `www.hotscripts.com`.

This list, although not complete, will get you started finding the information you need.

When you start researching your ideas, try to find something similar to what you have in mind. It does not really matter if what you find is written in PHP because if it is on the Web and it is dynamic, you can do it with PHP. For example, it is easy to reproduce a site written in Perl or Active Server Pages (ASP) once you learn the ropes.

For the project example I have already given you in this chapter, I had to research some of the ideas, such as how to build a PHP and MySQL search engine, how to use cookies with PHP, and so on. Through my research findings, I determined the best approaches for my project, and I moved into the next phase: planning and information gathering. Keep in mind that as the development phase progresses, you will more than likely have to research additional problems, so do not overdo the initial research. Hold off on researching every intricate detail until the coding portion.

Planning and Information Gathering

Have you ever heard of the concept known as the "peanut butter and jelly of programming?" Basically, it does not matter whether you put on the peanut butter or the jelly first—you still get the same result: a peanut butter and jelly sandwich. Working with that metaphor, you have already found the bread (the idea and the details) required to make the sandwich. Now you need to spread on the peanut butter and jelly—in no certain order. I prefer to put the peanut butter (layout and design) on first, instead of the jelly (the coding portion) so that is where you will head right now.

Planning a Website Layout, Sections, and Features

Now that you have an idea and some details, and you have done some research, it is time to start a layout. Some people prefer to do the coding first and the layout later, but I can assure you from experience, it is much more practical to do the layout first. When you have something visual to look at during development, you can see how your code fits the layout and reduce your development time dramatically. Once again, this is the "peanut butter and jelly of programming."

When you plan your layout for a project, try to determine the best way to use the layout space you have. If you are going to advertise on your project's website, consider where you want the advertising to "plug in" without distracting the readers from the reason they are at your site. Try to make your layout as smooth and clean as possible.

When I developed the project mentioned in this chapter, I knew that the company wanted to advertise on their website, and I also knew that I needed to provide an easy navigation system of links on the left side of the website. From there, I started to build the layout. I tried every means possible to avoid using frames and stuck to using HTML tables and cells to build the layout. Once I built the layout files, I started to code the website into the layout.

For the sections of the project's website, I started using my brainstorming process to see what would actually fit the best, and I looked for logical ways to put them all together. I knew that I would create the directory index with all the categories listed, the custom telephone list feature, and the administration functions. Using the same layout files for the "shell" of the website, I modified them accordingly to navigate through all of the sections I built. If you plan smartly, you can modify any section of your website easily throughout the development. Chapter 4, "Building a Website Template with PHP," covers how to build a reusable website template and covers more layout concepts.

Planning a MySQL Database

When it's time for you to begin planning a database, you need to have the basic ideas for what you are going to do. A database consists of *tables* and *columns* (or *fields*). A table is the section, and the columns or fields are the subsections of the table. For example, a table called news is a main section of the database, and the columns or fields in the news section—such as title, date, author, and article—are the subsections.

When it is time to plan a MySQL database for your project, you should follow the ideas you came up with in the brainstorming phase. Let's expand some more on the example for this chapter; I will give you an example of the database layout I used for the phone numbers section of the project.

First, I decided which tables to use. For this example, I created a table called `phonebook_listings`. I try to use a prefix for all of my tables that matches their relevance. For example, this table will be prefixed with `phonebook_`. This also allows me to use the database for other sections that I create later, for example, `news_articles` and `news_categories` for a news section of my website. Now I know that I have a phonebook section and a news section, and I know what tables belong to what section. This is only a personal preference, but it may help you keep your database looking tidy.

Now that I have chosen a table name, I need to create columns. I began thinking of what I would need for each phone number listing, and I came up with a list similar to this:

- Company name or person's name
- Category ID (comes from a separate table)
- Primary phone number
- Secondary phone number
- Fax number
- Address
- Website address
- E-mail address
- Business hours
- Other information

This list covers all of the information I will need to gather about each phone number listing in my database. With my basic list, I will create "MySQL-friendly" names for each of the columns; when it is time to design the database, I will refer back to this plan.

Along with planning the sections, you should consider a table layout such as the example I just gave you for each of the sections where you desire to use MySQL. Try to think of each element for the section you are going to use and make a list of them. The next chapter covers in depth how to create and administrate the MySQL databases.

Planning for a Target Audience

Another important planning consideration is the target audience. You should decide at an early stage for whom you want your website to be built. I built my PHP Freaks.com website specifically for web developers who desired a more advanced application of their skills. Based on that information, I decided how to create my layout and plan the sections for the site.

Your website may have a wide or narrow target audience, depending on what you are building. A website such as Google is built for almost anyone to search for information, whereas a site such as PayPal is built for people wanting to transfer money between other PayPal members. For the phone book example, the target audience is anyone who needs to look up a phone number. That means the site should be easy to use. Every site needs to be planned, laid out, and developed accordingly for your target audience. You should make an attempt to eliminate anything that is not applicable to your target audience.

Setting Up the Project Logistics

Depending on the scale of your project, you may need to build a team to compensate for the logistics required. Whether your team consists of a graphic artist, additional developers, server managers, team coordinators, and so on, you must carefully consider each of these roles. You know that you will definitely need a developer, but what about the other people?

PHP Developers

If you decide you need a PHP developer other than yourself, you are in luck. Good PHP developers are spawning all over at a rapid pace. Because PHP is evolving quickly, you should have no problem putting together a team of developers for your project. A good place to look for people hunting for work is usually in message boards or web-based forums. My PHP Freaks.com website has a separate forums system with a subforum for freelance developers. Usually, you can post your request in these forums, and someone will reply shortly if interested. You can visit the PHP Freaks.com forums at `www.phpfreaks.com/forums` and click the PHP Freelancing forum.

Currently, the going rate for an experienced PHP developer ranges from $25 to $75 per hour, depending on the skills required. However, if you are compiling a project team, the developer may be interested in a percentage of the earnings. If you are putting together a freeware project, the developer may be interested in developing just for the recognition. Many developers have their own opinions on projects; some do not care about the money and only develop as a hobby. Once again, this shows the dynamics involved with this type of skill and expertise.

Graphic Artists

Graphic artists, in my experience, are the most difficult to find. Sometimes you will get lucky and find someone experienced enough with Adobe Photoshop, and they may only be interested in getting their name in the credits for your project or adding another page into their portfolio. However, you may also find money-hungry graphic artists who are only seeking a quick way to make cash. Regardless, you will need to find someone who will fulfill your requirements and be readily available to accomplish the project's demands. Keep in mind that most projects you develop will require some sort of alterations and graphic elements throughout the stages of development. A perfect example of this is the need for icons, bullets, and web banners; in my experience, these are items people think of as the project progresses. When you negotiate with your graphic artist, try to keep something open in your agreement for additional work beyond the initial layouts. If you need to hire a graphic artist, you can easily find one at `www.elance.com`.

Server Administrators

Server administrators are becoming fairly easy to find these days, depending on the level of skill and trust you desire. Linux, the preferred operating system for web servers, is growing rapidly in popularity. A Linux administrator should not be too hard to find if you keep your eyes open. Try to keep in mind when searching for a good Linux administrator that you will need someone who is proficient in *all* aspects of web server administration. This means you not only need someone who knows how to configure PHP for your server but who can also handle a wide range of duties. The following is a short list of technologies that I would want a Linux administrator to have familiarity with:

Apache web server   Of course, in Linux, I prefer to use Apache because of its speed and reliability, so I would require someone who knows how to install and maintain Apache. A few important skills to look for specifically are the ability to manage Secure Sockets Layer (SSL) connections, virtual hosts, and security.

PHP   PHP is not always a plug-and-play operation. You will need someone who knows how to configure PHP, edit the configuration files, compile additional modules, and, most important, ensure security is set properly. PHP could potentially be any server's worse security nightmare if not configured properly, so make sure your server administrator really knows what they are doing!

MySQL database server   This is fairly easy to configure and maintain. You should still consider someone who has experience in this area. Even though you may easily manage MySQL by using some great third-party applications, knowledge of the MySQL configuration files, security, and options should still be an important consideration.

FTP server   Using the File Transfer Protocol (FTP) to update your files on the server is an absolute requirement. Once again, someone who knows how to configure FTP to be secure and prevent access to root file systems is a definite consideration. FTP, like most applications that run on your server, could potentially be dangerous if not configured properly.

Domain Name Server (DNS)   DNS allows you to translate a domain name into the server's address on the Internet. DNS management involves a large learning curve, and DNS server administration is something that should not be taken lightly. A few different types of DNS servers are available, but for Linux, I prefer to use the BIND package.

E-mail server   Although there are more than a few handfuls of e-mail servers out there, the most popular ones are Sendmail (default mail server on Linux, www.sendmail.org) and Qmail (www.qmail.org) for Linux servers. Regardless of which one you choose, security should be the number-one issue.

An incorrectly configured e-mail server could damage your communication requirements involved in any website. For example, if your e-mail server is an open relay, some companies or individuals could use your server to relay their *spam*, or bulk mail, through your server. After a few spam reports to selected agencies, your server could be blacklisted, and those using spam mail filters might block important e-mails coming from your server, thus reducing your communication capabilities and, in turn, reducing your business capabilities.

The bottom line is that e-mail is important; find someone who knows exactly what they are doing!

Updates and security   All but the least of your worries is the security and updates required to maintain your servers. Someone who knows how to configure a firewall, disable anonymous access, harness root access, and perform required updates on the core operating system and the applications involved is essential to the operation of your server.

Linux servers are known for being secure because people make every attempt to find exploits in the software; when an exploit is found, it is usually reported to the Linux developers, and patches are released within days.

Some Linux operating systems will notify your server administrator when an update is required. You will need a server administrator who will stay up-to-date and ensure that you have all of the latest versions and patches installed on your system.

Miscellaneous   Although most flavors of Linux will manage themselves through smart planning and implementation of the operating system, they will always need some sort of management to ensure things are running smoothly. This task may be minimal, depending on the activity on your server, or it could be time consuming. Either way, you would be able to sleep well at night knowing that someone is monitoring your systems to ensure that maximum uptime is achieved.

The bottom line to choosing the right server administrator is to find someone you can trust. You will find that not every experienced Linux administrator has a certification. Personally, I would hire someone regardless of a certification, based upon their skills and experience. Linux certifications are not given out as frequently as the Microsoft certifications, so the certified administrators are hard to find.

If you are determined to use your own servers, I think the best place to find a person who can fit all of the requirements for the previous list is someone who has run or worked at a web hosting company. These people will more than likely have experience in all of the requirements for a good server administrator. Most of the requirements may be learned fairly easily through documentation on the Web, but it requires some talent and ambition to become competent at these tasks. If you need assistance with learning Linux, check out www.linuxforum.com.

Project Managers/Team Coordinators

Depending on how many people you have on your project team, you may need a project manager/team coordinator to keep things moving in the right direction. A project manager is the person who will maintain a list of tasks involved, build timelines, coordinate between the project team members, and compile all of the elements involved with the project into phases.

To be the most effective, your project manager should not perform any other task besides project management. However, this may not be practical, so you may find that one person will perform many different elements. Besides, the fewer people you have on the project, the easier the project could be to manage, so you will have to take this into consideration when you decide who to involve and what positions to fill.

What's Best for You?

Not every project requires a large team to be successful. You have to alter the requirements depending on the scale and budget of your project. For example, most of the projects I work on, I go solo and fill most of the positions myself. I find it easier to work by myself than wait around for other people to catch up to me. I find it difficult and frustrating to wait for another developer to get back from vacation or to find time in their busy schedules to work on the sections that I need before I can move on to the next phase. That is one disadvantage of building a team of people—the actual time loss involved in waiting for other people to complete their portions of work.

Regardless, if you have a strict timeline, what happens if someone does not complete their work at the expected deadline? What happens if someone backs out on your project, and you have to start over? For instance, consider the amount of time lost to figure out what happened and to find a replacement to do that person's work while the rest of the team has to wait. If you are on a critical timeline, this could be devastating to your project. However, when things work smoothly, everyone benefits from a team effort.

When I was asked to develop the phone book project I discussed earlier in this chapter, I developed all aspects of the project on my own. This was a good learning experience because I got to see what it takes to build a project like this and I had a taste of what each of the positions on a team would go through. Based on that experience, I learned to better manage a team on later projects.

Considering the Hardware Requirements

Every project has different needs for hardware requirements. Surprisingly, hardware considerations are the least of your problems. PHP and MySQL do not require massive top-of-the-line hardware systems to run efficiently. To be honest, I have found that most web servers will run smoothly on the minimum system requirements to run Linux. Because Linux utilizes your hardware and processor much differently than Windows-based systems, you are not required to have massive amounts of hardware to run a Linux server that does not use a graphical interface.

Another great advantage of running a dedicated server is the fact that you do not need hyped-up sound and video cards. In fact, you can remove the sound card completely and step down to a standard Video Graphics Adapter (VGA) video card that would cost you around $20.

Let's look at a standard system required for a web server.

- Computer case
- Motherboard
- Central Processing Unit (CPU)
- Random Access Memory (RAM)
- Hard drive
- CD-ROM (for installation of the operating system)
- Memory (RAM)
- Video card (basic)
- Network adapter

With this system, you can probably find a nice motherboard that has the integrated network and video adapters. You only need the CD-ROM for installation; otherwise, you can remove it if you like.

To consider the size of the hardware you require to run your websites from, you need to know more about your project. One of my web servers runs from an AMD Athlon 650MHZ processor with 512MB of RAM and a single 40GB hard drive. This is probably the smallest computer I would use for a project, but it efficiently runs 25 websites, an e-mail server, a DNS server, and an FTP server, along with some other applications I use. During the first few months of running the phone book project, we utilized this server with high traffic loads with no problems.

It really does not matter about the size of the hardware. If you are building a website that will be viewed by 10,000 or 100,000 users per day and that uses PHP and MySQL, you do not need a massive server that costs a lot of money. Even though I say this, many people will still try to purchase as top-of-the-line servers as they can. This is not a bad idea because once you move through the steps involved in configuring a new server, I am sure you would not want to move to another server anytime soon.

The bottom line with hardware requirements is to find something you can afford without breaking your budget. If you can afford a top-of-the-line server, then go for it because as you move on to new projects, you will probably be able to share the same server with multiple websites. However, if you do not want to break the bank, purchase something a little bit slower but expandable in memory size. You can always attempt to upgrade later.

What's Next?

This chapter covered quite a bit of information about planning your project. It is up to you to choose how to plan, design, and implement your project. This chapter was written to aid and to share with you the methods I use to develop a project. The chapter covered many areas such as thinking of an idea, brainstorming, planning features and sections, planning your database, building your team, and considering hardware requirements.

In Chapter 3, "Building a Database Schema with MySQL," you will start working with MySQL. You will learn about using different column types, creating a database, creating tables, creating columns, and working with some excellent third-party software to manage your MySQL databases.

Building a Database Schema with MySQL

One of the most important elements to building a website with PHP and MySQL is the database. MySQL is a robust database server that supports a wide range of features. With MySQL you have the ability to insert, update, drop, index, replicate (file), and lock tables, and much more. If you build your database properly and configure your tables accordingly, you should have no performance problems running your site from a MySQL back end. After reading this chapter, you will be able to use MySQL and some of the associated third-party software for MySQL management.

Before you go any further in this chapter, you should grab a copy of MySQL and install it. You can download MySQL at `www.mysql.com` for free. I recommend you download all of the associated files for your operating system with the MySQL base installation so that you receive the MySQL Admin Tools.

Understanding MySQL

To effectively plan and use MySQL, you need to know some basics about the different types of tables and columns you will use in building your databases. Using tables and columns properly will ensure that your databases run smooth and efficiently. Let's look at tables first.

MySQL Table Types

MySQL supports a few different types of tables for using with your databases. As of MySQL version 3.23, you can choose from HEAP, ISAM, and MyISAM table types. Let's take a quick look at the differences:

HEAP   This table type uses hashed indexes that are stored in memory, which makes them very fast. However, if MySQL crashes, you will lose all the data stored in them. Thus, this table type is great for temporary tables!

ISAM   This type of table will be deprecated in future versions of MySQL. Furthermore, it has no major advantages over the MyISAM table type. The following are some of the properties and features of ISAM:

- Compressed and fixed-length keys.
- Fixed and dynamic record length.
- Sixteen keys with 16 key parts per key.
- Maximum key length of 256 (default).
- Data is stored in machine format; this is fast, but it is machine/operating system dependent.

MyISAM   This is the default table type and is compatible with nearly any requirements you may have for a database. It is based on the ISAM code and has many more useful extensions, including error checking, error repair, compression, and much more.

Furthermore, you can compile MySQL with additional table support such as InnoDB and BDB (BerkeleyDB). Please check the MySQL manual for information regarding these table types.

NOTE   Throughout this book, I will use MyISAM table types by default.

MySQL Column Types

Before you begin building your database structure, you should understand the column types and the purposes for which they are used. These are the most commonly used column types:

TINYINT   A very small integer. The signed range is -128 to 127. The unsigned range is 0 to 255.

SMALLINT   A small integer. The signed range is -32,768 to 32,767. The unsigned range is 0 to 65,535.

MEDIUMINT   A medium-sized integer. The signed range is -8,388,608 to 8,388,607. The unsigned range is 0 to 16,777,215.

INT   A normal-sized integer. The signed range is -2,147,483,648 to 2,147,483,647. The unsigned range is 0 to 4,294,967,295.

BIGINT   A large integer. The signed range is -9,223,372,036,854,775,808 to 9,223,372,036,854,775,807.

FLOAT   A floating-point number. Precision can be less than or equal to 24 for a single-precision floating-point number and between 25 and 53 for a double-precision floating-point number.

DOUBLE   A normal-sized (double-precision) floating-point number. Allowable values are -1.7976931348623157E+308 to -2.2250738585072014E-308, zero, and 2.2250738585072014E-308 to 1.7976931348623157E+308.

DECIMAL   An unpacked floating-point number.

DATE   A date. The supported range is 1000-01-01 to 9999-12-31.

DATETIME   A date and time combination. The supported range is '1000-01-01 00:00:00' to '9999-12-31 23:59:59'.

TIMESTAMP   A timestamp. The range is '1970-01-01 00:00:00' to sometime in the year 2037.

TIME   A time. The range is '-838:59:59' to '838:59:59'.

YEAR   A year in two-digit or four-digit format (the default is four-digit format). The allowable values are 1,901 to 2,155.

VARCHAR   A variable-length string.

TINYBLOB or TINYTEXT   A BLOB or TEXT column with a maximum length of 255 (2^8 – 1) characters.

BLOB or TEXT   A BLOB or TEXT column with a maximum length of 65,535 (2^16 – 1) characters.

MEDIUMBLOB or MEDIUMTEXT   A BLOB or TEXT column with a maximum length of 16,777,215 (2^24 – 1) characters.

LONGBLOB or LONGTEXT   A BLOB or TEXT column with a maximum length of 4,294,967,295 (2^32 – 1) characters.

ENUM   An enumeration. A string object that can have only one value, chosen from the list of values `'value1'`, `'value2'`, ..., NULL, or the special `' '` error value. An ENUM can have a maximum of 65,535 distinct values.

This list contains the most commonly used column types for your purposes. There are many more column types, and you can find a complete list in the MySQL manual at `www.mysql.com/ documentation`. Do not worry if you do not understand these column types yet. Throughout the database design in this book, I will give you practical examples of the column types you will need.

NOTE   When working with MySQL, you may notice in various places the terms *column* and *field*. A column relates to the database table structure, and a field relates to data stored for a particular column in a row, which is stored inside the table.

What Is ADOdb?

ADOdb is a set of classes that attempts to hide the differences between the nonstandardized PHP database access functions. It is most commonly used in applications such as PHAkt (a third-party Macromedia Dreamweaver extension) and the PostNuke content management system.

ADOdb currently supports the following database types:

- MySQL
- Oracle

- Microsoft SQL Server
- Sybase
- Sybase SQL Anywhere
- Informix
- PostgreSQL
- FrontBase
- Interbase (Firebird and Borland variants)
- Foxpro
- Access
- ADO
- ODBC

If you are interested in learning more about ADOdb, refer to the official website at php.weblogs.com/adodb.

Using MySQL Database Tools

The best part about working with excellent software such as MySQL is that someone is always working on third-party software to make your life better. In my experience, I have found some great third-party software applications and web-based scripts that allow me to create, delete, modify, and manage elements of my MySQL servers fairly easily without the need to learn command-line arguments for each action I take. This chapter will not cover how to manage MySQL from the command line, but it will show you some great point-and-click software that will make your life much easier.

> **WARNING** When managing a MySQL Server with root privileges, *do not* delete, or *drop*, the database named mysql. This database contains all of the necessary information to run your MySQL server. Deleting this database will render MySQL inoperative.

Using phpMyAdmin: Web-Based MySQL Administration

What better way to manage the MySQL portion of your PHP/MySQL website than using a set of PHP scripts with an excellent interface? The folks over at phpMyAdmin.net have created a set of scripts that you download and unpack (unzip or untar) on your website's directories. Simply open your web browser and point to the directory where you unpacked the files, and you now have an easy way to manage your MySQL.

Even if you do not plan to use phpMyAdmin, I encourage you to read this section to get a better understanding of different column types and why you use them.

Let's begin by grabbing phpMyAdmin:

1. Go to www.phpmyadmin.net and pick the file format of your choice. Download the files either directly to your web server or to your local computer.

2. Unpack the files and place them in your website's directory. For this example, I have placed my copy of phpMyAdmin in a directory called phpMyAdmin in my website's document root.

3. Modify the file called config.inc.php with your PHP editor and follow the directions for entering your MySQL server information, usernames, passwords, and so on. See Figure 3.1 where I configured the config.php file for the $cfg['PmaAbsoluteUri'] setting and Figure 3.2 where I configured the username and password in the phpMyAdmin config.php file.

FIGURE 3.1:

Configuring phpMyAdmin's config.inc.php file for the Pma-AbsolueURI setting

```
36    * If the auto-detection code does work properly, you can set to TRUE the
37    * $cfg['PmaAbsoluteUri_DisableWarning'] variable below.
38    */
39    $cfg['PmaAbsoluteUri'] = 'http://sybex/phpMyAdmin';
40
41
42    /**
```

FIGURE 3.2:

Configuring phpMyAdmin's config.inc.php file for username and password settings

```
62 $i++;
63 $cfg['Servers'][$i]['host']          = 'localhost'; // MySQL hostname
64 $cfg['Servers'][$i]['port']          = '';          // MySQL port - leave blank for default port
65 $cfg['Servers'][$i]['socket']        = '';          // Path to the socket - leave blank for default socket
66 $cfg['Servers'][$i]['connect_type']  = 'tcp';       // How to connect to MySQL server ('tcp' or 'socket')
67 $cfg['Servers'][$i]['compress']      = FALSE;       // Use compressed protocol for the MySQL connection
68                                                     // (requires PHP >= 4.3.0)
69 $cfg['Servers'][$i]['controluser']   = '';          // MySQL control user settings
70                                                     // (this user must have read-only
71 $cfg['Servers'][$i]['controlpass']   = '';          // access to the "mysql/user"
72                                                     // and "mysql/db" tables)
73 $cfg['Servers'][$i]['auth_type']     = 'config';    // Authentication method (config, http or cookie based)?
74 $cfg['Servers'][$i]['user']          = 'root';      // MySQL user
75 $cfg['Servers'][$i]['password']      = 'your_password';  // MySQL password (only needed
76                                                     // with 'config' auth_type)
77 $cfg['Servers'][$i]['only_db']       = '';          // If set to a db-name, only
78                                                     // this db is displayed
```

---

4. Open your web browser and type the address to the phpMyAdmin files. For example, because I created a directory called phpMyAdmin on my web server's document root, I go to www.mysite.com/phpMyAdmin in my web browser (see Figure 3.3).

WARNING phpMyAdmin has various types of authentication. The method used in this chapter is a direct authentication method where you do not have to enter a username and password to access phpMyAdmin. Ensure that you protect your server by password protecting the phpMyAdmin directory with your web server or use the cookie-based authentication for the auth_type directive.

FIGURE 3.3:

Introduction screen of
phpMyAdmin

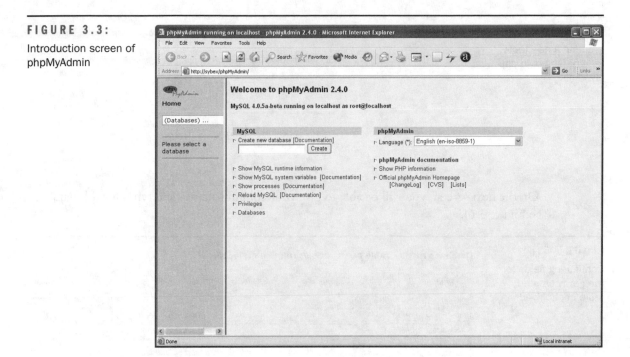

FIGURE 3.3:

Introduction screen of
phpMyAdmin

While you are in the main screen, you will have options to select your databases via the drop-down menu on the left panel, create new databases in the right (main) panel to view statistics, reload your MySQL server, and so on.

Creating Databases Using phpMyAdmin

Probably the first thing you will do when designing the database is to create one. In php-MyAdmin, this is simple. In the right window, simply type your database name and then click the Create button. For now, let's create a database named mydb (see Figure 3.4).

FIGURE 3.4:

Creating a new data-
base in phpMyAdmin

MySQL
⌐ Create new database [Documentation]
mydb   Create

⌐ Show MySQL runtime information
⌐ Show MySQL system variables [Documentation]

Once you have created your database, you will see a new screen that allows you to create tables in your database. Let's create a new table called news_articles and add five columns to it (see Figure 3.5).

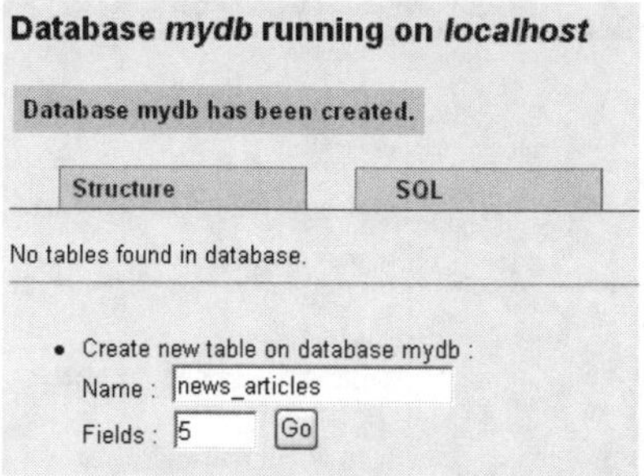

FIGURE 3.5:

Creating a new table
for a database in php-
MyAdmin

FIGURE 3.5:

Creating a new table
for a database in php-
MyAdmin

Database *mydb* running on *localhost*

Database mydb has been created.

Structure	SQL

No tables found in database.

• Create new table on database mydb :
  Name : news_articles
  Fields : 5   [Go]

On the next screen, you will be able to give your columns names and types for this database (see Figure 3.6).

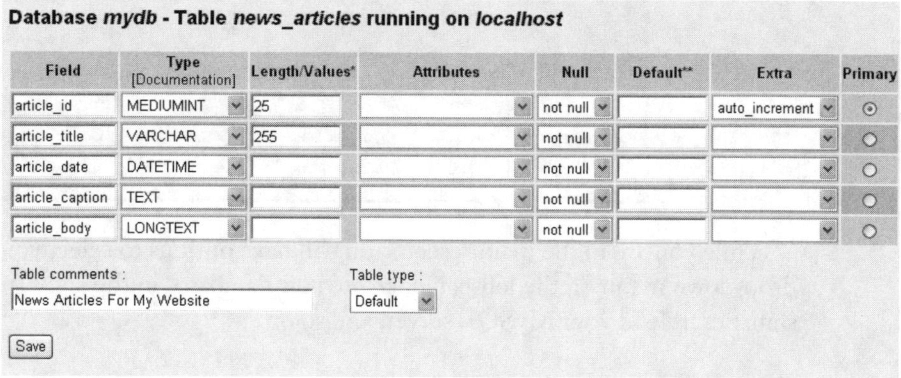

FIGURE 3.6:

Configuring fields for
the newly created
table in phpMyAdmin

Database *mydb* - Table *news_articles* running on *localhost*

Field	Type [Documentation]	Length/Values*	Attributes	Null	Default**	Extra	Primary
article_id	MEDIUMINT	25		not null		auto_increment	⦿
article_title	VARCHAR	255		not null			○
article_date	DATETIME			not null			○
article_caption	TEXT			not null			○
article_body	LONGTEXT			not null			○

Table comments :
News Articles For My Website

Table type :
Default

[Save]

After you have entered your column information, click Save; you will see the screen in Figure 3.7.

Let's take a moment to discuss the column types used in this example. This will give you an opportunity to explore the column types you learned about earlier in this chapter.

news_articles.article_id

The first column is called `article_id`. I created this column to give each article a unique and simple method of identification: an ID number. This field is a medium integer (number) with a length of 25 values. When you assign a length to a column, it does not mean that you can only enter up to that length in numbers or characters; however, it means that the length of the field can be up to 25 numbers long, for example: 9999999999999999999999999.

FIGURE 3.7:

Confirmation screen for creating a new table in phpMyAdmin

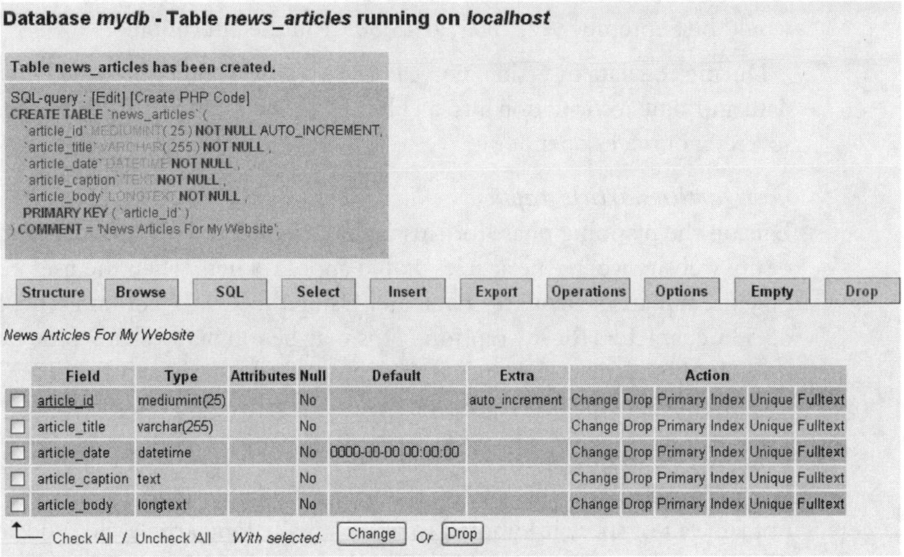

Database *mydb* - Table *news_articles* running on *localhost*

Table news_articles has been created.

SQL-query : [Edit] [Create PHP Code]
CREATE TABLE `news_articles` (
  `article_id` MEDIUMINT(25) NOT NULL AUTO_INCREMENT,
  `article_title` VARCHAR(255) NOT NULL ,
  `article_date` DATETIME NOT NULL ,
  `article_caption` TEXT NOT NULL ,
  `article_body` LONGTEXT NOT NULL ,
  PRIMARY KEY (`article_id`)
) COMMENT = 'News Articles For My Website';

| Structure | Browse | SQL | Select | Insert | Export | Operations | Options | Empty | Drop |

News Articles For My Website

	Field	Type	Attributes	Null	Default	Extra		Action				
☐	article_id	mediumint(25)		No		auto_increment	Change	Drop	Primary	Index	Unique	Fulltext
☐	article_title	varchar(255)		No			Change	Drop	Primary	Index	Unique	Fulltext
☐	article_date	datetime		No	0000-00-00 00:00:00		Change	Drop	Primary	Index	Unique	Fulltext
☐	article_caption	text		No			Change	Drop	Primary	Index	Unique	Fulltext
☐	article_body	longtext		No			Change	Drop	Primary	Index	Unique	Fulltext

↑— Check All / Uncheck All　*With selected:*　[Change]　*Or* [Drop]

This column also has an `auto_increment` value assigned to it. MySQL has the ability to automatically increment the row numbers for you. In other words, every time you make a new database entry, a unique value will be assigned to the new row. This value will be incremented by one each time a new row is entered into the database, for example, 1, 2, 3, 4....

The last important element about this column is that it is the *primary key* for this table. A *key* is used as a method to index the information inside the table. You can have more than one key, and the keys can be primary or unique. For this example, you will stick to using the primary key and assign it to this column.

news_articles.article_title
When I planned this table in my database, I decided I would need a column to store the title of the article. I then decided that each title should be fewer than 255 characters, and I chose the VARCHAR type of column for it.

VARCHAR stands for *variable characters*. VARCHAR columns are great because they can store simple information, and they also truncate the values if you exceed the maximum limit of 255 characters. Also, another value of using VARCHAR is that the trailing spaces are trimmed from the data entered.

news_articles.article_date
A great method to keep track of your dates and times is to use the DATE or DATETIME column type. In the `article_date` column, for example, I used DATETIME, which will

return a value such as YYYY-MM-DD HH:MM:SS. For example, 2003-09-22 13:30:01 would be September 22, 2003, at 13:30:01 in the afternoon.

During the data insertion, you can use a MySQL function called now() to enter the current date and time information into a column. You will use this function quite often in this book, so keep your eyes open for it!

news_articles.article_caption

During the planning phase for this table, I decided I would have a caption on the front page of my website where the articles would appear. Then, when the user clicks a link, I would display the full article from the database. Using the TEXT column type, I can enter up to 65,535 characters for my caption. This may be too many characters, but that is okay because it is a lot better than having data truncated when using the TINYTEXT column, which has a maximum value of 255 characters.

news_article.article_body

For my article body, the column that stores the full article, I wanted to ensure that I would not run out of space if I wanted to write a really long article. So, I decided to use a LONGTEXT column. The LONGTEXT column allows 4,294,967,295 characters. MySQL has field types for every usage scenario, so you will not have any problems with space when designing your applications either.

Adding Additional Table Fields in phpMyAdmin

The greatest feature of phpMyAdmin is flexibility. You never know when you will need to go back and add, delete, or alter tables and fields. Let's look at how to add additional columns to the table you created in the previous section. Follow these steps:

1. Open phpMyAdmin and choose the database you created from the drop-down menu on the left column. You'll see the screen shown in Figure 3.8.

2. Click the Properties link next to the table name. You will see a new screen that shows you the columns for that table. Toward the bottom of your screen, you will see a section that looks like Figure 3.9.

3. In the Add New Field text box, change the number to however many fields you want to add and then select where you want to add the columns from the drop-down menu. For this example, let's add one new field at the end of the table. Click the Go button, and you will see the screen in Figure 3.10.

4. In Figure 3.10, I added a new VARCHAR column named article_author and assigned it a 255-character length. Once again, I value those VARCHAR column types. Click the Save button, and you'll see Figure 3.11.

FIGURE 3.8:

Database properties
screen in phpMyAdmin

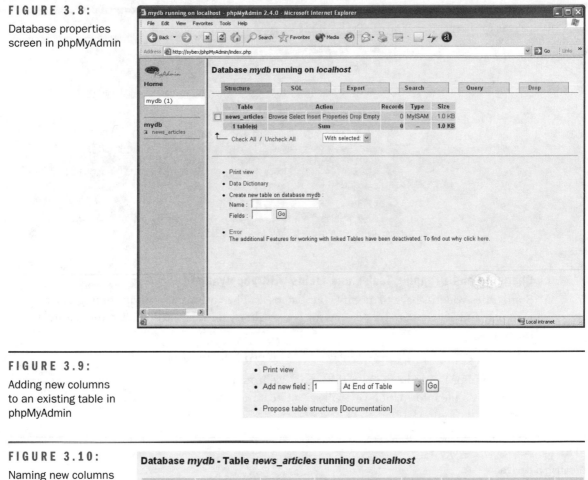

FIGURE 3.9:

Adding new columns
to an existing table in
phpMyAdmin

- Print view
- Add new field : 1   At End of Table   Go
- Propose table structure [Documentation]

FIGURE 3.10:

Naming new columns
in phpMyAdmin

Database *mydb* - Table *news_articles* running on *localhost*

Field	Type [Documentation]	Length/Values*	Attributes	Null	Default**	Extra	Primary
article_author	VARCHAR	255		not null			○

Save

Now you should have a good understanding of how to create new columns with php-
MyAdmin. Next, you will learn how to change and drop fields.

FIGURE 3.11:

Verification screen for
creating new columns
in phpMyAdmin

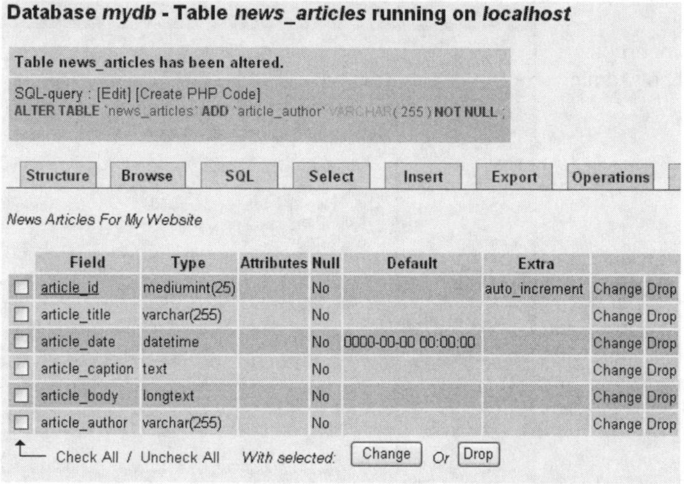

Database *mydb* - Table *news_articles* running on *localhost*

Table news_articles has been altered.

SQL-query : [Edit] [Create PHP Code]
ALTER TABLE `news_articles` ADD `article_author` VARCHAR (255) NOT NULL ;

| Structure | Browse | SQL | Select | Insert | Export | Operations |

News Articles For My Website

	Field	Type	Attributes	Null	Default	Extra		
☐	article_id	mediumint(25)		No		auto_increment	Change	Drop
☐	article_title	varchar(255)		No			Change	Drop
☐	article_date	datetime		No	0000-00-00 00:00:00		Change	Drop
☐	article_caption	text		No			Change	Drop
☐	article_body	longtext		No			Change	Drop
☐	article_author	varchar(255)		No			Change	Drop

Check All / Uncheck All   With selected: [Change] Or [Drop]

Changing and Dropping Tables and Fields with phpMyAdmin

Sometimes you just have to modify your database. The authors at phpMyAdmin.net recognize that and have incorporated ways for you to alter your table structures rather easily. Let's see how!

For this example, let's create a new table with two columns to it:

1. Open phpMyAdmin and select the database from the left drop-down menu. Below the current table information you will see a Create a New Table on Database mydb box, as shown in Figure 3.12.

FIGURE 3.12:

Creating a new table
to an existing data-
base in phpMyAdmin

- Print view
- Data Dictionary
- Create new table on database mydb :
  Name : [junk]
  Fields : [2] [Go]

2. Enter **junk** in the Name box and **2** in the Fields box and then click Go. You should be in familiar territory if you followed the steps for creating a table and columns earlier in this chapter. For the first column, enter **junk1** as the name, select INT as the column type, select 25 as the length values, select AUTO_INCREMENT for the EXTRA section, and select Primary Key.

3. In the second column, enter the name **junk2**, select VARCHAR as the column type, and enter **255** for the column length. See Figure 3.13 for this table setup.

Naming new fields for a new table in php-MyAdmin

Database *mydb* - Table *junk* running on *localhost*

Field	Type [Documentation]	Length/Values*	Attributes	Null	Default**	Extra	Primary
junk1	INT	25		not null		auto_increment	⦿
junk2	VARCHAR	255		not null			○

Table comments :
Junk Table

Table type :
Default

4. Finally, click the Save button, and you should see the acknowledgement screen that displays the new table.

Now that you have the junk table created, you can practice changing column names, dropping columns, and finally dropping the entire table.

Let's start by opening your database from scratch. Open your web browser, go to phpMyAdmin, and select your database from the left drop-down menu. When you have your database selected, you should now see two tables, junk and news_articles (see Figure 3.14).

Database properties screen in phpMyAdmin

Database *mydb* running on *localhost*

Structure	SQL	Export	Search

	Table	Action	Records	Type	Size
☐	**junk**	Browse Select Insert Properties Drop Empty	0	MyISAM	1.0 KB
☐	**news_articles**	Browse Select Insert Properties Drop Empty	0	MyISAM	1.0 KB
	2 table(s)	Sum	0	--	2.0 KB

Check All / Uncheck All   With selected.

- Print view
- Data Dictionary
- Create new table on database mydb :
  Name :
  Fields :   Go

Click the Properties link next to the junk table. Now you should see the detailed information for this column. Next to the junk2 column, let's click the Change hyperlink. You will see a screen similar to Figure 3.15.

In this screen, you can change the name, column type, and so on. Let's change the name from junk2 to junk3, set the Length/Values to 155, and then click Save (see Figure 3.16).

Database *mydb* - Table *junk* running on *localhost*

Field	Type [Documentation]	Length/Values*	Attributes	Null	Default**	Extra
junk2	VARCHAR ∨	255	∨	not null ∨		∨

Save

Database *mydb* - Table *junk* running on *localhost*

Table junk has been altered.

SQL-query : [Edit] [Create PHP Code]
ALTER TABLE `junk` CHANGE `junk2` `junk3` VARCHAR (155) NOT NULL

| Structure | Browse | SQL | Select | Insert | Export | Operations | Options |

Junk Table

	Field	Type	Attributes	Null	Default	Extra	Action					
☐	junk1	int(25)		No		auto_increment	Change	Drop	Primary	Index	Unique	Fulltext
☐	junk3	varchar(155)		No			Change	Drop	Primary	Index	Unique	Fulltext

└ Check All / Uncheck All   *With selected:* Change *Or* Drop

As you may notice, the column has been modified. You are definitely on the right track now! Let's see how to drop a column.

Because this screen is similar to the properties screen, click the Drop hyperlink next to the junk3 column. This will delete the column after you confirm your intentions (see Figure 3.17).

Microsoft Internet Explorer   ☒

? Do you really want to :
ALTER TABLE `junk` DROP `junk3`

OK   Cancel

Click OK to confirm your deletion and refresh your screen. You should see that the junk3 column has disappeared, as shown in Figure 3.18.

Now that you know how to manage columns, you will learn how to drop tables. Open your database from scratch again, and you'll see the two tables, junk and news_articles. Next to the junk table, click the Drop hyperlink, and then you will be asked if you want to drop the table junk (see Figure 3.19). Click the OK button to confirm, and your screen will refresh with only the news_articles column visible. You have successfully deleted your junk table!

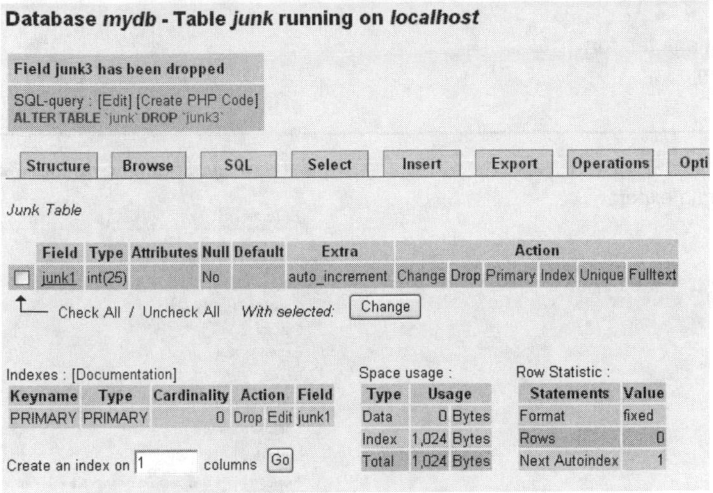

FIGURE 3.18:

You have successfully deleted junk3.

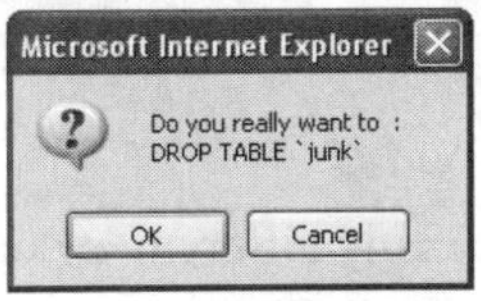

Database *mydb* - Table *junk* running on *localhost*

Field junk3 has been dropped

SQL-query : [Edit] [Create PHP Code]
ALTER TABLE `junk` DROP `junk3`

| Structure | Browse | SQL | Select | Insert | Export | Operations | Opti |

Junk Table

	Field	Type	Attributes	Null	Default	Extra	Action				
☐	junk1	int(25)		No		auto_increment	Change	Drop	Primary	Index	Unique	Fulltext

⌐ Check All / Uncheck All   *With selected:*   [Change]

Indexes : [Documentation]

Keyname	Type	Cardinality	Action	Field
PRIMARY	PRIMARY	0	Drop Edit	junk1

Create an index on 1 columns [Go]

Space usage :

Type	Usage
Data	0 Bytes
Index	1,024 Bytes
Total	1,024 Bytes

Row Statistic :

Statements	Value
Format	fixed
Rows	0
Next Autoindex	1

FIGURE 3.19:

Drop table verification message in phpMyAdmin

Microsoft Internet Explorer ☒

? Do you really want to :
DROP TABLE `junk`

[OK]   [Cancel]

Now that you have mastered the ability to create, change, and delete tables and columns, the last cool thing I will show you with phpMyAdmin is how to back up and restore entire databases.

Performing Backups and Restores with phpMyAdmin

Let's face it—you never know when you are going to need a good backup and restore of your database. I generally make it a point to create a backup on a live site before I do *any* modifications to my database. You never know when the server is going to take a "lunch break" on you and cause havoc on your website. It's a good feeling to know you have something standing by to fix your problems.

To make a backup, follow these steps:

1. Open phpMyAdmin.

2. Select your database from the drop-down menu on the left panel, and you will see your database open on the right panel.

3. Click the Export hyperlink, as shown in Figure 3.20. You'll see a new page that has the export options in Figure 3.21.

FIGURE 3.20:

Export options tab for phpMyAdmin

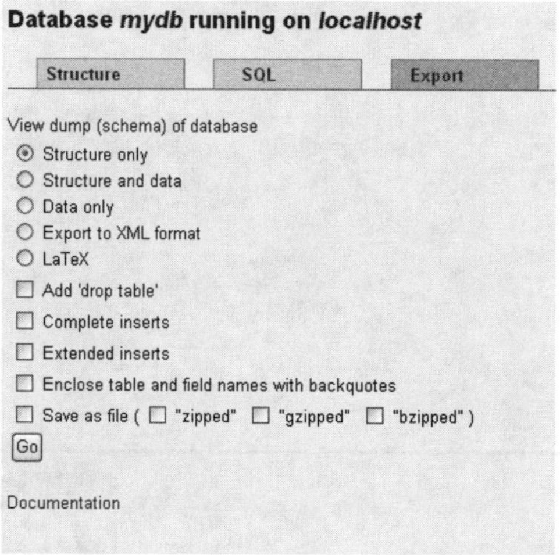

FIGURE 3.21:

phpMyAdmin export options

phpMyAdmin has many different export options. The following are the major ones:

Structure Only   This allows you to back up on the structure of the database and not the data.

Structure and Data   Create a full backup of the database including structure and data.

Data Only   Only back up the data, not the structure.

Add 'Drop Table'   This is useful when performing a restore on an existing database. It will drop or delete the tables and data before rebuilding the database with the backup file. It is important to select this option if you want to perform a restore. If you are going to dump this backup into a new server, you do not have to select this option; however, I recommend it anyway.

Save As File   If you select this option you will be prompted to download the database backup as a file. If you chose to compress the file, your backed-up file will be in the compression format that you choose.

Now that you better understand these options, let's perform a simple backup of the structure and data. Select the following options: Structure and Data, Add 'Drop Table,' and Save As File (see Figure 3.22). You will be prompted to download the file to your hard drive (see Figure 3.23).

FIGURE 3.22:

FIGURE 3.22:

Your phpMyAdmin export options

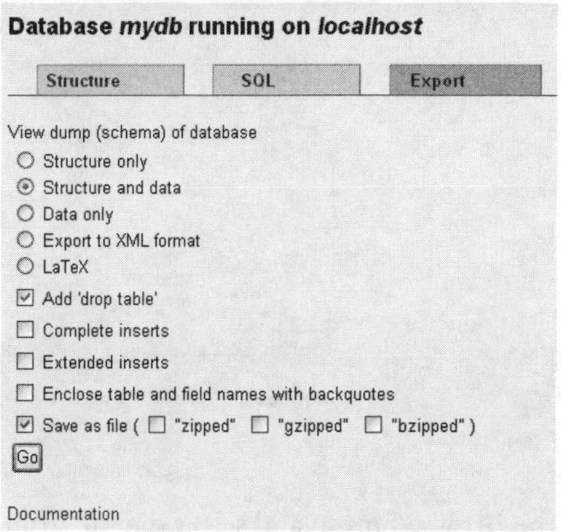

Database *mydb* running on *localhost*

Structure	SQL	Export

View dump (schema) of database
- ○ Structure only
- ⦿ Structure and data
- ○ Data only
- ○ Export to XML format
- ○ LaTeX
- ☑ Add 'drop table'
- ☐ Complete inserts
- ☐ Extended inserts
- ☐ Enclose table and field names with backquotes
- ☑ Save as file (☐ "zipped" ☐ "gzipped" ☐ "bzipped")

[Go]

Documentation

FIGURE 3.23:

phpMyAdmin download export file

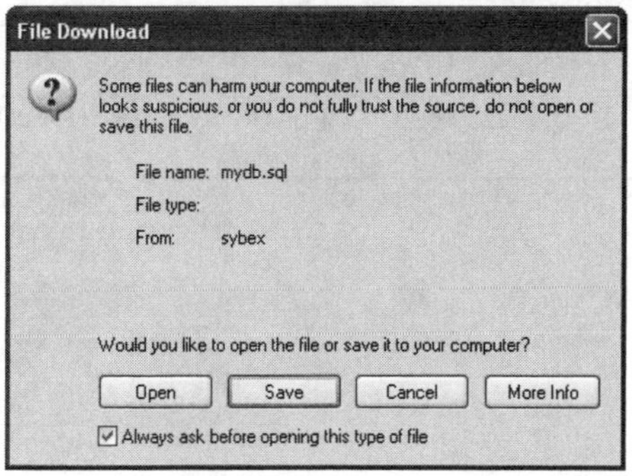

File Download   ⊠

(?) Some files can harm your computer. If the file information below looks suspicious, or you do not fully trust the source, do not open or save this file.

    File name: mydb.sql

    File type:

    From: sybex

Would you like to open the file or save it to your computer?

[Open] [Save] [Cancel] [More Info]

☑ Always ask before opening this type of file

Tuck this file away in a safe place because you will use it again in a moment when you restore the database.

To restore a database, follow these steps:

1. Select your database from the drop-down menu.

2. In the database screen, click the SQL hyperlink, as shown in Figure 3.24.

FIGURE 3.24:

phpMyAdmin SQL options tab

SQL

3. You'll see a screen similar to Figure 3.25. This screen allows you to copy and paste a MySQL query directly or select a file that contains a query from your hard drive.

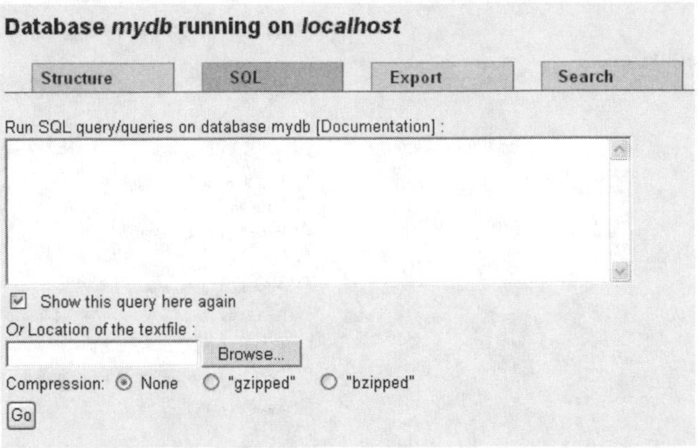

FIGURE 3.25:

phpMyAdmin SQL
options page

4. Click the Browse button and select the file from your hard drive that you saved in the backup procedure. Next, click the Go button to initiate the upload and query process on the file you chose.

5. Once you have uploaded your file, you should see the query performed on the next screen. Thus, the restore will be complete (see Figure 3.26).

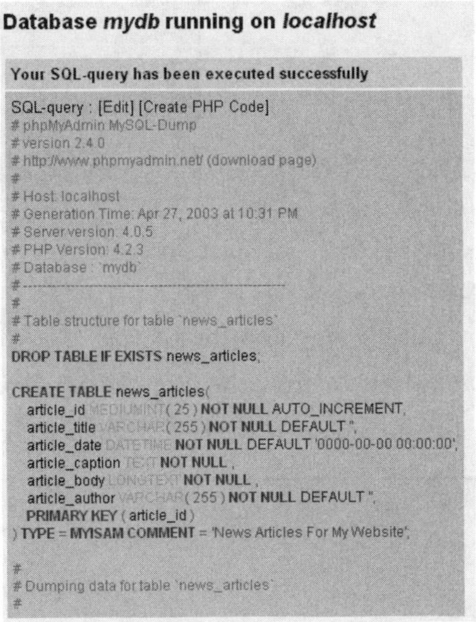

FIGURE 3.26:

phpMyAdmin SQL
query success
message

This section has covered the basic tasks involved in managing your MySQL database with phpMyAdmin. Although it only touched on the potential of what phpMyAdmin can do with MySQL, you are off to a good start. I recommend you explore this awesome application as much as possible; you will find that there are many more features that phpMyAdmin has to offer.

SQLyog MySQL Manager for Windows

I love Linux, and I attempt to use it every chance I get; however, working on Windows makes life much easier—when it works properly. I am extremely happy that I have found SQLyog to manage MySQL easily through my Windows Desktop.

SQLyog is an application developed by the folks over at Webyog.com. It was designed to be lightweight, super fast, and user friendly, and I believe the authors have achieved their goals. You can download SQLyog at www.webyog.com/sqlyog/.

After you have downloaded SQLyog, all that you have to do to install it is click the file; it will set itself up like many other Windows Installer applications do.

When you run SQLyog for the first time, you will see the Connection Manager (see Figure 3.27). From this screen, you will be able to manage connections to multiple servers and multiple usernames and passwords. Simply enter the connection information for your server, and click Save to save the information for later use or click Connect to connect using your settings.

FIGURE 3.27:
SQLyog Connection Manager

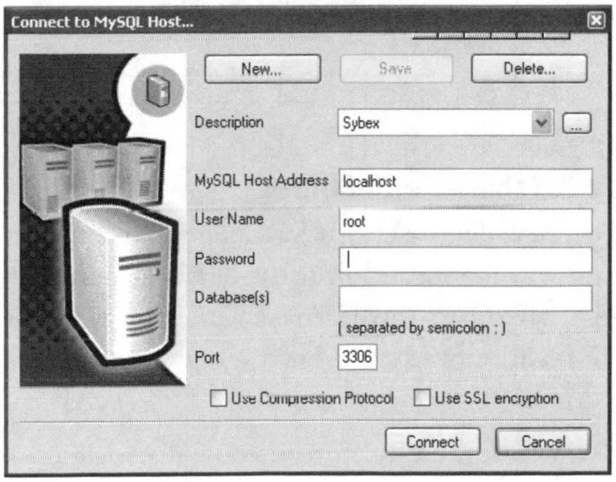

NOTE   It is important you understand how to create MySQL connections to remote servers and user permissions. Usually, when a hosting provider configures a user account, it does not allow connections outside of the "localhost" environment. If you are attempting to connect to a remote server, you must allow the user you are connecting with to use remote connections. Please refer to the MySQL manual to get a better understanding of this.

Once you have made a connection, you will see the main screen for SQLyog. This screen provides you with a list of databases, information screens on the right, and more (see Figure 3.28).

FIGURE 3.28:

SQLyog main screen

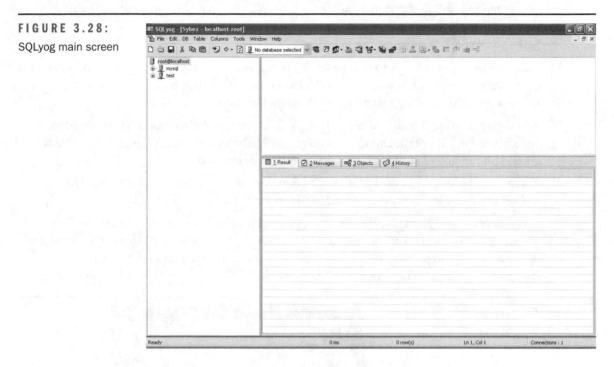

Creating Databases with SQLyog

Creating a new database with SQLyog is simple. Press Ctrl+D on your keyboard, and a new window will appear. Enter the database name you want and then click OK. For this example, I will create the database named mydb. If you followed the same steps in the previous section with phpMyAdmin, you may want to name yours mydb2 or something similar (see Figure 3.29).

After you click the OK button, you will see your database appear in the list of databases on the left panel (see Figure 3.30).

FIGURE 3.29:

SQLyog Create Database screen

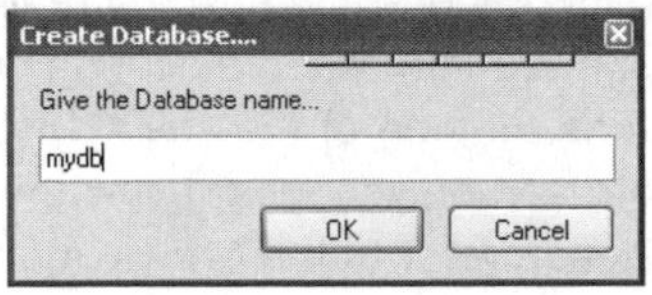

FIGURE 3.30:

SQLyog database
list panel

FIGURE 3.30:

SQLyog database
list panel

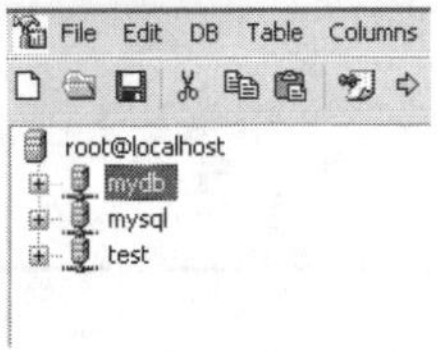

Now that you have your database created, you will add a new table to it. Click the database in the list and press the Insert key on your keyboard. A new window will appear, and you can now enter your column information in this new window (see Figure 3.31).

FIGURE 3.31:

SQLyog field
setup screen

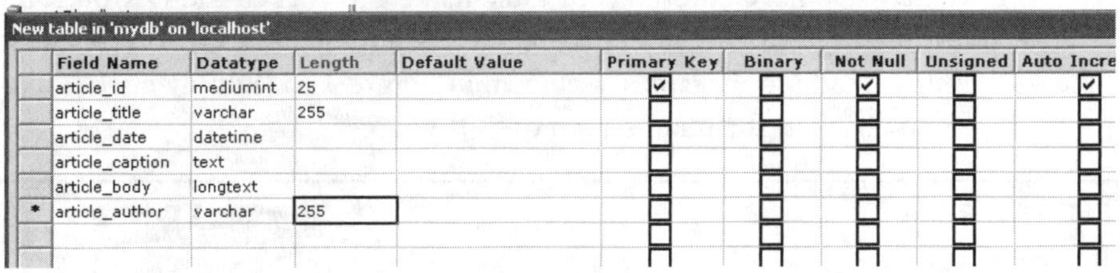

You will now set up this table the same as you did with news_articles using phpMyAdmin. Table 3.1 lists the table fields.

TABLE 3.1: Field Setup for the articles Table

Field Name	Data Type	Length	Extra
article_id	MEDIUMINT	25	Primary key, auto increment
article_title	VARCHAR	255	
article_date	DATETIME		
article_caption	TEXT		
article_body	LONGTEXT		
article_author	VARCHAR	255	

If you have any questions about these field types, please refer to the "Using phpMyAdmin: Web-Based MySQL Administration" section earlier in this chapter.

After you are done entering your field information, click the Create Table button at the bottom-left corner of this window (see Figure 3.32). You will be prompted for a table name, so enter **news_articles**, as shown in Figure 3.33.

FIGURE 3.32:

SQLyog field setup
screen actions

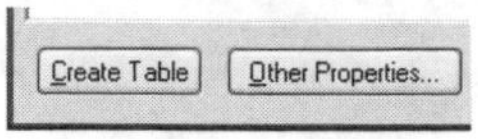

FIGURE 3.33:

SQLyog new table
name entry screen

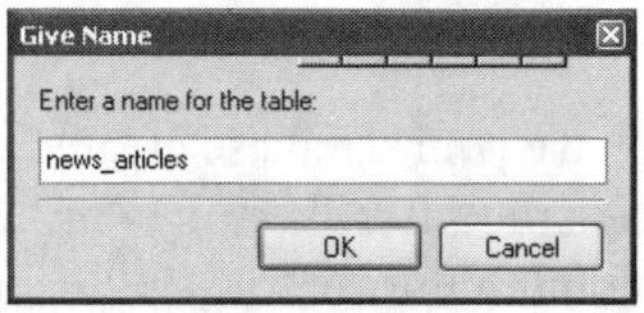

After you have entered your table name and clicked the OK button, you should see a success message, as shown in Figure 3.34. After you click OK on this window, you will have the
ability to add more tables, as shown in Figure 3.35. Simply click No on this window, and you
will be back in the main screen of SQLyog.

FIGURE 3.34:

SQLyog new table suc-
cess message

FIGURE 3.35:

SQLyog prompt
message

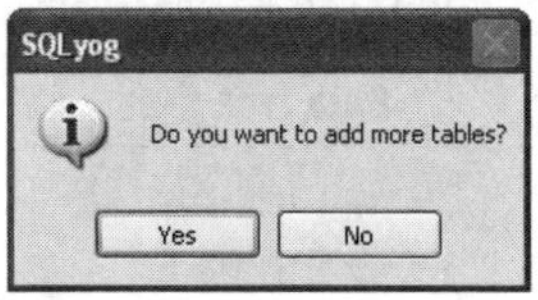

Modifying Tables with SQLYog

A major strength of SQLyog is the ability to perform multiple actions from one screen.
When you open SQLyog and make a connection to the MySQL server, you will see your
database list on the left. Double-click the database you want to work with, and you will
notice the tables list expand below the database name (see Figure 3.36).

FIGURE 3.36:

SQLyog database
table listings

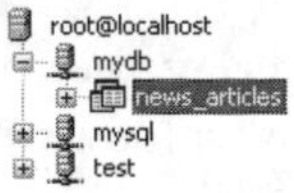

If you click the table you want to modify, press the F6 key or right-click, and then choose Alter Table Structure, you will see a screen that allows you to perform multiple tasks such as adding new fields and dropping fields from the same screen (see Figure 3.37).

FIGURE 3.37:

SQLyog modify fields screen

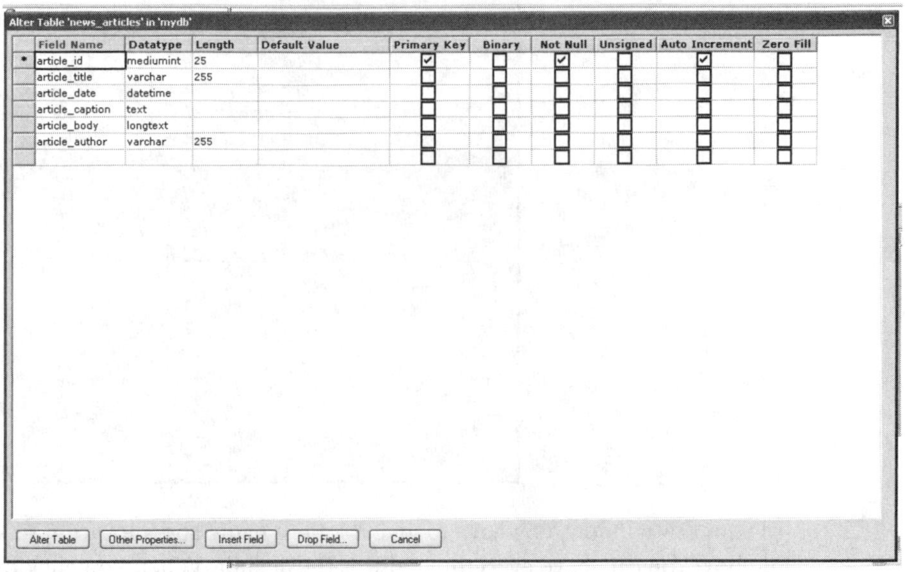

To add a new field to your table, simply enter the information for the new field on the first empty row and click the Alter Table button on the bottom-left corner of this window.

If you need to modify a field, simply make the changes and click the Alter Table button on the bottom-left corner of this window.

If you would like to delete or "drop" a field, click the field name and click the Drop Field button on the lower button bar. You will be prompted to acknowledge the deletion of a table before the program carries out the action.

That is all there is to modifying table structures in SQLyog! It is pretty easy to use and very user friendly. The authors have really planned this software well, and they have taken into account ways to make working with your databases easier and quicker!

Performing a Database Backup with SQLYog

This application would not be complete without a method of creating database backups. It is really simple to back up your database, as well! All you have to do is open SQLyog and make a connection to the server. Once in the main screen, right-click your database and select Export Database As Batch Scripts. You will see the window shown in Figure 3.38.

FIGURE 3.38:

SQLyog Export Data
screen

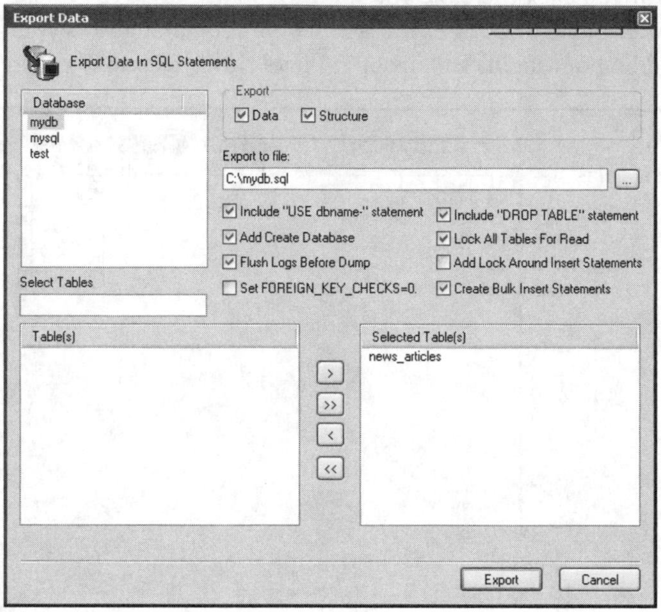

From this window, you have to give the file a name and a location to save to in the Export to File box. You can leave everything else as the default. When you click the Export button at the bottom, a new file will be saved on your hard drive. The file should look something like this:

```
/*
SQLyog v3.11
Host - localhost : Database - mydb
******************************************************************
Server version 3.23.55-nt
*/

create database if not exists `mydb`;

use `mydb`;

/*
Table struture for news_articles
*/

drop table if exists `news_articles`;
CREATE TABLE `news_articles` (
  `article_id` mediumint(25) NOT NULL auto_increment,
  `article_title` varchar(255) default NULL,
  `article_date` datetime default NULL,
  `article_caption` text,
```

```
    `article_body` longtext,
    `article_author` varchar(255) default NULL,
    PRIMARY KEY (`article_id`)
) TYPE=MyISAM;
```

This file is compatible with phpMyAdmin and command-line tools because it is a simple set of commands that will build the database structure.

NOTE   SQLyog does not provide any dialog boxes after the export procedure completes. You will see the message "Exporting of data successful. Total Time Taken = nnn ms" directly above the Export and Cancel buttons in the Export Data window. You must manually close the Export Data dialog box after you see this message.

If you would like to restore a database from a batch file, simply select Tools ➤ Execute Batch Script from the menu. Browse to the batch file you created in the previous step and click the Execute button. You will see a status message appear in the window, as shown in Figure 3.39, which means you are done!

NOTE   SQLyog does not provide any dialog boxes upon completion of the restore process. You will see a message similar to "N Query(s) Executed Successfully. Total Time Take = n ms." You must close the Execute Query(s) from a File window manually.

FIGURE 3.39:

SQLyog Execute
Query(s) from a File
screen

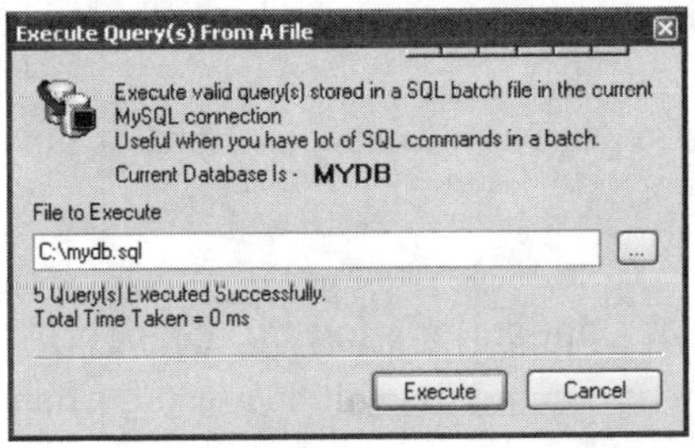

This section covered the basics of using SQLyog, including creating databases, adding tables, adding and modifying columns, exporting backups, and restoring backups to your database. I encourage you to learn more about this excellent application for managing your MySQL databases.

Connecting to MySQL Databases with PHP

Now that you know how to create a MySQL database with some third-party applications, it is time to make a connection to the database using PHP. The following sections discuss how to make a connection, the differences between a persistent and nonpersistent connection, and how to set up a global file that you will include throughout your website to establish the connection to your database for you.

Persistent and Nonpersistent MySQL Connections

What are the persistent and nonpersistent connections? With PHP, you have a few different methods to connect to your database. How you want to manage these connections is entirely up to you as the developer to choose. You may share the database connections with persistent connections, or you may close them and open new connections on demand with nonpersistent connections. Let's take a look at the differences.

Persistent Connections (*mysql_pconnect*)

I prefer to use this method of connecting to the MySQL server with all of my websites. With a persistent connection, PHP will first check for a connection that has already been established using the same username and password as the same host. If one is found and it is not currently being used by anyone else, PHP will pick up that connection and use it. When PHP is done with the connection, it will return it to the "pool" and free it up until it is needed again instead of closing the connection.

There are major advantages of using persistent connections, mainly efficiency. However, you should be aware that if you are limited to any number of persistent connections and your server's workload is high, if you exceed your connection limits, your script may not be able to connect and an error message will be displayed.

> **NOTE** If you have any questions about persistent connections, please refer to Chapter 21 of the PHP manual.

Nonpersistent Connections (*mysql_connect*)

A nonpersistent connection will be opened when the `mysql_connect` function is called and will remain open until the script has completed execution or until you use the `mysql_close` function to close the resource identifier. A nonpersistent connection simply opens the connection, performs the operations, and closes when the script is done with it.

Making the Connection

Now that we have discussed the types of connections, let's make one with PHP now. For this example, assume that your server is going to have an address of *localhost*, and your username will be *root* with a password of *password*. You can also assume that you are using the database that you created in the previous examples of this chapter, `mydb`. Let's check out the PHP code:

```php
<?php
$sql = mysql_pconnect('localhost', 'root', 'password');
```

```
mysql_select_db('mydb', $sql) or die (mysql_error());
?>
```

Let's break down this code into sections.

First, you started the PHP engine to parse the code with the <?php open tag. Next, you used a function called mysql_pconnect and the applicable arguments for this function. Here's the usage of the mysql_pconnect function:

> ***mysql_pconnect*** — *Open a persistent connection to a MySQL server*
> **Description**
> *resource **mysql_pconnect** ([string server [, string username [, string password [, int client_flags]]]])*

As you can see, you entered the server address for string server, the username for string username, and the password for string password in this function usage. Notice that you assigned a variable called $sql to the mysql_pconnect function. This simply returns a resource identifier to use in the mysql_select_db function.

Finally, you select a database with the mysql_select_db function. Let's look at this function usage:

> ***mysql_select_db*** — *Select a MySQL database*
> **Description**
> *bool **mysql_select_db** (string database_name [, resource link_identifier])*

Using the mysql_select_db function, you entered the database name mydb for the string database_name, and you used the $sql variable for the resource link_identifier. This allows you to use the persistent connection function with the select database function.

You can compound these two functions if you want. You achieve this similar to this example:

```
<?php
mysql_select_db('mydb', mysql_pconnect('localhost', 'root', 'password'))
    or die (mysql_error());
?>
```

The last portion of this code I want to point out is the mysql_error function. This function, when used with or die, will terminate the script execution and display the error from the MySQL server regarding the connection attempt and failure. If no errors were detected, the script will execute as advertised without error messages.

Finally, save this file as database.php and place it inside a directory called includes in your web server's document root. You will use this file when you start performing MySQL queries in Chapter 5, "Creating a Website Membership System."

What's Next?

Throughout this chapter, I introduced you to some information about MySQL, table types, and field and column types, as well as using some excellent third-party applications and web scripts to make life with MySQL much easier. Finally, I gave you examples to create connections with PHP to your MySQL server.

In the next chapter, I will show you how using PHP will make your life as a webmaster much easier when it comes to building a PHP-driven web template. I will also introduce you to PHP classes to build a META Content class.

CHAPTER 4

Building a Website Template with PHP

Building a website template with PHP has to be one of the most fascinating elements of synchronizing the look and feel of your website. By creating one file that includes the Hypertext Markup Language (HTML) layouts of your site, you can dramatically reduce the time and effort needed to manage changes in your site's layout.

I have been using this method for the past few years to develop all of my websites. It is much easier to work with one file and then include the layout sections I need by using custom functions; that way, I can develop the PHP code for each portion of my website without looking at the HTML. Furthermore, you can change the look and feel of your entire website by merely changing the one template file.

In this chapter, I will show you the methods I have used to successfully design a website template with PHP. I will also share one of the greatest secrets to getting ranked high in the search engines and, at the same time, introduce you to PHP classes and Object-Oriented Programming (OOP).

Designing Your Layout

In this chapter, you'll design a simple table-based layout in HTML for our examples. Alternatively, you may use many different types of software that allow you to easily design your website. Software such as Adobe Photoshop and Adobe Image Ready allow you to create a graphical layout and then "slice" the image file into separate images for an HTML layout. Using the Image Ready software, for example, you can export an HTML file with all of your slices in place. This allows you to get true What-You-See-Is-What-You-Get (WYSIWYG) results when designing in applications such as Photoshop.

Let's begin the initial layout based on the concepts from Chapter 2, "Planning Your Project." To keep this as simple as possible, let's design a basic table-based layout. After you work through this chapter, you should have no problem designing a more advanced graphical-based layout using tables and cells.

For my initial design, I used Adobe Photoshop to create a simple logo for the site (see Figure 4.1). Although this may not be important now, I will use this example logo as a reference point for the HTML layout. You should create a similar logo that matches your site.

FIGURE 4.1:
Adobe Photoshop logo design

Creating the HTML

Let's move on to the HTML design. Using your favorite HTML editor, create a table with a 100-percent width, three table rows, and three columns in the second and third rows. Set the cell padding to 0, the cell spacing to 0, and the border to 0. Figure 4.2 shows the table (I colored the borders for the table so that you can see exactly what I am talking about).

FIGURE 4.2:

Table example

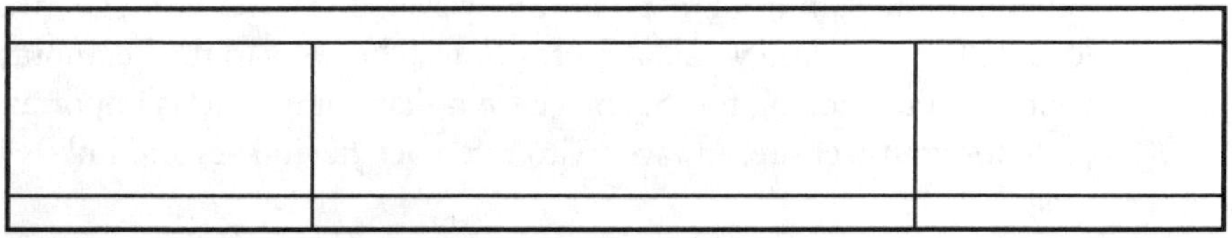

The code in Listing 4.1 is used for the table layout page. Do not worry about any of the head section information; you will get to that later:

Listing 4.1   HTML Layout

```html
<!DOCTYPE HTML PUBLIC "-//W3C//DTD HTML 4.01 Transitional//EN">
<html>
<head>
<title>Untitled Document</title>
<meta http-equiv="Content-Type" content="text/html; charset=iso-8859-1">
</head>

<body>
<table width="100%" border="2" cellpadding="0"
 cellspacing="0" bordercolor="#000000">
  <tr>
    <td colspan="3"> </td>
  </tr>
  <tr>
    <td> </td>
    <td> </td>
    <td> </td>
  </tr>
  <tr>
    <td> </td>
    <td> </td>
    <td> </td>
  </tr>
</table>
</body>
</html>
```

Now that you have the layout, if you want, you can insert your logo into the page in the first cell. I inserted my logo so that I have something to reference during this chapter; you can insert the logo you created. The following is an important tip: When building a layout like this, you always want to use hyperlinks and image links that relate to the site root or the document root of your website. For example, if you were to simply type `images/logo.gif` as the image source path, you are not telling the web browser to go to the root of your website and begin the path from that point. However, if you were to type `/images/logo.gif`, the leading forward slash would direct your web browser to the beginning of your document root and start looking for the image from that point. This is important when building a template for your website. Always try to reference the images and links with the leading forward slash!

You have your layout started now. Let's save this file and name it `layout.php` in your website's document root. Inside this new PHP document, you will start out by creating custom functions around the header and footer portions of the layout script. To better understand what you are about to do, look at Figures 4.3 through 4.5. These figures depict how you separate the HTML table into parts with the custom functions you are about to use. The shaded areas are the areas in use for the function. Specifically, Figure 4.3 shows the use of a custom header function, Figure 4.4 shows the use of a custom footer function, and Figure 4.5 shows the use of a content area.

FIGURE 4.3:

HTML usage for custom header function

FIGURE 4.4:

HTML usage for custom footer function

FIGURE 4.5:

HTML usage for content area

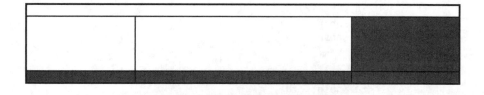

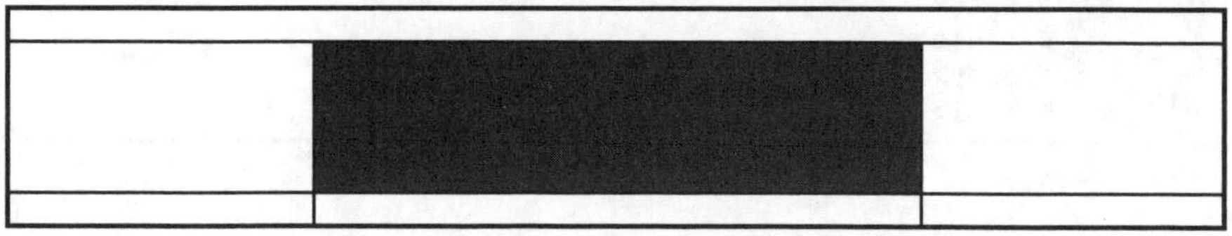

Creating the PHP Code

Now that you have an understanding of how this HTML layout is going to be divided so you can sandwich your content between the header and footer, let's take a look at the PHP code you are going to use to create the functions required to make this happen. See Listing 4.2.

Listing 4.2   *layout.php* **File**

```php
<?php
function myheader($ptitle){
?>
<!DOCTYPE HTML PUBLIC "-//W3C//DTD HTML 4.01 Transitional//EN">
<html>
<head>
</head>

<body>
<table width="100%" border="2" cellpadding="0"
cellspacing="0" bordercolor="#000000">
  <tr>
    <td colspan="3"> </td>
  </tr>
  <tr>
    <td> </td>
    <td>
    <!-- End Header and Begin Content -->
<?php
} // close myheader()
function footer(){
?>
<!-- End Content and Begin Footer -->
    </td>
    <td> </td>
  </tr>
  <tr>
    <td> </td>
    <td> </td>
    <td> </td>
  </tr>
</table>
</body>
</html>
}  //close footer()
?>
```

Now that you have seen the code, let's break it down for further understanding. First, you are going to start the PHP engine by initiating a <?php open tag. Next, you are going to create your own function by naming it myheader and giving the argument that you are going to pass into the function. You are going to use the variable name $ptitle, which stands for *page*

title. You will understand why you use this argument when you get to the "Creating the META Content Class" section later in this chapter. Here are the first few lines of code:

```php
<?php
function myheader($ptitle){
?>
```

As you can see, after you name the function and define the arguments, you use a close tag for PHP. Next, you insert the HTML that you want to be above the main content area of the website. At this point, you can also insert the image logo into the first cell of the first table row. Here is the HTML code for the myheader function:

```html
<!DOCTYPE HTML PUBLIC "-//W3C//DTD HTML 4.01 Transitional//EN">
<html>
<head>
</head>

<body>
<table width="100%" border="2" cellpadding="0"
  cellspacing="0" bordercolor="#000000">
  <tr>
    <td colspan="3"><img src="/images/logo.jpg" ALT="My PHP Site"></td>
  </tr>
  <tr>
    <td> </td>
    <td>
    <!-- End Header and Begin Content -->
```

Next, you issue another open tag that allows you to end the custom myheader function and start the footer function that is going to contain the footer HTML:

```php
<?php
}
function footer(){
?>
```

You may have noticed that I put HTML comments in my code such as `<!-- End Header and Begin Content -->`. This allows me to debug my scripts more easily when using the source view of my web browser. If you create hidden comments such as the examples in my code, you will be able to determine where your header and footer begin much more easily. Here is the rest of the HTML code for the footer function:

```html
<!-- End Content and Begin Footer -->
    </td>
    <td> </td>
  </tr>
  <tr>
    <td> </td>
```

```
   <td> </td>
   <td> </td>
  </tr>
 </table>
</body>
</html>
```

Now that you have the HTML code inserted, let's close out the footer function by issuing a PHP close tag and complete this file for now:

```
<?php
} // close myheader()
?>
```

Using the *layout.php* File

With your layout file coded into PHP, you are ready to put it to use for the first time. Create a text file, call it index.php, and save it in the same directory, preferably in your document root, along with the layout.php file. Here are the contents of the index.php file:

```
<?php
// include the layout file
include $_SERVER['DOCUMENT_ROOT'].'/layout.php';

// Use the myheader function from layout.php
myheader("Welcome to My Website!");

// Enter some content such as this message:
echo "Welcome to My Website!";

// Use the footer function from layout.php
footer();
?>
```

On the first line after the open tag, I used a comment in PHP. You can start a comment with the two forward slashes for a single-line comment such as `// include the layout file`. On the next line of code, you include the layout.php file using the PHP include function. Now that the file is included, you can use the functions available in the included file. In the next example, you will see how to call the myheader function that is located inside the layout.php from within the index.php file:

```
// Use the myheader function from layout.php
myheader("Welcome to My Website!");
```

Notice how you call the function and pass an argument into the function. In this example, I have included the page title in place of the $ptitle variable I used when creating the function in the layout.php file. You will use this argument later in this chapter in the "Creating the META Content Class" section.

Your next objective is to fill in the middle of the web page with your content. In the following code example, you use a simple echo statement to put the words *Welcome to My Website* between the custom header and footer functions:

```
// Enter some content such as this message:
echo "Welcome to My Website!";
```

This example is as simple as it can be. Keep in mind that you can include HTML files or dynamic content to fill this section, but for now, I am keeping this simple for this demonstration.

Your final objective in this script is to display the footer portion of your layout.php file. So, you will call the footer function from the layout.php file into the current file. You achieve this much like the example when you called your myheader function. You will also issue the PHP close tag to end the script:

```
// Use the footer function from layout.php
footer();
?>
```

When you open this script in your web browser, using a URL such as http://yourphpsite.com/index.php, you should see something similar to Figure 4.6.

FIGURE 4.6:

Viewing the index.php script

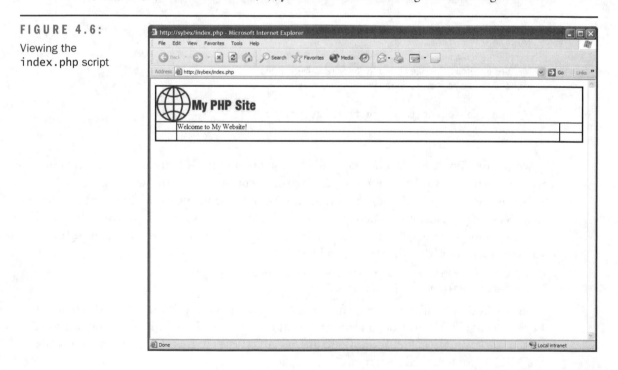

In Figure 4.6, you will see the borders around in the table. In the final `layout.php` file, you will remove the borders because they are not going to be used in the real layout. For Figure 4.6, I left the borders turned on to show you a clear picture of the results for this example.

You have created a basic HTML layout and chopped it up for PHP to use as custom header and footer functions with which to surround your content. With this layout, you can always include files in the left and right columns that allow you to add more links or whatever you desire.

Introducing Classes

As you are developing websites, you will find that you often need to use a piece of code that you have used before. Fortunately, the developers of PHP have taken into consideration that developing the same code repeatedly is a waste of time; as such, they have created a method of using pieces of code with variables to alter the way the code is used. This is called a *class*.

A class is a collection of functions and variables associated within a group. When you begin developing with PHP, you may discover Object Oriented Programming (OOP). OOP allows you to create reusable code and use it whenever and wherever you desire. A good example of OOP is to build an HTML META Content class that you can use throughout any of your websites. You can store this file on your hard drive and use it in as many projects as you like, and it will still serve the same purpose with minimal changes.

In the following sections, you will create the META Content class and include it into your `layout.php` file. Furthermore, by using the arguments you passed through the `myheader` function, you will dynamically generate unique page titles, keywords, and descriptions for your META Content for every page on your website. This is one of my most secretly kept techniques for building web pages throughout my PHP career, and it has proven to work well with search engines. Let's get started with the OOP by designing the first class.

Creating the Basic Class Structure

Based on my experience, I try to create classes inside their own file, and then I name the file with the prefix cls*XXXX* where *XXXX* is the name of the class. This is not required, but it will definitely help you figure out what file performs certain actions by just viewing the filename. The following code is a standard class structure:

```php
<?php
class ClassName{
    var $var1;
    var $var2;

    function myfunction1(){
```

```php
        // Import the vars into this function
        $result = "$this->var1 and $this->var2";

        // Return the result
        return $result;
    }

    function myfunction2(){
        // Reference myfunction1 within this function
        $myfunction1 = $this->myfunction1();

        // Return result
        return $myfunction1;
    }

}
?>
```

In this code, you see the basic class structure. First, you use your open tag for PHP, initi-ate a new class, and then give the class a name. The var in this code simply references a variable that has been defined after the class has been initialized. Next, you will see the first function that is used within this class. Within the first function, it assigns the variables defined into this function using the $this-> operator.

The previous example also depicts how you would call functions or variables from within the class. The $this-> operator is best thought of as meaning "within *this* class." I will give you a more practical example when you design the META Content class.

The following example shows you how to include the class file from the previous example in your current PHP script, initialize it, and put this class and its functions to use:

```php
<?php
include $_SERVER['DOCUMENT_ROOT']."/classes/clsMyClass.php";

$myclass = &new ClassName;

$myclass->var1 = "Apples";
$myclass->var2 = "Oranges";

echo $myclass->myfunction1()."<br />";
echo $myclass->myfunction2()."<br />";
?>
```

First, you start PHP with the open tag, and then you include the class filename. Notice how you use $_SERVER['DOCUMENT_ROOT'] and then the full path of the file when you use an include function. This ensures that the reference path to the file will be accurate every time. This is my preference, and it never fails—unless I type something wrong or the file does not exist.

After you have the file included, you call the class by using `$myclass = &new ClassName;`. The `$myclass` is simply a reference name to the class, and the `&new` is an operator that calls the class object by the class name. From this point forward, any time you want to use a function or an object from within that class, you will call it by using `$myclass->` followed by the function name.

The output from the previous example would be as follows:

```
Apples and Oranges
Apples and Oranges
```

The first *Apples and Oranges* text was generated by the `myfunction1`, and the second *Apples and Oranges* was generated from `myfunction1` from within `myfunction2`.

Now that you have been introduced to a basic class structure, let's create a more practical class for everyday use, the META Content class.

Creating the META Content Class

It is now time to create your first OOP class. This class will generate all of the META Content from an argument passed to the function. You will get this argument from the `$ptitle` in the `myheader` function from your `layout.php`. From the `$ptitle` string, you will break apart each word into a keyword, fill in the META data, and then generate the META Content description, copyright information, and page titles.

Create a new text file, name this file `clsMetaContent.php`, and save it in a separate directory of your choice in your web server's document root. I prefer to put mine in a directory called `classes` for a more organized web structure. The example in Listing 4.3 is the complete META Content class. I will break this class down into small portions and explain it one step at a time:

Listing 4.3   **META Content Class**

```php
<?php
class Meta{

    function metadata($ptitle){

        // Formulate the description for each page.
        if(empty($ptitle)){
            $description = $this->description;
        } else {
            $description = "$ptitle - $this->description";
        }

        // Make the keywords of the title lower case
        $keywords = strtolower($ptitle);
```

```php
        // Replace double spaces with single spaces
        $keywords = str_replace("  ", " ", $keywords);

        // Make string comma seperated
        $meta_words = str_replace(" ", ", ", $keywords);

        // If no Page Title, Use Alternative
        if(!$ptitle){
            $meta .= "<TITLE>$this->sitename - ".
            $meta .= "$this->slogan</TITLE>\n";
        } else {
            $meta .= "<TITLE>$this->sitename: ".
            $meta .= "$ptitle</TITLE>\n";
        }

        // Append META content to the $meta string for output
        $meta .= "<META NAME=\"KEYWORDS\"
         CONTENT=\"$meta_words, $this->keywords2\">\n";
        $meta .= "<META NAME=\"DESCRIPTION\"
         CONTENT=\"$this->description\">\n";
        $meta .= "<META NAME=\"ROBOTS\"
        CONTENT=\"INDEX,FOLLOW\">\n";
        $meta .= "<META NAME=\"GENERATOR\"
         CONTENT=\"$this->company_name\">\n";
        $meta .= "<META NAME=\"AUTHOR\"
         CONTENT=\"$this->company_name\">\n";
        $meta .= "<META NAME=\"REVISIT-AFTER\"
         CONTENT=\"2 DAYS\">\n";
        $meta .= "<META NAME=\"RESOURCE-TYPE\"
        CONTENT=\"document\">\n";
        $meta .= "<META NAME=\"COPYRIGHT\"
        CONTENT=\"Copyright (c) 2003
         $this->company_name\">\n";
        $meta .= "<META NAME=\"DISTRIBUTION\"
         CONTENT=\"Global\">\n";
        $meta .= "<META NAME=\"GENERATOR\"
         CONTENT=\"$this->generator\">\n";
        $meta .= "<META NAME=\"RATING\"
        CONTENT=\"GENERAL\">\n";
        $meta .= "<META HTTP-EQUIV=\"REPLY-TO\"
        CONTENT=\"webmaster@yourdomain.com\">\n";
        $meta .= "<META HTTP-EQUIV=\"Content-Type\"
        CONTENT=\"text/html;
         charset=iso-8859-1\">\n";

        return $meta;
    }
}
?>
```

This class is a great learning tool for understanding many different PHP functions, especially text formatting and manipulation functions. Let's begin:

```
<?php
class Meta{
```

With any PHP script, you must issue the open tag <?php. Next, you initialize a class and give it a name by using the code class Meta. This class is named Meta. Also, you will enclose the entire contents of this class with the brackets {}.

Your first and only function in this META class is the function that generates the META content and returns it to the reference that executes this function in your PHP script. You create a custom function by giving it a name and defining the arguments allowed for that function; in this case, it is the $ptitle that you will get from your layout.php myheader function:

```
function metadata($ptitle){
```

Now you begin having fun with PHP! The first portion of the META function will use an IF ELSE control structure to determine if the $ptitle has any value assigned to it. If it does not, or the string is empty, you will use an alternative META description. Notice how you reference the var $description in this example from within this function. I will show you how to assign the value to the var $description later in this chapter. For now, take notice of how I used the $this->description operator:

```
// Formulate the description for each page.
if(empty($ptitle)){
   $description = $this->description;
} else {
   $description = "$ptitle - $this->description";
}
```

For text formatting, I will convert all of the words in the $ptitle string into lower case and assign this new converted string to the variable named $keywords:

```
// Make the keywords of the title lower case
$keywords = strtolower($ptitle);
```

Before you break apart the $keywords string, you need to remove any double spaces and replace them with a single space to ensure that your str_replace function works properly:

```
// Remove extra spaces
$keywords = str_replace("  ", " ", $keywords);
```

The next portion of code takes the $keywords string and convert it to a comma-separated word list for each word in the string. You achieve this by using the str_replace function once again:

```
// Make string comma seperated
$meta_words = str_replace(" ", ", ", $keywords);
```

Using the same method to determine if the $ptitle string is empty, you use the empty function along with the IF ELSE control structure. If the $ptitle string is empty, you will make a page title from the $sitename var and the $slogan var. This prevents no page title from being displayed at all:

```
// If no Page Title, Use Alternative
if(!$ptitle){
    $meta .= "<TITLE>$this->sitename - ".
    $meta .= "$this->slogan</TITLE>\n";
} else {
    $meta .= "<TITLE>$this->sitename: ".
    $meta .= "$ptitle</TITLE>\n";
}
```

The next portion of code uses the string appending technique to append to the output of $meta. You also use the $this-> operator and all of the strings you have been creating and manipulating throughout the meta function so far:

```
// Append META content to the $meta string for output
$meta .= "<META NAME=\"KEYWORDS\"
CONTENT=\"$meta_words, $this->keywords2\">\n";
    $meta .= "<META NAME=\"DESCRIPTION\"
CONTENT=\"$this->description\">\n";
$meta .= "<META NAME=\"ROBOTS\"
CONTENT=\"INDEX,FOLLOW\">\n";
$meta .= "<META NAME=\"GENERATOR\"
CONTENT=\"$this->company_name\">\n";
$meta .= "<META NAME=\"AUTHOR\"
CONTENT=\"$this->company_name\">\n";
$meta .= "<META NAME=\"REVISIT-AFTER\"
CONTENT=\"2 DAYS\">\n";
$meta .= "<META NAME=\"RESOURCE-TYPE\"
CONTENT=\"document\">\n";
$meta .= "<META NAME=\"COPYRIGHT\"
CONTENT=\"Copyright (c) 2003
$this->company_name\">\n";
$meta .= "<META NAME=\"DISTRIBUTION\"
CONTENT=\"Global\">\n";
$meta .= "<META NAME=\"GENERATOR\"
CONTENT=\"$this->generator\">\n";
$meta .= "<META NAME=\"RATING\"
CONTENT=\"GENERAL\">\n";
$meta .= "<META HTTP-EQUIV=\"REPLY-TO\"
CONTENT=\"webmaster@yourdomain.com\">\n";
$meta .= "<META HTTP-EQUIV=\"Content-Type\"
CONTENT=\"text/html;
charset=iso-8859-1\">\n";
```

Now you have one long string named $meta that contains the entire HTML, you need to pass back to your PHP script and fill in your <HEAD></HEAD> section for your page titles, META data, and so on. Now all you have left for this function is to return the string when the function inside this class is called within a PHP script. You achieve this last operation by using the return control structure:

```
return $meta;
```

Finally, you need to close this function and complete the class as well as issue the PHP close tag:

```
    }
}
?>
```

Congratulations! You have now completed your first useful PHP object-oriented Class. Let's put this OOP lesson to use!

Using the Meta Content Class

Now that you have your class created, it's time to test it out! Currently, the layout.php file does not have any META content, and the <HEAD></HEAD> sections are empty. Let's open the layout.php files and fill in those blanks with your spiffy new class!

The newly modified layout.php file will look like Listing 4.4 when you are done adding the META content class.

Listing 4.4   **Modified *layout.php* File**

```php
<?php
function myheader($ptitle){

include $_SERVER['DOCUMENT_ROOT']."/classes/clsMetaContent.php";
$meta = &new Meta;

$meta->company_name = "My Company";
$meta->description = "This is my first PHP enabled website.";
$meta->keywords2 = "PHP, MySQL, Web Development";
$meta->sitename = "My PHP Site";
$meta->slogan = "Be patient, I'm learning!";
$meta->generator = "PHP";
?>
<!DOCTYPE HTML PUBLIC "-//W3C//DTD HTML 4.01 Transitional//EN">
<html>
<head>
<?php echo $meta->metadata($ptitle); ?>
</head>

<body>
```

```
<table width="100%" border="2" cellpadding="0"
 cellspacing="0" bordercolor="#000000">
  <tr>
    <td colspan="3"><img src="/images/logo.jpg" ALT="My PHP Site"></td>
  </tr>
  <tr>
    <td> </td>
    <td>
    <!-- End Header and Begin Content -->
<?php
}
function footer(){
?>
<!-- End Content and Begin Footer -->
    </td>
    <td> </td>
  </tr>
  <tr>
    <td> </td>
    <td> </td>
    <td> </td>
  </tr>
</table>
</body>
</html>
<?php
}
?>
```

The only part of the layout.php file that you have modified is the portion that contains the myheader function. You will begin right below the section where you named and initialized the myheader function. First, you need to include the clsMetacontent.php file:

```
include $_SERVER['DOCUMENT_ROOT']."/classes/clsMetaContent.php";
```

Once again, notice how you use the $_SERVER['DOCUMENT_ROOT'] to ensure you have the complete path to the actual file included. Next, you will initialize the class and assign a reference variable to it:

```
$meta = &new Meta;
```

Do you remember all of that var $varname stuff I was talking about when you created the META Content class? Well, here is how you assign values to those vars:

```
$meta->company_name = "My Company";
$meta->description = "This is my first PHP enabled website.";
$meta->keywords2 = "PHP, MySQL, Web Development";
$meta->sitename = "My PHP Site";
$meta->slogan = "Be patient, I'm learning!";
$meta->generator = "PHP";
```

Skip down to below the <head> tag in your HTML portion and change it as follows:

```
<head>
<?php echo $meta->metadata($ptitle); ?>
</head>
```

NOTE If you desire to use the shortcut syntax for echo, you may use <?=$meta->metadata ($ptitle) ?> instead of the full <?php echo $meta->metadata($ptitle); ?>. If you want to use the shortcut syntax, you must ensure that the short_open_tag value is set to On in your php.ini file.

You can leave the rest of your layout.php script as you originally coded it in this chapter. Open your script in your web browser from your web server and take a look at the source of the HTML. You can do this via Internet Explorer by selecting View ➢ Source. You should see the HTML in Listing 4.5.

Listing 4.5 **HTML Output to Web Browser from Test Scripts**

```
<!DOCTYPE HTML PUBLIC "-//W3C//DTD HTML 4.01 Transitional//EN">
<html>
<head>
<TITLE>My PHP Site: Welcome to My Website!</TITLE>
<META NAME="KEYWORDS" CONTENT="welcome, to, my, website!,
 PHP, MySQL, Web Development">
<META NAME="DESCRIPTION" CONTENT="This is my first PHP enabled website.">
<META NAME="ROBOTS" CONTENT="INDEX,FOLLOW">
<META NAME="GENERATOR" CONTENT="My Company">
<META NAME="AUTHOR" CONTENT="My Company">
<META NAME="REVISIT-AFTER" CONTENT="2 DAYS">
<META NAME="RESOURCE-TYPE" CONTENT="document">
<META NAME="COPYRIGHT" CONTENT="Copyright (c) 2003 My Company">
<META NAME="DISTRIBUTION" CONTENT="Global">
<META NAME="GENERATOR" CONTENT="PHP">
<META NAME="RATING" CONTENT="GENERAL">
<META HTTP-EQUIV="REPLY-TO" CONTENT="webmaster@yourdomain.com">
<META HTTP-EQUIV="Content-Type" CONTENT="text/html; charset=iso-8859-1">
</head>

<body>
<table width="100%" border="2" cellpadding="0"
  cellspacing="0" bordercolor="#000000">
  <tr>
    <td colspan="3"><img src="/images/logo.jpg" ALT="My PHP Site"></td>
  </tr>
  <tr>
    <td> </td>
    <td>
    <!-- End Header and Begin Content -->
Welcome to My Website!
```

```
<!-- End Content and Begin Footer -->
    </td>
    <td> </td>
  </tr>
  <tr>
    <td> </td>
    <td> </td>
    <td> </td>
  </tr>
</table>
</body>
</html>
```

If you see the same output, or something similar, depending on the settings you chose for your code, then congratulations! You have just created your first portable OOP class that you can use in all of your websites. The search engines will love your site, and you will have page titles on all of your pages.

What's Next?

In this chapter, you have designed a simple layout and used that layout to create a theme for your entire website. You now have a method of simply modifying one file and changing every single page on your site easily. Throughout the rest of this book, you are going to be building on this basic template to create a complete website, so please do not delete your files created in this chapter yet!

You are moving right along, and it is now time to start working with databases, user input forms, and e-mail systems in the next chapter.

CHAPTER 5

Creating a Website Membership System

website membership system offers visitors a sense of attachment to your site. This chapter covers how to use PHP and MySQL to create a website membership system that allows your users to sign up, validate, log in, and gain access to special areas of your site. Additionally, the chapter will expand on the Object-Oriented Programming (OOP) techniques you learned in the previous chapter; you will learn how to use the PHP mail functions, how to work with MySQL to perform queries, and how to expand upon the website layout you created in the previous chapter.

Preparing the Membership System

In the previous chapter, you learned how to create a reusable website theme with PHP. Before you begin to create your membership system, you need to modify your website files to utilize the MySQL database and META Content class. This is what you will do:

- Create a common file that will include all of the classes and essential files required throughout the website.

- Modify the index.php file to include a Hypertext Markup Language (HTML) document with your welcome message.

- Secure directories on your website with a special index file to keep out unwanted visitors.

Creating the *common.php* File

Let's begin by creating a file called common.php and saving it to your document root. This file will use the PHP include function to include all of the files you need. The file will look like this example:

```php
<?php

// Include Meta Content Class
include $_SERVER['DOCUMENT_ROOT'].'/classes/clsMetaContent.php';

// Include Database Connection File
include $_SERVER['DOCUMENT_ROOT'].'/includes/database.php';

?>
```

NOTE   When including files, it is good practice to prefix the path of the file with $_SERVER['DOCU-MENT_ROOT'] followed by the relative path to the actual file. This assures successful portability with your website.

This file simply includes the META Content class file from Chapter 4, "Building a Website Template with PHP," and the database.php file from Chapter 3, "Building a Database Schema with MySQL." You will include more files when you create them throughout this book.

Editing the *layout.php* File

You need to edit your layout.php file to include the common.php file you have just created. Open your layout.php file and delete the line where you included the clsMetaContent.php file. Directly under the PHP open tag, add an include statement for the common.php file. The first portion of the new layout.php file will look like this example:

```php
<?php

include $_SERVER['DOCUMENT_ROOT']."/common.php";

function myheader($ptitle){
$meta = &new Meta;
$meta->company_name = "My Company";
```

Including a Welcome Message HTML File

To better understand the technique of keeping large chunks of HTML code in separate files, you will create an HTML file with your welcome message inside it. I use this method because working with PHP can be complicated, and the less code you have to look at, the easier it should be to understand.

First, create a directory in your document root called html, and then create an HTML file called index_page.html. This file should contain a welcome message formatted with some fonts of your choosing, and you can strip out any of the HTML code from above and below the <BODY></BODY> tags. This is important because some browsers and search engines do not like multiple header tags. Your index_page.html file should look something like this:

```html
<p><font size="3" face="Verdana, Arial, Helvetica, sans-serif"><strong>Welcome
    to my PHP driven website! </strong></font></p>
<p><font size="2" face="Verdana, Arial, Helvetica, sans-serif">The purpose of
    this site
    is for me to learn and practice using PHP and MySQL, so stick around and stay
    tuned, this is going to be exciting!</font></p>
```

Next, open your index.php file from Chapter 4, "Building a Website Template with PHP", in your document root and change the welcome message content to an include statement with this file. This is the new index.php file:

```php
<?php
// include the layout file
include $_SERVER['DOCUMENT_ROOT'].'/layout.php';

// Use the myheader function from layout.php
myheader("Welcome to My Website!");

// Include the welcome html page.
include $_SERVER['DOCUMENT_ROOT'].'/html/index_page.html';
```

```
// Use the footer function from layout.php
footer();
?>
```

When you open your index.php file in the web browser, it should now look like Figure 5.1.

Securing Web Directories

When you have a directory structure with files that are to be included and not accessed directly, it is a good idea to secure that directory with some method to prevent people from inadvertently viewing a list of the files. Some web servers are configured to automatically list all of the files in the visitor's browser if there is no index page present. You can use a file that will redirect the user back to the index of the site if they try to access these directories.

Let's secure your images, html, includes, and classes directories by placing a file named index.php in each of them. The index.php file should contain this code:

```php
<?php
header("Location: http://".$_SERVER['SERVER_NAME']);
?>
```

Using the PHP header function, you can redirect the visitor back to your index page forcefully.

FIGURE 5.1:

Modified
index.php file

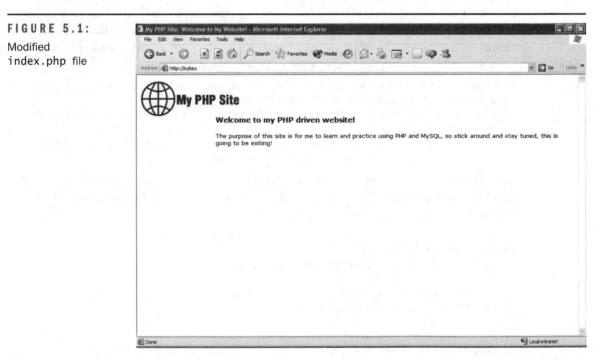

NOTE   `$_SERVER['SERVER_NAME']` is a PHP superglobal. These superglobals were introduced in recent versions of PHP. You can find a complete list of superglobals in the PHP manual in the "Predefined Variables" section.

Now you are all set up, so you can begin your membership system!

Setting Up the Membership System Database Tables

When your members sign up for access to your website, you will collect information about them. To store this information, you will need to create a table with some columns in your database. Using your preferred method to edit the MySQL database, follow these steps:

1. Add a table called members to your database.

2. Create columns for the members table as depicted in Table 5.1.

TABLE 5.1: Column Setup for the members Table

Field Name	Data Type	Length/Values	Default	Extra
id	MEDIUMINT	25		Primary key, auto increment
first_name	VARCHAR	50		
last_name	VARCHAR	50		
email_address	VARCHAR	50		
signup_date	DATETIME			
verified	ENUM	'0' and '1'	0	
last_login	DATETIME			
bio	TINYTEXT			
admin_access	ENUM	'0' and '1'	0	
username	VARCHAR	25		
password	VARCHAR	100		

These columns will gather information such as first name, last name, e-mail address, signup date, date of last login, and a short biography about the person. Additionally, you will use the ENUM column type, which is a list of specific values that operate similarly to radio buttons in an HTML form. When you code the signup and verification scripts, you will better understand the ENUM column types and why you use them.

If you want to manually enter this table structure into MySQL, you can use this example:

```
CREATE TABLE members (
  id mediumint(25) NOT NULL auto_increment,
  first_name varchar(50) NOT NULL default '',
  last_name varchar(50) NOT NULL default '',
  email_address varchar(50) NOT NULL default '',
  signup_date datetime NOT NULL default '0000-00-00 00:00:00',
  verified enum('0','1') NOT NULL default '0',
  last_login datetime NOT NULL default '0000-00-00 00:00:00',
  bio tinytext NOT NULL,
  admin_access enum('0','1') NOT NULL default '0',
  username varchar(25) NOT NULL default '',
  password varchar(100) NOT NULL default '',
  PRIMARY KEY (id)
) TYPE=MyISAM COMMENT='Membership System for My PHP Site';
```

Creating a Membership Signup Script

In the following sections, you will create the signup script that will gather and validate the user input. Then you will compare the database for existing information; if no matches are found, you will allow the user to be created in the database. After you achieve all of this, you will send the new member a welcome e-mail and also notify the site administrator (which is you) about the signup with an e-mail.

Creating the HTML Signup Form

The first step you need to accomplish is to create an HTML form that will collect information about your visitor and present a method of displaying errors based on the input of the visitor and your criteria. Using your HTML editor, create an HTML form similar to the example in Listing 5.1.

Listing 5.1   **HTML Signup Form**

```
<p><font size="4" face="Verdana, Arial, Helvetica, sans-serif"><strong>Become
  a Member!</strong></font></p>
<p><font size="2" face="Verdana, Arial, Helvetica, sans-serif">Join our website
  and enjoy the benefits of becoming a member!</font></p>
<?php
if($errors){
echo "<p align=\"center\"><font size=\"2\" face=\"Verdana, Arial, Helvetica,
sans-serif\" color=\"#FF0000\">$errors</font></p>\n";
}
?>
```

```html
<form method="post" action="/join.php">
  <table width="50%" border="1" align="center" cellpadding="4" cellspacing="0">
    <tr>
      <td width="200" align="left" valign="top" nowrap><font size="2"
face="Verdana, Arial, Helvetica, sans-serif">First Name</font></td>
      <td width="179" align="left" valign="top"><input name="first_name"
type="text" id="first_name" value="<?=$_POST['first_name'];?>"></td>
    </tr>
    <tr>
      <td width="200" align="left" valign="top" nowrap><font size="2"
face="Verdana, Arial, Helvetica, sans-serif">Last Name</font></td>
      <td align="left" valign="top"><input name="last_name" type="text"
id="last_name" value="<?=$_POST['last_name'];?>"></td>
    </tr>
    <tr>
      <td width="200" align="left" valign="top" nowrap><font size="2"
face="Verdana, Arial, Helvetica, sans-serif">Email Address</font></td>
      <td align="left" valign="top"><input name="email_address" type="text"
id="email_address" value="<?=$_POST['email_address'];?>"></td>
    </tr>
    <tr>
      <td align="left" valign="top" nowrap><font size="2" face="Verdana, Arial,
Helvetica, sans-serif">Verify Email Address</font></td>
      <td align="left" valign="top"><input name="email_address2" type="text"
id="email_address3" value="<?=$_POST['email_address2'];?>"></td>
    </tr>
    <tr>
      <td width="200" align="left" valign="top" nowrap><font size="2"
face="Verdana, Arial, Helvetica, sans-serif">Desired Username</font></td>
      <td align="left" valign="top"><input name="username" type="text"
id="username" value="<?=$_POST['username'];?>"></td>
    </tr>
    <tr>
      <td width="200" align="left" valign="top" nowrap><font size="2"
face="Verdana, Arial, Helvetica, sans-serif">Password</font></td>
      <td align="left" valign="top"><input name="password" type="password"
id="password" value="<?=$_POST['password'];?>"></td>
    </tr>
    <tr>
      <td width="200" align="left" valign="top" nowrap><font size="2"
face="Verdana, Arial, Helvetica, sans-serif">Password Again</font></td>
      <td align="left" valign="top"><input name="password2" type="password"
id="password2" value="<?=$_POST['password2'];?>"></td>
    </tr>
    <tr>
      <td width="200" align="left" valign="top" nowrap><font size="2"
face="Verdana, Arial, Helvetica, sans-serif">Tell us about yourself!</font></td>
      <td align="left" valign="top"><textarea
name="bio"><?=$_POST['bio'];?></textarea></td>
    </tr>
    <tr>
```

```
      <td align="left" valign="top"> </td>
      <td align="left" valign="top"><input name="req" type="hidden" id="req"
value="process">
         <input type="submit" name="Submit" value="Submit Information!"></td>
   </tr>
  </table>
 </form>
```

Save the HTML in Listing 5.1 as a file in your website document root in the directory html/forms and name it membership_signup.html. Let's talk about some of the features this form contains.

The first portion of your form is a simple welcome message with a heading and a sentence to convince the visitor to sign up for your site. This is basic HTML with some font formatting:

```
<p><font size="4" face="Verdana, Arial, Helvetica, sans-serif"><strong>Become
   a Member!</strong></font></p>
<p><font size="2" face="Verdana, Arial, Helvetica, sans-serif">Join our website
   and enjoy the benefits of becoming a member!</font></p>
```

Next, you will embed some PHP code that will display any errors from your PHP form validation when you post the form information to this script. Do not worry; I will cover how to generate these errors shortly. Here is the error message display code:

```
<?php
if($errors){
echo "<p align=\"center\"><font size=\"2\" face=\"Verdana, Arial, Helvetica,
sans-serif\" color=\"#FF0000\">$errors</font></p>\n";
}
?>
```

The rest of this HTML document is a standard HTML form with PHP imbedded into the VALUE field for each form element. When the visitor posts the information to your script, each form element such as text input types are stored into the $_POST array within PHP. Take a look at this form element example:

```
<input type="text" name="first_name" value="<?=$_POST['first_name'];?>">
```

With the previous example, I used a basic text input type for my form. In the value, I entered the shortcut PHP syntax to echo the $_POST array value for the first_name key. The reason I use these form values in this HTML document is for error checking purposes. If your visitor does not enter all of the required information or enters invalid information, you will include this HTML document into the error checking part of your script—the values they entered into the form that passed the error check will automatically fill into the form, and the invalid information they entered will be deleted. I will cover the error checking portion in the processing part of this script.

The last portion of this HTML form that I will point out is the `hidden` input type form element. I use these form elements for script navigation, which I will show you when you structure your `join.php` script. Let's look at the example, and then I will explain it in more detail:

```
<input type="hidden" name="req" value="process">
```

The `hidden` type of input type means that there will be nothing visible to the user regarding this form element. With PHP, you will create a navigation system inside your script called `req`; with the values assigned to this name, you can jump to different sections inside your script and perform the actions in those sections. This is a neat feature of PHP, which is useful for minimizing the amount of files for your website. A good example of this is the traditional method of posting forms; you would post from file A to file B. With PHP, you can use file A to perform multiple actions by using this `switch` as a navigation system. You will set up this navigation system in the next section.

Creating the *join.php* Script Structure

Now that you have your form created, it is time to set up the script. Create a file named `join.php` in your website's document root. In this file, you will start out by including the `layout.php` file you created in Chapter 4, "Building a Website Template with PHP." Take a look at the top portion of this script:

```php
<?php
include $_SERVER['DOCUMENT_ROOT'].'/layout.php';
```

Next, you start structuring the navigation system mentioned earlier in this chapter. You will use a `switch` control structure in PHP to divide your script into subsections to perform certain actions. To start your `switch`, you use this code:

```
switch($_REQUEST['req']){
```

In this `switch`, you pass the argument `$_REQUEST['req']`. You are assigning the values of the `$_REQUEST` superglobal array from PHP with the key value of `req` that is passed to the PHP script from the browser. There are a few different types of superglobal arrays within PHP, such as `$_POST`, `$_GET`, and `$_REQUEST`. To learn more about superglobals, please refer to the PHP manual; however, I will cover most of them in this book.

When working with the `switch`, if no value is passed to the arguments, the `switch` will go directly to the "default" section specified. In this case, you will allow the default to include the signup form. This allows the signup form to automatically display when the user accesses the `join.php` file for the first time. The following is the code for the default section of the switch:

```
default:
      myheader("Become a Member!");
```

```
        include $_SERVER['DOCUMENT_ROOT'].
                '/html/forms/membership_signup.html';
        footer();
    break;
```

The default value for the switch displays the header portion of the website from the custom function myheader with the custom page title from your layout.php file. It also includes the HTML membership signup form you created and displays the footer function inside the layout.php file.

After each section of a switch, you must issue a break; for that section to end. Otherwise, each section of your switch will display simultaneously.

Next, close out your switch and the script by using this code:

```
    }
?>
```

To understand the logical flow of this script at this point, see Listing 5.2.

Listing 5.2   *join.php* Default Case

```php
<?php
include $_SERVER['DOCUMENT_ROOT'].'/layout.php';

switch($_REQUEST['req']){
    default:
        myheader("Become a Member!");
        include $_SERVER['DOCUMENT_ROOT'].
                '/html/forms/membership_signup.html';
        footer();
    break;
}
?>
```

If you were to display the script in Listing 5.2 in your web browser, you would see the HTML form you created with your layout surrounding it. At this time, your PHP script will not process any information from the form. If you were to fill the form fields in your web browser and click the button Submit Information, you would see the same form displayed with the information you entered already filled in. This shows you that the $_POST values are working properly.

Let's save this file for now and begin working on the processing portion of this script.

Processing the Form Information

Now that you have the ability to post the information to your PHP script, it's time to figure out what you want to do with it. You can relate this to the planning section of Chapter 2,

"Planning Your Project"; however, I have already taken care of the planning for you. I have decided that the course of action you need to take with this information is as follows:

- Validate if the visitor has posted all of the required form information; for this script, everything is required.

- Check if the username already exists in the database; if it does, have the visitor change it before accepting this visitor as a new member.

- Check if the e-mail address has already been used; if it has, do not allow the visitor to join with that e-mail address. This is for security purposes.

- Validate that the password and the confirm password fields match. If they do not, have the visitor verify their password again.

- Validate that the e-mail address and the verify e-mail address fields match. This prevents the visitor from entering an incorrect e-mail address.

- Insert the visitor into the database if all validation checks pass.

- Send the visitor and yourself an e-mail notification of the new signup. Inside the e-mail sent to the visitor, create a hyperlink that will validate that the user has properly received the e-mail and validated their e-mail address. Once the user clicks the link, their membership will become active, and they can log in to the system.

You are ready to begin coding the next portion of your join.php script. Earlier in this chapter, I introduced you to the switch method of navigation in your script. You now need to create a new section of switch called a case. A switch validates the argument passed to it and looks for a case name that matches the argument's value. When the match is found, it will then execute the code for that case until PHP processes a break. When the break is found, the case you are working with will end, and PHP will look for the next match. In your script, you will only have one match per case, so the script will finish executing and will not perform anymore actions.

You may have noticed in the HTML form that you used <INPUT TYPE="HIDDEN" NAME="req" VALUE="process">. This HTML code presents the value of $_REQUEST['req'] to your switch argument, and it tells that the VALUE of this is "process", which will cause PHP to execute the code in the process case.

Let's go ahead and create a case called process in your script directly below the switch initialization. In theory, you should always put your default case at the end of the switch according to the PHP documentation; however, I have found that this does not really matter. Your switch code should now look similar to this example:

```
switch($_REQUEST['req']){
    case "process":
```

```
        break;

    default:
        myheader("Become a Member!");
        include $_SERVER['DOCUMENT_ROOT'].
            '/html/forms/membership_signup.html';
        footer();
    break;
}
```

TIP

If you would like to check what information is posted from your HTML form to your PHP script in your process case, type the following code: **print_r($_POST);**. This will present you with the $_POST array printed with all of the keys and values that were sent to the script using the $_POST method.

In this process case, you will start developing a system that will validate all of the information required by the visitor. See Listing 5.3 for the process case containing the form validation code and the rest of the actions you will perform upon successful signup. I will break Listing 5.3 down step by step in a moment.

Listing 5.3   **The *process case* from *join.php***

```
case "process":
    myheader("Become a Member: Step 2");

    // Validate all required fields were posted
    if(!$_POST['first_name'] ||
       !$_POST['last_name'] ||
       !$_POST['email_address'] ||
       !$_POST['email_address2'] ||
       !$_POST['username'] ||
       !$_POST['password'] ||
       !$_POST['password2'] ||
       !$_POST['bio']){

        $error = true;
        $errors .= "<strong>Form Input Errors:".
                    "</strong>\n\n"

        if(!$_POST['first_name']){
            $errors .= "Missing First Name\n";
        }

        if(!$_POST['last_name']){
            $errors .= "Missing Last Name\n";
        }

        if(!$_POST['email_address']){
```

```php
            $errors .= "Missing Email Address\n";
            $email_error = true;
        }

        if(!$_POST['email_address2']){
            $errors .= "Missing Email Address".
                        "Verification\n";
            $email_error = true;
        }

        if(!$_POST['username']){
            $errors .= "Missing Username\n";
        }

        if(!$_POST['password']){
            $errors .= "Missing Password\n";
            $password_error = true;
        }

        if(!$_POST['password2']){
            $errors .= "Missing Password Verification\n";
            $password_error = true;
        }

        if(!$_POST['bio']){
            $errors .= "Missing Information About ".
                        "Yourself\n";
        }
    }

// If both emails were posted, validate they match.
if($email_error == false){
        if($_POST['email_address'] !=
                $_POST['email_address2']){
            $error = true;
            $errors .= "Email addresses do not match!\n\n";
            $email_error = true;
        }
}

// If both passwords were posted, validate they match.
if($password_error == false){
        if($_POST['password'] != $_POST['password2']){
            $error = true;
            $errors .= "Passwords do not match!\n\n";
            $password_error = true;
        }
}

if($email_error == false){
    // Verify if email address has been used already.
    $ecount = mysql_result(mysql_query("SELECT COUNT(*)
```

```
                              AS ecount FROM members
                              WHERE email_address =
                              '{$_POST['email_address']}'"),0);

        // If email exists, generate error and message.
        if($ecount > 0){
            $error = true;
            $errors .= "This email address has already ".
                       "been used ".
                       "please choose another.\n\n";
        }
    }

    // Verify if username already exists.
    $ucount = mysql_result(mysql_query("SELECT COUNT(*)
                    AS ucount FROM members
                    WHERE username =
                    '{$_POST['username']}'"),0);

    // If username exists, generate error and message.
    if($ucount > 0){
        $error = true;
        $errors .= "Username already exists, ".
                   "please choose another.\n\n";
    }

    // If $error is TRUE, then include the signup form
    // and display the errors we found.

    if($error == true){
        $errors = nl2br($errors);
        include $_SERVER['DOCUMENT_ROOT'].
                '/html/forms/membership_signup.html';
        footer();
        exit();
    }

    // All checks have passed, insert user in database

    // Email user

    // Email Admin

    // That's it! Done!
break;
```

It appears that I have a lot of explaining to do for your process case in Listing 5.3. Let's start breaking this code down by pieces.

The first portion of code will validate that each of the fields that you decided are required have been completed and posted by the visitor. This code example uses an IF control structure to validate the fields. Additionally, you use the not (!), equals (==), and or (| |) comparison operators to validate multiple arguments at the same time. If you would like to learn more about comparison operators, please see the "Comparison Operators" section in the PHP manual. Here is the code:

```php
// Validate all required fields were posted
   if(!$_POST['first_name'] ||
      !$_POST['last_name'] ||
      !$_POST['email_address'] ||
      !$_POST['email_address2'] ||
      !$_POST['username'] ||
      !$_POST['password'] ||
      !$_POST['password2'] ||
      !$_POST['bio']){
```

If any of these posted fields are empty or do not exist, they will return TRUE for this IF statement, and the code between the curly braces {} will execute. Otherwise, the statement will bypass the code in the curly braces because the IF statement was declared FALSE.

The next portion of code executes inside the IF statement if the visitor has not posted all of the required fields. You are going to figure out exactly which fields were not posted and create an error message for each one. Let's go through this code now:

```php
$error = true;
$errors .= "<strong>Form Input Errors:".
           "</strong>\n\n"
```

The $error variable is a Boolean. Because it does not exist, if you attempt to validate it using a comparison operator, it will evaluate to FALSE by default. For now, because you have errors, you want to assign a TRUE value to it. You will use this later in this script to determine if any errors were detected. Also, you have created an appended string named $errors with the HTML code and error messages inside of it. Take special notice of the newline characters \n in these examples. You will format your final error message when it is time to display it on the error page.

You are going to start verifying one by one which $_POST variables caused the FALSE value of the IF statement now. You will use an IF statement on each one of these values and create an error message for each one that was not present when the visitor posted the information. Here are the examples for the First Name and Last Name form fields:

```php
if(!$_POST['first_name']){
    $errors .= "Missing First Name\n";
}

if(!$_POST['last_name']){
    $errors .= "Missing Last Name\n";
}
```

The next validation is a little bit different because now you are going to assign a new Boolean named $email_error to the e-mail address verification. You do this because you are going to perform a match on the e-mail addresses later in this script. If the user did not post the required fields to check the match, there is really no sense in presenting an extra error stating that they do not match. Check out this code:

```
if(!$_POST['email_address']){
    $errors .= "Missing Email Address\n";
    $email_error = true;
}


if(!$_POST['email_address2']){
    $errors .= "Missing Email Address ".
                "Verification\n";
    $email_error = true;
}
```

The next check for the username is the same as the previous ones without any additional Booleans assigned to them. They will check the information is there and, if it is not, generate an error message for that field:

```
if(!$_POST['username']){
    $errors .= "Missing Username\n";
}
```

Once again, you are going to assign a Boolean to avoid another check for the password field. If both passwords were not posted, you will assign a Boolean for these fields and generate an error message:

```
if(!$_POST['password']){
    $errors .= "Missing Password\n";
    $password_error = true;
}

if(!$_POST['password2']){
    $errors .= "Missing Password Verification\n";
    $password_error = true;
}
```

The final step to determining which form fields were not posted is the About Yourself field. You also need to close out this IF statement with a curly brace:

```
    if(!$_POST['bio']){
        $errors .= "Missing Information About ".
                "Yourself\n";
    }
}
```

Now that you know which form fields were posted, you will run a check on the e-mail address posted by the Email and Email Confirmation form fields as well as the Password and Password Confirmation fields.

You start by checking the Boolean that would have been assigned if either of the two required fields to verify the match exists. If the visitor did not post the information required, the Boolean would have been assigned and the IF statement would skip generating a different error message for it:

```
// If both emails were posted, validate they match.
if($email_error == false){
    if($_POST['email_address'] !=
            $_POST['email_address2']){
        $error = true;
        $errors .= "Email addresses do not match!\n\n";
        $email_error = true;
    }
}
```

In the previous example, you checked that $email_error is a FALSE Boolean. If it is a FALSE Boolean or it does not exist by using the comparison operator because the visitor did post both required fields, you will run a check that they match by comparing the two posted items with the not equal (!=) comparison operator. In this case, if Email Address is "not equal" to the confirmation e-mail address, you will assign the $error Boolean a TRUE value and append to the $errors string a message about this error.

Next, you will use the same method as the previous one for the passwords the user has posted:

```
// If both passwords were posted, validate they match.
if($password_error == false){
    if($_POST['password'] != $_POST['password2']){
        $error = true;
        $errors .= "Passwords do not match!\n\n";
        $password_error = true;
    }
}
```

Now it is time to start using MySQL! You have created your tables using the examples from the "Setting Up the Membership System Database Tables" section earlier in this chapter, and it is time to start performing some checks against the database to ensure that the username and e-mail address your visitors are trying to use do not exist in your database already.

Once again, you will use the $email_error Boolean and ensure that no previous e-mail errors exist from the validation code. If the Boolean is FALSE or does not exist, then it is time to perform a MySQL check on the e-mail address.

You will use a MySQL function called COUNT in a compounded MySQL function query. COUNT is an alternative to, and much more efficient than, using the PHP function mysql_num_rows. Take a look at this code:

```
if($email_error == false){
    // Verify if email address has been used already.
```

```
$ecount = mysql_result(mysql_query("SELECT COUNT(*)
            AS ecount FROM members
            WHERE email_address =
            '{$_POST['email_address']}'"),0);

// If email exists, generate error and message.
if($ecount > 0){
   $error = true;
   $errors .= "This email address has already ".
            "been used ".
            "please choose another.\n\n";
}
}
```

Let's break this down a little further. The first portion is the Boolean check on the variable $email_error, and then you pull your MySQL query from the database. Keep in mind that the MySQL connection is created from your database.php file, which is included in the common.php file you created in the "Preparing the Membership System" section at the beginning of this chapter.

The following is your MySQL query that uses the PHP functions mysql_result and mysql_query combined to return a value to the $ecount variable:

```
$ecount = mysql_result(mysql_query("SELECT COUNT(*)
            AS ecount FROM members
            WHERE email_address =
            '{$_POST['email_address']}'"),0);
```

This query will return a number value and assign it to the $ecount variable.

I want to take a moment to explain the query. Here, you are selecting COUNT from all of the fields in the table members where the email_address field matches the user-posted e-mail address and assigning the result the name ecount in the query.

Do not worry if you do not completely understand SQL queries yet. I will cover them throughout the rest of this book. You should be proficient at building queries with SQL when you are done reading this book and completing the code examples. If you desire to learn about building queries now, you can check out sql.org.

To conclude the e-mail database check, you will perform an IF statement on the $ecount variable to see if it is greater than zero by using the comparison operator for greater than (>). If the value of $ecount is greater than zero, then you will assign a TRUE value to the $error Boolean and append an error message to the $errors string.

Next, you perform the same database checks for the username the visitor wants to use:

```
// Verify if username already exists.
$ucount = mysql_result(mysql_query("SELECT COUNT(*)
            AS ucount FROM members
```

```
                 WHERE username =
                 '{$_POST['username']}'"),0);

// If username exists, generate error and message.
if($ucount > 0){
    $error = true;
    $errors .= "Username already exists, ".
                "please choose another.\n\n";
}
```

Now all of the error checking is done. If any errors existed or if the $error Boolean is TRUE, you will halt the operation and present the signup form with the errors above it and the form fields completed with the information they posted:

```
// If $error is TRUE, then include the signup form
// and display the errors we found.

if($error == true){
    $errors = nl2br($errors);
    include $_SERVER['DOCUMENT_ROOT'].
            '/html/forms/membership_signup.html';
    footer();
    exit();
}
```

The first IF statement checked the value of $error. If it was TRUE, then you moved on to formatting the $errors string. Here you are using a PHP text formatting function called nl2br, which converts newline characters into HTML line breaks (<br />). This will ensure that your error message is clean looking and easy to read.

After you format the $errors string, you include the form that you created in the "Creating the HTML Signup Form" section earlier in this chapter. I mentioned earlier that the form is embedded with PHP to automatically complete the form fields the visitor has already submitted. This presents a more professional appearance to your website, and it prevents the user from using the Back button in their web browser.

Next, you will display the footer of the website using your footer function from the layout .php file, and then you use the exit PHP function, which will halt any further processing of the script. When you exit the script, it will prevent the visitor's information from being entered into the database, and it will additionally prevent the e-mails from being sent. This is good a trick you can use anytime you want to stop subsequent code from executing.

Take a look at Figure 5.2 through Figure 5.5 for examples of the error checking code you have created in this script. Specifically, Figure 5.2 shows a form entry with missing fields, and Figure 5.3 shows the error message that results. Figure 5.4 shows a form entry with mismatched e-mail address and password information, and Figure 5.5 shows the errors that result.

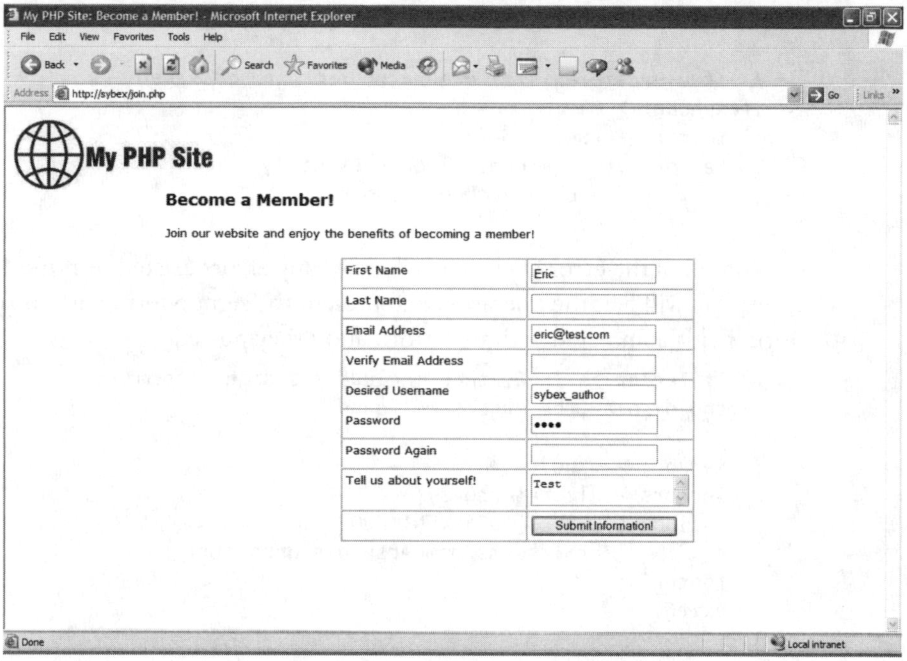

FIGURE 5.2: Form entry with missing fields

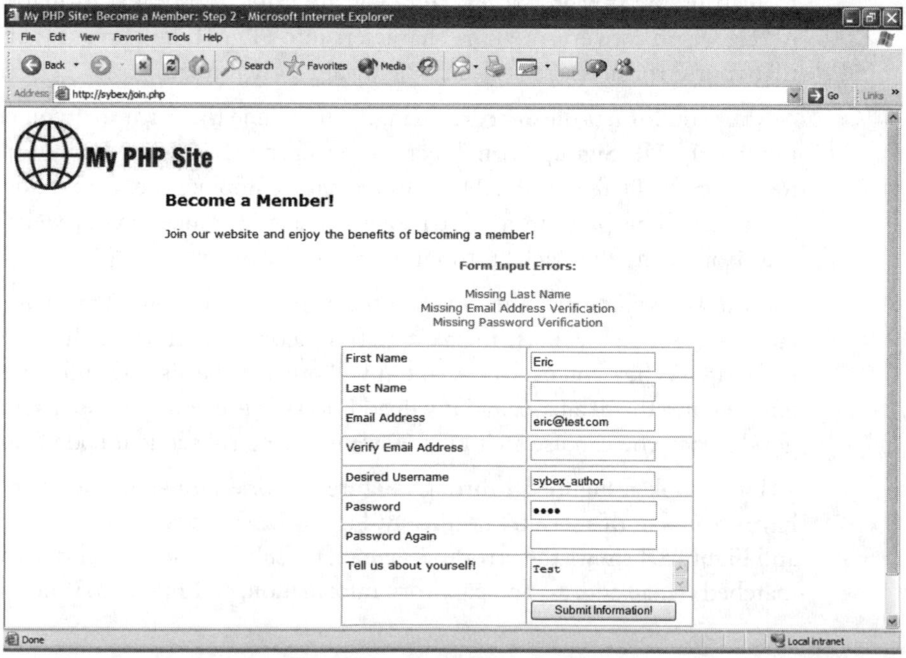

FIGURE 5.3: Form validation errors displayed in browser from Figure 5.2

FIGURE 5.4:

Form entry with mismatched e-mail address and password information

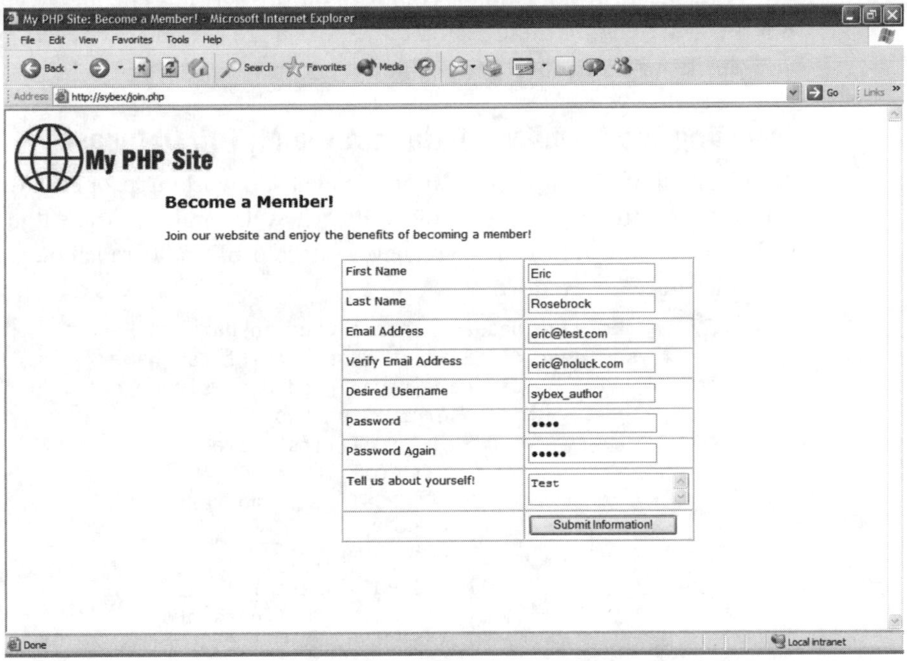

FIGURE 5.5:

Form validation errors displayed in browser from Figure 5.4

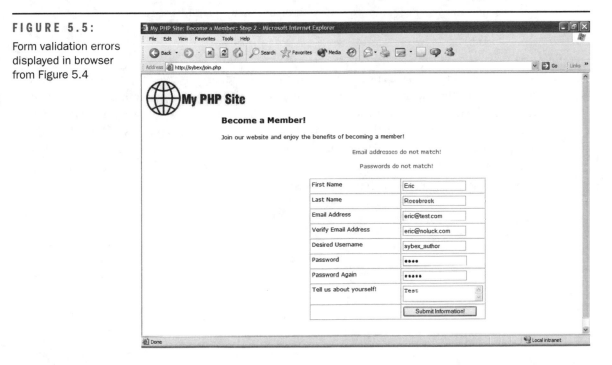

All of your form validation is complete for this script. I encourage you to test your script out if you are coding these examples while you are reading. Try every possible combination and check out how robust this script is.

Inserting the Members' Data into the MySQL Database

Now that all of your form validation is coded and working properly, you need to store the information into the members table of the MySQL database. You will use the PHP function mysql_query to store the data you have collected and validated about your new member. Take a look at this code example:

```
// All checks have passed, insert user in database
$sql = @mysql_query("INSERT INTO members (first_name,
                     last_name, email_address, signup_date,
                     bio, username, password)
                     VALUES ('$_POST[first_name]',
                             '$_POST[last_name]',
                             '$_POST[email_address]',
                             now(),
                             '$_POST[bio]',
                             '$_POST[username]',
                             '".md5($_POST[password])."')
                     ");
if(!$sql){
    echo "Error inserting your information into MySQL: ".mysql_error();
    footer();
    exit();
}
```

Let's break this down step by step for better understanding. First, you use a mysql_query function to INSERT the data into the appropriate columns. The first set of parentheses is the column names of the table into which you are inserting the data. The next set of parentheses is the actual values you are inserting into the columns defined in the first set of parentheses. MySQL will not accept a mismatch query, meaning that you must have an equal amount of columns defined in the first set of parentheses and an equal number of values in the second set. Here is the code:

```
$sql = @mysql_query("INSERT INTO members (first_name,
                     last_name, email_address, signup_date,
                     bio, username, password)
                     VALUES ('$_POST[first_name]',
                             '$_POST[last_name]',
                             '$_POST[email_address]',
                             now(),
                             '$_POST[bio]',
                             '$_POST[username]',
                             '".md5($_POST[password])."'
                             )");
```

When you assign a variable name to the mysql_query function, such as $sql in this case, the value of the $sql variable name will be a Boolean TRUE or FALSE, depending on if there were errors found in the query. This allows you to suppress the output errors of the mysql_query function using an at (@) symbol in front of the function call.

The next important item I want to point out in this query is the now() function. The now() function will format any DATE, DATETIME, TIMESTAMP, and related MySQL columns with the current date and time of the MySQL query. This is a perfect function for time stamping information in your database.

When dealing with passwords in your MySQL database, it is always best to encrypt them in some way. PHP offers a function called md5, which is a one-way encryption and cannot be decrypted. This may sound confusing at first, but when you need to validate a value against md5 encrypted data, you convert the new data to md5 and then compare the two values together. If they match, you have validated the information. In this case, you will encrypt the user's password in the database using the md5 one-way encryption. Be safe, be secure!

After you have performed the query, you use an IF statement to check the value of the $sql Boolean. If the query failed, you will give the user an error in the browser and embed the response from the MySQL server by using the mysql_error function. Once again, you will display the footer of your website with the custom footer function from the layout.php file and exit the script with the exit function. This method is much cleaner in appearance than using the common method you may have seen, or die, which exits the script immediately upon receiving the error from the MySQL server during the query:

```
if(!$sql){
    echo "Error inserting your information into MySQL: ".
        mysql_error();
    footer();
    exit();
}
```

The final step to the MySQL query is to get the ID number from the AUTO_INCREMENT ID column in your database. This number is incremented one value from the previous row each time a new row is created, hence the term *auto increment*. The AUTO_INCREMENT column types are good for creating unique numbers for just about any type of table you create. In this example, you are assigning a number to each new user and making it their user ID. Let's grab this information from MySQL so you can send it to the user in e-mail. You will use the mysql_insert_id function to get the number:

```
$userid = mysql_insert_id();
```

Sending E-mail with PHP

When the form validation has passed the test and you have successfully entered the user into the database, you will send the user and the website administrator an e-mail notifying them of the new user signup. You will be using a custom e-mail class that you will create in this section.

For Windows-based web servers, you will need a Simple Mail Transfer Protocol (SMTP) server to send e-mails from PHP. Windows does not ship with an SMTP server by default, so you will have to find a third-party application that can handle this task. When I am developing on Windows, I use Workgroup Mail (www.workgroupmail.com). Workgroup Mail is a shareware application that offers a free 30-day trial.

TIP   Windows users can create a fake domain name and edit a file called hosts in your C:\Windows\System32\drivers\etc directory to set up a domain name to point to your local computer. With this domain name, you can check your e-mail using Workgroup Mail and even set up Apache for virtual hosts and then access your website.

Because sending e-mails is a common task that requires some memorization of the mail function, you can reduce the amount of code to memorize by creating a custom class to send e-mails. In this chapter, I will show you a simple text-based class that you are going to use. If you want to expand on this class to add HTML mail and file attachments, you could have a fully functional mail class for virtually every use you desire. For now, you will keep it simple and build the e-mail headers required by mail servers. Let's look at this class now:

```php
<?php
class Email {

    function SendMail(){
        $Message = stripslashes($this->Message);
        $Message = stripslashes($this->Message);
        $headers .="From: ".$this->FromName.
                    "<".$this->FromMail.">\n";
        $headers .="Reply-To: ".$this->FromName.
                    "<".$this->FromMail.">\n";
        //$headers .="X-Priority: 1\n";
        //$headers .="X-MSMail-Priority: High\n";
        $headers .="X-Mailer: My PHP Mailer\n";
        $headers .="Origin: ".$_SERVER['REMOTE_ADDR']."\n";
        mail($this->ToMail, $this->Subject, $Message,
            $headers);
    }
}
?>
```

This file initializes a new class, and then it creates a new custom function named SendMail. This function will remove any backslashes that PHP inserts before the quotes and escape characters in form-posted values. You do this by using the stripslashes function on the string that is passed through the internal pointer $this->Message from the variables defined above the function inside the class. Here is the code I have just described:

```php
<?php
class Email {

    function SendMail(){
        $Message = stripslashes($this->Message);
        $Message = stripslashes($this->Message);
```

This class will also build a nice set of e-mail headers that mail servers and mail clients use to identify elements of the e-mail that is sent through them. These headers are the main reason I create a custom e-mail class. I like to ensure that I have all of the proper headers, and I do not want to memorize all of them. This is the advantage of classes: to reduce the amount of code you have to type when you need to perform an action. Here are the e-mail headers for this class:

```php
$headers .="From: ".$this->FromName.
           "<".$this->FromMail.">\n";
$headers .="Reply-To: ".$this->FromName.
           "<".$this->FromMail.">\n";
//$headers .="X-Priority: 1\n";
//$headers .="X-MSMail-Priority: High\n";
$headers .="X-Mailer: My PHP Mailer\n";
$headers .="Origin: ".$_SERVER['REMOTE_ADDR']."\n";
```

NOTE I have coded the e-mail priorities for certain mail clients into this class; however, I have disabled them. If you want to use these priorities, remove the two forward slashes on the applicable lines.

Next, you will use the PHP mail function to send the e-mail using the values you have compiled into this class. Also, you are finished with the function, so you close the function and the class. Here is the code:

```php
mail($this->ToMail, $this->Subject, $Message,
        $headers);
    }
}
?>
```

Save this class file in your classes directory and name it clsEmail.php.

Before you can use the class, though, you have to include it. Using your common.php file, enter a new include line for this class. You will use this in multiple places throughout your website, so this is a great file to be included all the time. Here is my current common.php file:

```php
<?php

// Include Meta Content Class
```

```
include $_SERVER['DOCUMENT_ROOT'].
        '/classes/clsMetaContent.php';

// Include Database Connection File
include $_SERVER['DOCUMENT_ROOT'].
        '/includes/database.php';

// Include Email Class
include $_SERVER['DOCUMENT_ROOT'].
        '/classes/clsEmail.php';
?>
```

Now it is time to go back to your join.php file and send out an e-mail to the client. Below the MySQL queries, you will add the following code:

```
$verify_url = "http://".$_SERVER['SERVER_NAME'].
              "/join.php?req=verify&id=$userid&vcode=".
              md5($_POST['first_name']);

$mailer = &new Email;
// Email user
$mailer->ToMail = $_POST['email_address'];
$mailer->FromMail = "admin@test.com";
$mailer->FromName = "My PHP Site Administrator";
$mailer->Subject = "Your Membership at My PHP Site";
$mailer->Message = "Dear $_POST[first_name],\n".
                   "Thanks for joining our website! We".
                   " welcome you and look forward to".
                   " your participation.\n\n".
                   "Below you will find the ".
                   "information required to ".
                   "Login to our website!\n\n".
                   "First, you will need to verify".
                   " your email address ".
                   "by clicking on this ".
                   "hyperlink:\n$verify_url\nand ".
                   "following the directions in your ".
                   " web browser.\n\n".
                   "=====================\n".
                   "Username: $_POST[username]\n".
                   "Password: $_POST[password]\n".
                   "UserID: $userid\n".
                   "Email Address: ".
                   "$_POST[email_address]\n".
                   "=====================\n\n".
                   "Thank you,\n".
                   "My PHP Site Administrator\n".
                   "http://$_SERVER[SERVER_NAME]\n";
```

```
$mailer->SendMail();
```

I will break down the usage of this class for better understanding.

You want to find a way to verify the user's e-mail address. The best way to verify an e-mail address is to send an e-mail with a Uniform Resource Locator (URL) that contains a method of verifying the user with a special code embedded into it. You create this special code by using the ID number that MySQL returned from the database insert query, and then you can validate the person by a number of methods. The method I chose to use is to encrypt their first name using the md5 function and put the output into the URL. You will create the verification code later in this chapter. This is the code you will use to create this special URL to be e-mailed to the user:

```
$verify_url = "http://".$_SERVER['SERVER_NAME'].
              "/join.php?req=verify&id=$userid&vcode=".
              md5($_POST['first_name']);
```

Next, you will initialize the mail class that was included through your common.php file, and you assign a variable $mailer with which to associate that class:

```
$mailer = &new Email;
```

With the class initialized, you can start using it. First, you need to define the variables the class will use. You tell the class to whom you will send the e-mail:

```
$mailer->ToMail = $_POST['email_address'];
```

Next, you will define the e-mail address from whom the e-mail will be sent. In this case, it is admin@test.com:

```
$mailer->FromMail = "admin@test.com";
```

Next, define the name of the person who sent the e-mail:

```
$mailer->FromName = "My PHP Site Administrator";
```

Then, define the subject of the e-mail:

```
$mailer->Subject = "Your Membership at My PHP Site";
```

Now you need to create the e-mail message body for the e-mail being sent. This body identifies the user by first name, welcomes them with a nice message, describes how to verify their e-mail address with the special URL, and gives them their username, password, and e-mail. You can customize this e-mail to your needs. Here is the code:

```
$mailer->Message = "Dear $_POST[first_name],\n".
                   "Thanks for joining our website! We".
                   " welcome you and look forward to".
                   " your participation.\n\n".
                   "Below you will find the ".
                   "information required to ".
                   "Login to our website!\n\n".
```

```
                      "First, you will need to verify".
                      " your email address ".
                      "by clicking on this ".
                      "hyperlink:\n$verify_url\nand ".
                      "following the directions in your ".
                      " web browser.\n\n".
                      "=====================\n".
                      "Username: $_POST[username]\n".
                      "Password: $_POST[password]\n".
                      "UserID: $userid\n".
                      "Email Address: ".
                      "$_POST[email_address]\n".
                      "=====================\n\n".
                      "Thank you,\n".
                      "My PHP Site Administrator\n".
                      "http://$_SERVER[SERVER_NAME]\n";
```

Finally, the last step to sending this e-mail is to use the SendMail function from your class:

```
$mailer->SendMail();
```

When this code executes successfully, an e-mail will be sent to the user upon signup. Figure 5.6 shows the e-mail I received upon signup.

Now that you have e-mailed the user, let's send the administrator an e-mail. You achieve this by using the same method as the user e-mail. Here is the code:

```
// Email Admin
$mailer->ToMail = "eric@test.com";
$mailer->FromMail = "admin@test.com";
$mailer->FromName = "My PHP Site Administrator";
$mailer->Subject = "New Member at My PHP Site [$userid]";
$mailer->Message = "Hi,\n\n".
                      "A new member has just signed up ".
                      "at My PHP Site! Here's their ".
                      " information:\n\n".
                      "=====================\n".
                      "First Name: $_POST[first_name]\n".
                      "Last Name: $_POST[last_name]\n".
                      "Email Address: ".
                      "$_POST[email_address]\n".
                      "UserID: $userid\n".
                      "=====================\n\n".
                      "Thank you,\n".
                      "My PHP Site Administrator\n".
                      "http://$_SERVER[SERVER_NAME]\n";
$mailer->SendMail();
```

Figure 5.7 shows the e-mail the administrator receives after signup.

FIGURE 5.6:

E-mail received by
user after signing up

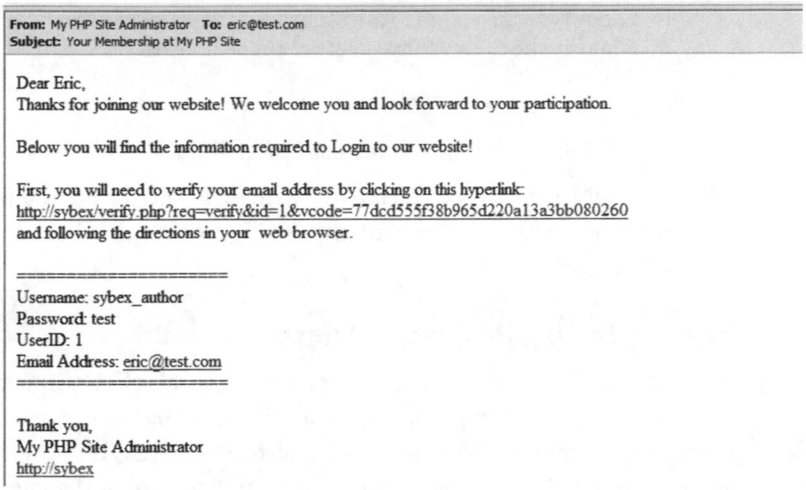

> From: My PHP Site Administrator   To: eric@test.com
> Subject: Your Membership at My PHP Site
>
> Dear Eric,
> Thanks for joining our website! We welcome you and look forward to your participation.
>
> Below you will find the information required to Login to our website!
>
> First, you will need to verify your email address by clicking on this hyperlink:
> http://sybex/verify.php?req=verify&id=1&vcode=77dcd555f38b965d220a13a3bb080260
> and following the directions in your web browser.
>
> =====================
> Username: sybex_author
> Password: test
> UserID: 1
> Email Address: eric@test.com
> =====================
>
> Thank you,
> My PHP Site Administrator
> http://sybex

FIGURE 5.7:

E-mail received by
administrator after
signup

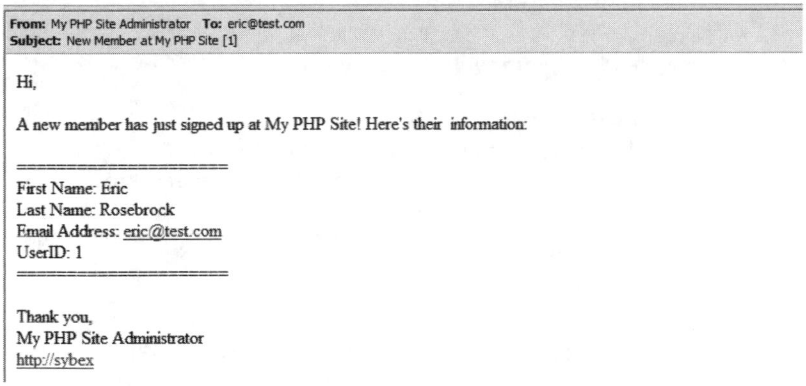

> From: My PHP Site Administrator   To: eric@test.com
> Subject: New Member at My PHP Site [1]
>
> Hi,
>
> A new member has just signed up at My PHP Site! Here's their information:
>
> =====================
> First Name: Eric
> Last Name: Rosebrock
> Email Address: eric@test.com
> UserID: 1
> =====================
>
> Thank you,
> My PHP Site Administrator
> http://sybex

Displaying Success Message After Signup

The next task to perform for the process case of the signup procedure is to display a welcome
message to notify the user to check their e-mail for login information. This message is only
displayed upon a successful signup. If the signup is not successful, you have already taken care
of displaying an error message in the previous code from this chapter. Because this message is
short and simple, you do not need to create an HTML file and include it; you can just echo it
in the PHP script. Let's display a message and complete this portion of your script:

```
// Display Success Message
echo '<p align="center"><font size="4" '.
     'face="Verdana, Arial, Helvetica, sans-serif">'.
     '<strong>Your Signup Was Successful!'.
     '</strong></font></p>'.
```

```
            '<p align="center"><font size="4" '.
            'face="Verdana, Arial, Helvetica, sans-serif">'.
            'Please check your email for instructions.'.
            '</font></p>';
    // That's it! Done!
```

Figure 5.8 depicts the success message after signup.

This concludes the process case for your join.php script. You only have one more portion of the join.php script to complete: the verify case that validates the user's e-mail when they click the URL.

Verifying the User's E-mail Address

The next task is to create the code to verify the special URL you embedded into the welcome e-mail sent to the user upon signup. You will begin by creating a new case in your switch and naming it verify. This switch will perform a MySQL query using the information in the URL and will check your database for a row matching the encrypted first name values and the ID number. Let's view the code:

```
case "verify":
    myheader("Verify Information");

    // Perform MySQL Query:
    $sql = mysql_result(mysql_query("SELECT COUNT(*)
                        AS vcount FROM members WHERE
                        id='{$_GET['id']}' AND
                        md5(first_name) = '{$_GET['vcode']}'
                        "),0);

    if($sql == 1){
        $update = mysql_query("UPDATE members SET
                        verified='1' WHERE
                        id='{$_GET['id']}'");
        if(!$update){
            echo "Error with MySQL Query: ".mysql_error();
        } else {
            echo '<p align="center"><font size="4" '.
            'face="Verdana, Arial, Helvetica, sans-serif">'.
            '<strong>You Have Been Verified!'.
            '</strong></font></p>';
            include $_SERVER['DOCUMENT_ROOT'].
                        '/html/forms/login_form.html';
        }
    } else {
        echo "Sorry, Could not be verified!";
    }
break;
```

FIGURE 5.8:

Signup successful
screen in web browser

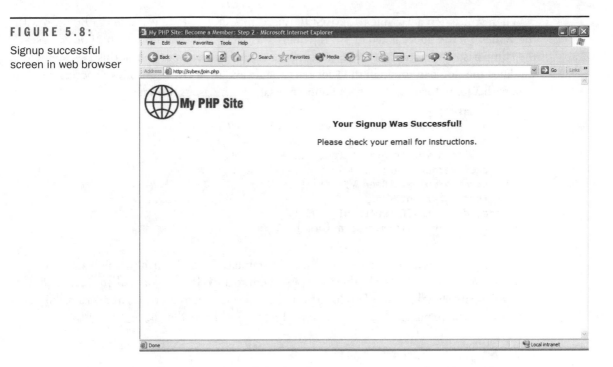

First, you initialize the case and display the custom myheader function with a custom page title from the layout.php:

```
case "verify":
    myheader("Verify Information");
```

Next, you perform the MySQL query to match the values. In this query, you use the COUNT MySQL function again to return the number of rows found in the database that matched the criteria. Also, you use the md5 PHP function to encrypt the first_name column before you can match it against your encrypted value for the vcode in the URL:

```
// Perform MySQL Query:
$sql = mysql_result(mysql_query("SELECT COUNT(*)
                    AS vcount FROM members WHERE
                    id='{$_GET['id']}' AND
                    md5(first_name) = '{$_GET['vcode']}'
                    "),0);
```

Now your $sql variable contains a number of rows found matching your criteria. You will perform an IF statement to decide what exactly you want to do with this value. In this case, if the value is 1, you will update the user in your database and change the ENUM verified field from 0 to 1, symbolizing that the user has clicked this link and validated their e-mail address.

When you assign a variable to a MySQL query, the return of the variable is a Boolean with the values 0 if the query failed or 1 if the query was successful. With Booleans, you can use the comparison operator ! to see if there was an error. The first portion of this IF statement validates the Boolean found in the $update variable and then either displays a success message with a login form or displays a failure message to the user's browser:

```php
if(!$update){
    echo "Error with MySQL Query: ".mysql_error();
} else {
    echo '<p align="center"><font size="4" '.
    'face="Verdana, Arial, Helvetica, sans-serif">'.
    '<strong>You Have Been Verified!'.
    '</strong></font></p>';
    include $_SERVER['DOCUMENT_ROOT'].
            '/html/forms/login_form.html';
}
```

In the previous example, I have also created a standard HTML form that will accept the user's username and password values and post them to a PHP script named login.php that you will create shortly. This file is located in the website document root /html/forms directory, and it will be named login_form.html. Listing 5.4 shows the login_form.html file.

Listing 5.4   *login_form.html* **File**

```html
<div align="center"><strong><font size="4" face="Verdana, Arial, Helvetica,
sans-serif">Please
  Login </font></strong></div>
<form action="/login.php" method="post">
  <table width="30%" border="0" align="center" cellpadding="4" cellspacing="0">
    <tr>
      <td width="19%"><font size="2" face="Verdana, Arial, Helvetica, sans-
serif"><strong>Username:</strong></font></td>
      <td width="81%"><input name="username" type="text" id="username"
value="<?=$_POST['username'];?>"></td>
    </tr>
    <tr>
      <td><font size="2" face="Verdana, Arial, Helvetica, sans-
serif"><strong>Password:</strong></font></td>
      <td><input name="password" type="password" id="password"></td>
    </tr>
    <tr>
      <td> </td>
      <td><div align="center">
          <input type="hidden" name="req" value="validate">
          <input type="submit" name="Submit" value="Submit">
        </div></td>
    </tr>
  </table>
</form>
```

FIGURE 5.9:

Successful verification
and login form

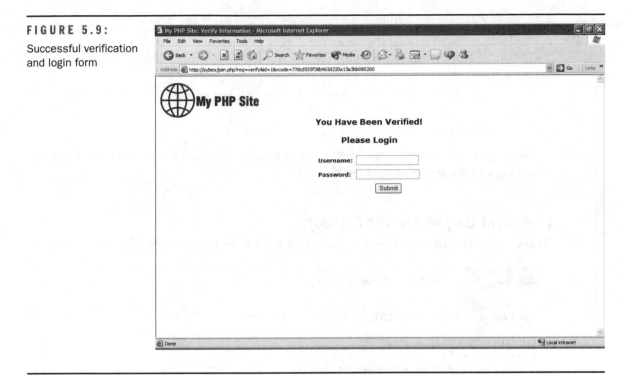

FIGURE 5.10:

Invalid e-mail verifica-
tion message

Figure 5.9 depicts the verification success message and the login form.

The last portion of this `verify` case is to display an error message if the criteria in your first MySQL query failed and the `$sql` variable has any other value than 1:

```
} else {
    echo "Sorry, Could not be verified!";
}
```

Figure 5.10 depicts the "Sorry, Could not be verified!" message.

Finally, you display your custom `footer` function from the `layout.php`, and then you issue a `break` to end the code execution for this `case`:

```
break;
```

Looking at the *join.php* File Summary

Before moving to any other files, let's take a look at the complete `join.php` file (see Listing 5.5).

Listing 5.5   **The Complete *join.php* File**

```php
<?php
include $_SERVER['DOCUMENT_ROOT'].'/layout.php';

switch($_REQUEST['req']){
case "process":
    myheader("Become a Member: Step 2");

    // Validate all required fields were posted
    if(!$_POST['first_name'] ||
        !$_POST['last_name'] ||
        !$_POST['email_address'] ||
        !$_POST['email_address2'] ||
        !$_POST['username'] ||
        !$_POST['password'] ||
        !$_POST['password2'] ||
        !$_POST['bio']){

            $errors .= "<strong>Form Input Errors:".
                        "</strong>\n\n";
            $error = true;

            if(!$_POST['first_name']){
                $errors .= "Missing First Name\n";
            }

            if(!$_POST['last_name']){
                $errors .= "Missing Last Name\n";
            }

            if(!$_POST['email_address']){
                $errors .= "Missing Email Address\n";
```

```php
            $email_error = true;
        }

        if(!$_POST['email_address2']){
            $errors .= "Missing Email ".
                       "Address Verification\n";
            $email_error = true;
        }

        if(!$_POST['username']){
            $errors .= "Missing Username\n";
        }

        if(!$_POST['password']){
            $errors .= "Missing Password\n";
            $password_error = true;
        }

        if(!$_POST['password2']){
            $errors .= "Missing Password Verification\n";
            $password_error = true;
        }

        if(!$_POST['bio']){
            $errors .= "Missing Information About Yourself\n";
        }
}

// If both emails were posted, validate they match.
if($email_error == false){
        if($_POST['email_address'] !=
               $_POST['email_address2']){
            $error = true;
            $errors .= "Email addresses do not match!\n\n";
            $email_error = true;
        }
}

// If both passwords were posted, validate they match.
if($password_error == false){
        if($_POST['password'] != $_POST['password2']){
            $error = true;
            $errors .= "Passwords do not match!\n\n";
            $password_error = true;
        }
}

// Verify if username already exists.
$ucount = mysql_result(mysql_query("SELECT COUNT(*)
                AS ucount FROM members
                WHERE username =
                '{$_POST['username']}'"),0);
```

```php
// If username exists, generate error and message.
if($ucount > 0){
    $error = true;
    $errors .= "Username already exists, ".
            "please choose another.\n\n";
}

if($email_error == false){
    // Verify if email address has been used already.
    $ecount = mysql_result(mysql_query("SELECT COUNT(*)
                AS ecount FROM members
                WHERE email_address =
                '{$_POST['email_address']}'"),0);

    // If username exists, generate error and message.
    if($ecount > 0){
        $error = true;
        $errors .= "This email address has already ".
                "been used ".
                "please choose another.\n\n";
    }
}

// If $error is TRUE, then include the singup form
// and display the errors we found.

if($error == true){
    $errors = nl2br($errors);
    include $_SERVER['DOCUMENT_ROOT'].
            '/html/forms/membership_signup.html';
    footer();
    exit();
}

// All checks have passed, insert user in database
$sql = @mysql_query("INSERT INTO members (first_name,
                last_name, email_address, signup_date,
                bio, username, password)
                VALUES ('$_POST[first_name]',
                        '$_POST[last_name]',
                        '$_POST[email_address]',
                        now(),
                        '$_POST[bio]',
                        '$_POST[username]',
                        '".md5($_POST[password])."'
                        )");
if(!$sql){
    echo "Error inserting your information ".
        "into MySQL: ".mysql_error();
    footer();
```

```php
        exit();
}

$userid = mysql_insert_id();
$verify_url = "http://".$_SERVER['SERVER_NAME'].
             "/join.php?req=verify&id=$userid&vcode=".
             md5($_POST['first_name']);

$mailer = &new Email;
// Email user
$mailer->ToMail = $_POST['email_address'];
$mailer->FromMail = "admin@test.com";
$mailer->FromName = "My PHP Site Administrator";
$mailer->Subject = "Your Membership at My PHP Site";
$mailer->Message = "Dear $_POST[first_name],\n".
                   "Thanks for joining our website! We".
                   " welcome you and look forward to".
                   " your participation.\n\n".
                   "Below you will find the ".
                   "information required to ".
                   "Login to our website!\n\n".
                   "First, you will need to verify".
                   " your email address ".
                   "by clicking on this ".
                   "hyperlink:\n$verify_url\nand ".
                   "following the directions in your ".
                   " web browser.\n\n".
                   "=====================\n".
                   "Username: $_POST[username]\n".
                   "Password: $_POST[password]\n".
                   "UserID: $userid\n".
                   "Email Address: ".
                   "$_POST[email_address]\n".
                   "=====================\n\n".
                   "Thank you,\n".
                   "My PHP Site Administrator\n".
                   "http://$_SERVER[SERVER_NAME]\n";
$mailer->SendMail();

// Email Admin
$mailer->ToMail = "eric@test.com";
$mailer->FromMail = "admin@test.com";
$mailer->FromName = "My PHP Site Administrator";
$mailer->Subject = "New Member at My PHP Site [$userid]";
$mailer->Message = "Hi,\n\n".
                   "A new member has just signed up ".
                   "at My PHP Site! Here's their ".
                   " information:\n\n".
                   "=====================\n".
                   "First Name: $_POST[first_name]\n".
                   "Last Name: $_POST[last_name]\n".
```

```php
                              "Email Address: ".
                              "$_POST[email_address]\n".
                              "UserID: $userid\n".
                              "=====================\n\n".
                              "Thank you,\n".
                              "My PHP Site Administrator\n".
                              "http://$_SERVER[SERVER_NAME]\n";
        $mailer->SendMail();
        // Display Success Message
        echo '<p align="center"><font size="4" '.
             'face="Verdana, Arial, Helvetica, sans-serif">'.
             '<strong>Your Signup Was Successful!'.
             '</strong></font></p>'.
             '<p align="center"><font size="4" '.
             'face="Verdana, Arial, Helvetica, sans-serif">'.
             'Please check your email for instructions.'.
             '</font></p>';
        // That's it! Done!
    break;

    case "verify":
        myheader("Verify Information");

        // Perform MySQL Query:
        $sql = mysql_result(mysql_query("SELECT COUNT(*)
                             AS vcount FROM members WHERE
                             id='{$_GET['id']}' AND
                             md5(first_name) = '{$_GET['vcode']}'
                             "),0);

        if($sql == 1){
            $update = mysql_query("UPDATE members SET
                             verified='1' WHERE
                             id='{$_GET['id']}'");
            if(!$update){
               echo "Error with MySQL Query: ".mysql_error();
            } else {
               echo '<p align="center"><font size="4" '.
               'face="Verdana, Arial, Helvetica, sans-serif">'.
               '<strong>You Have Been Verified!'.
               '</strong></font></p>';
               include $_SERVER['DOCUMENT_ROOT'].
                       '/html/forms/login_form.html';
            }
        } else {
           echo "Sorry, Could not be verified!";
        }
        footer();
    break;
```

```
        default:
            myheader("Become a Member!");
            include $_SERVER['DOCUMENT_ROOT'].
                    '/html/forms/membership_signup.html';
            footer();
        break;
    }
    ?>
```

Creating the Login System

You have created a method for your user to sign up and validate their e-mail address. Now that you have validated them, you have to create a method for them to log in to your website. In the following sections, you will use PHP sessions for the first time in this book, and you will perform more MySQL queries. Let's get started!

Starting PHP Sessions

Before you validate your members against the database, you need to start a PHP session. PHP sessions are arrays of information that you can modify with information about your users. They can contain virtually anything you want, such as names, e-mail addresses, pages viewed, and other text-based information.

Sessions are stored on the web server in files, and they are only kept during the duration of the user's visit. Once the user leaves the website, PHP will destroy the files. Each session also has its own unique identifier automatically generated by PHP when the session is created.

A session must be started before any text or HTML is output to the web browser, or you will receive errors from PHP. To start a session, you will use the session_start function. You will also create a unique session name for your sessions using the session_name function. I do not like to type the same code over and over again, so I have created a custom file that will start the session for me. I include this file into the common.php file so my sessions will be available on every page of the website. Here is the file named session.php in the includes directory:

```
<?php
session_start();
session_name('MyPHPSite');
header("Cache-control: private"); // Fix for IE
?>
```

Please ensure that you include the file in the previous example in your common.php file.

Some web browsers such as Microsoft Internet Explorer have problems caching PHP sessions. This problem is most noticeable when posting form information and using the web browser's Back button to modify information in the form. You may notice a "Page Cannot Be Displayed" error. To fix this, you use the PHP code header("Cache-control: private");. If the header function I have just described does not work properly, you may set the session_cach_limiter setting to none in your php.ini file.

To use a PHP session in a file, you must ensure that the session_start function is on every page. In the previous example, you have included the session.php file into the layout.php to ensure you are always using sessions throughout your entire website.

Creating the Login Verification Script

You have already created an HTML form that accepts the username and password and posts them to the script named login.php. Create a new text file and name it login.php in your website's document root. Once again, you will use a switch to perform multiple actions within a single PHP file. This file will contain the HTML form to log in by default, and when you pass a hidden value through your HTML form, you will use the validate case to do the validation. Listing 5.6 shows the login file.

Listing 5.6   **The *login.php* File**

```php
<?php
include $_SERVER['DOCUMENT_ROOT'].
        '/layout.php';
switch($_REQUEST['req']){

case "validate":
    $validate = @mysql_query("SELECT * FROM members
                WHERE username='{$_POST['username']}'
                AND password = md5('{$_POST['password']}')
                AND verified='1'");

    if(mysql_num_rows($validate) == 1){
        while($row = mysql_fetch_assoc($validate)){
            $_SESSION['login'] = true;
            $_SESSION['userid'] = $row['id'];
            $_SESSION['first_name'] = $row['first_name'];
            $_SESSION['last_name']  = $row['last_name'];
            $_SESSION['email_address'] = $row['email_address'];

            if($row['admin_access'] == 1){
                $_SESSION['admin_access'] = true;
            }
```

```
        $login_time = mysql_query("UPDATE members
                      SET last_login=now()
                      WHERE id='{$row['id']}'");
      }
      header("Location: /loggedin.php");
  } else {
     myheader("Login Failed!");
     echo '<p align="center">Login Failed</p>';
     echo '<p align="center">If you have already joined '.
          'our website, you may need to validate '.
          'your email address. '.
          'Please check your email for instructions.';
     footer();
  }
break;

default:
  myheader("Login!");
     include $_SERVER['DOCUMENT_ROOT'].
             '/html/forms/login_form.html';
  footer();
break;
}
?>
```

Let's break the file in Listing 5.6 down. The first portion of the file starts the PHP engine, includes your layout.php, and starts the structure for the switch:

```
<?php
include $_SERVER['DOCUMENT_ROOT'].
        '/layout.php';
case "validate":
```

You will not use the custom myheader function in the validate case yet. You will use it when you need it because you will later use a PHP function called header to redirect the user to a different page. The header function is similar to session_start—you must issue it before you output any text or HTML to the web browser, or you will get errors.

Next, you will perform a MySQL query on the information the user posted from the login form. This time, you will perform a direct mysql_query with the criteria you need to validate the user. You will use this same mysql_query statement again in a couple of different places within this script.

You should also notice that you are using the md5 function on the password the user posted. The password in the database was already passed through the md5 when the user signed up, so now you need to match the password the user is posting to the one in the database. This query is also going to use error suppression with the @ symbol in front of the mysql_query function. You do not want nasty errors displayed on your page from MySQL because you want to project a professional image and create your own error handling. Here is the code:

```
$validate = @mysql_query("SELECT * FROM members
                WHERE username='{$_POST['username']}'
                AND password = md5('{$_POST['password']}')
                AND verified='1'
                ");
```

After you have performed the query, you will use an IF statement combined with the mysql_num_rows function. The mysql_num_rows function will return a result for the number of rows found in a mysql_query by the query identifier. In this case, the identifier is $validate. The IF statement checks that the number of rows found is equal to 1; if the expression matches, the code within the IF statement executes:

```
if(mysql_num_rows($validate) == 1){
```

Now you are going into new territory. With your mysql_query you told MySQL to SELECT * FROM members based upon the set of criteria in the WHERE clause. This is the second time you get to use the same query in this code. You will extract all of the data in the row returned from the query into an array:

```
while($row = mysql_fetch_assoc($validate)){
```

With the previous code example, you will have an array named $row with keys and values for each column in your table, for example: $row['first_name'], $row['last_name'], and so on.

Now you have your data extracted and an array named $row, so you can start using it to register session variables. Take a look at this example of how to build your sessions:

```
$_SESSION['login'] = true;
$_SESSION['userid'] = $row['id'];
$_SESSION['first_name'] = $row['first_name'];
$_SESSION['last_name']  = $row['last_name'];
$_SESSION['email_address'] = $row['email_address'];
```

You set a session value just like adding new keys and values to an array. You define the key $_SESSION['first_name'] and then assign the value to it: $_SESSION['first_name'] = value;.

For these purposes, you first assign a Boolean value to the login key of the session, and then you assign values to the rest of the custom keys.

You want to verify if the user who has just logged in has administrative access to your website, so you perform a check on the admin_access field returned from the database. If it contains a value of 1, you add a Boolean key to the user's session for admin_access (you will utilize this in the next chapter when you create a website news system):

```
if($row['admin_access'] == 1){
        $_SESSION['admin_access'] = true;
}
```

The next step is to update the last_login field in the database for this user. You want to record the last time they logged in with the current time this script was executed. You use this field for maintenance purposes. If the user has not logged in for six months, you could probably assume they are not active any longer and delete them from your database if you want:

```
$login_time = mysql_query("UPDATE members
                SET last_login=now()
                WHERE id='{$row['id']}'");
```

The previous example is a mysql_query. To better understand it, verbalize it in your head like this: "Update the members table and SET the last_login field to the current time WHERE the id field matches the $row['id'] from my database query."

Next, you will close out the while loop you used to build the array with the database query:

```
}
```

The final portion of a successful login is to redirect the user to a new script named loggedin.php. This will allow the web browser to refresh itself and update any areas in your layout.php file that display information if the user is logged in. I will cover these areas later in this chapter.

To redirect the user with PHP, you will use the header PHP function with the Location argument to redirect the user to the loggedin.php script:

```
header("Location: /loggedin.php");
```

If your user could not be validated by the mysql_num_rows result from the mysql_query, you will display the custom myheader function and give them a message stating that the login has failed. You will also include your custom footer function to complete the layout of the website. Also, you will issue a break for this case to stop PHP from executing the rest of the switch. Here is the code for the ELSE statement for failure:

```
} else {
    myheader("Login Failed!");
    echo '<p align="center">Login Failed</p>';
    echo '<p align="center">If you have already joined '.
         'our website, you may need to validate your email '.
         'address. Please check your email for instructions.';
    footer();
}
break;
```

Figure 5.11 depicts the "Login Failed" message.

FIGURE 5.11:
"Login Failed" message

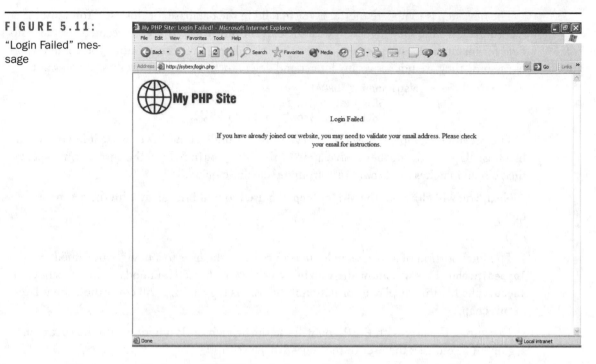

You want to display the HTML login form when the user accesses the `login.php` by default, so you will create the `default case` that will display your custom `myheader` function, the login form, and the custom `footer` function. Take a look at the `default case`:

```
default:
    myheader("Login!");
        include $_SERVER['DOCUMENT_ROOT'].
                '/html/forms/login_form.html';
    footer();
break;
}
?>
```

In the previous example, I closed the `default case`, the `switch`, and the PHP script.

That's it for the login verification script. That wasn't too bad! By now, you should be starting to understand how things flow together with the custom layout you created in Chapter 4, "Building a Website Template with PHP." You still have a few more things to do with the membership system. Next, you will create the script that is displayed to welcome the member after a successful login.

The Post Login Script

After the user has logged in and been verified, you will redirect them to a script called loggedin.php. You do this to refresh the web browser, update the hyperlinks in your layout.php file, and start displaying the session information.

Let's create an HTML file and save it in your html directory. Name this file loggedin_message.html. Here is how mine looks:

```
<p><font size="4" face="Verdana, Arial, Helvetica, sans-serif">Welcome
<?=$_SESSION['first_name'];?>!</font></p>
<p><font size="2" face="Verdana, Arial, Helvetica, sans-serif">You have
successfully
   logged in! You have special access to the <a href="/members.php">Members
Area!</a></font></p>
<p><font size="2" face="Verdana, Arial, Helvetica, sans-serif">Would you like
   to <a href="/logout.php">logout now</a>?</font></p>
```

FIGURE 5.12:

Post login script message

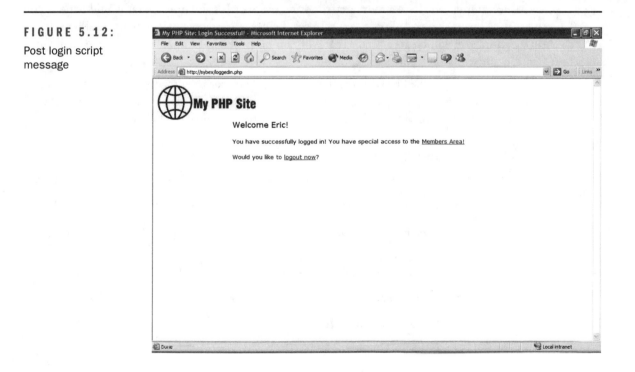

Create a new file and name it `loggedin.php` in your website's document root. This script is going to include the welcome message with your custom layout functions. This script will look like this example:

```php
<?php
include $_SERVER['DOCUMENT_ROOT'].
        '/layout.php';

myheader("Login Successful!");
include $_SERVER['DOCUMENT_ROOT'].
        '/html/loggedin_message.html';
footer();
?>
```

Figure 5.12 shows the `loggedin.php` script with the welcome message displayed.

Creating a Lost Password Script

Users are funny; they have a tendency to forget passwords sometimes, so it would benefit you to create a script that will allow them to reset their passwords easily if they forget them. In this section, you will create a script that will randomly generate a password upon e-mail verification and e-mail it to the user.

First, create a simple HTML form that will allow the user to enter their e-mail address to recover their username and password. Second, save this file in your /html/forms directory and name it `lostpw_form.html`. Listing 5.7 shows what my form looks like.

Listing 5.7   **Lost Password Form HTML File (*lostpw_form.html*)**

```html
<p><font size="4" face="Verdana, Arial, Helvetica, sans-serif"><strong>Reset My
  Password</strong></font></p>
<p><font size="2" face="Verdana, Arial, Helvetica, sans-serif">If you have lost
your password,
  you may enter your email address below and a new password will be sent to your
  email address.</font></p>
<form name="form1" method="post" action="/lostpw.php">
  <table width="42%" border="0" cellspacing="0" cellpadding="4">
    <tr>
      <td width="20%" nowrap><font size="2" face="Verdana, Arial, Helvetica,
sans-serif">Your
        Email Address:</font></td>
      <td width="21%"><input name="email_address" type="text"
id="email_address">
      </td>
      <td width="59%"><input name="req" type="hidden" id="req" value="recover">
```

```
                <input name="Go!" type="submit" id="Go!" value="Go!"></td>
        </tr>
     </table>
  </form>
```

Next, create a script named lostpw.php and save it in your website's document root. You
will once again use a switch to create multiple uses for a single PHP file in this script. Listing 5.8 shows how my lostpw.php file looks.

Listing 5.8   **Reset Lost Password File (*lostpw.php*)**

```php
<?php

include $_SERVER['DOCUMENT_ROOT'].
        '/layout.php';

switch($_REQUEST['req']){

case "recover":
   myheader("Reset Password");
   $sql = mysql_query("SELECT * FROM members
           WHERE
           email_address = '{$_POST['email_address']}'
           ");
   if(mysql_num_rows($sql) == 1){
      while($row = mysql_fetch_assoc($sql)){
         $alphanum = "abchefghjkmnpqrstuvwxyz0123456789";
         for($i=0; $i <= 10; $i++) {
                 $num = rand() % 33;
                 $tmp = substr($alphanum, $num, 1);
                 $newpass = $newpass . $tmp;
         }
         $update = mysql_query("UPDATE members
                 SET password = '".md5($newpass)."'
                 WHERE id='{$row['id']}'");
         stripslashes(extract($row));
      }
      if(!$update){
         echo '<p align="center">Password Could '.
             'not be reset! Sorry!</p>';
      } else {
         echo '<p align="center">Password Reset! '.
             'Please check your email for your new'.
             'password.</p>';

             include $_SERVER['DOCUMENT_ROOT'].
                     '/html/forms/login_form.html';
```

```
                // mail user.
                $mailer = &new Email;
                $mailer->ToMail = $email_address;
                $mailer->FromMail = "admin@test.com";
                $mailer->FromName = "My PHP Site Administrator";
                $mailer->Subject = "New Password For My PHP Site";
                $mailer->Message = "Dear $first_name,\n\n".
                                   "You have requested a new ".
                                   "password for My PHP Site. ".
                                   "Below is your new login ".
                                   "informaiton:\n\n".
                                   "=====================\n".
                                   "Username: $username\n".
                                   "New Password: $newpass\n".
                                   "=====================\n\n".
                                   "You may login at any time ".
                                   "at http://".
                                   "$_SERVER['SERVER_NAME']".
                                   "/login.php\n\n".
                                   "Thank You!\n".
                                   "My PHP Site Administrator";
            $mailer->SendMail();


            }
        } else {
            echo '<p align="center">We could not find '.
                 'any matches for that email address! '.
                 'Please try again!</p>';
        }
        footer();
    break;

    default:
        myheader("Reset Password");
        include $_SERVER['DOCUMENT_ROOT'].
                '/html/forms/lostpw_form.html';
        footer();
    break;
    }
    ?>
```

Let's break the script in Listing 5.8 down. First, you start the PHP engine and include your
layout.php file. Next, you initialize your switch and create the first case named recover.
Take a look at this code:

```
<?php

include $_SERVER['DOCUMENT_ROOT'].
```

```
         '/layout.php';

  switch($_REQUEST['req']){

  case "recover":
```

The `recover` case will first call the custom `myheader` function from the `layout.php` file, then compare the e-mail address (the user input from the form), and then check to see if there is a match in the database by performing a `mysql_query` and then by using an `IF` statement on the `mysql_number_rows` function:

```
myheader("Reset Password");
$sql = mysql_query("SELECT * FROM members
       WHERE
       email_address = '{$_POST['email_address']}'
       ");
if(mysql_num_rows($sql) == 1){
```

When the `IF` statement is validated by the `mysql_num_rows` function returning a value of 1, you will start to generate a new password with which to update the user's information in the database.

Next, you will fetch the associated values of this `mysql_query` into an array using the `mysql_fetch_assoc` function:

```
while($row = mysql_fetch_assoc($sql)){
```

You start generating a random password by creating a string containing values to randomly pick from using your `FOR` loop combined with a few other functions to randomly pick from the string. This next portion of code also uses an appended string, so each time the PHP loops through the `FOR` loop, it will append a new letter to this `$new_pass` string:

```
$alphanum = "abchefghjkmnpqrstuvwxyz0123456789";
for($i=0; $i <= 10; $i++) {
        $num = rand() % 33;
        $tmp = substr($alphanum, $num, 1);
        $newpass = $newpass . $tmp;
}
```

After the previous portion of code has executed, you will end up with a randomly generated password. It is now time to update the database with the `md5` encrypted version of it:

```
$update = mysql_query("UPDATE members
        SET password = '".md5($newpass)."'
        WHERE id='{$row['id']}'");
```

The next function you will use is called `extract`, and it creates variables from all of the keys and values in an array. For example, `$row['id']` would be converted to `$id`. Also, you will use the `stripslashes` function, which will remove any backslashes on any escaped characters in the values of these new variables:

```
stripslashes(extract($row));
```

Because you are done with your `while loop` from the database query, close out the loop by using the right curly brace:

```
}
```

With your `$update` Boolean that was returned from the `mysql_query`, you can check to see if the password was successfully updated in the database. If the update failed, you will show a message to the user notifying them of the failure. If it did not fail, you will display a success message followed by a login form and then send the user an e-mail notifying them of the new password generated for their membership:

```
if(!$update){
    echo '<p align="center">Password Could '.
        'not be reset! Sorry!</p>';
} else {
    echo '<p align="center">Password Reset! '.
        'Please check your email for your new '.
        'password.</p>';

        include $_SERVER['DOCUMENT_ROOT'].
                '/html/forms/login_form.html';
    // mail user.
    $mailer = &new Email;
    $mailer->ToMail = $email_address;
    $mailer->FromMail = "admin@test.com";
    $mailer->FromName = "My PHP Site Administrator";
    $mailer->Subject = "New Password For My PHP Site";
    $mailer->Message = "Dear $first_name,\n\n".
                    "You have requested a new ".
                    "password for My PHP Site. ".
                    "Below is your new login ".
                    "informaiton:\n\n".
                    "=====================\n".
                    "Username: $username\n".
                    "New Password: $newpass\n".
                    "=====================\n\n".
                    "You may login at any time ".
                    "at http://".
                    "$_SERVER['SERVER_NAME']".
                    "/login.php\n\n".
                    "Thank You!\n".
```

```
                        "My PHP Site Administrator";
    $mailer->SendMail();


    }
```

Take special notice of the e-mail portion of the previous code for the method used to display the e-mail address and username. Because you use the `extract` function, the keys were turned into variables from the MySQL query. This enables you to use a variable such as `$email_address` that came from `$row['email_address']` in the `mysql_fetch_assoc` `while loop`.

In the previous example, you performed your error checking, created a new instance of the custom e-mail class included through your `common.php` file, and then sent the e-mail. You also have closed out the first `IF` statement that used `mysql_num_rows` to determine if you had a match to the e-mail address the user entered in the form.

The next portion of the code is the `ELSE` statement if your `mysql_num_rows` result returned any value other than 1. If you could not find a match in the database, you will notify the user accordingly:

```
} else {
    echo '<p align="center">We could not find '.
        'any matches for that email address! '.
        'Please try again!</p>';
}
```

For the rest of this current `case` you are working with, you will use the custom footer function and issue the break to stop the code execution for this portion of your `switch`:

```
    footer();
break;
```

The last portion of this script is the default `case` you use to display the e-mail form with your custom `myheader` and `footer` functions. This is the form you saw in Listing 5.7.

```
default:
    myheader("Reset Password");
    include $_SERVER['DOCUMENT_ROOT'].
            '/html/forms/lostpw_form.html';
    footer();
break;
}
?>
```

Figures 5.13 through 5.15 show you the process of resetting a password. Specifically, Figure 5.13 shows that the user enters their e-mail address to get a new password, Figure 5.14 shows the message they get after entering their e-mail address, and Figure 5.15 shows the e-mail message they receive.

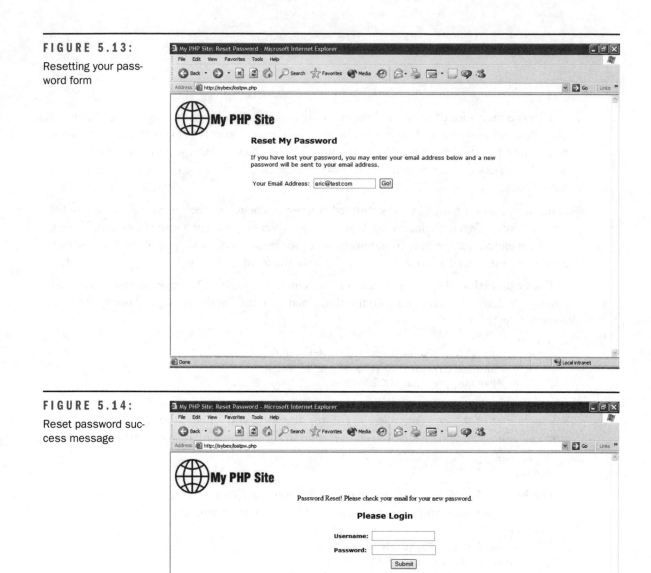

FIGURE 5.15:
Reset password e-mail

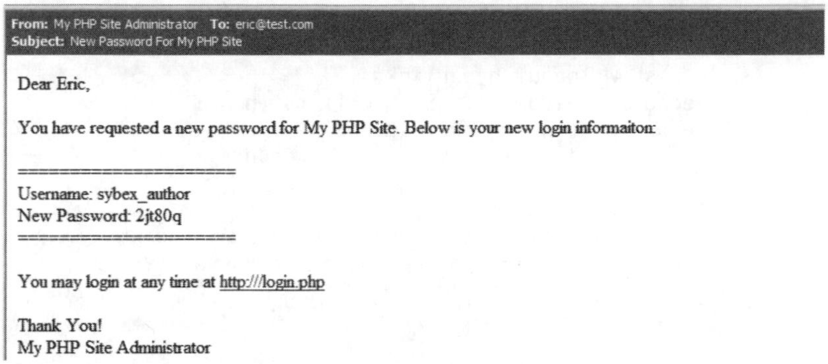
From: My PHP Site Administrator To: eric@test.com
Subject: New Password For My PHP Site

Dear Eric,

You have requested a new password for My PHP Site. Below is your new login informaiton:

=====================
Username: sybex_author
New Password: 2jt80q
=====================

You may login at any time at http:///login.php

Thank You!
My PHP Site Administrator

Now your users have the ability to reset those lost passwords. This handy script will save you a lot of time when dealing with a large amount of users.

Creating the Membership Hyperlinks Box

When you designed your site layout in the previous chapter, you built a table that has a left column, a middle column, and a right column. The left column is used primarily for hyperlinks. Sometimes these hyperlinks are grouped into *blocks*, or *boxes*, as some people refer to them. The names came from the traditional PHP portal systems, and they were named this because they were "blocky" in appearance.

Let's create a box that will display a login hyperlink if the user is not logged in as a member or that will display a logout hyperlink if they are logged in already. You will determine if the user is logged in with the PHP sessions you created in your login script.

Create a new PHP file, name it `member_box.php`, and save it in your website's document root in a directory named `boxes`.

Listing 5.9 shows the `member_box.php` code.

Listing 5.9 Membership Box File (*member_box.php*)

```
<table width="160" border="0" cellspacing="0" cellpadding="0">
  <tr bgcolor="#000066">
    <td width="5" height="10"><font color="#FFFFFF"> </font></td>
    <td width="150"><div align="center"><font color="#FFFFFF" size="2"
face="Verdana, Arial, Helvetica, sans-
serif"><strong>Membership</strong></font></div></td>
    <td width="5"> </td>
  </tr>
  <tr>
    <td height="5"> </td>
    <td align="left" valign="top">
```

```php
<?php
if($_SESSION['login'] == true){
    // show logout hyperlinks
    echo '- Welcome '.$_SESSION[first_name].'!<br />';
    echo '- <a href="/access.php">Member\'s Area</a><br />';
    echo '- <a href="/logout.php">Logout</a>';
} else {
    // show login form
    echo '<a href="/login.php">Member Login</a><br />';
    echo '<a href=="/lostpw.php">Lost Password?</a>';
}
?>

    </td>
    <td> </td>
    </tr>
    <tr>
    <td width="5" height="10"><font color="#FFFFFF"> </font></td>
    <td width="150"> </td>
    <td width="5"> </td>
    </tr>
</table>
<hr size="1">
```

This file starts out with basic HTML. The HTML will build a table with the first row colored and the word *Membership* in the middle column.

The next table row will break out into PHP in the middle column and check if the user is logged in using your $_SESSION['login'] value, which is a TRUE or FALSE Boolean. You assigned the TRUE value when the user logged in successfully. If this session value does validate TRUE, you will display a welcome message with the user's first name, a member's area hyperlink, and a logout hyperlink. If the $_SESSION['login'] value does not exist, it will not validate TRUE, and then this script will display a login hyperlink in the ELSE statement:

```php
<?php
if($_SESSION['login'] == true){
    // show logout hyperlinks
    echo '- Welcome '.$_SESSION[first_name].'!<br />';
    echo '- <a href="/access.php">Member\'s Area</a><br />';
    echo '- <a href="/logout.php">Logout</a>';
} else {
    // show login form
    echo '<a href="/login.php">Member Login</a><br />';
    echo '<a href=="/lostpw.php">Lost Password?</a>';
}
?>
```

Next, you will finish the HTML of the table and save the file so you can include it in your layout.php file for the left column! Open the layout.php file and make the modifications now.

For my columns to look proper when I open them in a web browser, I had to create a new table inside the left HTML table column where I wanted my hyperlinks to go. The only reason I added this column is for padding and alignment. In the middle column for the new table, I simply included the member_box.php file and then saved the file. Listing 5.10 shows the middle portion of the layout.php file.

Listing 5.10   **Middle Section of *layout.php***

```
<body>
<table width="100%" border="0" cellpadding="0" cellspacing="0"
bordercolor="#000000">
  <tr>
    <td colspan="3"><a href="/"><img src="/images/logo.jpg" ALT="My PHP Site"
BORDER="0"></a><hr size="1"></td>
  </tr>
  <tr>
    <!-- Left Links Column -->
    <td width="170" valign="top">
    <table width="170" border="0" cellpadding="0" cellspacing="0">
    <tr>
    <td width="10"> </td>
    <td valign="top">

    <?php
    include $_SERVER['DOCUMENT_ROOT'].
            '/boxes/member_box.php';
    ?>

    </td>
    <!-- End Left Links Column -->
    <td width="10"> </td>
    </tr>
    </table>
    </td>
    <td>
    <!-- End Header and Begin Content -->
<?php
}
function footer(){
?>
```

Looks pretty simple eh? You should be familiar with including files by now! The one thing I want to note is that I made some cosmetic modifications to the layout.php file when I included the member_box.php. Specifically, I created a hyperlink on the website logo to go back to the index, and then I added a one-pixel HTML horizontal line below the logo. This gives the website a little bit more definition, especially because it has a white background.

Figure 5.16 shows the member block when the user is not logged in, and Figure 5.17 shows when the member is logged into the website.

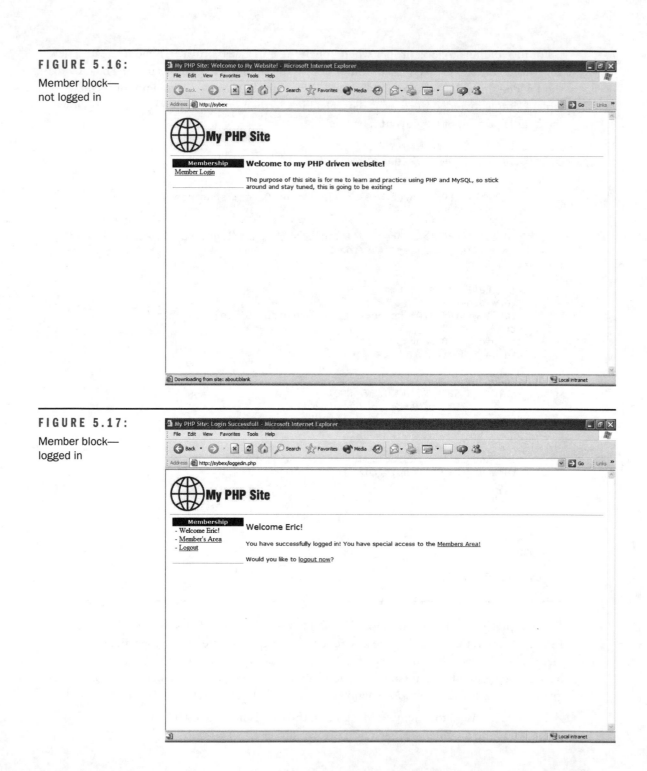

Granting Member-Only Access

When the member has logged into the website, you can use the same method you used to show the logout hyperlinks in the previous section to display hyperlinks to special areas. Furthermore, you can control access to these areas by checking the $_SESSION['login'] Boolean value and then granting access if the value exists.

I am going to take this opportunity to touch on another element of OOP. In the previous examples of OOP in this book, you always used PHP classes. I am going to give you an example of OOP without using a class structure. In your session.php file, you will create a custom function named login_check directly below the functions used to start the session.

The custom function will use an IF statement that will check that $_SESSION['login'] is equal to TRUE. If it is not, you will display the myheader function, login HTML form, and footer function and then exit the script using the exit function.

Open your session.php file inside your includes directory that you created earlier in this chapter and modify it as follows:

```php
<?php
session_start();
session_name('MyPHPSite');
header("Cache-control: private"); // Fix for IE

function login_check(){
    if($_SESSION['login'] != TRUE){
        myheader("Login Required!");
        include $_SERVER['DOCUMENT_ROOT'].
                '/html/forms/login_form.html';
        footer();
        exit();
    }
}
?>
```

The new function is now available throughout your PHP scripts through the hierarchy of the include structure you used. It is included like the classes, and you can use this function any time by simply calling it.

The next file will be named access.php, and it will reside in your website's document root. This file corresponds with the hyperlink you made in the member_box.php file, and the link is displayed when the member is logged in. Let's take a look at this script and the usage of the login_check function:

```php
<?php
include $_SERVER['DOCUMENT_ROOT'].
        '/layout.php';
```

```php
login_check();

myheader("Members Area");

echo '<p align="center">Welcome to the '.
     'Members Area '.$_SESSION['first_name'].
     '!';
footer();
?>
```

The most important element of the previous example is the `login_check();` line. This code will call the `login_check` function and check for the session value. If the session value does not exist, it will exit the script and the rest of the code in the script will not be visible to the user. If the session value does exist, the rest of the code in this script below the `login_check();` function call will be visible, hence you have just granted access to a member that has been logged in!

Congratulations! You now have a method to control access to virtually any portion of your website using PHP sessions!

Logging Out

The last portion of the membership system is a method to allow the member to log out. This method is not really required because the member will automatically get logged out when they close their web browser; however, it provides an additional sense of security to your members.

Let's create a script named `logout.php` and save it in your web server's document root. You will use a `switch` to create multiple uses with the same physical file. This file will ask the member if they want to log out and provide them with hyperlinks for a "Yes" or "No" response. If they click the Yes hyperlink, you will destroy their session and log them out. If they choose No, you will send them back to the previous page using a JavaScript back hyperlink. Listing 5.11 shows the `logout.php` file.

Listing 5.11   **Logout Script (*logout.php*)**

```php
<?php
include $_SERVER['DOCUMENT_ROOT'].
        '/layout.php';

switch($_REQUEST['req']){
   case "logout":
      session_destroy();
      header("Location: /logout.php?req=loggedout");
```

```
      break;

   case "loggedout":
      myheader("Logout");
      echo '<p align="center">You are now logged out!</p>'.
      footer();
      break;

   default:
      myheader("Logout");
      echo '<p align="center">Are You Sure '.
           'you want to logout?</p>'.
           '<p align="center">'.
           '<a href="/logout.php?req=logout">Yes</a>'.
           ' | <a href="javascript:history.back()">No</a>'.
           '</p>';
      footer();
      break;
}
?>
```

Let's break the script in Listing 5.11 down. You should already be familiar with the first portion. You start the PHP engine and then include your `layout.php` file. Next, you build your `switch` structure and create the cases you need to perform the logout:

```
<?php
include $_SERVER['DOCUMENT_ROOT'].
       '/layout.php';

switch($_REQUEST['req']){
```

The `logout` case is the second step to the logout process. This is the portion of your `switch` that will be used when the member clicks the Yes hyperlink in the `default case`.

This `case` uses a PHP session function called `session_destroy`. This function will completely remove all session values and destroy any references to the session and the member's web browser. After the session has been destroyed, you will redirect the user directly to the next `case`, which is `loggedout`, and this case will display a message to the member stating they have been logged out:

```
case "logout":
   session_destroy();
   header("Location: /logout.php?req=loggedout");
   break;
```

The next `case` is the portion of your `switch` that the member is redirected to from the logout `case`. It simply displays a message to the member upon successful logout:

```
case "loggedout":
   myheader("Logout");
```

```
      echo '<p align="center">You are now logged out!</p>'.
      footer();
  break;
```

The `default` case, which is the first step in the logout process, simply displays two hyperlinks to the member, giving them the option to log out or to continue their session as a member. I prefer to use this confirmation method because I think it is rude to immediately log the member out if they inadvertently clicked the Logout hyperlink:

```
default:
    myheader("Logout");
    echo '<p align="center">Are You Sure '.
        'you want to logout?</p>'.
        '<p align="center">'.
        '<a href="/logout.php?req=logout">Yes</a>'.
        ' | <a href="javascript:history.back()">No</a>'.
        '</p>';
    footer();
break;
```

Let's complete the `switch` structure and the PHP script:

```
}
?>
```

Now your membership system is complete!

What's Next?

This chapter covered some common routines used to work with PHP. You created an advanced system that allows you to gather information from user inputs, validate form information, utilize MySQL query functions, use PHP sessions, reset passwords, and log out your members.

In the next chapter, you will start building content for your website. You will build a news system using PHP and MySQL that will allow you to write, display, edit, and delete news articles directly on your website. You will also look at using news feeds from other websites to populate your news section automatically.

CHAPTER 6

Developing a Website News System

A valuable key to any website's success is fresh content. Many websites use some sort of news system to keep their readers updated with information about the site or a topic related to the site. When your readers see fresh content, they will probably return to your site repeatedly to see what is new and, in turn, boost your website statistics. This method has proven to be true for my website at www.phpfreaks.com.

This chapter gives you a practical solution for everyday routines involving PHP and MySQL while at the same time showing these routines put to use in a website news system. These routines involve the standard insert, update, display, and delete procedures required for most website management systems developed in PHP and MySQL. With these methods, you will be able to manage your website's content with your web browser and not your File Transfer Protocol (FTP) client.

Specifically, you will plan a news system, configure the database, and develop PHP scripts to manage your news articles from your website interface. You will create a two-part archive page that will either display all of the news articles in the database or display a category and all of the news articles related to that category.

Another great technique I will show you is how to link news articles to categories. By creating a category-based article system, you will have the ability to archive your articles and sort them in relationship to their categories. Let's begin planning this news system!

Planning the News System

With any script or section of your website that you create, planning is required. For this news system, you will link each article to a category. By linking all of the news articles to categories, you have better options for storing and sorting the articles. In this chapter, you will create an index page for the news articles that will display all of the categories and the number of articles linked to each category.

You have already planned the MySQL table for the news articles; however, in the "Preparing the MySQL Database" section of this chapter, you will modify the table structure a little to enhance the original plan. Get used to modifying your original structures, files, and plans because you will probably find yourself doing so quite often.

Preparing the Website Administrator Access

Some areas of this website will require special administrator access assigned to your users (specifically, you) when they log in. In Chapter 5, "Creating a Website Membership System," you created a special column in the members table that allows you to grant administrative access to certain members of your website. When a user logs in and has the special flag enabled in the admin_access column, they get a special $_SESSION value assigned to them. With this value, they are able to access privileged areas of the website.

If you have not done so yet, create a membership for yourself, and using your MySQL administrator application, edit your information in the members table and enable admin_access for yourself. The next time you log into your site, you will have administrative access, and you will be able to pass the administrative checks you are about to create.

You will modify the session.php file in your includes directory to add a new function named admin_check. This new function will be available throughout the website, and it will help you to control access to your sensitive files. Open the session.php file and add this function to the bottom of it:

```
function admin_check(){
    if($_SESSION['admin_access']){
       myheader("Access Denied!");
        echo "<center>This area is restricted".
            " for website administrators!";
       footer();
       exit();
    }
}
```

You will use this function throughout the development of your news article management system.

Preparing the MySQL Database

For the article portion of the database, I have determined that you will need to use a table named news_articles. This is the same table you created in Chapter 3, "Building a Database Schema with MySQL," with a few additional columns. Table 6.1 shows the table structure; modify your news_articles table accordingly.

TABLE 6.1: Structure Setup for the news_articles Table

Field Name	Data Type	Length	Extra
article_id	MEDIUMINT	25	Primary key, auto increment
cat_id	MEDIUMINT	25	
article_title	VARCHAR	255	
article_date	DATETIME		
article_caption	TEXT		
article_body	LONGTEXT		
article_author	VARCHAR	255	
article_read_count	MEDIUMINT	25	

In the example for Table 6.1, I added three new columns to the existing `news_articles` table: `cat_id` to link to the category ID from the new table you will create in a moment, `article_author` to display the name of the author, and `article_read_count` to count the number of times an article has been read.

The next step is to create the `news_categories` table. Table 6.2 shows the structure; create your table accordingly.

TABLE 6.2: Structure Setup for the `news_categories` Table

Field Name	Data Type	Length	Extra
cat_id	MEDIUMINT	25	Primary key, auto increment
cat_name	VARCHAR	155	
cat_description	TINYTEXT		

Now that you have created your tables, it is time to start coding some PHP to interact with the MySQL database!

Creating the News Article Category Management System

Before you begin writing news articles, you need to create a system to manage the news article categories. The following sections are a great introduction to the common routines of inserting, updating/modifying, and deleting that make up any web-based management system when working with PHP.

Creating the News Article Category Insert Script

You have already created the `news_categories` database table from Table 6.2, so let's start by creating a script that will enter the data into the database and create the new categories.

In Chapter 5, "Creating a Website Membership System," you utilized a `switch` control structure to create multiple uses for a single PHP file. In the news article category management script, you will use a `switch` structure as well.

The first Hypertext Markup Language (HTML) file you will create serves as an index page for the `default case` that allows you to click whichever action you want to perform for the category management. This HTML file is named `news_cat_admin.html` and is stored in the website document root under the `html` directory (see Listing 6.1).

Listing 6.1   **Category Management Index HTML File**

```
<div align="center">
  <p><font size="4" face="Verdana, Arial, Helvetica, sans-serif">News Article
    Category Administration</font></p>
  <p><font size="3" face="Verdana, Arial, Helvetica, sans-serif">Please select
    an option:</font></p>
  <p><font size="2" face="Verdana, Arial, Helvetica, sans-serif"><a
href="/admin/newscategory.php?req=new_cat"><strong>Add
    News Article Categories</strong></a></font></p>
  <p><a href="/admin/mod_news_category.php"><font size="2" face="Verdana, Arial,
Helvetica, sans-serif"><strong>Delete
    or Modify News Article Categories</strong></font></a></p>
</div>
```

The next file will serve as an input HTML form that will post the category name and description to the PHP script for validation and insertion into the MySQL database's news_categories table. This HTML file is named news_category_insert.html and is stored in your website document root under the html/forms directory (see Listing 6.2).

Listing 6.2   **Category Management Insert Form**

```
<p><font size="4" face="Verdana, Arial, Helvetica, sans-serif">Create a News
Article
  Category</font></p>
<form action="/admin/newscategory.php" method="post">
  <table width="33%" border="0" align="center" cellpadding="4" cellspacing="0">
    <tr>
      <td width="17%" align="left" valign="top"><font size="2" face="Verdana,
Arial, Helvetica, sans-serif"><strong>Category
        Name</strong></font></td>
      <td width="83%"><input name="cat_name" type="text" id="cat_name"></td>
    </tr>
    <tr>
      <td align="left" valign="top" nowrap><font size="2" face="Verdana, Arial,
Helvetica, sans-serif"><strong>Category
        Description</strong></font></td>
      <td><textarea name="cat_description" id="cat_description"></textarea></td>
    </tr>
    <tr>
      <td> </td>
      <td><div align="center">
          <input name="req" type="hidden" value="create_cat">
          <input type="submit" name="Submit" value="Create Category!">
        </div></td>
    </tr>
  </table>
</form>
<p><font size="4" face="Verdana, Arial, Helvetica, sans-serif"></font></p>
```

Let's now create the PHP script that will handle these HTML files and perform the MySQL insert operations for the categories. Create a file named `newscategory.php` and place it in a directory under your website document root named `admin` (see Listing 6.3).

Listing 6.3   News Category Management Script

```php
<?php
include $_SERVER['DOCUMENT_ROOT'].
        '/layout.php';

// Quick Admin session check
admin_check();

switch($_REQUEST['req']){
   // Category Insert Case
   case "create_cat":
     myheader("Add News Category");

     // Double check form posted values are there
     // before performing INSERT query
     if(!$_POST['cat_name'] || !$_POST['cat_description']){
         echo '<p align="center">Missing Form '.
              'Information!</p>'.
              '<p align="center">Please use your '.
              'browser back button and complete '.
              'the form.</p>';
         footer();
         exit();
     }

     // Insert Query
     $sql = mysql_query("INSERT INTO news_categories
                (cat_name, cat_description)
                VALUES('{$_POST['cat_name']}',
                    '{$_POST['cat_description']}')");

     // Insert query results
     if(!$sql){
         echo "Error with MySQL Query: ".mysql_error();
     } else {

         echo '<p align="center">Category
              '.$_POST[cat_name].
              ' created!<br />New category id:
              '.mysql_insert_id();
         echo '<br /><a href="/admin/newscategory.php?req=new_cat">Create '.
              'another category</a>';
     }
   break;
```

```
// Create category form case
case "new_cat":
  myheader("Create News Category");
  include $_SERVER['DOCUMENT_ROOT'].
          '/html/forms/news_category_insert.html';
  footer();
break;

default:
  myheader("News Category Administration");
  include $_SERVER['DOCUMENT_ROOT'].
          '/html/news_cat_admin.html';
  footer();
break;

}
?>
```

Let's break down the previous code example. The first portion of the script starts the PHP engine and includes the `layout.php` file. You should be familiar with this by now.

Because this script is going to be restricted only to your administrative members, you will use the special function you created earlier in the "Preparing the Website Administrator Access" section of this chapter. Once this function has been used and the person accessing the script is not an administrator, they will be presented a message stating they are not authorized to access this portion of the website. If the person accessing the script is granted the special administrative flag in their session, they will be able to view the intended code of this script:

```
// Quick Admin session check
admin_check();
```

Next, you initialize the `switch` structure and develop your first `case`. This case will accept the form input and perform a simple form validation on the posted fields. After the form validation has passed, a `mysql_query` is performed to insert the data into the table. After the query has been performed, a simple check on the Boolean value of the `$sql` variable identifies failure or success on the query and displays an error or success message. The last portion of this `case` will display a hyperlink to the previous form and close out the `case` with a `break`:

```
switch($_REQUEST['req']){
  // Category Insert Case
  case "create_cat":
    myheader("Add News Category");

    // Double check form posted values are there
    // before performing INSERT query
    if(!$_POST['cat_name'] || !$_POST['cat_description']){
        echo '<p align="center">Missing Form '.
             'Information!</p>'.
```

```
                        '<p align="center">Please use your '.
                        'browser back button and complete '.
                        'the form.</p>';
               footer();
               exit();
        }

        // Insert Query
        $sql = mysql_query("INSERT INTO news_categories
                        (cat_name, cat_description)
                        VALUES('{$_POST['cat_name']}',
                                '{$_POST['cat_description']}')");

        // Insert query results
        if(!$sql){
                echo "Error with MySQL Query: ".mysql_error();
        } else {

                echo '<p align="center">Category
                        '.$_POST[cat_name].
                        ' created!<br />New category id:
                        '.mysql_insert_id();
                echo '<br /><a href="/admin/newscategory.php?req=new_cat">Create '.
                        'another category</a>';

        }
    break;
```

The next case will actually display the HTML form from Listing 6.2 in the web browser:

```
    // Create category form case
    case "new_cat":
        myheader("Create News Category");
        include $_SERVER['DOCUMENT_ROOT'].
                '/html/forms/news_category_insert.html';
        footer();
    break;
```

The default case will include the HTML index file you created for the category management system in Listing 6.1:

```
    default:
        myheader("News Category Administration");
        include $_SERVER['DOCUMENT_ROOT'].
                '/html/news_cat_admin.html';
        footer();
    break;
```

Let's close the switch structure and the PHP script:

```
    }
    ?>
```

Now the insert portion of your script is complete, so run it in your web browser and insert a couple of categories.

Figure 6.1 displays the news category management index, or the `default case` in this script.

FIGURE 6.1:

News category management index

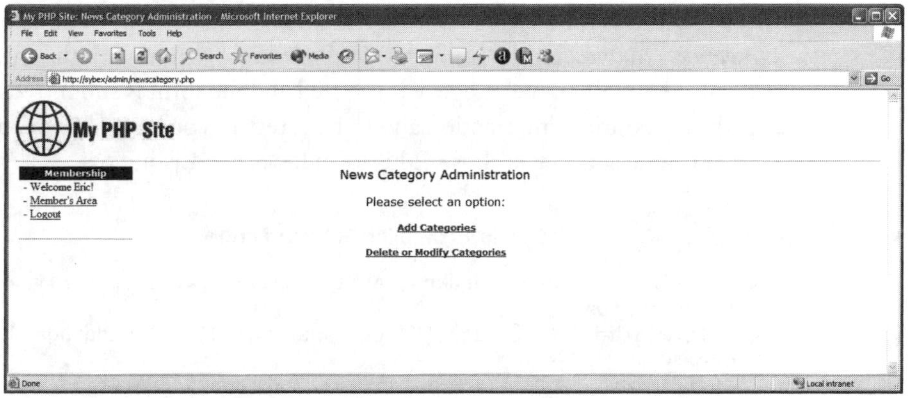

In Figure 6.2, I have entered a category named *World News*, and in Figure 6.3, I have entered a category named *Computer Stuff*. Figure 6.4 depicts the confirmation screen after creating the category.

FIGURE 6.2:

Creating a World News category

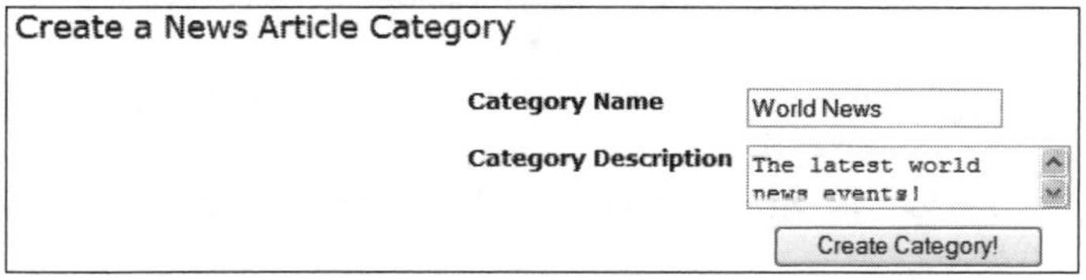

FIGURE 6.3:

Creating a Computer Stuff category

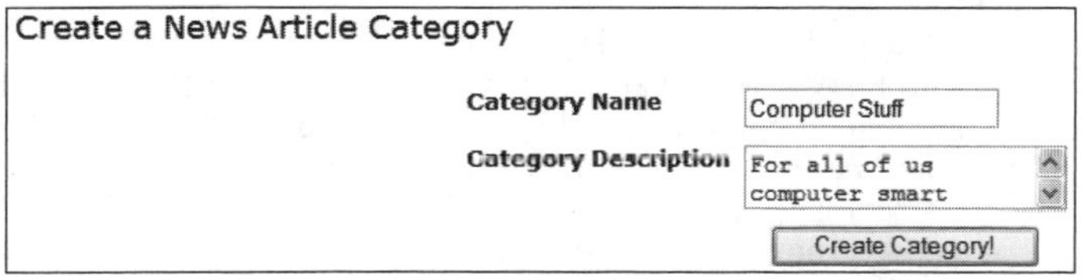

FIGURE 6.4:

Confirming the new Computer Stuff category

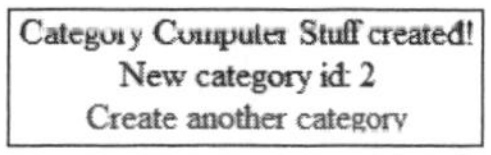

Creating the News Article Category Update and Delete Script

The next task is to create script that will allow you to update categories with new titles and descriptions and to delete categories you no longer want.

First, you will create the HTML forms required to perform these actions. The first form is named mod_news_category_index.html, and it goes in your html/forms directory. This HTML form will serve as the starting point for modifying and deleting your categories. It will contain two sections of dynamically generated HTML select menus with the category information inside of them. When the category is selected and the form is submitted, a mysql_query will fetch the appropriate information about the category you have chosen and display a new page based upon the action you chose. This form looks like Listing 6.4.

| Listing 6.4 | Modify News Categories Index Form |

```
<font size="4" face="Verdana, Arial, Helvetica, sans-serif">Modify News Article
Category </font>
<table width="90%" border="0" cellspacing="0" cellpadding="4">
  <tr>
    <td width="200" align="left" valign="top"><font size="2" face="Verdana,
Arial, Helvetica, sans-serif">Select
      a category to modify:</font></td>
    <td align="left" valign="top"><form name="form1" method="post"
action="/admin/mod_news_category.php">
        <?php cat_list(NULL);?>
        <input name="req" type="hidden" id="req" value="mod_category">
        <input type="submit" name="Submit" value="Go">
      </form></td>
  </tr>
</table>
<hr size="1">
<p><font size="4" face="Verdana, Arial, Helvetica, sans-serif">Delete News
Article
  Category:</font></p>
<table width="90%" border="0" cellspacing="0" cellpadding="4">
  <tr>
    <td width="200" align="left" valign="top"><font size="2" face="Verdana,
Arial, Helvetica, sans-serif">Select a category to delete:</font></td>
    <td align="left" valign="top"><form name="form1" method="post"
action="/admin/mod_news_category.php">
        <?php cat_list(NULL);?>
        <input name="req" type="hidden" id="req" value="del_category">
        <input type="submit" name="Submit" value="Go">
      </form></td>
  </tr>
</table>
<hr size="1">
<p><font size="4" face="Verdana, Arial, Helvetica, sans-serif"><a
href="/admin/newscategory.php?req=new_cat">Create
  a News Article Category</a></font></p>
<hr size="1">
```

The next form you will create is named mod_news_category_form.html, and it will be stored in your html/forms directory. This next form will look like the form you created earlier that gathered the information you needed to insert a new category into the database. This form has embedded PHP for the input fields. You will extract the information to complete these fields from the database before the form displays in the web browser.

When you initially see this form in action, the information will be completed in the input fields from the database; from there you will be able to make the changes to the information and submit the form to the PHP script to update the database. Listing 6.5 shows the form.

Listing 6.5   Category Modification Form

```
<p><font size="4" face="Verdana, Arial, Helvetica, sans-serif">Modify News
Article
  Category</font></p>
<form action="/admin/mod_news_category.php" method="post">
  <table width="33%" border="0" align="center" cellpadding="4" cellspacing="0">
    <tr>
      <td width="17%" align="left" valign="top"><font size="2" face="Verdana,
Arial, Helvetica, sans-serif"><strong>Category
        Name</strong></font></td>
      <td width="83%"><input name="cat_name" type="text" id="cat_name"
value="<?=stripslashes($row[cat_name]);?>"></td>
    </tr>
    <tr>
      <td align="left" valign="top" nowrap><font size="2" face="Verdana, Arial,
Helvetica, sans-serif"><strong>Category
        Description</strong></font></td>
      <td><textarea name="cat_description"
id="cat_description"><?=stripslashes($row[cat_description]);?></textarea></td>
    </tr>
    <tr>
      <td> </td>
      <td><div align="center">
          <input name="cat_id" type="hidden" id="cat_id"
value="<?=$row['cat_id'];?>">
          <input name="req" type="hidden" value="update_category">
          <input type="submit" name="Submit" value="Modify Category!">
        </div></td>
    </tr>
  </table>
</form>
```

Now it is time to create a script named mod_news_category.php in your website document root in the admin directory (see Listing 6.6).

Listing 6.6   **Modify and Delete News Article Category Script**

```php
<?php
include $_SERVER['DOCUMENT_ROOT'].
        '/layout.php';

// Quick Admin session check
admin_check();

// Dynamic Form Select Menu
// For Categories
function cat_list($selected){
   // Perform the query
   $sql = mysql_query("SELECT * FROM
         news_categories");

   // Begin select menu
   echo "<select name=\"cat_id\">\n";
   echo "<option value=\"NULL\">Please Select</option>\n";

   // Do the loop for the categories
   while($row = mysql_fetch_array($sql)){
        echo "<option value=\"".
        stripslashes($row[cat_id])."\"";

        // if $selected is equal
        // to current row, select
        // this item in menu.

        if($selected == $row[cat_id]){
           echo "selected";
        }

        echo ">".stripslashes($row[cat_name]).
        "</option>\n";
   }
   // Close select statement
   echo "</select>\n";
}
// Initiate myheader function
myheader("Modify or Delete News Categories");

// Start switch
switch($_REQUEST['req']){

   // Modify category form
   case "mod_category":
      $sql = mysql_query("SELECT * FROM
            news_categories WHERE
            cat_id='{$_POST['cat_id']}'");
```

```php
            $row = mysql_fetch_assoc($sql);

            include $_SERVER['DOCUMENT_ROOT'].
            '/html/forms/mod_news_category_form.html';
    break;

    // Modify category query
    case "update_category":
        $sql = mysql_query("UPDATE news_categories
            SET cat_name='{$_POST['cat_name']}',
            cat_description='{$_POST['cat_description']}'
            WHERE cat_id='{$_POST['cat_id']}'}");
        if(!$sql){
            echo "Error performing query: ".
                mysql_error();
        } else {
          echo '<p align="center">Category Updated!</p>';
          echo '<p align="center">'.
                '<a href="/admin/mod_news_category.php">'.
                'Modify Another Category</a>';
        }
    break;

    // Delete category confirmation
    case "del_category":
        echo '<p align="center">Are you sure '.
            'you want to delete this category?'.
            '</p>';

        echo '<p align="center">'.
            '<a
href="/admin/mod_news_category.php?req=delete_category&amp;cat_id='
            .$_POST['cat_id'].'">Yes</a>  '.
            '| <a href="/admin/mod_news_category.php">No</a></p>';
    break;

    // Delete category query
    case "delete_category":
        $sql = mysql_query("DELETE FROM news_categories
            WHERE cat_id='{$_GET['cat_id']}'");

        if(!$sql){
            echo 'Error performing DELETE query: '.
                mysql_error();
        } else {
          echo '<p align="center">Category Deleted!</p>';
          echo '<p align="center">'.
                '<a href="/admin/mod_news_category.php">'.
                'Modify another category</a></p>';
        }
    break;
```

```
    // Modify and delete category forms
    default:
        include $_SERVER['DOCUMENT_ROOT'].
                '/html/forms/mod_news_category_index.html';
    break;

}

// Footer
footer();

?>
```

Let's break this script down for further understanding. First, you include your `layout.php` file and then perform your administrative session check:

```
<?php

include $_SERVER['DOCUMENT_ROOT'].
        '/layout.php';

// Quick Admin session check
admin_check();
}
```

Next, you create a custom function that dynamically generates an HTML select menu with the category names and the category ID numbers. This function will be used in the HTML from Listing 6.4 that will be included in your `default case`:

```
// Dynamic Form Select Menu
// For Categories
function cat_list($selected){
    // Perform the query
    $sql = mysql_query("SELECT * FROM
            news_categories");

    // Begin select menu
    echo "<select name=\"cat_id\">\n";
    echo "<option value=\"NULL\">Please Select</option>\n";

    // Do the loop for the categories
    while($row = mysql_fetch_array($sql)){
            echo "<option value=\"".
            stripslashes($row[cat_id])."\"";

            // if $selected is equal
            // to current row, select
            // this item in menu.

            if($selected == $row[cat_id]){
```

```
            echo "selected";
        }

        echo ">".stripslashes($row[cat_name]).
        "</option>\n";
    }
    // Close select statement
    echo "</select>\n";
}
```

In this script, I have determined that you will use any special code functions that will prevent you from using the myheader and footer functions from the layout.php file outside of the switch, so I have included these functions as necessary:

```
myheader("Modify or Delete News Categories");
```

Next, you initialize the switch and build your first case. The first case, modify_category, will include the form from Listing 6.5, and it will contain all of the information about the category you have selected by performing a mysql_query and embedding the result values into the form using PHP:

```
// Start switch
switch($_REQUEST['req']){

    // Modify category form
    case "mod_category":
        $sql = mysql_query("SELECT * FROM
                news_categories WHERE
                cat_id='{$_POST['cat_id']}'");

                $row = mysql_fetch_assoc($sql);

                include $_SERVER['DOCUMENT_ROOT'].
                '/html/forms/mod_news_category_form.html';
    break;
```

The intent of the previous case is to allow you to make changes to an existing category in the database and then post the changes to the next case, which updates the affected row in the MySQL database. Let's take a look at the next case, update_category:

```
// Modify category query
case "update_category":
    $sql = mysql_query("UPDATE news_categories
            SET cat_name='{$_POST['cat_name']}',
            cat_description='{$_POST['cat_description']}'
            WHERE cat_id='{$_POST['cat_id']}'");
    if(!$sql){
        echo "Error performing query: ".
            mysql_error();
```

```
        } else {
          echo '<p align="center">Category Updated!</p>';
          echo '<p align="center">'.
               '<a href="/admin/mod_news_category.php">'.
               'Modify Another Category</a>';
        }
    break;
```

In the previous code example, you used a mysql_query with the UPDATE syntax. The UPDATE syntax must contain the columns and their new values as well as a WHERE clause defining exactly which row the query will update. The previous code example also uses an error checking method to determine if the query was a success or failure and presents a message accordingly.

The next case in your script contains the delete category confirmation screen. As stated previously, I think it is rude to omit a confirmation screen before deleting any data from the database. This next case is simply a confirmation screen that will ask you if you want to delete the category you have selected. You will present a Yes or No option to perform the action. If the user chooses Yes, the hyperlink will take them to the next case, which is delete_category. If the user chooses No, they will go back to the default case, which is the index of this script:

```
// Delete category confirmation
case "del_category":
    echo '<p align="center">Are you sure '.
         'you want to delete this category?'.
         '</p>';

    echo '<p align="center">'.
         '<a href="/admin/mod_news_category.php?req=delete_category&amp;cat_id='
         .$_POST['cat_id'].'">Yes</a>  '.
         '| <a href="/admin/mod_news_category.php">No</a></p>';
    break;
```

To perform the actual delete operation, you will use a mysql_query with the DELETE FROM syntax. This particular syntax must also include a WHERE clause to identify exactly which row you are attempting to delete:

```
// Delete category query
case "delete_category":
    $sql = mysql_query("DELETE FROM news_categories
             WHERE cat_id='{$_GET['cat_id']}'");

    if(!$sql){
      echo 'Error performing DELETE query: '.
           mysql_error();
    } else {
      echo '<p align="center">Category Deleted!</p>';
      echo '<p align="center">'.
```

```
                        '<a href="/admin/mod_news_category.php">'.
                        'Modify another category</a></p>';
        }
    break;
```

A common mistake is improperly using the DELETE syntax. Do not use DELETE * or any other column definition in the query. The proper use is DELETE FROM table WHERE col-umn='value'.

The last portion of the `switch` is the `default case`, which will include the HTML forms identified in Listing 6.4. This case will allow you to select a category and either delete or modify it from one of the previous `case` examples in this script:

```
// Modify and delete category forms
default:
    include $_SERVER['DOCUMENT_ROOT'].
            '/html/forms/mod_news_category_index.html';
break;
```

As stated earlier when explaining this script, I have determined that the `myheader` and `footer` functions could be initiated outside of the `switch` because you are not worrying about displaying HTML from these functions before using any special functions such as `header` or `session_start`, which are picky about output buffers. Therefore, you use the custom `footer` function outside of the `switch` in this script:

```
}

// Footer
footer();

?>
```

This script is complete. You are at a point now where you need to create some hyperlinks in the left column that only the website administrators will see. Let's do that now.

Creating the News Article Category Administrator Hyperlinks

You have a smooth system going at this point. When a user logs into your website, you assign session values to identify the user and their access levels throughout the website. If a user is flagged as an administrator by the `admin_access` value in your `members` table, you will assign them a special flag in their session. Based upon this concept, you can display special hyperlinks for the administrators that the regular users will not see.

Create a new file called box_admin_links.php inside your website document root boxes directory. Take a look at this code example:

```
<?php
if($_SESSION['admin_access'] == true){
?>
<table width="160" border="0" cellspacing="0" cellpadding="0">
  <tr bgcolor="#000066">
    <td width="5" height="10"><font color="#FFFFFF"> </font></td>
    <td width="150"><div align="center"><font color="#FFFFFF" size="2"
face="Verdana, Arial, Helvetica, sans-serif"><strong>Admin
Links</strong></font></div></td>
    <td width="5"> </td>
  </tr>
  <tr>
    <td height="5"> </td>
    <td align="left" valign="top">
    <p><font size="2" face="Verdana, Arial, Helvetica, sans-serif">
      <a href="/admin/newscategory.php">Create News Article
Categories</a></font></p>
      <p><font size="2" face="Verdana, Arial, Helvetica, sans-serif"> <a
href="/admin/mod_news_category.php">Modify/Delete
        News Article Categories</a></font></p>
      <p><font size="2" face="Verdana, Arial, Helvetica, sans-serif"><a
href="/admin/news_insert.php">Add
        News Article</a></font></p>
      <p><font size="2" face="Verdana, Arial, Helvetica, sans-serif"><a
href="/admin/mod_news_article.php">Modify/Delete
        News Article</a></font></p>
      <p> </p>
    </td>
    <td> </td>
  </tr>
</table>
<hr size="1">
<?
}
```

This code example simply creates a nice-looking table around the hyperlinks that point to the administration functions of the website.

In your layout.php file directly below the point where you included your member_box.php file, include the new file you just created. Here is what this portion of the layout.php file looks like:

```
<!-- Left Links Column -->
<td width="170" valign="top">
```

```
<table width="170" border="0" cellpadding="0" cellspacing="0">
<tr>
<td width="10"> </td>
<td valign="top">
<?php
include $_SERVER['DOCUMENT_ROOT'].
           '/boxes/member_box.php';

include $_SERVER['DOCUMENT_ROOT'].
        '/boxes/box_admin_links.php';
?>
</td>
<!-- End Left Links Column -->
```

When you reload your website in the browser, you should now see your hyperlinks in the administration links on the left side if you are logged in as an administrator, as shown in Figure 6.5. 

FIGURE 6.5:

Administration links

Testing the News Article Category Management System

The scripts are built and the administrative links are in place, so it is time to put all this hard work to the test. Load your web browser and follow these steps to test your management system:

1. Log in to your website with the username and password to which you have granted administrator access.

2. Click the Create News Article Categories hyperlink under the "Admin Links" heading and then click the Add News Article Categories hyperlink in the middle of the page, as shown in Figure 6.6.

3. Next, create a new category named *Test Category 1* with a description of your choice in the Category Description field, as shown in Figure 6.7. You will receive a confirmation message, as shown in Figure 6.8.

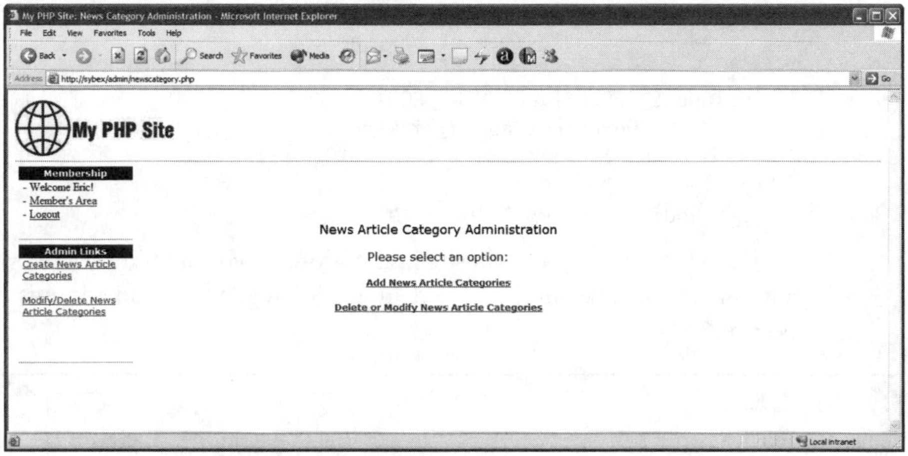

FIGURE 6.6:

The news article category index page

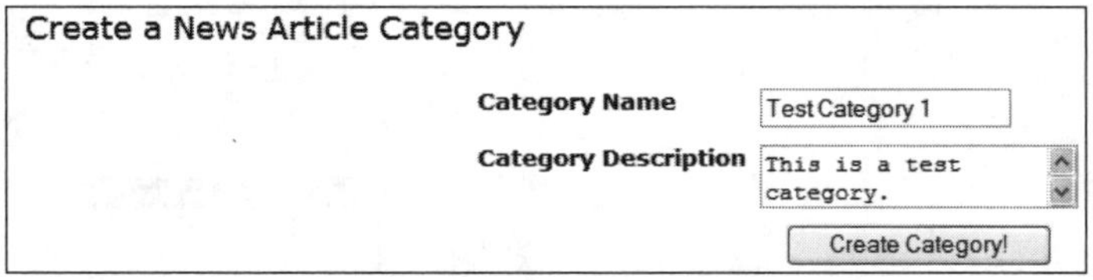

FIGURE 6.7:

Creating the test category

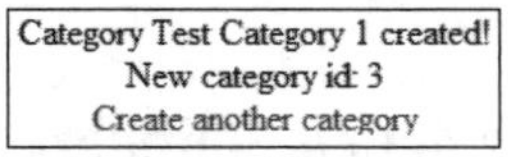

FIGURE 6.8:

Confirming a new category

4. Click the Modify/Delete News Article Categories hyperlink under the "Admin Links" heading in the left column, as shown in Figure 6.9.

5. Select Test Category 1 in the first select menu and click the Go button. You will see the screen shown in Figure 6.10.

6. Modify your category by renaming the category name to *Test Category 2* and changing the description. When you are done making changes, click the Modify Category button. You will see the screen in Figure 6.11.

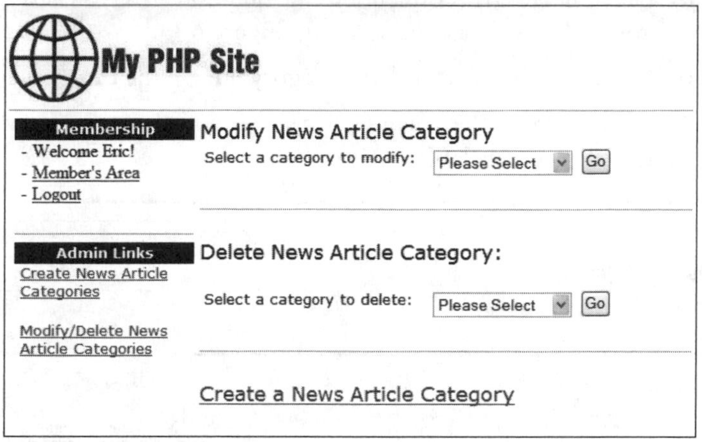

FIGURE 6.9:

The category
modify/delete
index screen

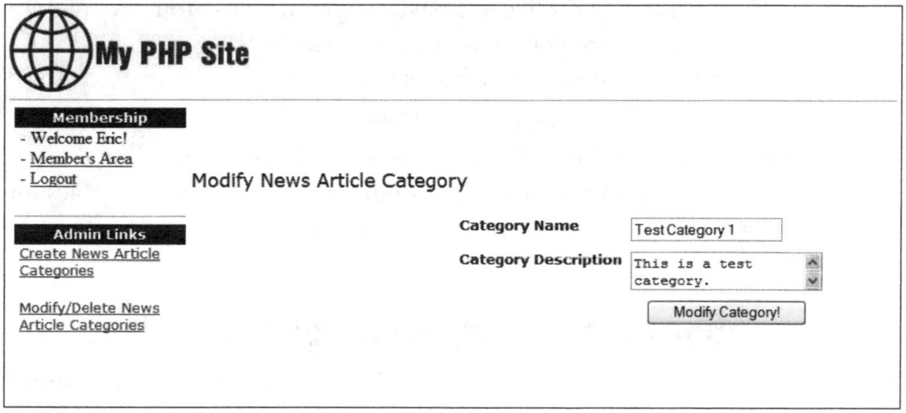

FIGURE 6.10:

The modify category
screen

FIGURE 6.11:

The modify category
confirmation screen

7. Click the Modify Another Category hyperlink on the confirmation screen or click the
Modify/Delete News Article Categories link from the administration links in the left column. You will see the index screen again.

8. Select Test Category 2 from the Delete News Article Category select menu and click the
Go button. You will see the screen in Figure 6.12.

9. Click the Yes hyperlink under the question "Are you sure you want to delete this category?" You will see the screen in Figure 6.13.

10. Click the Modify Another Category link on the category deleted confirmation screen.

11. Check either select menu on this screen, and you should notice that the Test Category 2 is no longer available.

FIGURE 6.12:

Requesting confirmation screen

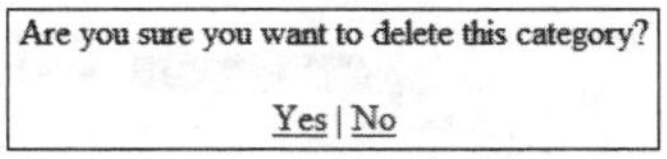

> Are you sure you want to delete this category?
>
> Yes | No

FIGURE 6.13:

Category deleted confirmation screen

> Category Deleted!
>
> Modify another category

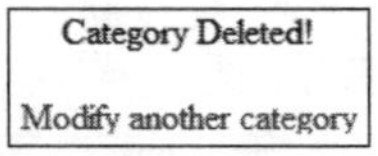

If everything works like it should, congratulations! You have just created a complete management system for your news article categories. Believe it or not, all of this work is a routine task for any web-based management system.

You will have to decide if you like this method over using a MySQL manager such as phpMyAdmin or SQLyog; however, there are advantages to using this method. The main advantage is to prevent granting access to the MySQL database or tables for administration helpers (users granted administrative access) on websites.

Creating the News Article Management System

Now that you have mastered the skill of creating a management system for your news article categories, it is time to create a similar system for your news articles. I will cover this process again to show you some variants involved in creating different types of administration systems in your websites.

Creating the News Article Insert Script

You need to make a script that will allow you to type the news articles into a form and store the information into the database. This script is not too difficult compared to the scripts you have already created in this chapter; however, you will link the news articles to the categories, so this may be new to you.

Create a new script in your website document root in the `admin` directory. Name this script `news_insert.php`. For this script, you will create an HTML form named `news_insert_form.html` and store it in the `html/forms/` directory. Listing 6.7 is the HTML form that will gather the article title, caption, body, and the `cat_id` value for the category with which you want to associate the article.

Listing 6.7 **News Article HTML Insert Form**

```
<p><font size="4" face="Verdana, Arial, Helvetica, sans-serif">News Article
Submission</font></p>
<form name="form1" method="post" action="/admin/news_insert.php">
  <table width="51%" border="0" align="center" cellpadding="4" cellspacing="0">
    <tr>
      <td width="25%" align="left" valign="top" nowrap><font size="2"
face="Verdana, Arial, Helvetica, sans-serif"><strong>Article
        Title</strong></font></td>
      <td width="75%"><input name="article_title" type="text" id="article_title"
size="60"></td>
    </tr>
    <tr>
      <td align="left" valign="top" nowrap><font size="2" face="Verdana, Arial,
Helvetica, sans-serif"><strong>Article
        Category</strong></font></td>
      <td><?php cat_list(NULL); ?></td>
    </tr>
    <tr>
      <td align="left" valign="top" nowrap><font size="2" face="Verdana, Arial,
Helvetica, sans-serif"><strong>Article
        Caption</strong></font></td>
      <td><textarea name="article_caption" cols="60"
id="article_caption"></textarea></td>
    </tr>
    <tr>
      <td align="left" valign="top" nowrap><font size="2" face="Verdana, Arial,
Helvetica, sans-serif"><strong>Full
        article</strong></font></td>
      <td><textarea name="article_body" cols="60" rows="15"
id="article_body"></textarea></td>
    </tr>
    <tr>
      <td align="left" valign="top"> </td>
      <td><div align="center">
          <input name="req" type="hidden" id="req" value="submit_article">
          <input type="submit" name="Submit" value="Submit News Article!">
        </div></td>
    </tr>
  </table>
</form>
```

Listing 6.8 depicts the PHP script that will insert the news article into the database.

Listing 6.8   **News Article Insert PHP Script**

```php
<?php

include $_SERVER['DOCUMENT_ROOT'].
    '/layout.php';

// Quick Admin session check
admin_check();

// Dynamic Form Select Menu
// For Categories
function cat_list($selected){
    // Perform the query
    $sql = mysql_query("SELECT * FROM
            news_categories");

    // Begin select menu
    echo "<select name=\"cat_id\">\n";
    echo "<option value=\"NULL\">Please Select</option>\n";

    // Do the loop for the categories
    while($row = mysql_fetch_array($sql)){
            echo "<option value=\"".
            stripslashes($row[cat_id])."\"";

            // if $selected is equal
            // to current row, select
            // this item in menu.

            if($selected == $row[cat_id]){
                echo "selected";
            }

            echo ">".stripslashes($row[cat_name]).
            "</option>\n";
    }
    // Close select statement
    echo "</select>\n";
}
// Initiate myheader function

myheader("Insert News Article");

switch($_REQUEST['req']){
    case "submit_article":
        if(!$_POST['article_title'] ||
            !$_POST['article_caption'] ||
            !$_POST['article_body'] ||
            $_POST['cat_id'] == 0){
            echo '<p align="center">Missing
                Form Information!</p>'.
```

```php
                '<p align="center">Please use
                 your browser back '.
                'button and complete the form.</p>';
        footer();
        exit();
    }

    $full_name = $_SESSION['first_name']." "
                .$_SESSION['last_name'];
    $sql = mysql_query("INSERT INTO news_articles
            (cat_id, article_title, article_caption,
             article_body, article_author,
             article_date)
            VALUES ('{$_POST['cat_id']}',
                    '{$_POST['article_title']}',
                    '{$_POST['article_caption']}',
                    '{$_POST['article_body']}',
                    '$full_name',
                    now())");

    if(!$sql){
        echo "Error performing query: ".
             mysql_error();
    } else {
        echo '<p align="center">Article Inserted!<br />'.
'ID Number: '.
             mysql_insert_id().'</p>';
        echo '<p align="center">'.
             '<a href="/admin/news_insert.php">'.
             'Enter Another News Article</a>';
    }

    break;

    default:
        include $_SERVER['DOCUMENT_ROOT'].
            '/html/forms/news_insert_form.html';
    break;
}

footer();

?>
```

Let's break down this script for further understanding. First, you start PHP, include your layout.php file, and perform an administrative check on the session. Looks pretty familiar, doesn't it?

```php
<?php
```

```
include $_SERVER['DOCUMENT_ROOT'].
    '/layout.php';

// Quick Admin session check
admin_check();
```

Next, you build your dynamic form select menu function that will be called from within the HTML form by the embedded PHP code. This function is the same as in the news article category management scripts:

```
// Dynamic Form Select Menu
// For Categories
function cat_list($selected){
    // Perform the query
    $sql = mysql_query("SELECT * FROM
            news_categories");

    // Begin select menu
    echo "<select name=\"cat_id\">\n";
    echo "<option value=\"NULL\">Please Select</option>\n";

    // Do the loop for the categories
    while($row = mysql_fetch_array($sql)){
            echo "<option value=\"".
            stripslashes($row[cat_id])."\"";

            // if $selected is equal
            // to current row, select
            // this item in menu.

            if($selected == $row[cat_id]){
                echo "selected";
            }

            echo ">".stripslashes($row[cat_name]).
            "</option>\n";
    }
    // Close select statement
    echo "</select>\n";
}
```

Once again, I have determined that the custom myheader function may be used outside of the switch, so I have initiated it here and then started the switch:

```
// Initiate myheader function

myheader("Insert News Article");

switch($_REQUEST['req']){
```

The first case in this switch will perform a form validation against the posted fields to ensure everything you need has been posted. Once the form validation passes, the mysql_query will insert the applicable information into the database.

Notice that you have also built a variable called $full_name with the session values first_name and last_name to insert as the article_author in the news article.

The next important thing I want you to notice about this code is the usage of the now() function in MySQL. The now() function will set the date on any date- or time-related column type in MySQL to the current date at the time of the query:

```php
case "submit_article":
    if(!$_POST['article_title'] ||
        !$_POST['article_caption'] ||
        !$_POST['article_body'] ||
        $_POST['cat_id'] == 0){
        echo '<p align="center">Missing
            Form Information!</p>'.
            '<p align="center">Please use
             your browser back '.
            'button and complete the form.</p>';
        footer();
        exit();
    }

    $full_name = $_SESSION['first_name']." "
                .$_SESSION['last_name'];
    $sql = mysql_query("INSERT INTO news_articles
            (cat_id, article_title, article_caption,
             article_body, article_author,
             article_date)
            VALUES ('{$_POST['cat_id']}',
                    '{$_POST['article_title']}',
                    '{$_POST['article_caption']}',
                    '{$_POST['article_body']}',
                    '$full_name',
                    now())");

    if(!$sql){
        echo "Error performing query: ".
            mysql_error();
    } else {
        echo '<p align="center">Article Inserted!<br />'.
            'ID Number: '.
            mysql_insert_id().'</p>';
        echo '<p align="center">'.
            '<a href="/admin/news_insert.php">'.
```

```
          'Enter Another News Article</a>';
   }

break;
```

The default case in this code simply includes the HTML form you created from Listing 6.7:

```
default:
   include $_SERVER['DOCUMENT_ROOT'].
      '/html/forms/news_insert_form.html';
break;
```

And finally, you close the switch, include your custom footer function, and close the PHP script.

This completes the news article insert script. It's getting much easier now, isn't it? Let's move onto the next portion of the news article management, the news article modify and delete script!

Creating the News Article Modify and Delete Script

The next script you will create is the news article modify and delete script. With this script, I will show you how to create an alternating row color index with all of your news articles inside of a table. Every other row in the table will contain an alternated color that allows users to read the table much more easily.

Let's get started on this script. First, you will need one HTML form that allows you to modify the existing information in the database and post it to your PHP script to perform an UPDATE query. Create an HTML form named news_modify_form.html and save it in your html/forms directory (see Listing 6.9).

Listing 6.9   **News Article Modification HTML Form**

```
<p><font size="4" face="Verdana, Arial, Helvetica, sans-serif">News Article
Modification</font></p>
<form method="post" action="/admin/mod_news_article.php">
  <table width="51%" border="0" align="center" cellpadding="4" cellspacing="0">
    <tr>
      <td width="25%" align="left" valign="top" nowrap><font size="2"
face="Verdana, Arial, Helvetica, sans-serif"><strong>Article
        Title</strong></font></td>
      <td width="75%"><input name="article_title" type="text" id="article_title"
value="<?= stripslashes($row['article_title']);?>" size="60"></td>
    </tr>
    <tr>
      <td align="left" valign="top" nowrap><font size="2" face="Verdana, Arial,
Helvetica, sans-serif"><strong>Article
```

```
          Category</strong></font></td>
        <td><?php cat_list($row[cat_id]); ?></td>
      </tr>
      <tr>
        <td align="left" valign="top" nowrap><font size="2" face="Verdana, Arial,
Helvetica, sans-serif"><strong>Article
          Caption</strong></font></td>
        <td><textarea name="article_caption" cols="60"
id="article_caption"><?=stripslashes($row['article_caption']);?></textarea></td>
      </tr>
      <tr>
        <td align="left" valign="top" nowrap><font size="2" face="Verdana, Arial,
Helvetica, sans-serif"><strong>Full
          article</strong></font></td>
        <td><textarea name="article_body" cols="60" rows="15"
id="article_body"><?=stripslashes($row['article_body']);?></textarea></td>
      </tr>
      <tr>
        <td align="left" valign="top"> </td>
        <td><div align="center">
            <input name="article_id" type="hidden" id="article_id"
value="<?=$row['article_id'];?>">
            <input name="req" type="hidden" id="req" value="update_news_article">
            <input type="submit" name="Submit" value="Modify News Article!">
          </div></td>
      </tr>
    </table>
</form>
```

The form in Listing 6.9 will display the information about the news article using embedded PHP tags that you create with the extracted information from the database. The news article information that you modify will be posted to a case inside your PHP script to perform the UPDATE query. This form also uses the dynamic category select menu function you created in the modify categories scripts.

The next task is to create the PHP script that will perform all of your update and delete functions. Create a script named mod_news_article.php and save it in your admin directory (see Listing 6.10).

Listing 6.10   Modify and Delete News Articles PHP Script

```
<?php

include $_SERVER['DOCUMENT_ROOT'].
    '/layout.php';

// Quick Admin session check
admin_check();
```

```php
// Dynamic Form Select Menu
// For Categories
function cat_list($selected){
    // Perform the query
    $sql = mysql_query("SELECT * FROM
            news_categories");

    // Begin select menu
    echo "<select name=\"cat_id\">\n";
    echo "<option value=\"NULL\">Please Select</option>\n";

    // Do the loop for the categories
    while($row = mysql_fetch_array($sql)){
            echo "<option value=\"".
            stripslashes($row[cat_id])."\"";

            // if $selected is equal
            // to current row, select
            // this item in menu.

            if($selected == $row[cat_id]){
                echo "selected";
            }

            echo ">".stripslashes($row[cat_name]).
            "</option>\n";
    }
    // Close select statement
    echo "</select>\n";
}

// Display myheader
myheader("Modify or Delete News Articles");

// Switch navigation
switch($_REQUEST['req']){

    // Modify article form
    case "mod_news_article":
        $sql = mysql_query("SELECT * FROM
            news_articles WHERE
            article_id='{$_GET['article_id']}'
            ");
        $row = mysql_fetch_assoc($sql);
        include $_SERVER['DOCUMENT_ROOT'].
            '/html/forms/news_modify_form.html';
    break;

    // Modify article query
    case "update_news_article":
```

```php
        // Form validation
        if(!$_POST['article_title'] ||
           !$_POST['article_caption'] ||
           !$_POST['article_body'] ||
           $_POST['cat_id'] == 0){
            echo '<p align="center">Missing '.
                 'Form Information!</p>'.
                 '<p align="center">Please use your '.
                 'browser back '.
                 'button and complete the form.</p>';
            footer();
            exit();
        }

        // Update query
        $sql = mysql_query("UPDATE news_articles SET
                article_title='{$_POST['article_title']}',
                article_caption='{$_POST['article_caption']}',
                article_body='{$_POST['article_body']}',
                cat_id='{$_POST['cat_id']}'
                WHERE article_id='{$_POST['article_id']}'");

        // Query error check
        if(!$sql){
            echo "Error performing query: ".
                 mysql_error();
        } else {
            echo '<p align="center">Article Updated!!</p>';
            echo '<p align="center">'.
                 '<a href="/admin/mod_news_article.php">'.
                 'Modify Another News Article</a>';
        }
    break;

    // Delete article confirmation
    case "confirm_delete":
        echo '<p align="center">Are you sure '.
             'you want to delete this article?'.
             '</p>';

        echo '<p align="center">'.
             '<a
href="/admin/mod_news_article.php?req=delete_news_article&amp;article_id='
             .$_GET['article_id'].'">Yes</a> '.
             '| <a href="/admin/mod_news_article.php">No</a></p>';

    break;

    // Delete article query
    case "delete_news_article":
        $sql = mysql_query("DELETE FROM news_articles
```

```
                    WHERE article_id='{$_GET['article_id']}'");

          if(!$sql){
             echo 'Error performing DELETE query: '.
                 mysql_error();
          } else {
             echo '<p align="center">Article Deleted!</p>';
             echo '<p align="center">'.
                 '<a href="/admin/mod_news_article.php">'.
                 'Modify Another Article</a></p>';
          }
       break;

       // Default case: modify/delete index
       default:
          // Define alternating row colors
          $color1 = "#E6E6E6";
          $color2 = "#F4FEFF";
          // Set row_count
          $row_count = 0;

          // Build top of the table
          echo '<p><font size="4" face="Verdana, '.
              'Arial, Helvetica, sans-serif">'.
              'Modify or Delete News Articles'.
              '</font></p>';
          echo '<table align="center" width="90%" border="0" '.
              'cellpadding="4" cellspacing="0">';
          echo '<tr>';
          echo '<td width="300">Article</td>';
          echo '<td width="150">Article Date</td>';
          echo '<td width="5">Modify</td>';
          echo '<td width="5">Delete</td>';
          echo "</tr>";

          // Perform MySQL Query to get rows
          $sql = mysql_query("SELECT * FROM news_articles") or die (mysql_error());
          while($row = mysql_fetch_array($sql)){

             // Determine which row color to use
             $row_color = ($row_count % 2) ? $color1 : $color2;

             // Display table row with data
             echo '<tr bgcolor="'.$row_color.'">';
             echo '<td width="300">'.
                 '<a href="/articles.php?req=read&amp;article_
id='.$row['article_id'].
                 '">'.$row['article_title'].'</a></td>';
             echo '<td width="150">'.$row['article_date'].'</td>';
             echo '<td width="5"><a href="/admin/mod_news_article.php?req='.
                 'mod_news_article&amp;article_id='.$row['article_id'].'">'.
```

```
                'Modify</a></td>';
        echo '<td width="5"><a href="/admin/mod_news_article.php?req='.
                'confirm_delete&amp;article_id='.$row['article_id'].'">'.
                'Delete</a></td>';
        echo "</tr>";

            $row_count++; // Increment row count
    } // end while loop
    // Close the table
    echo '</table>';

    break;
}
footer();

?>
```

You should already understand the first half of the script. You start the PHP engine, include your layout, perform a session check for the administrator values, create the dynamic category select menu function, and include the custom myheader function.

Let's move onto the first case in the script. This case is similar to the category modification script. Here, you will extract the data from the database about the article you have selected from the default case. Based on that information, you will populate the HTML form you included in this script from Listing 6.9:

```
// Modify article form
case "mod_news_article":
    $sql = mysql_query("SELECT * FROM
            news_articles WHERE
            article_id='{$_GET['article_id']}'
            ");
    $row = mysql_fetch_assoc($sql);
    include $_SERVER['DOCUMENT_ROOT'].
        '/html/forms/news_modify_form.html';
break;
```

The next case will be used when you submit the information from the HTML form in Listing 6.9. This case performs a quick form validation to ensure you have all of the required fields in the posted information. If all the required fields are there, you will update the news article in the database with the posted information and then show a message based on the result of the query:

```
// Modify article query
case "update_news_article":

    // Form validation
    if(!$_POST['article_title'] ||
```

```
            !$_POST['article_caption'] ||
            !$_POST['article_body'] ||
            $_POST['cat_id'] == 0){
            echo '<p align="center">Missing '.
                'Form Information!</p>'.
                '<p align="center">Please use your '.
                'browser back '.
                'button and complete the form.</p>';
            footer();
            exit();
        }

        // Update query
        $sql = mysql_query("UPDATE news_articles SET
                article_title='{$_POST['article_title']}',
                article_caption='{$_POST['article_caption']}',
                article_body='{$_POST['article_body']}',
                cat_id='{$_POST['cat_id']}'
                WHERE article_id='{$_POST['article_id']}'");

        // Query error check
        if(!$sql){
            echo "Error performing query: ".
                mysql_error();
        } else {
            echo '<p align="center">Article Updated!!</p>';
            echo '<p align="center">'.
                '<a href="/admin/mod_news_article.php">'.
                'Modify Another News Article</a>';
        }
    break;
```

Now it is time to work on the delete article portion of this script. As previously stated, I think it is rude to delete information without a confirmation screen, so your first case will present the user with a question, and they will have to click Yes to delete the news article. If they click Yes, they will move to the case in your switch that performs the delete query. If they click No, they will be presented the news article management index page:

```
// Delete article confirmation
case "confirm_delete":
    echo '<p align="center">Are you sure '.
        'you want to delete this article?'.
        '</p>';

    echo '<p align="center">'.
        '<a href="/admin/mod_news_article.php?req=delete_news_
article&amp;article_id='
```

```
          .$_GET['article_id'].'">Yes</a>  '.
        '| <a href="/admin/mod_news_article.php">No</a></p>';
```

break;

The next case simply deletes the news article from the database and presents a message about the query results:

```
// Delete article query
case "delete_news_article":
    $sql = mysql_query("DELETE FROM news_articles
        WHERE article_id='{$_GET['article_id']}'");

    if(!$sql){
        echo 'Error performing DELETE query: '.
            mysql_error();
    } else {
        echo '<p align="center">Article Deleted!</p>';
        echo '<p align="center">'.
            '<a href="/admin/mod_news_article.php">'.
            'Modify Another Article</a></p>';
    }
break;
```

The last portion of this script is the default case. I will take this opportunity to cover how to make your HTML table rows alternate in color for a MySQL result set because this is currently a hot item on the Internet. Let's break this case down into portions to better understand how to alternate these row colors!

The first task is to define the default case:

```
// Default case: modify/delete index
  default:
```

To allow your rows to alternate in color, you need to pick two HTML colors and assign them to variables such as $color1 and $color2:

```
// Define alternating row colors
$color1 = "#E6E6E6";
$color2 = "#F4FEFF";
```

Next, you need to create a variable named $row_count with the value of 0. This $row_count variable will determine which of the $color1 or $color2 variables to use when displaying the row color:

```
// Set row_count
$row_count = 0;
```

Now you need to build the top of the table and the first row for the column headings. This table is a simple HTML table with four columns:

```
// Build top of the table
echo '<p><font size="4" face="Verdana, '.
    'Arial, Helvetica, sans-serif">'.
    'Modify or Delete News Articles'.
    '</font></p>';
echo '<table align="center" width="90%" border="0" '.
    'cellpadding="4" cellspacing="0">';
echo '<tr>';
echo '<td width="300">Article</td>';
echo '<td width="150">Article Date</td>';
echo '<td width="5">Modify</td>';
echo '<td width="5">Delete</td>';
echo "</tr>";
```

Performing MySQL queries should be becoming easier and easier by now! Let's perform a query to get all of the information about the news articles from the database:

```
// Perform MySQL Query to get rows
$sql = mysql_query("SELECT * FROM news_articles") or die (mysql_error());
```

Because you will fetch the results into an array, you will use a while loop to display the results one by one:

```
while($row = mysql_fetch_array($sql)){
```

Inside the while loop, you will perform a simple math query to determine if $row_count is divisible by two. If the result is true, you will use $color2; if it is not true, you will use $color1. The $row_count value is incremented each time a row is extracted from the database, so this value will be divisible by two every other time the while loop is performed:

```
// Determine which row color to use
$row_color = ($row_count % 2) ? $color1 : $color2;
```

Now that your $row_color has been determined, you will display the HTML row with the BGCOLOR value in the new variable $row_color. You now have the row color for this row selected and in place:

```
// Display table row with data
echo '<tr bgcolor="'.$row_color.'">';
```

The next portion of the code simply displays the information about the current article in the while loop. Additionally, you will display hyperlinks to the applicable case inside this switch to perform the administrative action you desire:

```
echo '<td width="300">'.
    '<a href="/articles.php?req=read&amp;article_id='.$row['article_id'].
    '">'.$row['article_title'].'</a></td>';
echo '<td width="150">'.$row['article_date'].'</td>';
echo '<td width="5"><a href="/admin/mod_news_article.php?req='.
```

```
        'mod_news_article&amp;article_id='.$row['article_id'].'">'.
        'Modify</a></td>';
    echo '<td width="5"><a href="/admin/mod_news_article.php?req='.
        'confirm_delete&amp;article_id='.$row['article_id'].'">'.
        'Delete</a></td>';
    echo "</tr>";
```

To ensure that the correct color that will be used in the next row, you increment the $row_count variable by using a post increment operator (++) each time this loop occurs. This will cause the math query you created earlier to be either odd or even in value and will choose the applicable row color:

```
$row_count++; // Increment row count
```

NOTE To learn more about incrementing operators, please see the "Incrementing/Decrementing Operators" section of the PHP manual.

Next, you close the while loop for the MySQL query and then close the HTML table:

```
} // end while loop
// Close the table
echo '</table>';
```

Terminate the current case with the break; statement:

```
break;
```

Finally, you close the switch, display your custom footer, and then terminate the PHP script:

```
}
footer();

?>
```

The news article administration scripts are now complete! Do not forget to add some new hyperlinks to your box_admin_links.php file so that you can find these files more easily. Listing 6.11 shows my current box_admin_links.php file.

Listing 6.11　　**Current Admin Hyperlinks Box**

```
<?php
if($_SESSION['admin'] == true){
?>
<table width="160" border="0" cellspacing="0" cellpadding="0">
  <tr bgcolor="#000066">
    <td width="5" height="10"><font color="#FFFFFF"> </font></td>
    <td width="150"><div align="center"><font color-"#FFFFFF" size-"2"
face="Verdana, Arial, Helvetica, sans-serif"><strong>Admin
Links</strong></font></div></td>
    <td width="5"> </td>
```

```
    </tr>
    <tr>
      <td height="5"> </td>
      <td align="left" valign="top">
      <p><font size="2" face="Verdana, Arial, Helvetica, sans-serif">
        <a href="/admin/newscategory.php">Create News Article
Categories</a></font></p>
        <p><font size="2" face="Verdana, Arial, Helvetica, sans-serif"> <a
href="/admin/mod_news_category.php">Modify/Delete
          News Article Categories</a></font></p>
        <p><font size="2" face="Verdana, Arial, Helvetica, sans-serif"><a
href="/admin/news_insert.php">Add
          News Article</a></font></p>
        <p><font size="2" face="Verdana, Arial, Helvetica, sans-serif"><a
href="/admin/mod_news_article.php">Modify/Delete
          News Article</a></font></p>
        <p> </p>
      </td>
      <td> </td>
    </tr>
    <tr>
      <td width="5" height="10"><font color="#FFFFFF"> </font></td>
      <td width="150"> </td>
      <td width="5"> </td>
    </tr>
  </table>
  <hr size="1">
  <?
  }
  ?>
```

Testing the News Article Management System

Because you have been working so hard on these scripts, it is time to test them and ensure that everything is working properly! Follow these steps to make sure your system works:

1. Log in to your website with the administrator-enabled membership.

2. Click the Add News Article hyperlink in the "Admin Links" section of the left column. You will see the screen shown in Figure 6.14.

3. Add a news article with the following information, as shown in Figure 6.15:

   - Article Title: Test News Article 1

   - Article Category: Computer Stuff

   - Article Caption: This is a test news article!

   - Full Article: Test article body

4. Click Submit News Article to see the confirmation screen shown in Figure 6.16.

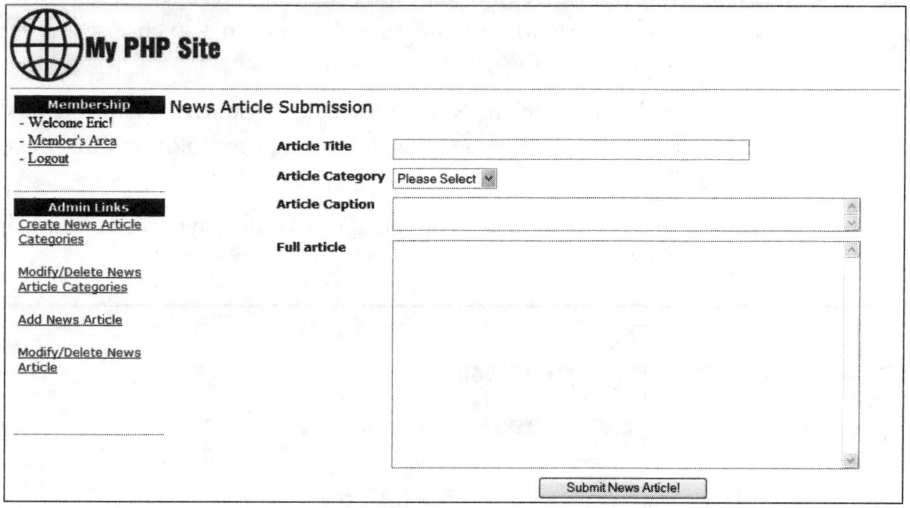

FIGURE 6.14:

Adding a news article

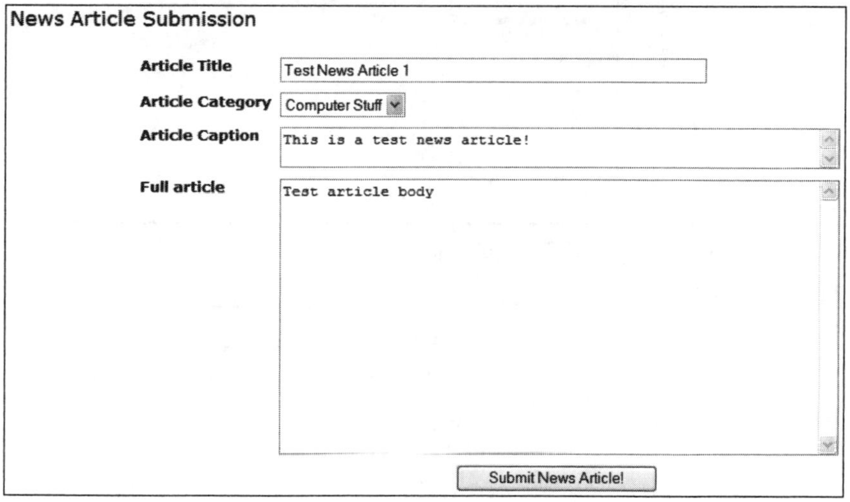

FIGURE 6.15:

Adding the test article

FIGURE 6.16:

The confirmation screen for adding a test article

5. Next, click the Enter Another News Article link, repeat step 3 two times, and change the number of the title for each new article. You can also choose a different category for each news article if you want.

6. Click the Modify/Delete News Article link from the "Admin Links" section of the left column. You should now see the alternating row colors on this page, as shown in Figure 6.17.

7. In the Test News Article 1 row, click the Modify hyperlink. You will see the screen in Figure 6.18.

FIGURE 6.17:

Modify or delete index screen with alternating row colors

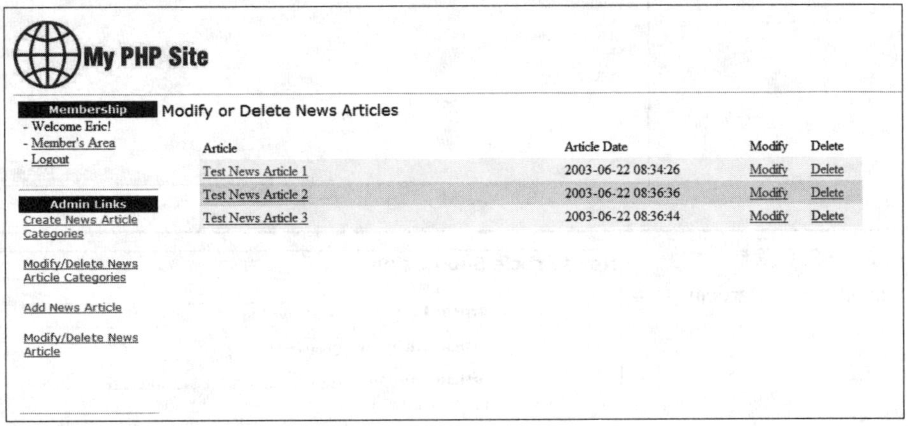

FIGURE 6.18:

Modifying the news article form

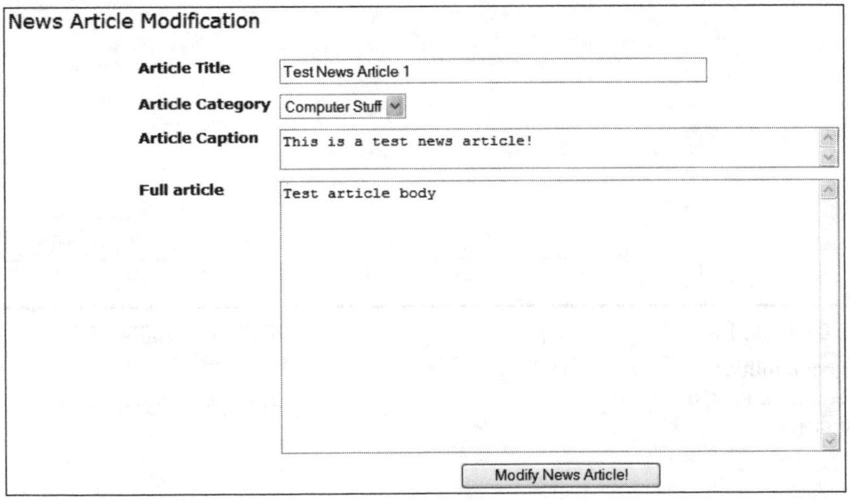

8. Change the title from *Test News Article 1* to *My PHP Site Opening Soon!* and then change the category to Computer Stuff using the drop-down box. Alter the news article caption to announce the opening of your website and write an article about it if you want, as shown in Figure 6.19. You can use HTML in the Article Caption and Full Article fields to present hyperlinks, images, tables, or whatever you like.

9. Click Modify News Article to see the confirmation screen, as shown in Figure 6.20.

10. Next, click the Modify/Delete News Article link from the "Admin Links" section of the left column. In the second row, click the Delete hyperlink for the Test News Article 2 article, as shown in Figure 6.21.

11. Click the Yes hyperlink to delete the hyperlink from the delete article confirmation screen, as shown in Figure 6.22. You will see a message notifying you that the article has been deleted, as shown in Figure 6.23.

FIGURE 6.19:

Modifying the news article

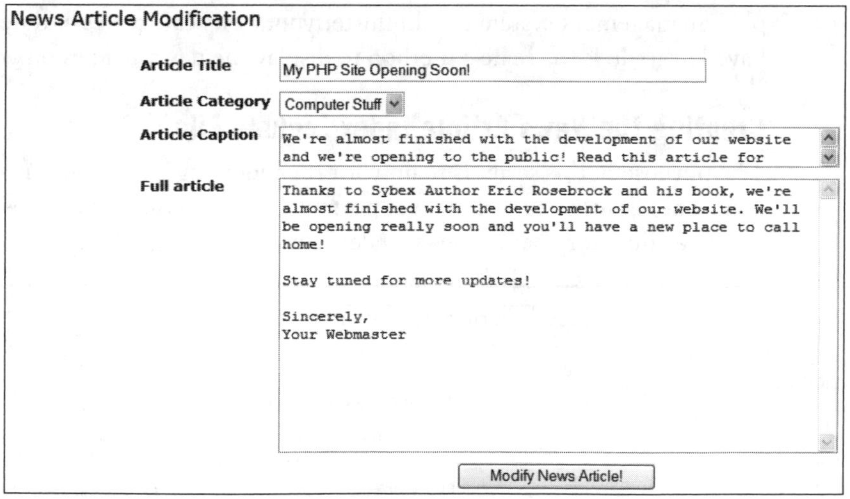

News Article Modification

Article Title	My PHP Site Opening Soon!
Article Category	Computer Stuff
Article Caption	We're almost finished with the development of our website and we're opening to the public! Read this article for
Full article	Thanks to Sybex Author Eric Rosebrock and his book, we're almost finished with the development of our website. We'll be opening really soon and you'll have a new place to call home! Stay tuned for more updates! Sincerely, Your Webmaster

Modify News Article!

FIGURE 6.20:

Article modified confirmation screen

Article Updated!!

Modify Another News Article

FIGURE 6.21:

The Delete link

Test News Article 2   2003-06-22 08:36:36   Modify   Delete

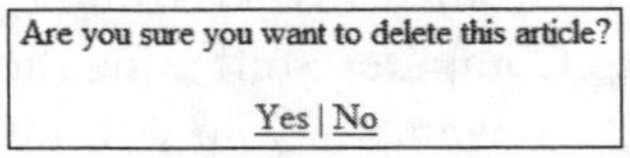

FIGURE 6.22:

Article delete confir-
mation screen

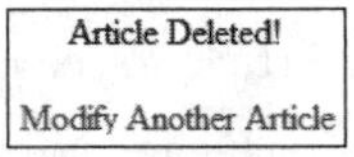

> Are you sure you want to delete this article?
>
> Yes | No

FIGURE 6.23:

Article deleted message

> Article Deleted!
>
> Modify Another Article

12. Next, click the Modify/Delete News Article link from the "Admin Links" section of the left column. Modify the Test News Article 3 to whatever you would like it to say or delete it. For my Test News Article 3, I went to CNN.com, found an interesting news article, and entered some information with a link to the full article at CNN.com. I also assigned this article to the World News category, as shown in Figure 6.24.

If everything has worked until this point, you are on the right track. You now have a complete management system to administer your news categories and news articles! Now all you have left to do is to create a method to display the news articles on your website.

Creating the News Article Index Include File

The purpose of this script is mainly for the index page, but you can also include it anywhere you want because you will make it portable. Create a file in the website document root includes directory named news_index.php (see Listing 6.12).

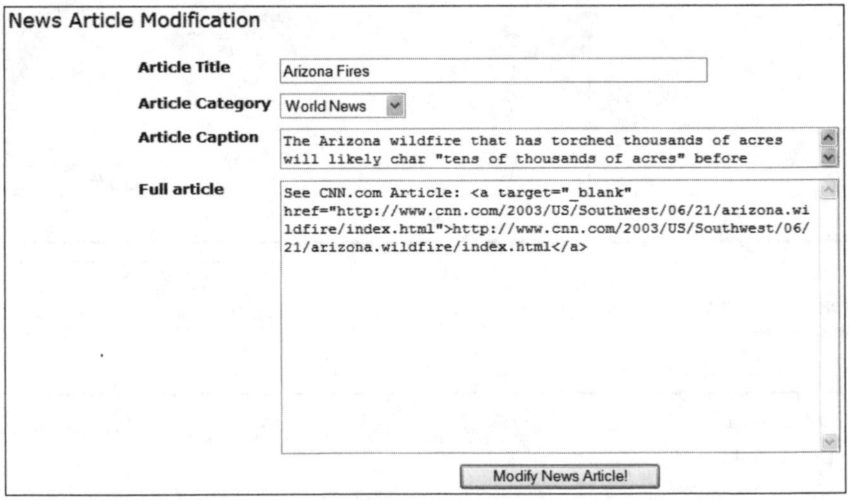

FIGURE 6.24:

Adding a link to an
outside article

News Article Modification

Article Title	Arizona Fires
Article Category	World News
Article Caption	The Arizona wildfire that has torched thousands of acres will likely char "tens of thousands of acres" before
Full article	See CNN.com Article: \<a target="_blank" href="http://www.cnn.com/2003/US/Southwest/06/21/arizona.wildfire/index.html">http://www.cnn.com/2003/US/Southwest/06/21/arizona.wildfire/index.html\</a>

Modify News Article!

Listing 6.12   News Index Include Script

```
<!-- Articles Begin-->
<hr size="1">
<table width="100%" border="0" cellpadding="0" cellspacing=0>
<tr>
<td>
<font size="4" face="Verdana, Arial, Helvetica, sans-serif">
<strong>News Articles</strong></font>
</td>
</tr>
<tr>
<td>
<?php
$sql = mysql_query("SELECT *,
    date_format(article_date, '%M %D, %Y') as article_date
    FROM news_articles
    ORDER BY article_id
    DESC LIMIT 5");


while($row = mysql_fetch_array($sql)){
    stripslashes(extract($row));

    $cat_name = mysql_result(mysql_query("SELECT cat_name
                FROM news_categories
                WHERE cat_id='$cat_id'"),0);

?>
    <table width="100%" border="0" cellpadding="2" cellspacing="0">
    <tr>
    <td valign="bottom">
    <font size="3" face="Verdana, Arial, Helvetica, sans-serif">
    <a href="/articles.php?req=read&amp;article_id=<?=$article_id?>">
    <?=stripslashes($cat_name).": ".$article_title?></a>   </font><br />
    <font size="1" face="Verdana, Arial, Helvetica, sans-serif">
    By: <em><?=$article_author?></em> - <?=$article_date?></font>
    </td>
    </tr>
    <tr>
    <td valign="top">
    <p align="justify">
    <font size="2" face="Verdana, Arial, Helvetica, sans-serif">
    <?=$article_caption?>
    </font>
    </p>
    </td>
    </tr>
    <tr>
    <td valign="top">
    <font size="2" face="Verdana, Arial, Helvetica, sans-serif">
    <a href="/articles.php?req=read&amp;article_id=<?=$article_id?>">
```

```
    Read Full Article</a>
    </font>
    </td>
    </tr>
    </table>
    <hr size="1">
<?php
}
?>
</td>
</tr>
</table>
<!-- Articles End-->
```

Let's break this script down. First, you build an HTML table outline for the articles to fit inside. I also included a hidden comment inside the HTML to help debug any problems you may have when viewing the source code of the web browser output:

```
<!-- Articles Begin-->
<hr size="1">
<table width="100%" border="0" cellpadding="0" cellspacing=0>
<tr>
<td>
<font size="4" face="Verdana, Arial, Helvetica, sans-serif">
<strong>News Articles</strong></font>
</td>
</tr>
<tr>
<td>
```

Next, you fire up the PHP engine and perform a MySQL query to get the last five entries in the news_articles table and put them into an array with which to use a while loop:

```
<?php
$sql = mysql_query("SELECT *,
    date_format(article_date, '%M %D, %Y') as article_date
    FROM news_articles
    ORDER BY article_id
    DESC LIMIT 5");
```

Let's talk about the previous MySQL query example. There is a lot of new information in this query. First, you may notice that you selected everything in the table by using * and that you also selected the date by using the date_format MySQL function.

When you store dates in MySQL, you have the ability to format them any way you like by using a built-in MySQL function called date_format. To format a date using MySQL, you need to perform a date_format query like this:

```
SELECT date_format(date_column, 'FORMAT RULES') as output_name FROM table_name
WHERE field='value'
```

You can find a complete list of formatting values for your dates in the MySQL manual under "Date and Time Functions." You can find the MySQL manual at `www.mysql.com/documentation` or at `www.phpfreaks.com/mysqlmanual.php`.

The next important part of this query is the `ORDER BY` clause. MySQL allows you to order your results by a particular column with the ascending (ASC) or descending (DESC) rules. In this query, you want the last articles entered into the database to be displayed first and then the previous four articles displayed in descending order.

The last element of this query is the `LIMIT` clause. MySQL allows you to limit the number of results. You can limit the results to the first *x* number of results, or you can limit the number of rows using an offset. For example, this will return the first five results:

```
SELECT * FROM table WHERE field='value' LIMIT 5
```

This will return five results starting with the fifth row, or rows 5–9:

```
SELECT * FROM table WHERE field='value' LIMIT 5, 5
```

This will return five results starting with the tenth row, or rows 5–14.

```
SELECT * FROM table WHERE field='value' LIMIT 5, 10
```

Next, you will create the `while` loop using `mysql_fetch_array` with your query:

```
while($row = mysql_fetch_array($sql)){
stripslashes(extract($row));
```

In previous MySQL examples, I have given you the long method of displaying your information. In this example, you will use the `extract` function combined with the `stripslashes` function to turn each of your array keys from the `$row` array into their own variable names with their values assigned to them, with the backslashes stripped out.

For example, if you had an array named `$row` and its contents were as follows:

```
Array
(
    [article_id] => 1
    [aricle_title] => My PHP Site
)
```

when you use the `extract` function on `$row`: `extract($row)`, you will create the following variables and values:

```
$article_id = 1;
$article_title = "My PHP Site";
```

Because you went through all the trouble of assigning the news article to a category, let's get the category name from the database in a single-field `mysql_result` query using the

`$cat_id` that was extracted from the `$row` array. You will display this category name in front of the article title:

```
$cat_name = mysql_result(mysql_query("SELECT cat_name
            FROM news_categories
            WHERE cat_id='$cat_id'"),0);
```

Next, you build the HTML for the news articles to be displayed on the front page or wherever you choose on the site. Notice how you close the PHP engine. Also, throughout this HTML example, you are using the PHP `echo` shortcut syntax to fill in the blanks for your HTML news article layout:

```
<table width="100%" border="0" cellpadding="2" cellspacing="0">
<tr>
<td valign="bottom">
<font size="3" face="Verdana, Arial, Helvetica, sans-serif">
<a href="/articles.php?req=read&amp;article_id=<?=$article_id?>">
<?=stripslashes($cat_name).": ".$article_title?></a>
</font><br />
<font size="1" face="Verdana, Arial, Helvetica, sans-serif">
By: <em><?=$article_author?></em> - <?=$article_date?></font>
</td>
</tr>
<tr>
<td valign="top">
<p align="justify">
<font size="2" face="Verdana, Arial, Helvetica, sans-serif">
<?=$article_caption?>
</font>
</p>
</td>
</tr>
<tr>
<td valign="top">
<font size="2" face="Verdana, Arial, Helvetica, sans-serif">
<a href="/articles.php?req=read&amp;article_id=<?=$article_id?>">
Read Full Article</a>
</font>
</td>
</tr>
</table>
<hr size="1">
```

Next, you start PHP to close out your `while` loop; then you immediately issue the PHP close tag and close out your HTML tables:

```
<?php
}
?>
```

```
</td>
</tr>
</table>
<!-- Articles End-->
```

All that you have to do now is open your `index.php` file in the website document root and include this file below your `welcome_message.html` file. Go ahead and modify your `index.php` script according to Listing 6.13; when you are done making the changes, open the index page in your web browser to see a site similar to Figure 6.25.

Listing 6.13   **Index.php File**

```php
<?php
// include the layout file
include $_SERVER['DOCUMENT_ROOT'].
    '/layout.php';

// Use the myheader function from layout.php
myheader("Welcome to My Website!");

// Include the welcome html page.
include $_SERVER['DOCUMENT_ROOT'].
    '/html/index_page.html';

// Include News Index File
include $_SERVER['DOCUMENT_ROOT'].
    '/includes/news_index.php';

// Use the footer function from layout.php
footer();
?>
```

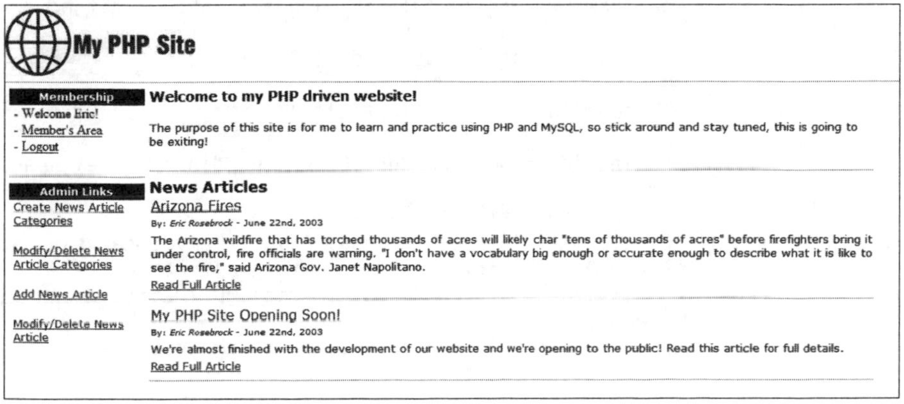

FIGURE 6.25:

News articles included on the front page

The site is really coming together now! You may have noticed that there are some hyperlinks in your news articles on the front page that do not go anywhere yet. Let's fix this problem by creating the actual script that will display the full news articles on your website.

Creating the Read Full Articles Script

It is time to create the script that allows you to read the full news article that is inside the article_body column of your database. But wait, there's more! Now you finally get to test the full capabilities of your dynamic page title and META Content functions of your layout.php script. Each news article you display in this new script will have its own dynamically generated page title and META Content! Listing 6.14 shows the read full articles script.

Listing 6.14   Read Full Articles Script

```php
<?php
include $_SERVER['DOCUMENT_ROOT'].
    '/layout.php';

switch($_REQUEST['req']){
    case "read":
        $sql = mysql_query("SELECT *,
        date_format(article_date, '%M %D, %Y') as article_date
        FROM news_articles
        WHERE article_id='{$_GET['article_id']}'");

        mysql_query("UPDATE news_articles
        SET article_read_count =
        (article_read_count +1) WHERE
        article_id = '{$_GET['article_id']}'");

        $row = mysql_fetch_assoc($sql);
        stripslashes(extract($row));
        $cat_name = mysql_result(mysql_query("SELECT cat_name
            FROM news_categories
            WHERE cat_id='$cat_id'"),0);

        myheader("News: $article_title");
        ?>
        <table width="90%" border="0" cellpadding="2" cellspacing="0">
        <tr>
        <td valign="bottom">
        <font size="3" face="Verdana, Arial, Helvetica, sans-serif">
        <strong><?=$article_title?></strong></font><br />
        <font size="2" face="Verdana, Arial, Helvetica, sans-serif">
        Category:
        <a href="/articles.php?req=category&amp;cat_id=<?=$cat_id?>">
        <?=stripslashes($cat_name)?></a>
        </font><br />
```

```
<font size="1" face="Verdana, Arial, Helvetica, sans-serif">
By: <em><?=$article_author?></em> - <?=$article_date?><br />
This article has been read: <?=$article_read_count?> times.</font>
</td>
</tr>
<tr>
<td valign="top">
<p align="justify">
<font size="2" face="Verdana, Arial, Helvetica, sans-serif">
<?=nl2br($article_body)?></font></p>
</td>
</tr>
</table>
<hr size="1">
<font size="2" face="Verdana, Arial, Helvetica, sans-serif">
<a href="/articles.php">Back to News Articles</a><br />
<a href="/articles.php?req=category&amp;cat_id=<?=$cat_id?>">
View Articles From <?=stripslashes($cat_name)?> Category</a>
</font>
<?php
break;

case "category":
    $cat_name = mysql_result(mysql_query("SELECT cat_name
        FROM news_categories
        WHERE cat_id='{$_GET['cat_id']}'"),0);

    myheader("News Articles: ".stripslashes($cat_name));
    ?>
    <!-- Articles Begin-->
    <table width="100%" border="0" cellpadding="0" cellspacing=0>
    <tr>
    <td>
    <font size="4" face="Verdana, Arial, Helvetica, sans-serif">
    <strong>News Article Category: <?=stripslashes($cat_name)?>
    </strong></font>
    </td>
    </tr>
    <tr>
    <td>

    <?php
    $sql = mysql_query("SELECT *,
        date_format(article_date, '%M %D, %Y') as article_date
        FROM news_articles
        WHERE cat_id='{$_GET['cat_id']}'
        ORDER BY article_id
        DESC");

    while($row = mysql_fetch_array($sql)){
        stripslashes(extract($row));
```

```php
        $cat_name = mysql_result(mysql_query("SELECT cat_name
            FROM news_categories
            WHERE cat_id='$cat_id'"),0);
    ?>
     <table width="100%" border="0" cellpadding="2" cellspacing="0">
     <tr>
     <td valign="bottom">
     <font size="3" face="Verdana, Arial, Helvetica, sans-serif">
     <a href="/articles.php?req=read&amp;article_id=<?=$article_id?>">
      <?=stripslashes($cat_name).": ".$article_title?></a>
     </font><br />
     <font size="1" face="Verdana, Arial, Helvetica, sans-serif">
     By: <em><?=$article_author?></em> - <?=$article_date?></font>
     </td>
     </tr>
     <tr>
     <td valign="top">
     <p align="justify">
     <font size="2" face="Verdana, Arial, Helvetica, sans-serif">
     <?=$article_caption?>
     </font>
     </p>
     </td>
     </tr>
     <tr>
     <td valign="top">
     <font size="2" face="Verdana, Arial, Helvetica, sans-serif">
     <a href="/articles.php?req=read&amp;article_id=<?=$article_id?>">
     Read Full Article</a>
     </font>
     </td>
     </tr>
     </table>
     <hr size="1">
    <?php
    }
    ?>
    </td>
    </tr>
    </table>
    <!-- Articles End-->

    <?
break;

default:
myheader("News Articles Archive");
?>
<!-- Articles Begin-->
<table width="100%" border="0" cellpadding="0" cellspacing=0>
<tr>
```

```
<td>
<font size="4" face="Verdana, Arial, Helvetica, sans-serif">
<strong>News Articles Archive</strong></font>
</td>
</tr>
<tr>
<td>

<?php
$sql = mysql_query("SELECT *,
    date_format(article_date, '%M %D, %Y') as article_date
    FROM news_articles
    ORDER BY article_id
    DESC");

while($row = mysql_fetch_array($sql)){
    stripslashes(extract($row));
    $cat_name = mysql_result(mysql_query("SELECT cat_name
            FROM news_categories
            WHERE cat_id='$cat_id'"),0);
?>
    <table width="100%" border="0" cellpadding="2" cellspacing="0">
    <tr>
    <td valign="bottom">
    <font size="3" face="Verdana, Arial, Helvetica, sans-serif">
    <a href="/articles.php?req=read&amp;article_id=<?=$article_id?>">
     <?=stripslashes($cat_name).": ".$article_title?></a>
    </font><br />
    <font size="1" face="Verdana, Arial, Helvetica, sans-serif">
    By: <em><?=$article_author?></em> - <?=$article_date?></font>
    </td>
    </tr>
    <tr>
    <td valign="top">
    <p align="justify">
    <font size="2" face="Verdana, Arial, Helvetica, sans-serif">
    <?=$article_caption?>
    </font>
    </p>
    </td>
    </tr>
    <tr>
    <td valign="top">
    <font size="2" face="Verdana, Arial, Helvetica, sans-serif">
    <a href="/articles.php?req=read&amp;article_id=<?=$article_id?>">
    Read Full Article</a>
    </font>
    </td>
    </tr>
    </table>
    <hr size="1">
```

```
<?php
}
?>
</td>
</tr>
</table>
<!-- Articles End-->

<?
break;
}

?>
```

Listing 6.14 is a fairly large script. This is one of the drawbacks of coding HTML directly into your scripts, but sometimes it is more practical to use this method. I will break down the important elements of this script.

First, you build the top portion of your script using the methods covered thoroughly in this book. The most important element you should notice is that you are not going to use the custom myheader function outside of the switch. The purpose for this is that you want to pass a dynamically generated page title for each news article the user reads. So, you must include the function only after you have extracted the article title from the database.

The first case named read in this switch displays when the reader clicks the hyperlinks to access the article. Take a look at the MySQL query portions of this case:

```
switch($_REQUEST['req']){
    case "read":
        $sql = mysql_query("SELECT *,
        date_format(article_date, '%M %D, %Y') as
        article_date
        FROM news_articles
        WHERE article_id='{$_GET['article_id']}'");

        mysql_query("UPDATE news_articles
        SET article_read_count =
        (article_read_count +1) WHERE
        article_id = '{$_GET['article_id']}'");

        $row = mysql_fetch_assoc($sql);
        stripslashes(extract($row));
        myheader("News: $article_title");
        ?>
```

Once again in this example, you use the `date_format` function to format your date in the first MySQL query.

The second MySQL query is an interesting one. You perform an `UPDATE` query and a math function at the same time to update the `article_read_count` field in the database table:

```
mysql_query("UPDATE news_articles
SET article_read_count =
 (article_read_count +1) WHERE
article_id = '{$_GET['article_id']}'");
```

Next, you create an `associative` array named `$row` using the `mysql_fetch_assoc` function utilizing the `mysql_query`. You do not need to use a `while` loop on this function because you are only extracting one row of information in the database.

Here you use the `stripslashes` and `extract` functions again to create simple variable names to use in the rest of this `case`:

```
stripslashes(extract($row));
```

Next, you grab the category name from the `news_categories` table using the same query you used in the `news_index.php` file. The category name will display directly under the title of the news article, and it will contain a hyperlink to a list of articles that are linked to that category:

```
$cat_name = mysql_result(mysql_query("SELECT cat_name
     FROM news_categories
     WHERE cat_id='$cat_id'"),0);
```

I have been building up the suspense of generating dynamic page titles long enough! Because you now have the news article title available to you from the database, you can create a dynamic page title that will be different for each news article on your website. Check out the custom `myheader` function call in the next example:

```
myheader("News: $article_title");
?>
```

From this point of this case forward, you close PHP and create your HTML formatting for the news article.

When you allow user input into HTML form text areas, many people assume that by pressing the Enter key on the keyboard PHP and HTML can automatically translate the special ASCII characters into a human-readable format; however, this is not true. The computer knows there is a line break there, but the web browser does not decode these line breaks for you. So, you fix this by using the n12br function covered in Chapter 1, "Introducing PHP." Take a look at this example for the article body:

```
<p align="justify">
<font size="2" face="Verdana, Arial, Helvetica,
sans-serif">
<?=n12br($article_body)?></font>
</p>
```

This example allows an HTML <br /> to be generated each time the user presses the Enter key while typing an article into the text fields while using an HTML form to input data.

The news article archive system, which is part of this script as well, will consist of two parts. The first part will contain a category-based listing and all of the news articles that are linked to that category. You achieve this with the code found in the category case. The category case does not require any special explanation; it's basically the same code from the news_index.php file that you created earlier with minor HTML formatting and a modified MySQL query.

You will find the full list of news articles in your archive in the default case. The default case does not need an in-depth explanation either. It is simply a modified version of the news_index.php file you included in your index page. The only differences are minor formatting, and I have removed the LIMIT clause from the MySQL query because I wanted this to serve as an archive displaying all of the news articles on the website.

Your website should be looking much better already! You have created a fairly advanced news management system that gives your readers fresh content.

Creating a Hyperlinks Box

Now that you have some content to display and some sections to link to on your site, you need to create a hyperlinks box for your users to navigate through the site. In your website document root boxes directory, create a new PHP file and name it box_main_links.php. This box will contain all of the applicable links that point inside the website, as shown in Listing 6.15.

Listing 6.15   **Main Website Hyperlinks Box**

```
<table width="160" border="0" cellspacing="0" cellpadding="0">
  <tr bgcolor="#000066">
    <td width="5" height="10"><font color="#FFFFFF"> </font></td>
    <td width="150">
    <div align="center">
    <font color="#FFFFFF" size="2" face="Verdana, Arial, Helvetica, sans-serif">
    <strong>Site Links</strong></font>
    </div>
```

```
        </td>
        <td width="5"> </td>
      </tr>
      <tr>
        <td height="5"> </td>
        <td align="left" valign="top">
<a href="/">Index</a><br />
<a href="/articles.php">News Articles</a>
        </td>
        <td> </td>
      </tr>
      <tr>
        <td width="5" height="10"><font color="#FFFFFF"> </font></td>
        <td width="150"> </td>
        <td width="5"> </td>
      </tr>
</table>
<hr size="1">
```

Next, include this new file into your `layout.php` file directly under the `box_admin_links.php` file. Here is my include section of the `layout.php` file:

```
<?php
include $_SERVER['DOCUMENT_ROOT'].
        '/boxes/member_box.php';

include $_SERVER['DOCUMENT_ROOT'].
        '/boxes/box_admin_links.php';

include $_SERVER['DOCUMENT_ROOT'].
        '/boxes/box_main_links.php';
?>
```

When a user is not logged into the website, the layout will appear as in Figure 6.26.

FIGURE 6.26:

Main website hyper-links box

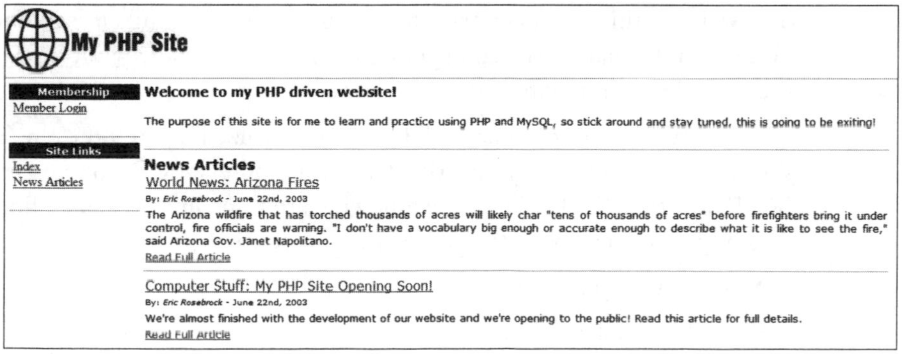

Challenge: Create a News Article Comment System

By this point, you should be comfortable with creating HTML forms and inserting information into the database. As a challenge, I recommend you practice the skills you have learned by creating a comment system for your news articles. The following are some of the steps I have come up with to create this assignment:

- Create a table in your database that has a comment ID, comment subject, comment body, comment date, and a link to the article ID number.

- Create a PHP script that will insert the required information about the comment, such as the comment subject, comment date, comment body, username of the person submitting the comment, and the article ID to which the comment belongs.

- Create the links required to access the form from the news article at the bottom of the news article itself.

- Control access to the comment system to allow only members to post the comments using the `login_check()` function inside the `session.php` file you created in Chapter 5, "Creating a Website Membership System."

- Display the comments from your comments table for the article being viewed in a `while` loop at the bottom of each article.

Have some fun with creating this comment system. If you are having a hard time planning your comment system, refer to `www.phpfreaks.com` to see the one I created for my personal site. It may help you to figure out what you need to do. Good luck!

Adding News Feeds

If you desire to add news from other websites to your site automatically, you are looking for a *news feed*. A news feed is usually received by a script that you can download or create on your own website; this script connects to an external site and pulls information into your database. With the information stored in your database, you may format it however you like to fit the theme and requirements of your website.

At this time, news feeds are still being standardized throughout the Internet. Some websites use Really Simple Syndication (RSS), and others use Resource Description Framework (RDF) or other XML feeds. The following are some links you may find useful to determine which type of feed fits the requirements you desire:

Newsfeed Type	URL
RSS 2.0 at Backend.Userland.Com	`backend.userland.com/rss`
RDF information	`www.w3.org/TR/1999/REC-rdf-syntax-19990222/`

Newsfeed Type	URL
XML news feeds with PHP	`martin.f2o.org/php/xml-feed`
Syndic8.com news feed information	`www.syndic8.com`

Some of the content management systems such as PostNuke come with third-party add-on modules that will automatically populate your database with other website news from their feeds. If you would like to learn more about PostNuke, refer to `www.postnuke.com`.

What's Next?

This chapter contained quite a bit of information regarding the daily routines involved in creating a news management system for your website. Even though it covered mainly a news system, there are a lot of hidden tips, tricks, and techniques throughout the chapter. If you missed them, it is a good idea to review the chapter again because it could make life much easier for you as a PHP developer.

In the next chapter, you will learn about working with web services and Application Programming Interfaces (APIs). I will discuss how to add some valuable services from popular websites to your site, such as search engine bars from Google, website statistics from Alexa, and language translation from Google.com.

CHAPTER 7

Enhancing Your Website with Web Services and APIs

The Internet is growing at a rapid pace these days. The rumors of the "dot-com" boom being over are not as true as some of you may think. With the evolution of new technology on the Internet, some websites and companies are beginning to offer methods for webmasters to enhance their site's capabilities. These technologies are usually offered through web services or an Application Programmer Interface (API).

This chapter covers how to use the language translation tools available at www.google.com/language_tools to display your site in different languages automatically and how to use the Google search engine (www.google.com) to provide your readers with a method of searching within your website or the Internet from your site. The chapter also shows you how to work with the Amazon Web Services API to provide your users with a method of searching Amazon.com for books, music, or other merchandise from within your site.

Working with Web Services

A *web service* is usually a simple and easy-to-use method of enhancing your website using another site's technology. Web services are usually easier to use than an API. Let's begin with the Google language translation tools.

Using Google Language Translation Services

Google offers language tools to translate text and web pages for most languages. There is no API available for this feature yet, so you will have to use it as a web service. You will create a method to pass the current Uniform Resource Locator (URL) the user is viewing to the Google translator to translate the page into the language the user has selected from a form on your site.

For this web service, you will create a form inside a box on the left column of your site. This form will send the proper information to Google to translate the page, and then the Google website will appear with your translated results.

The only script required for sending information to Google's language translator is the form itself. This may sound like it has nothing to do with PHP, but you will use PHP in this form to pass the current URL that the reader is viewing to the translator, as shown in Listing 7.1.

Listing 7.1 **Language Translation Select Box**

```php
<?php
$URL = "http://".$_SERVER['SERVER_NAME'].$_SERVER['REQUEST_URI'];
?>
<table width="160" border="0" cellspacing="0" cellpadding="0">
  <tr bgcolor="#000066">
    <td width="5" height="10"><font color="#FFFFFF"> </font></td>
    <td width="150">
```

```
     <div align="center">
     <font color="#FFFFFF" size="2" face="Verdana, Arial, Helvetica, sans-serif">
     <strong>Translate</strong></font>
     </div>
     </td>
     <td width="5"> </td>
   </tr>
   <tr>
     <td height="5"> </td>
     <td align="left" valign="top">
<center><font size="1" face="Verdana, Arial, Helvetica, sans-serif">
<strong>Choose Your Language:</strong>
</font>
<form action="http://translate.google.com/translate">
<input type="hidden" name="u" value="<?=$URL?>">
<select name=langpair>
<option value="en|de">German</option>
<option value="en|es">Spanish</option>
<option value="en|fr">French</option>
<option value="en|it">Italian</option>
<option value="en|pt">Portuguese</option>
</select>
<input type=submit value="Go!">
</form>
<font size="1" face="Verdana, Arial, Helvetica, sans-serif">Powered by<br>
<a href="http://www.google.com/language_tools" target="_blank">
Google Language Tools</a>
</font>
        </center>
    </td>
     <td> </td>
   </tr>
</table>
<hr size="1">
```

You may notice that this script starts with a portion of PHP code. This code allows maximum portability by reading the $_SERVER['SERVER_NAME'] superglobal array value and determining the name of your server, for example, http://www.yourphpsite.com. Next, you want to obtain the name of the script and arguments passed to the script by using $_SERVER['REQUEST_URI']. Together, these two superglobal values provide you with a complete URL for the page being viewed. For example, if you were viewing http://www.yourphpsite.com/news .php?read=13, by using the previous code example, $_SERVER['SERVER_NAME'] would return www.yourphpsite.com, and $_SERVER['REQUEST_URI'] would return /news.php?read=13. Now you have a method to post the full URL into the Google translator form. This is the code example just discussed:

```php
<?php
$URL = "http://".$_SERVER['SERVER_NAME'].$_SERVER['REQUEST_URI'];
?>
```

Next, you build the HTML layout for the box to include in your `layout.php` file. In the content portion of your HTML table, put the following form, which will post the information to Google:

```
<form action="http://translate.google.com/translate">
<input type="hidden" name="u" value="<?=$URL?>">
<select name=langpair>
<option value="en|de">German</option>
<option value="en|es">Spanish</option>
<option value="en|fr">French</option>
<option value="en|it">Italian</option>
<option value="en|pt">Portuguese</option>
</select>
<input type=submit value="Go!">
</form>
```

Take a look at the second line of the previous code example. You embed the $URL variable you created at the top of this script into the URL value that Google requires to translate the website:

```
<input type="hidden" name="u" value="<?=$URL?>">
```

The rest of the form consists of the languages and their form post values that Google uses to determine to which language to translate. For your site, because it is in English, you are translating from English to another language.

Next, save this file as box_translate.php in your website's document root boxes directory. You will also include this box into your layout.php file directly below the box_main_links.php file. Take a look at the include portion of this layout.php file:

```
<?php
include $_SERVER['DOCUMENT_ROOT'].
        '/boxes/member_box.php';

include $_SERVER['DOCUMENT_ROOT'].
        '/boxes/box_admin_links.php';

include $_SERVER['DOCUMENT_ROOT'].
        '/boxes/box_main_links.php';

include $_SERVER['DOCUMENT_ROOT'].
        '/boxes/box_translate.php';
?>
```

Open your website in your browser, and you should see the new box appear at the bottom of the left column, as shown in Figure 7.1.

FIGURE 7.1:

Translation tools box

Let's translate the site into Spanish. Click the drop-down menu, select Spanish as your option, and then click the Go button. When the next page loads, you should see your site translated in Spanish, as shown in Figure 7.2.

If everything has worked out, then congratulations! You have just used the Google translation tools as a web service to enhance the possibilities of your website!

FIGURE 7.2:

The Spanish translation

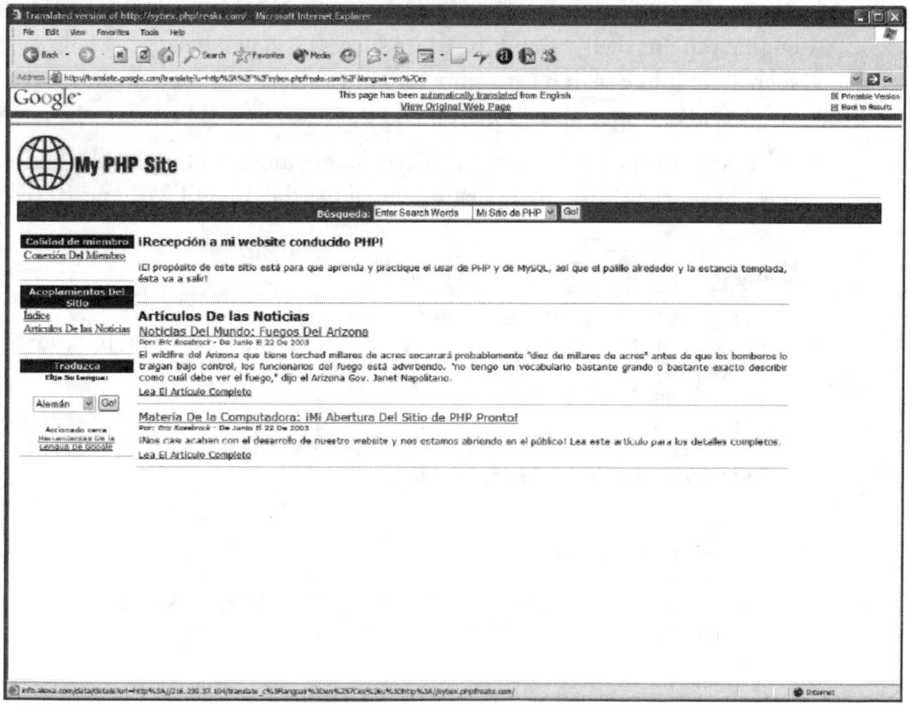

You must ensure that the server you are testing this script on is an actual web server with a domain name that can be translated on the Internet. When developing locally, you can use names and resolve them on your own Domain Name System (DNS) servers or through your Windows hosts file; however, Google cannot look those names up in DNS, and therefore this script will not work properly.

Using the Google Search Engine in Your Website

Google was created at Stanford University and become one of the top search engines on the Internet in a short time. In this section, I will show you a simple method of offering the Google search engine on your website so that your users will not have to leave your website to access the powerful Google search engine. You will also add a feature in this script that allows your user to choose to search for results within your site (if the Google search spiders have indexed your site).

You may be wondering why you would want to include Google on your site when a user can just go to www.google.com and perform the search on the Google website. I cannot stress this enough to you as a webmaster: The more features you have on your website and the longer you can keep the user on your site clicking on pages and accessing sections, the better your search engine rankings will be and the more success you will have as a webmaster. By adding features such as an inline search capability for your users, users may come to your site to browse news articles, access special sections, and do their searches. The more clicks, the better!

Let's create a new file in your website's document root under the html/forms directory; name this file search_form.html. Listing 7.2 shows the full HTML and PHP code for this file.

Listing 7.2   **Google Search Form**

```
<form method="post" action="/search.php">
<table width="100%" border="1" cellpadding="0" cellspacing="0"
bordercolor="#000000">
<tr align="left">
<td width="95%" align="center" valign="middle" bgcolor="#006699" align="center">
<font color="#FFFFFF" size="2" face="Verdana, Arial, Helvetica, sans-serif">
<strong>Search:</strong></font>

<?php
if(!$_POST['q']){
?>
<input name="q" onFocus="if(this.value=='Enter Search Words')this.value='';"
value="Enter Search Words">
<?php
} else {
?>
<input name="q" value="<?=stripslashes($_POST['q'])?>">
```

```php
<?php
}

?>
<select name="where">
<option value="local" <?if($_POST['where'] == "local") echo "selected"; ?>>My
PHP Site</option>
<option value="external" <?if($_POST['where'] == "external") echo "selected";
?>>The Web</option>
</select>
<input type="submit" value="Go!">
</td>
</tr>
</table>
</form>
```

The code in Listing 7.2 consists of an HTML form that will post to a script on your site named search.php that you will create later. This file also has some PHP embedded into it, so I will break down the important elements:

```php
<?php
if(!$_POST['q']){
?>
<input name="q" onFocus="if(this.value=='Enter Search Words')this.value='';"
value="Enter Search Words">
<?php
} else {
?>
<input name="q" value="<?=stripslashes($_POST['q'])?>">
<?php
}

?>
```

The previous code will check if you have posted the form value of q, which is short for *query* in the Google search engine. If the q value has been posted, you will remove any backslashes from the values using the PHP stripslashes function and automatically fill the text field values of the form with the posted values. If q is not posted or does not exist, you will use a nifty JavaScript feature that will display *Enter Search Words* in the text box; when the user clicks the box, the *Enter Search Words* text disappears so the user can enter their search words.

The next portion of PHP code in this example will help determine which form select item the user chose before posting the form information. The form select menu name is where, so you will check the value of $_POST['where']; then, using an IF statement, you will enter the "selected" value in the appropriate select menu option so that the selection the user made before they posted the form is now selected on the preceding search.php script:

```php
<select name="where">
```

```
<option value="local" <?if($_POST['where'] == "local") echo "selected"; ?>>My
PHP Site</option>
<option value="external" <?if($_POST['where'] == "external") echo "selected";
?>>The Web</option>
</select>
```

Now that you have the form developed, you will create the script to which this form will post. Make a new PHP script, name it search.php, and then place it in your website's document root. Listing 7.3 for the code.

Listing 7.3   *search.php* **Script**

```
<?php
include $_SERVER['DOCUMENT_ROOT'].
    '/layout.php';


if($_POST['where'] == "local"){
    $q = $_POST['q']." site:www.phpfreaks.com";
} else {
    $q = $_POST['q'];
}

$q = htmlentities(urlencode($q));
$url = "http://www.google.com/search?q=$q";

myheader("Search Results");
?>

  <IFRAME SRC="<?=$url?>"
  TITLE="Search Results"
  width="100%"
  height="500">
    <!-- Alternate content for non-supporting browsers -->
    Your web browser does not support inline frames, therefore
     this feature can not be used.
  </IFRAME>

<?php
footer();
?>
```

The code in Listing 7.3 includes your layout.php and accepts the form-posted values from search_form.html; then you determine what you want to do with them. I will break down each section and cover what it does:

```
if($_POST['where'] == "local"){
    $q = $_POST['q']." site:www.phpfreaks.com";
} else {
```

```
    $q = $_POST['q'];
}
```

Google offers many different search methods. When you go to the Google.com website and enter a search phrase, you are doing an open search with no constraints. You want to give your users the ability to search the Internet or search only within your website. Your users have this option when they select what search results they want returned from the form select menu. If they choose the My PHP Site option, the form select menu value of `where` will be `local`. Based on this factor, you append `site:www.yourphpsite.com` to the search query and only results found in `www.yourphpsite.com` will return on the page.

If the user chooses The Web option, then the value of `where` is not equal to `local` and the first `IF` statement will not be validated, which means they must have selected The Web option from the select menu. Therefore, you will perform an open search query without constraints.

Next, you will convert the search phrase into the proper format for the Google search engine to accept. This is known as *URL encoding*. To properly encode this URL for Google, you need to use the PHP `htmlentities` function and then use the `urlencode` function. By using only the `urlencode` function, all spaces are converted to %20. There are many special characters that are converted, as well. Some sites such as Google require that white spaces are converted to plus signs (+) instead, so you combine the two functions together to get the output you need. For example the phrase *this is a search phrase* would be converted to `this+is+a+search+phrase`:

```
$q = htmlentities(urlencode($q));
$url = "http://www.google.com/search?q=$q";
```

After you have the URL created that will open the Google search engine with your query, you open the HTML layout and display an inline frame (`IFRAME`) to present the results. Using an `IFRAME` is the easiest method to include content from one website to another, so that's what you will do:

```
<IFRAME SRC="<?=$url?>"
TITLE="Search Results"
width="100%"
height="500">
  <!-- Alternate content for non-supporting browsers -->
  Your web browser does not support inline frames, so
   this feature cannot be used.
</IFRAME>
```

Notice the `IFRAME SRC="<?=$url?>"` code in the previous example. You are simply telling the `IFRAME` what to open and display in the frame; in this case, it is the URL that you created from the PHP code.

Now, include the HTML form you created into the `layout.php` file. Directly below your logo, create a new table row (TR) and insert a column that spans three columns: TD COLSPAN="3". Include the `search_form.html` file into this new cell. Here is the modified `layout.php` section:

```
<table width="100%" border="0" cellpadding="0" cellspacing="0"
bordercolor="#000000">
  <tr>
    <td colspan="3"><a href="/"><img src="/images/logo.jpg" ALT="My PHP Site"
BORDER="0"></a><hr size="1"></td>
  </tr>
  <tr>
    <td colspan="3">
    <?php
    include $_SERVER['DOCUMENT_ROOT'].
      '/html/forms/search_form.html';
    ?>

    </td>
  </tr>
```

Open your website in your browser, and you should see the new search bar below your logo, as shown in Figure 7.3.

Before you begin testing this script, you should notice that the site I used for the My PHP Site value in `search.php` is www.phpfreaks.com. I used a website that I knew was indexed by the Google search engine for these tests. When you build your site and get in the search engines, you can change this value.

Let's test it out! First, type in the phrase *PHP htmlspecialchars*, leave the My PHP Site value selected, and click the Go button. You will see all of the results from www.phpfreaks.com in your inline frame, as shown in Figure 7.4.

Take special notice that the search words you entered are still presented in the form and that the My PHP Site value is selected.

Next, enter *PHP Freaks* in the Search box, select The Web option, and click the Go button. You will see the results shown in Figure 7.5.

FIGURE 7.3:
Search engine bar

FIGURE 7.4:

FIGURE 7.4:

Search results for My
PHP Site selection

FIGURE 7.5:

Search results for an
open search

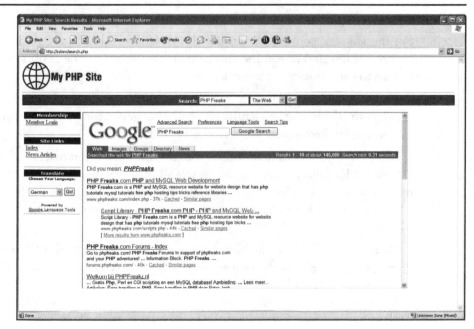

Take special notice that the select menu now has The Web option selected.

Your site is really shaping up with all of these nifty web services you have been using! Do not stop there! The Internet is full of useful web services you can use if you like. Also, just because something is not offered as a web service does not mean that it is not possible to use. Be sure to give credit where credit is due to stay out of trouble! Poke around on the Internet and see what you can find to enhance your site with PHP and web services.

Working with APIs

An API utilizes methods of sending information to the remote API server for processing and receiving results back to your script regarding the type of transaction that was intended. You will probably see APIs used most in applications for merchant account gateways to process credit card information. Chapter 9, "Processing Payments for Your Website," covers this usage in depth.

APIs are starting to become more available on the Internet as new development languages start to evolve. Companies are realizing the value of offering services such as an API to their customers, and the Web is moving strongly toward using APIs for nearly every solution that can support it. A perfect example is the Amazon Web Services API.

Amazon Web Services API Made Simple

For this chapter, you will use the Amazon Web Services API to retrieve information based on a search phrase and format the results to fit your website while at the same time getting a chance to earn money as a webmaster.

To begin using your Amazon Web Services API, you will need to obtain a developer token, which is an ID number to identify you as the person or company performing the query. Go to www.amazon.com/webservices to obtain your token key.

Next, it is a good idea to download the API documentation that is included in the API Developer Kit, also available at the previous URL. You do not have to download the documentation for this project, but I strongly recommend it. Because it is free, I suggest taking advantage of the download; you may be able to enhance the code you develop in this section with more features.

Sometimes API documentation is not practical to use for PHP. Only recently have API developers realized that the majority of the Internet is moving toward PHP as the development language of choice and started supporting it in their documentation. Regardless of the lack of documentation, there is usually a method around the downfalls due to lack of PHP support because web APIs are usually based on one principle: to send and receive data via a Hypertext Transfer Protocol (HTTP) request.

During my research phase of implementing the Amazon Web Services API with PHP, I found some exaggerated examples that required me to download three or four different scripts to achieve the same results I will show you, which uses the Amazon Web Services API with a custom PHP Extensible Markup Language (XML) parsing class and a simple code example to utilize the class. I will also cover how to make those cool page numbers also known as *pagination* for your script.

The Amazon Web Services API offers multiple ways of retrieving information through its usage. You have the ability to use Simple Object Access Protocol (SOAP) with a PHP class named NuSOAP (`sourceforge.net/projects/nusoap`), which is based on the principles of the Perl SOAP class, Extensible Stylesheet Language Transformations (XSLT), and finally the XML method you are going to use.

Regardless of which methods are available, you have to choose one that works best with PHP. The bottom line is that you will send and receive data from the Amazon Web Services API and format it to fit your page. The easiest method I have found is to use XML to retrieve the results.

Before you begin developing your front end for the Amazon Web Services API, you will need to obtain the XML parser class that I have made available for you to use:

1. Go to `www.phpfreaks.com/script/view/202.php` and download the file to your hard drive.

2. Extract the `clsParseXML.zip` file.

3. Copy the `clsParseXML.php` file to your website document root's `classes` directory.

Creating the HTML and PHP

Now you are ready to begin working with the Amazon Web Services API. To start, you will create an HTML file that will display the results of each book to your website. This file will be looped through all of the results you find and it will be included for each one. Create a file in your website's document root under the `html` directory and name it `books_layout.html` (see Listing 7.4).

Listing 7.4   **Book HTML Layout File**

```
<p><font size="4" face="Verdana, Arial, Helvetica, sans-serif"></font></p>
<table width="100%" border="0" cellspacing="0" cellpadding="4">
  <tr>
    <td colspan="2"><font size="4" face="Verdana, Arial, Helvetica, sans-
serif"><strong><a href="<?=$product_link?>" target="_blank">
      <?=$product_name?>
      </a></strong></font></td>
  </tr>
  <tr>
```

```html
        <td width="4%" align="left" valign="top"><a href="<?=$product_link?>"
target="_blank">
            <img src="<?=$product_image?>" alt="<?=$product_name?>" border="0">
</a></td>
        <td width="96%" align="left" valign="top"><p><font size="3" face="Verdana,
Arial, Helvetica, sans-serif">
        <strong>Publisher:
        <?=$product_manufacturer?>
        </strong></font><br>
        <font size="3" face="Verdana, Arial, Helvetica, sans-
serif"><strong>Author<?php if($product_author2){ echo "s"; }?>:</strong>
        <?php
            $authors = $product_author1;
            if($product_author2){
                $authors .= ", $product_author2";
            }
            if($product_author3){
                $authors .= ", $product_author3";
            }
            if($product_author4){
                $authors .= ", $product_author4";
            }
            if($product_author5){
                $authors .= ", $product_author5";
            }
            echo $authors;
        ?>
        </font><br>
        <font size="2" face="Verdana, Arial, Helvetica, sans-serif">Release
Date: <?=$product_release_date?></font><br>
        <font size="2" face="Verdana, Arial, Helvetica, sans-serif">ISBN:
<?=$product_isbn?></font></p>
        <p><font size="2" face="Verdana, Arial, Helvetica, sans-serif"><strong>New
        Price:
        <?=$product_new_price?>
        <?php if($product_used_price){?>
        / Used Price:
        <?=$product_used_price?>
        <? } ?>
        </strong></font><br>
        <font size="4" face="Verdana, Arial, Helvetica, sans-serif"><strong><a
href="<?=$product_link?>" target="_blank">Buy
        it Now! </a></strong></font>
    </td>
  </tr>
  <tr>
    <td colspan="2"><font size="4" face="Verdana, Arial, Helvetica, sans-
serif"><strong><a href="<?=$product_link?>" target="_blank">
        </a></strong></font></td>
  </tr>
</table>
<hr size="1">
```

I will break down the important elements of Listing 7.4 for you. Before you include this HTML file, you will do some work with the array of results returned from the XML parser that you will develop later in this section. You will display the values of the variables you find for each book in that layout, so you have embedded some PHP into this HTML.

The first important portion of embedded PHP is the part where you determine how many authors wrote each book. These results are returned from the Amazon Web Services API, and you want to make sure you have the grammar proper, so you determine if you need to display *Author* or *Authors* for the heading of that section in the HTML document. You achieve this with a simple IF statement to see if more than one author exists:

```
<font size="3" face="Verdana, Arial, Helvetica, sans-serif"><strong>Author<?php
if($product_author2){ echo "s"; }?>:</strong>
```

Next, you determine the best method of displaying the author names for the book title. If there is only one author, you do not want a comma behind the author's name, and if there are only two authors, you only want a comma after the first author's name and so on. So you develop this code that will format the author list properly:

```php
<?php
    $authors = $product_author1;
    if($product_author2){
        $authors .= ", $product_author2";
    }
    if($product_author3){
        $authors .= ", $product_author3";
    }
    if($product_author4){
        $authors .= ", $product_author4";
    }
    if($product_author5){
        $authors .= ", $product_author5";
    }
    echo $authors;
?>
```

The last part of code in this file will determine if the "used price" value exists for the book title. If it does, you put a forward slash and then the used price behind the new price:

```
<strong>New
Price:
<?=$product_new_price?>
<?php if($product_used_price){?>
/ Used Price:
<?=$product_used_price?>
<? } ?>
</strong>
```

You now have the HTML layout that will be looped through and completed by the results you find. It is time to start with the XML parsing code! The next file will be called books.php, and it will reside in the website document root directory (see Listing 7.5).

Listing 7.5   **Amazon Web Services API Script**

```php
<?php

include $_SERVER['DOCUMENT_ROOT'].
    '/layout.php';

// XML Parser Class
include $_SERVER['DOCUMENT_ROOT'].
    '/classes/clsParseXML.php';

myheader("Amazon Books");

if(!$_REQUEST['book']){
    $_REQUEST['book'] = "www dummy";
}

// Page Number Determination
if(!isset($_REQUEST['page'])){
    $page = 1;
} else {
    $page = $_REQUEST['page'];
}

$amazon_xml = "http://xml.amazon.com/onca/xml3?".
            "t=webservices-20". // Amazon Associate ID
            "&dev-t=XXXXXXXXXXXX". // Developer Token
            "&KeywordSearch=".
            .stripslashes(urlencode($_REQUEST['book'])). // Search Word
            "&mode=books". // Type of Product
            "&type=lite".  // Search Mode
            "&page=$page". // Current Page Number
            "&f=xml";

$xml_parse = &new ParseXML;
$xml_tree = $xml_parse->GetXMLTree($amazon_xml);

// Display RAW $xml_tree Results
/*
echo "<pre>";
print_r($xml_tree);
echo "</pre>";
footer();
exit();
*/
```

```
// Get Error Message if there is one.
$error_message = $xml_tree[PRODUCTINFO][0][ERRORMSG][0][VALUE];

if($error_message){
    echo "<center>".$error_message."<br />".
    "The service may be down at the moment.</center>";
    footer();
    exit();
}

// Get total number of pages for page code
$total_pages = $xml_tree[PRODUCTINFO][0][TOTALPAGES][0][VALUE];

// Get total number of results from the query
$total_results = $xml_tree[PRODUCTINFO][0][TOTALRESULTS][0][VALUE];

// Display top of page with search phrase, page numbers
// and total results found
echo '<font size="4" face="Verdana, Arial, Helvetica, sans-serif">'.
    '<strong>Books for: '.stripslashes(urldecode($_REQUEST['book'])).
    '</strong><br />'.
    'Page: '.$page.' of '.$total_pages.'<br />'.
    'Total Results: '.$total_results.
    '<hr size="1">';

// loop through and show products
foreach($xml_tree[PRODUCTINFO][0][DETAILS] AS $product){
    // Results Retrieved, make quick
    // variables from array values.
    $product_link = $product[ATTRIBUTES][URL];
    $product_isbn = $product[ASIN][0][VALUE];
    $product_name = $product[PRODUCTNAME][0][VALUE];
    $product_catalog = $product[CATALOG][0][VALUE];
    $product_manufacturer = $product[MANUFACTURER][0][VALUE];
    $product_release_date = $product[RELEASEDATE][0][VALUE];
    $product_image = $product[IMAGEURLMEDIUM][0][VALUE];
    $product_new_price = $product[OURPRICE][0][VALUE];
    $product_used_price = $product[USEDPRICE][0][VALUE];
    $product_author1 = $product[AUTHORS][0][AUTHOR][0][VALUE];
    $product_author2 = $product[AUTHORS][0][AUTHOR][1][VALUE];
    $product_author3 = $product[AUTHORS][0][AUTHOR][2][VALUE];
    $product_author4 = $product[AUTHORS][0][AUTHOR][3][VALUE];
    $product_author5 = $product[AUTHORS][0][AUTHOR][4][VALUE];

    // include layout file for looping results
    include $_SERVER['DOCUMENT_ROOT'].
      '/html/books_layout.html';
}


// Build Pagination System (Page Numbers)
echo '<center><font size="2" face="Verdana, '.
```

```
            'Arial, Helvetica, sans-serif">'.
            '<strong>Page Number:</strong><br />';

   for($i = 0; $i < $total_pages; $i++){
      $p = ($i + 1);
      if($page == $p){
         echo "<strong>$page</strong> ";
      } else {
         echo "<a href=\"".$PHP_SELF."?page=$p&book=".$_REQUEST['book']."\">".
            "$p</a> ";
      }
   }
   echo "</font></center>";

   // Display footer
   footer();
?>
```

It sure looks like I have a lot of explaining to do, so let's get started! The first portion of the script includes the `layout.php` file; it also includes the XML parser class that you downloaded earlier, and it displays the `myheader` function:

```
<?php

include $_SERVER['DOCUMENT_ROOT'].
   '/layout.php';

// XML Parser Class
include $_SERVER['DOCUMENT_ROOT'].
   '/classes/clsParseXML.php';
myheader("Amazon Books");
```

NOTE   The XML parser class is included in this script instead of the `common.php` file because you will only be using it one time.

Sometimes as a webmaster you just have to pull tricks on your users who like to test your skills by submitting empty form data. When a user submits a form without typing in the search phrase, you set a search phrase for them: www dummy:

```
if(!$_REQUEST['book']){
   $_REQUEST['book'] = "www dummy";
}
```

Creating Page Numbers

Now you begin the real fun: pagination. Page-numbered results have grown in popularity over the past few years; however, many people still struggle with the code to make them.

This example is about the easiest it can get, but it appears in parts throughout the code in Listing 7.5. First, you need to determine if you have a page number value set already and, if you do have one set, what its value is. If you do not have a page number value set yet, you need to set it to a value of 1, for the first page:

```
// Page Number Determination
if(!isset($_REQUEST['page'])){
    $page = 1;
} else {
    $page = $_REQUEST['page'];
}
```

Next, you need to build the URL to retrieve the Amazon web services XML document from its API. Let's break this code down into smaller portions. First, you start building the $amazon_xml variable that will be passed to the XML parser class later:

```
$amazon_xml = "http://xml.amazon.com/onca/xml3?".
```

Second, if you want to earn money and you have an Amazon Associates ID (www.amazon.com/associates), you can enter it here to receive a percentage of each sale made from users who clicked on the links from your website to purchase the item. For this example, you will use the default Amazon Associate ID, which is webservices-20:

```
"t=webservices-20". // Amazon Associate ID
```

Remember that developer token you had to get earlier? This is where you use it. I replaced my developer token with XXXXXXXXXXXX for my security purposes, so put your token in that place:

```
"&dev-t=XXXXXXXXXXXX". // Developer Token
```

Now you need to enter the URL-encoded search phrase into the URL. Also, you always use stripslashes on form-posted data to remove those backslashes automatically generated by PHP:

```
"&KeywordSearch="
.stripslashes(urlencode($_REQUEST['book'])). // Search Word
```

The next portion of this URL is the mode. You can choose from DVD, software, books, and more. Refer to the Amazon Web Services API documentation for more information. For this mode, use books:

```
"&mode=books". // Type of Product
```

The search type has two available flavors, light and heavy, depending on how detailed you want the results to be. For this purpose, light is more than sufficient:

```
"&type=lite".  // Search Mode
```

Here is another portion of the pagination code! You will tell the API what page you are viewing so you can retrieve the appropriate results from it. For your reference, the Amazon Web Services API only returns 10 results per page:

```
"&page=$page". // Current Page Number
```

The next portion of code simply specifies that you want XML as the result from the API:

```
"&f=xml";
```

Remember that XML parser class I had you download? It is time to put it to use. Initialize the class and call the function that builds your XML tree from the $amazon_xml variable you just created:

```
$xml_parse = &new ParseXML;
$xml_tree = $xml_parse->GetXMLTree($amazon_xml);
```

To help you understand what the XML parser class actually accomplishes, I have left this portion of the code in my examples. All you have to do is remove the comment tags /* and */ from above and below the code to see the raw output of the array generated from the class:

```
// Display RAW $xml_tree Results
/*
echo "<pre>";
print_r($xml_tree);
echo "</pre>";
footer();
exit();
*/
```

When you view the raw output of the XML parser class, you will see that the results are in one large array, depending on the number of results found. Typing the full name of each array key would be quite a pain, so you create simplified variable names for them.

Sometimes an API may go offline for maintenance or may simply return an error code. To prevent your script from displaying nasty error messages, you perform a check on a specific value of the results found in the results array:

```
// Get Error Message if there is one.
$error_message = $xml_tree[PRODUCTINFO][0][ERRORMSG][0][VALUE];

if($error_message){
    echo "<center>".$error_message."<br />".
    "The service may be down at the moment.</center>";
    footer();
    exit();
}
```

The previous example will check to see if the ERRORMSG value is present in the returned results. If this value is present, you will display a nice message to the user and exit the script to prevent further errors from being displayed.

The next example shows you how you retrieve the total number of available pages from the resulting search and turn it into the $total_pages variable. This variable is important because you use it in the pagination code later:

```
// Get total number of pages for page code
$total_pages = $xml_tree[PRODUCTINFO][0][TOTALPAGES][0][VALUE];
```

As a courtesy to your users, you can show how many total results are found, so you create the $total_results variable to display later:

```
// Get total number of results from the query
$total_results = $xml_tree[PRODUCTINFO][0][TOTALRESULTS][0][VALUE];
```

Now you will create a simple HTML section that displays the search phrase, the current page number, and the number of results found at the top of the results page:

```
// Display top of page with search phrase, page numbers
// and total results found
echo '<font size="4" face="Verdana, Arial, Helvetica, sans-serif">'.
    '<strong>Books for: '.stripslashes(urldecode($_REQUEST['book'])).
    '</strong><br />'.
    'Page: '.$page.' of '.$total_pages.'<br />'.
    'Total Results: '.$total_results.
    '<hr size="1">';
```

Do you remember that books_layout.html file you created? This is where all the variables from that file are created and the actual file is included into this loop. You use a foreach function that converts array keys into variables and loops through the array until it does not find any more keys to convert:

```
// loop through and show products
foreach($xml_tree[PRODUCTINFO][0][DETAILS] AS $product){
    // Results Retrieved, make quick
    // variables from array values.
```

First, you get the link to Amazon.com for the current product in the array:

```
$product_link = $product[ATTRIBUTES][URL];
```

Second, you want to display the book's ISBN number, which on Amazon.com is the Amazon Standard Identification Number:

```
$product_isbn = $product[ASIN][0][VALUE];
```

The rest of these variables are pretty easy to figure out by their names:

```
$product_name = $product[PRODUCTNAME][0][VALUE];
$product_catalog = $product[CATALOG][0][VALUE];
$product_manufacturer = $product[MANUFACTURER][0][VALUE];
$product_release_date = $product[RELEASEDATE][0][VALUE];
$product_image = $product[IMAGEURLMEDIUM][0][VALUE];
$product_new_price = $product[OURPRICE][0][VALUE];
```

```
$product_used_price = $product[USEDPRICE][0][VALUE];
$product_author1 = $product[AUTHORS][0][AUTHOR][0][VALUE];
$product_author2 = $product[AUTHORS][0][AUTHOR][1][VALUE];
$product_author3 = $product[AUTHORS][0][AUTHOR][2][VALUE];
$product_author4 = $product[AUTHORS][0][AUTHOR][3][VALUE];
$product_author5 = $product[AUTHORS][0][AUTHOR][4][VALUE];
```

Next, you include the `books_layout.html` file to display the HTML-formatted results:

```
// include layout file for looping results
include $_SERVER['DOCUMENT_ROOT'].
  '/html/books_layout.html';
}
```

The next portion of code is the bulk of the pagination code. Let's break it down. First, you create some HTML to show the words *Page Number:* and then you will display the results below it:

```
// Build Pagination System (Page Numbers)
echo '<center><font size="2" face="Verdana, '.
    'Arial, Helvetica, sans-serif">'.
    '<strong>Page Number:</strong><br />';
```

The next portion of code is one of my favorites. Using `for` loops allows you to increment numbers easily. You achieve this by performing three actions inside the `for` loop function itself. For example:

```
for(initial assignment, comparison, incrementation){
    // Perform this inside the loop each time
}
```

Follow these steps:

1. Identify the initial value of `$i`. In this case, `$i` is equal to zero.

2. Define how many times the loop will run. In this example, if `$i` is less than the total number of pages, keep running the `for` loop until `$i` is equal to or greater than the `$total_pages` value.

3. Increment the value of `$i` each time this loop is run using `$i++`:

```
for($i = 0; $i < $total_pages; $i++){
```

Next, you need to ensure your page numbers are set up properly, so you add 1 to the `$i` value and assign it to the `$p` variable:

```
$p = ($i + 1);
```

Because you will be creating hyperlinks for the page numbers you are not currently viewing, you need to determine if the current loop cycle is equal to the current page. If it is, you do not want a hyperlink for this page, so you use an IF statement to determine the course of action:

```
if($page == $p){
    echo "<strong>$page</strong> ";
} else {
```

All of the pages you will be returning except the current one will require a hyperlink. So, you create a hyperlink with the $page variable and the value for the page number, which is the current loop cycle. You also need to ensure that you pass the search phrase into the URL, or when the user clicks the page link, they will be presented with nothing:

```
echo "<a href=\"".$PHP_SELF."?page=$p&book=".$_REQUEST['book']."\">".
    "$p</a> ";
}
```

Next, close out the for loop:

```
}
```

Clean up the HTML:

```
echo "</font></center>";
```

Finally, display the footer and close PHP:

```
// Display footer
footer();
?>
```

Creating the Search Box

The last thing you need to accomplish before testing this is to create a search box for the left column of the website. I created a box with a form inside of it, named the file box_books.php, and placed it inside my website document root under the boxes directory. You should also include this file in your layout.php file. See Listing 7.6 for the box_books.php file and Listing 7.7 for the include file portion of my layout.php file.

Listing 7.6   Books Search Box

```
<table width="160" border="0" cellspacing="0" cellpadding="0">
  <tr bgcolor="#000066">
    <td width="5" height="10"><font color="#FFFFFF"> </font></td>
    <td width="150">
    <div align="center"> <font color="#FFFFFF" size="2" face="Verdana, Arial,
Helvetica, sans-serif">
      <strong>Search for Books!</strong></font></div>
    </td>
    <td width="5"> </td>
  </tr>
  <tr>
    <td height="5"> </td>
```

```
    <td align="left" valign="top">
<center>
        <font size="1" face="Verdana, Arial, Helvetica, sans-serif">
<strong>Enter
        a Search Phrase:</strong> </font>
        <form action="/books.php" method="post">
          <input name="book" type="text" size="10"
        value="<?
        if(isset($_REQUEST['book']))
        echo stripslashes($_REQUEST['book']);
        ?>">
          <input type=submit value="Go!">
</form>
<font size="1" face="Verdana, Arial, Helvetica, sans-serif">Powered by<br>
        <a href="http://www.amazon.com" target="_blank"> Amazon.com</a>
        </font>
      </center>
   </td>
   <td> </td>
  </tr>
</table>
<hr size="1">
```

Listing 7.7 **Include Portion of the *layout.php* File**

```
<!-- Left Links Column -->
<td width="170" valign="top">
<table width="170" border="0" cellpadding="0" cellspacing="0">
<tr>
<td width="10"> </td>
<td valign="top">
<?php
include $_SERVER['DOCUMENT_ROOT'].
        '/boxes/member_box.php';

include $_SERVER['DOCUMENT_ROOT'].
        '/boxes/box_admin_links.php';

include $_SERVER['DOCUMENT_ROOT'].
        '/boxes/box_main_links.php';

include $_SERVER['DOCUMENT_ROOT'].
        '/boxes/box_books.php';

include $_SERVER['DOCUMENT_ROOT'].
        '/boxes/box_translate.php';
?>
</td>
<!-- End Left Links Column -->
```

Let's test this new fancy Amazon Web Services API script! Open your site in your web browser, and you should see the heading "Search for Books" above your translation box, as shown in Figure 7.6. In that box, type in the word *Sybex* and click the Go button. You should see a nicely formatted page with the results for the word *Sybex*, as shown in Figure 7.7.

Take a look at the top of the page above the first result found. You should see some statistics regarding the search results for this query, as shown in Figure 7.8.

Scroll down to the bottom of the page, and you should see page numbers with hyperlinks on every page except for the current one, as shown in Figure 7.9.

FIGURE 7.6:

The "Search for Books" header

FIGURE 7.7:

Search results for the word *Sybex*

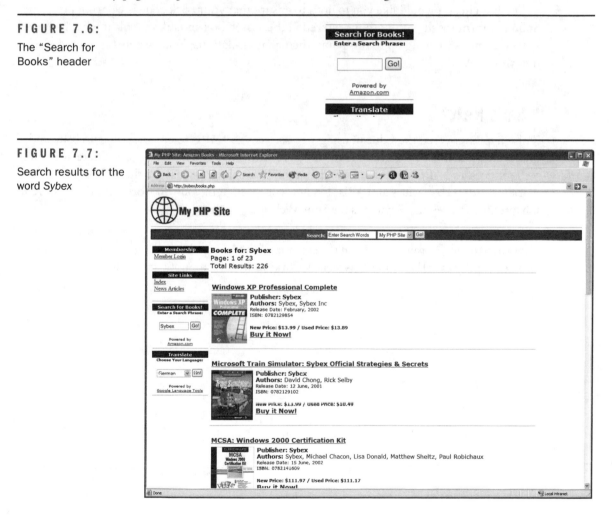

Books for: Sybex
Page: 1 of 23
Total Results: 226

Page Number:
1 2 3 4 5 6 7 8 9 10 11 12 13 14 15 16 17 18 19 20 21 22 23

The last check I would like you to do is to ensure that your trick code is working properly. Submit a form result with nothing entered in the search box and take a look at what happens. If everything is working up to this point, then congratulations! You have just mastered working with an API!

What's Next?

This chapter covered the value of using web services and APIs to enhance your website and give your users more options. Do not stop here with what you have learned. There are more web services and APIs out there for you to use! This chapter is just the tip of the iceberg for working with web services and APIs. Do not worry, though; you will work with them more in Chapter 9, "Processing Payments for Your Website."

The next chapter will cover the basics of creating a shopping cart system to allow you to sell products on your website. I will cover some of the basics about using cookies and generating shopping cart ID numbers as well as working with form input array values.

CHAPTER 8

Creating a Shopping Cart System

Websites that utilize online shopping cart systems are great places for you as a webmaster or a business owner to earn money selling your products. When you are ready to step up to the e-commerce part of the Internet, a shopping cart is the way to go. However, planning the shopping cart system can be tricky and will require some extensive testing and implementation to ensure you have done it right.

This chapter covers the core of the shopping cart system including creating unique cart identifier numbers, setting cookies to retrieve stored unique identifiers, posting arrays with form elements, and controlling your stock.

Furthermore, you will create a simple product display page that will pull product information from the MySQL database, format your products, and post the form information to the shopping cart system. If you desire, you can create your own administrative functions using the methods of insert, modify/update, and delete covered in Chapter 6, "Developing a Website News System." For this chapter, you will create the tables and insert your products using your favorite MySQL database management tool.

When you are done with this chapter, you will have a fully functioning shopping cart system that will lead you into the next chapter, which covers how to process credit card payments with merchant account gateways and Application Programming Interfaces (APIs).

Planning Your Shopping Cart

A shopping cart system must be handled delicately. When dealing with sales, you have to project a flawless image of quality in your sales system. It's almost the same as ensuring your store is clean before you open the doors in the morning for a line of customers waiting outside. If your products are not priced right or your stock is not handled properly, your customers may not want to purchase from you because they may doubt the quality of your products. Keep that in mind while you plan your shopping cart system, and you may prevent potential sales losses when your site goes live.

The tricky part about planning an e-commerce shopping cart system is finding a way to make it foolproof. You have to ask yourself a wide array of questions regarding how even the most computer-illiterate person would approach using your system. You are the developer, but you'll have to think of it from the novice's point of view when you're considering the functionality of your system.

Let's take into account some of the potential areas that users may find flaws in your shopping cart system. I will run through some scenarios and then present the workarounds for them.

Scenario 1   You have a storefront with products. At the bottom of each product listing, you will present a form field that allows the shopper to enter how many of each product they want to purchase. When they submit this form, your system will add the product to their cart.

But wait! What if they enter more than you have in stock? What if the item is one of a kind, and you can't purchase more to fill back orders? You need to prevent overselling your stock, especially for limited items. Stock control is your most important feature of the cart. It is much easier to prevent overselling and charging the shopper for products that you don't have than refunding their money and providing an explanation of what happened. To prevent these downfalls, I will cover stock control thoroughly in this chapter.

Scenario 2   When the shopper views their shopping cart page, they will have the ability to update the quantity of the item in their cart. If they have multiple items in their shopping cart, you will need to provide a convenient method for them to change the quantity of all of those products with one click. The easier you can make their shopping experience, the better chance you will sell your product to them. Stock control also provides a strong role in these features.

Scenario 3   The shopper has added an item to their shopping cart that they do not want to purchase. In your shopping cart system, you need to provide a method to remove a product without requiring the shopper to start over and add all of the products they want to purchase again.

Scenario 4   The shopper decided after adding multiple items to their shopping cart that they want to start again. You need to provide a method for them to empty their cart with one swift click of the button.

Scenario 5   The shopper has added items to their cart but does not want to purchase them at this time. They want to come back to the website at a later date, maybe sometime around next payday, and purchase the items. You will have to create a method to identify the shopper when they return and present them with their shopping cart and its contents from the last time they visited the site.

The previous scenarios are the common concepts you must build into your shopping cart. You should consider every possible situation to ensure you can get the customer to purchase your products without distracting them by faulty code or planning.

Preparing the Code for Your Shopping Cart

To prepare for the code for this chapter, you need to modify your database and create new scripts to support the objective—building your shopping cart system.

The first step you will take is to create a new column in your members table. You will name this new column cart_id and make it a VARCHAR column type with a length of 255. This column will store the unique ID that you create when the shopper adds an item to their shopping cart for the first time. If the shopper is logged in as a member, you will update their information in the database and insert the unique ID into this field.

Next, you will create a table named shopping_products with the information found in Table 8.1.

TABLE 8.1: Structure Setup for the shopping_products Table

Field Name	Data Type	Length	Extra
product_id	MEDIUMINT	25	Primary key, auto increment
product_title	VARCHAR	155	
product_price	FLOAT		
product_qty	MEDIUMINT	25	
caption	TINYTEXT		
long_description	TEXT		

The usage for these columns is as follows:

product_id   A unique automatically incremented number for each product in your table.

product_title   The title of the product that is used in the shopping cart system and storefront.

product_price   The price of the product. This field type is FLOAT for use with numbers such as prices.

product_qty   Used for stock control purposes. This field is the number of each item you have in stock.

caption   A short description of the product to be used for the products index page.

long_description   The full description of the product that will be displayed when viewing the product individually.

After you have created your product table, let's enter two products into the database. You can use your MySQL management tool of choice. I have entered the products in Table 8.2 and Table 8.3.

TABLE 8.2: Product 1, PHP Baseball Hat

Field Name	Value
product_id	
product_title	PHP Baseball Hat
product_price	12.95
product_qty	19
caption	These PHP hats are truly unique and hard to find. Grab yours while they last! Limited stock!
long_description	These PHP baseball hats are one size fits all and are made of wool. We only have one color in stock: blue. The PHP logo is embroidered on the front of the hat. Grab them while they last!

TABLE 8.3: Product 2, PHP Mousepad

Field Name	Value
product_id	
product_title	PHP Mousepad
product_price	5.99
product_qty	45
caption	Nice mousepad for those hard-core PHP developers out there!
long_description	Looking for a mousepad? Why not get this PHP mousepad? It has been proven to boost your PHP development time by 25 percent because of the slick surface for your mouse to move along. Order now, and we will include the special "Lint Free" edition!

Next, you will create the MySQL table to store the shopping cart information for your shoppers (see Table 8.4).

TABLE 8.4: Structure Setup for the shopping_carts Table

Field Name	Data Type	Length	Extra
id	MEDIUMINT	25	Primary key, auto increment
cart_identifier	VARCHAR	155	
product_id	MEDIUMINT	25	
product_qty	MEDIUMINT	25	
product_title	VARCHAR	155	
product_price	FLOAT		
date	DATETIME		

The usage for these columns is as follows:

id   Automatically incremented unique number for each row in the table.

cart_identifier   A unique ID that you will generate to identify the shopper in the shopping cart system.

product_id   Obtained from the `shopping_products` table for each product entered in the user's shopping cart.

product_qty   The quantity of the product the shopper wants to purchase.

product_title   Used to reduce the number of queries from multiple tables when viewing the shopping cart information.

product_price   Used to multiply the `product_qty` by the `product_price` to get the total product price in the shopping cart.

date   Date of the last activity on this shopping cart. It can be used to run a CRON job or a task that will clean up old and unused shopping carts after a certain period of time.

Creating a Simple Storefront

As mentioned earlier in this chapter, you will create a simple product page that will allow your shoppers to see the products and add them to the shopping cart. If you want, you can expand upon this storefront and add administrative functions based on the concepts to insert, update/modify, and delete your products as discussed in Chapter 6, "Developing a Website News System."

To begin, you will create an index page for all of your products. This page will display the product title, price, stock, a hyperlink to the product page, and a small form to quickly add the product to the cart. To get started, you will create two Hypertext Markup Language (HTML) templates for your products. The first template is the small description of the product that will reside on the index page. Name this file `product_small.html` and save it in your website document root under the `html` directory (see Listing 8.1).

Listing 8.1   *products_small.html* **Template File**

```
<table width="100%" border="0" cellspacing="0" cellpadding="4">
  <tr>
    <td colspan="2"><font size="3" face="Verdana, Arial, Helvetica, sans-serif">
    <a href="/products.php?req=view&product_id=<?=$product_id?>">
<?=$product_title?></a>
    </font></td>
  </tr>
  <tr>
```

```
        <td width="16%" align="left" valign="top"><font size="2" face="Verdana,
Arial, Helvetica, sans-serif"><strong>Description:</strong></font></td>
        <td width="84%">
          <?=$caption?>
        </td>
      </tr>
      <tr>
        <td align="left" valign="top"><strong><font size="2" face="Verdana, Arial,
Helvetica, sans-serif">Price:</font></strong></td>
        <td>$
          <?=$product_price?>
        </td>
      </tr>
      <tr>
        <td> </td>
        <td><form method="post" action="/cart.php">
          <font size="2" face="Verdana, Arial, Helvetica, sans-serif">
        <strong>Add To cart</strong></font>
        <input name="qty" type="text" value="1" size="3">
          <input type="hidden" name="req" value="add">
          <input type="hidden" name="product_id" value="<?=$product_id?>">
          <input type="submit" name="Submit" value="Go!">
          </form></td>
      </tr>
    </table>
    <hr size="1">
```

You have seen these file types numerous times in this book. The file is an HTML layout
for your product, and it also has embedded PHP. You will loop this file through your
MySQL results and complete the information inside the template with PHP.

The next file you need to create is the larger template that will display the product by itself
on its own page. Create a new file in your website document root under the html directory
and name it product_large.html (see Listing 8.2).

Listing 8.2   ***products_large.html* Template File**

```
<table width="100%" border="0" cellspacing="0" cellpadding="4">
  <tr>
    <td colspan="2"><font size="4" face="Verdana, Arial, Helvetica, sans-
serif"><?=$product_title?></font></td>
  </tr>
  <tr>
    <td width="16%" align="left" valign="top"><font size="2" face="Verdana,
Arial, Helvetica, sans-serif"><strong>Description:</strong></font></td>
    <td width="84%"><?=$long_description?></td>
  </tr>
  <tr>
    <td align="left" valign="top"><strong><font size="2" face="Verdana, Arial,
Helvetica, sans-serif">Price:</font></strong></td>
    <td>$<?=$product_price?></td>
```

```
        </tr>
        <tr>
          <td align="left" valign="top"><font size="2" face="Verdana, Arial,
Helvetica, sans-serif"><strong>In Stock:</strong></font></td>
          <td><?=$product_qty?></td>
        </tr>
        <tr>
          <td> </td>
          <td>
        <form method="post" action="/cart.php">
            <font size="2" face="Verdana, Arial, Helvetica, sans-serif">
          <strong>Add To cart </strong></font>
          <input name="qty" type="text" value="1" size="3">
            <input type="hidden" name="req" value="add">
          <input type="hidden" name="product_id" value="<?=$product_id?>">
            <input type="submit" name="Submit" value="Go!">
          </form>
        </td>
      </tr>
    </table>
```

This file also includes a template for your product information as well as a form that will post to the shopping cart file and pass the `product_id` and `product_qty` to the shopping cart.

Now that you have your templates created, it is time to create a file in your website's document root directory and name it `products.php`. This file will utilize the previous examples to complete the template and display your products (see Listing 8.3).

Listing 8.3   *products.php Products File*

```php
<?php

include $_SERVER['DOCUMENT_ROOT'].
    '/layout.php';

switch($_REQUEST['req']){
  case "view":
      $sql = mysql_query("SELECT *
                    FROM shopping_products
                    WHERE
                    product_id='{$_REQUEST['product_id']}'");
      $row = mysql_fetch_assoc($sql);
      stripslashes(extract($row));
      $page_title = "Our Products: "
                    .stripslashes($row[product_title]);
      myheader($page_title);
      $long_description = nl2br($long_description);
      include $_SERVER['DOCUMENT_ROOT'].
             '/html/product_large.html';
```

```
            footer();
        break;

    default:
        myheader("Our Products");
        $sql = mysql_query("SELECT *
                    FROM shopping_products
                    WHERE (product_qty > 0)
                    ORDER BY product_title");
        while($row = mysql_fetch_array($sql)){
            stripslashes(extract($row));
            $caption = nl2br($caption);

            include $_SERVER['DOCUMENT_ROOT'].
                '/html/product_small.html';

        }
        footer();
    break;
}
?>
```

The products.php file contains two cases in the switch. The default case will display your products in alphabetical order and provide the shopper with a chance to add the items to their shopping cart or access the view case that allows a full detailed description of the product. Figure 8.1 shows the default case, and Figure 8.2 shows the view case in action.

FIGURE 8.1:

Product index, default case

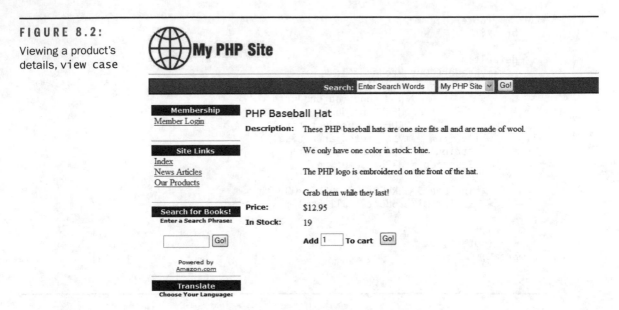

FIGURE 8.2:
Viewing a product's
details, `view case`

If everything is working well, you have a method to allow your shoppers to browse products and add them to your shopping cart. Let's move on to the core of the shopping cart system.

Making a Shopping Cart Class

Because your shopping cart is going to contain a large set of complex code, you will make things easier on yourself by creating a class that will contain all of the functions you need to utilize the features of your cart. The first file you will work with will reside in the website document root under the `classes` directory. Name this new file `clsShoppingCart.php` (see Listing 8.4).

Listing 8.4   Shopping Cart Class

```php
<?php

class ShoppingCart{
    // Get the cart id
    // If one is not available, make one.
    function get_cart_id(){
        if(!isset($_COOKIE['cid'])){
            $cart_id = FALSE;
        } else {
            $cart_id = $_COOKIE['cid'];
```

```php
        $_SESSION['cid'] = $_COOKIE['cid'];
    }
    if($_SESSION['cid']){
        $cart_id = $_SESSION['cid'];
        if($_SESSION['login']){
            @mysql_query("UPDATE members SET
                cart_id='$cart_id'
                WHERE id='".$_SESSION['userid']."'");
        }
    } else {
        $cart_id = FALSE;
    }
    if(!$cart_id){
        return FALSE;
    } else {
        return $cart_id;
    }
}

function cart_add($product_id, $product_qty){

    $cart_id = $this->get_cart_id();

    if(!$cart_id){
        // if no cart id found, generate one
        $unique_cid = md5(uniqid(rand(),1));

        // set cart id into the cookie
        setcookie('cid', $unique_cid, time()+24*3600*60);

        // Register session with cart id value
        $_SESSION['cid'] = $unique_cid;

        // if person is a member
        // modify their profile with
        // cart id in the database

        if($_SESSION['login']){
            $_SESSION['cid'] = $unique_cid;
            @mysql_query("UPDATE members SET
                    cart_id='$unique_cid'
                    WHERE id='".$_SESSION['userid']."'");
        }
    }
    $sql_get_product = mysql_query("SELECT * FROM shopping_products
                                    WHERE product_id='$product_id'");

    $sql_check = mysql_query("SELECT * FROM shopping_carts
                    WHERE
                    cart_identifier='{$_SESSION['cid']}'
                    AND product_id='$product_id'");
```

```php
            while($row = mysql_fetch_array($sql_check)){
                    $products = mysql_fetch_assoc($sql_get_product);
                    if(($product_qty + $products[product_qty]) >
                        $products[product_qty]){
                      $new_qty = $products[product_qty];
                    } else {
                      $new_qty = ($product_qty + $row[product_qty]);
                    }

                    $sql = mysql_query("UPDATE shopping_carts SET
                               product_qty = '$new_qty',
                               date = now()
                               WHERE
                               id='{$row['id']}'");
                    $skip = TRUE;
            }
        if(!$skip){
                $products = mysql_fetch_assoc($sql_get_product);
                if($products[product_qty] < $product_qty){
                    $product_qty = $products[product_qty];
                }

                if($product_qty > 0){

                $sql = mysql_query("INSERT INTO shopping_carts
                               (cart_identifier,
                                product_id,
                                product_title,
                                product_qty,
                                product_price,
                                date)
                                     VALUES ('{$_SESSION['cid']}',
                                        '$product_id',
                                        '{$products['product_title']}',
                                        '$product_qty',
                                        '{$products['product_price']}',
                                        now())");
                } else {
                    $sql = FALSE;
                }

        }

        if(!$sql){
            return FALSE;
        } else {
            return TRUE;
        }
}

function empty_cart(){
```

```
        $cart_identifier = $this->get_cart_id();
        $sql = @mysql_query("DELETE FROM shopping_carts
                    WHERE
                    cart_identifier='$cart_identifier'");
        if(!$sql){
                return FALSE;
        } else {
                return TRUE;
        }
    }
}
?>
```

I will break down each of the functions in your shopping cart class file in the following sections so you can understand what they do.

Shopping Cart Class: *get_cart_id* Function

The first function, get_cart_id, may be a little confusing when you first glance at it. The main purpose of this function is to return an error (a FALSE Boolean value) or to return a unique shopping cart ID to the script that calls this function. It could be pretty complicated if you have never used cookie functions before, but that is okay, I will break it down.

First, you define the function by the name get_cart_id and define the arguments passed to it. In this case, you do not pass any arguments to this function:

```
function get_cart_id(){
```

Second, because your shopping cart is going to provide a cookie feature, you will check for the cid value in your cookie using the PHP isset function. This IF statement would read "If $_COOKIE['cid'] is not set" because you used the ! operator on the function call. Inside your IF statement, if the cookie value is not set, you will assign $cart_id a FALSE value. I will explain the usage of $cart_id at the end of this function:

```
if(!isset($_COOKIE['cid'])){
    $cart_id = FALSE;
}
```

If the $_COOKIE['cid'] value is present, you will assign the current session value of $_SESSION['cid'] to the value in the cookie. By assigning a session value of the cookie, you can provide a redundant check to see if the shopping cart unique identifier has been assigned to the shopper:

```
else {
    $cart_id = $_COOKIE['cid'];
    $_SESSION['cid'] = $_COOKIE['cid'];
}
```

Next you will see if the $_SESSION['cid'] value is present. If it is, you will assign the $cart_id variable the value of the unique cart identifier, and you will also make an attempt to update the database to add the shopping cart ID to the member profile if the shopper is also a member on your site:

```
if($_SESSION['cid']){
    $cart_id = $_SESSION['cid'];
        if($_SESSION['login']){
            @mysql_query("UPDATE members SET
                    cart_id='$cart_id'
                    WHERE id='".$_SESSION['userid']."'");
        }
}
```

If the cookie check and the session check have failed, you ensure that the $cart_id variable has been assigned a FALSE value:

```
else {
    $cart_id = FALSE;
}
```

The next task is to determine the value of $cart_id. If it is FALSE because the checks have failed, you return FALSE as the output of this function. If the $cart_id variable actually contains a value other than FALSE, you will return the $cart_id value in the output of this function:

```
if(!$cart_id){
    return FALSE;
} else {
    return $cart_id;
}
}
```

Do not worry if you do not fully understand the purpose of this function yet; by the time you are done with this chapter, you will have a good understanding of it because you will use it in multiple places of your shopping cart in order to include the cart_add function in this class.

Shopping Cart Class: *cart_add* Function

The next function will be used when your shopper adds products to the cart. This function will utilize the get_cart_id function to determine if the unique shopping cart ID exists, and if it does, you will utilize it; if it does not, you will create one. I will now break it down.

First, you define the function and pass the arguments to it. You will pass two arguments to this function: $product_id, which is the product ID posted from the product pages, and $product_qty, which is the number of items the shopper wants to purchase:

```
function cart_add($product_id, $product_qty){
```

Second, you will determine if the shopping cart ID exists by using the nifty function you created earlier:

```
$cart_id = $this->get_cart_id();
```

As mentioned in the get_cart_id function, the output will be a FALSE value if no cart ID exists, or it will contain the cart ID. The next IF statement will create a unique ID if the $cart_id variable is a Boolean and contains a FALSE value:

```
if(!$cart_id){
```

To generate a unique ID, you will use the following PHP functions together: md5, uniqid, and rand. After you have your unique ID generated, you assign them to the $unique_cid variable:

```
// if no cart id found, generate one
$unique_cid = md5(uniqid(rand(),1));
```

Ah! Finally, cookies! The next task is to set the cookie value of the unique ID. To set a cookie, you simply use the setcookie function with the arguments passed to it like this: setcookie(*name of value, value, time limit to expire, additional arguments*). In this use, you will give the cookie value a name of cid and assign the value to it. You will use the PHP time function to get the current time, and then you add, in seconds, 24 * 3600* 60 for the time limit to expire. This math equation will add 60 days to the current time when this script was executed. After the setcookie function has executed, you will have the values required to rerun the $cart_id value from the get_cart_id function:

```
// set cart id into the cookie
setcookie('cid', $unique_cid, time()+24*3600*60);
```

After you have your cookie value set, you will also assign the value to the current session:

```
// Register session with cart id value
$_SESSION['cid'] = $unique_cid;
```

Next, you will update the database if the shopper is a member. This allows you to provide redundancy to keep track of this valuable shopping cart ID:

```
// if person is a member
// modify their profile with
// cart id in the database
if($_SESSION['login']){
    $_SESSION['cid'] = $unique_cid;
    @mysql_query("UPDATE members SET
            cart_id='$unique_cid'
            WHERE id='".$_SESSION['userid']."'");
}
} // end generate unique ID.
```

After you have taken care of getting or generating the unique shopping cart ID, you check to see if the shopper already has the product in their shopping cart. If they do, you will simply add the new quantity of the product to the current quantity. This check prevents having duplicate products in the shopping cart. The first query will retrieve the product information from your `shopping_products` table, and it will be used in multiple places throughout this function, so you go ahead and define it here:

```
$sql_get_product = mysql_query("SELECT * FROM shopping_products
                                WHERE product_id='$product_id'");
```

The next query will get the information about the user's shopping cart from your database:

```
$sql_check = mysql_query("SELECT * FROM shopping_carts
                WHERE
                cart_identifier='{$_SESSION['cid']}'
                AND product_id='$product_id'");
```

The results from the `$sql_check` function are utilized in a `while` loop, which allows you to loop through each `product_id` and update the quantity using a math function. The math function adds the current `product_qty` of their shopping cart to the `$product_qty` the user has chosen—if the product ID matches the result of the query:

```
while($row = mysql_fetch_array($sql_check)){
```

The next portion of code retrieves the current stock of the product and then checks to see how many more of the product the shopper wants to purchase. If the sum of the current shopping cart product quantity and the new quantity they want to purchase are greater than the amount of stock you have, then you will adjust the shopper's cart quantity to your maximum stock. If the sum is not greater, you will add the current shopping cart product quantity to the new quantity and use that number to update the cart. The `$new_qty` variable sets the quantity of the product in their cart:

```
$products = mysql_fetch_assoc($sql_get_product);
if(($product_qty + $products[product_qty]) >
    $products[product_qty]){
  $new_qty = $products[product_qty];
} else {
  $new_qty = ($product_qty + $row[product_qty]);
}
```

After you figure out the correct quantity of the product to allow the user to purchase, you update their shopping cart with this new value:

```
$sql = mysql_query("UPDATE shopping_carts SET
                product_qty = '$new_qty',
                date = now()
                WHERE
                id='{$row['id']}'");
```

To prevent adding another instance of this product into the shopping cart, you create a Boolean named $skip and assign a TRUE value for it to use for determining whether you need to perform the INSERT query later in this script:

```
        $skip = TRUE;
    }
```

At this point, you have already determined if the product already exists in the shopping cart; if it does, you update the quantity of the cart plus the new quantity of the item. If you find the item in the cart and the shopper is trying to add more of the item, you skip this next query because the $skip Boolean is TRUE from the previous listing. If it is not TRUE and the product does not exist already, you add the product to the shopper's cart:

```
 if(!$skip){
```

Earlier, you defined the MySQL query for $sql_get_product. This is the second place in your code that it is used. You will get the product information to include the stock quantity that you have and perform the query to update their cart with this new product and the correct quantity that you can sell them:

```
$products = mysql_fetch_assoc($sql_get_product);
if($products[product_qty] < $product_qty){
    $product_qty = $products[product_qty];
}
```

If the product quantity that the user has entered is greater than zero, you will perform the query. Otherwise, you will skip the query on the next else statement:

```
        if($product_qty > 0){

        $sql = mysql_query("INSERT INTO shopping_carts
                    (cart_identifier,
                     product_id,
                     product_title,
                     product_qty,
                     product_price,
                     date)
                    VALUES ('{$_SESSION['cid']}',
                            '$product_id',
                            '{$products['product_title']}',
                            '$product_qty',
                            '{$products['product_price']}',
                            now())") or die (mysql_error());

        } else {
            $sql = FALSE;
        }

    }
```

After all of your queries have completed, you will determine if the operation was successful. If it was, you will return the TRUE Boolean as the output for this function; otherwise you will return FALSE:

```
if(!$sql){
    return FALSE;
} else {
    return TRUE;
}
}
```

This function is complex to understand. You perform multiple checks and redundancies to ensure that your shopping cart is correct, that you are sure that the unique shopping cart ID exists or is created, and that your product stock is not oversold. Do not worry if you do not fully understand how it all comes together just yet; you will use these functions inside the actual shopping cart files, and you will see a more practical application of them later.

Shopping Cart Class: *empty_cart* Function

The last function in your shopping cart class will empty the shopping cart. This happens by getting the cart ID and performing a DELETE query based on the cart ID. After the query has been performed, you will return a Boolean for the success or failure of the query:

```
function empty_cart(){
    $cart_identifier = $this->get_cart_id();
    $sql = @mysql_query("DELETE FROM shopping_carts
                WHERE
                cart_identifier='$cart_identifier'");
    if(!$sql){
        return FALSE;
    } else {
        return TRUE;
    }
}
```

The class is now complete and ready for use. Be sure to include this class into your common.php file before you move on to creating the rest of the shopping cart. Let's dig in and create the core of the shopping cart system!

Building the Shopping Cart Interface: *cart.php*

You will create a single file that will allow the shopper to add products, update quantities, calculate prices, and delete items from their cart. This file is going to utilize the class you created previously. Create a file in your website document root directory and name it cart.php (see Listing 8.5).

Listing 8.5   Shopping Cart *cart.php* File

```php
<?php

include $_SERVER['DOCUMENT_ROOT'].
   '/layout.php';

$cart = &new ShoppingCart;
$cart_id = $cart->get_cart_id();

switch($_REQUEST['req']){
   case "add":
      $add2cart = $cart->cart_add($_REQUEST['product_id'],
                                  $_REQUEST['qty']);

      myheader("Shopping Cart");
      if(!$add2cart){
         echo "<center>The product could not be ".
             "to your shopping cart. You may ".
             "have entered an invalid quantity</center>";
      } else {
         echo "<center>Item added to your shopping cart!<br />".
             "<a href=\"/cart.php\">View ".
             "your cart</a></center>";
      }
      footer();
   break;

   case "update":
      while(list($product_id, $qty) = each($_POST[qty])){
         $sql = mysql_query("SELECT * FROM
                     shopping_products
                     WHERE product_id='$product_id'");

         $row = mysql_fetch_assoc($sql);
         if($qty == 0){
            mysql_query("DELETE FROM shopping_carts
                    WHERE cart_identifier='$cart_id'
                    AND
                    product_id='$product_id'");
         }

         if($qty > $row[product_qty]){
            mysql_query("UPDATE shopping_carts
                    SET product_qty='{$row[product_qty]}'
                    WHERE cart_identifier='$cart_id'
                    AND
                    product_id='$product_id'");

            $error = TRUE;
            $products[$product_id] =
```

```
                    stripslashes($row[product_title]);

        } else {
            mysql_query("UPDATE shopping_carts
                    SET product_qty='$qty'
                    WHERE cart_identifier='$cart_id'
                    AND
                    product_id='$product_id'");
        }
    }
    if($error){
        myheader("Shopping Cart");
        echo "<center>You have selected more ".
            "than our current stock for the following ".
            "product(s): <br />";

        while(list($product_id, $product_name) = each($products)){
            echo "<a href=\"/products.php?req=view&product_id=$product_id\">".
                "$product_name</a><br />";
        }

        echo "<br />";
        echo "We have updated your quantity to the maximum ".
            "value that we have in stock.</center><br />";
        echo "<center><a href=\"/cart.php\">".
            "Back to Cart</a></center>";
        footer();
    } else {
        header("Location: /cart.php");
    }

break;

case "remove":
    $sql = mysql_query("DELETE FROM
                shopping_carts
                WHERE cart_identifier='$cart_id'
                AND product_id='{$_REQUEST['product_id']}'");
    header("Location: /cart.php");

break;

case "empty_confirm":
    myheader("Shopping Cart");
    echo "<center>Are you sure ".
        "you want to empty your cart?<br />".
        "<a href=\"/cart.php?req=empty\">Yes</a>".
        " | ".
        "<a href=\"/cart.php\">No</a></center>";
    footer();

break;
case "empty":
```

```
        myheader("Shopping Cart");
        $cart->empty_cart();
        echo "<center>Your cart has been emptied!</center>";
        footer();
    break;



    default:
        myheader("Your Shopping Cart");

        if($cart_id){
            $num_items = mysql_result(mysql_query("SELECT
                            COUNT(*) as items
                            FROM shopping_carts
                            WHERE cart_identifier='$cart_id'"),0);
            if($num_items == 0){
                echo "<center>Your Shopping Cart is Empty!</center>";
                footer();
                exit();
            }
        } else {
                echo "<center>Your Shopping Cart is Empty!</center>";
                footer();
                exit;
        }
        ?>
        <p><font size="4" face="Verdana, Arial, Helvetica, sans-serif">
        Your Shopping Cart
        </font></p>
        <p><font size="2" face="Verdana, Arial, Helvetica, sans-serif">
        This page allows you to modify or empty your shopping cart contents.
        Simply change the number of each product you wish to purchase and
        select the "Update Cart" link at the bottom.</font></p>
        <form name="update" method="post" action="/cart.php">
        <input type="hidden" name="req" value="update">
        <table width="90%" border="1" cellspacing="0" cellpadding="4"
align="center">
        <tr>
        <td>Qty</td>
        <td>Product</td>
        <td align="right">Price</td>
        <td align="right">Product Total</td>
        </tr>

        <?php

        $total = mysql_result(mysql_query(
                    "SELECT sum(product_qty * product_price) AS
                     subtotal FROM shopping_carts
                     WHERE cart_identifier='$cart_id'"),0);

        $total = number_format($total, 2);
```

```php
        $sql = mysql_query("SELECT * FROM shopping_carts
                    WHERE cart_identifier='$cart_id'");

        while($row = mysql_fetch_array($sql)){
            $product_total =
                number_format(($row[product_qty] * $row[product_price]),2);
            echo "<tr>".
                    "<td>".
                    "<input type=\"text\" ".
                    "name=\"qty[$row[product_id]]\" ".
                    "size=\"2\" value=\"$row[product_qty]\">".
                    "<br /><font size=\"2\">".
                    "<a href=\"/cart.php?req=remove&".
                    "product_id=$row[product_id]\">".
                    "Remove</a>".
                    "</td>".
                    "<td><a href=\"/products.php?req=view&".
                    "product_id=$row[product_id]\">".
                    stripslashes($row[product_title]).
                    "</a></td>".
                    "<td align=\"right\">\$$row[product_price]</td>".
                    "<td align=\"right\">\$$product_total</td>".
                    "</tr>";
        }
        ?>
        <tr>
        <td colspan="2"> </td>
        <td align="right">Total:</td>
        <td align="right">$<?=$total?></td>
        </tr>
        <tr>
        <td colspan="4" align="center">
        <a href="javascript:void(document.update.submit())">Update Cart</a>
         | 
        <a href="/cart.php?req=empty_confirm">Empty Cart</a>
         | 
        <a href="/products.php">Continue Shopping</a>
         | 
        <a href="/checkout.php">Checkout</a>
        </td>
        </tr>
        </table>
        </form>

        <?php
        footer();
    break;
}
?>
```

I will now break this file down so you can understand what it is doing.

Shopping Cart Interface: *cart.php* Initialization

To start the code in the cart.php file, you fire up the PHP engine and include your layout.php file from your custom theme. Next you will initialize the shopping cart class and then get the shopping cart ID from the get_cart_id function within the class. You grab the shopping cart ID outside of the switch and at the top of the file because you will be using the $cart_id variable throughout cart.php. By getting the $cart_id here, you are able to reduce the code:

```php
<?php

include $_SERVER['DOCUMENT_ROOT'].
    '/layout.php';

$cart = &new ShoppingCart;
$cart_id = $cart->get_cart_id();
```

Next you will start your switch that allows you to perform multiple operations within the same physical file:

```php
switch($_REQUEST['req']){
```

Shopping Cart Interface: *cart.php add case*

This case allows the shopper to add products to their shopping cart. It utilizes the cart_add function from within your shopping cart class. When the shopper posts the form from the products.php file, the data is sent to this case, and you pass two arguments to the cart_add function in the class: the product ID number and the quantity they want to add to their cart:

```php
case "add":
        $add2cart = $cart->cart_add($_REQUEST['product_id'],
                                    $_REQUEST['qty']);
```

Next, you will display your custom myheader function from the layout.php file with the dynamic page title you want to display for this page:

```php
myheader("Shopping Cart");
```

Because the result of the cart_add function in the class is a Boolean value, you will determine which message to display to the shopper. You can display a message saying the product was added to their cart, or you can display an error message, depending on the value of the Boolean:

```php
if(!$add2cart){
    echo "<center>The product could not be ".
        "to your shopping cart. You may ".
        "have entered an invalid quantity</center>";
} else {
    echo "<center>Item added to your shopping cart!<br />".
        "<a href=\"/cart.php\">View ".
        "your cart</a></center>";
}
```

You also will need to display the `footer` function from the `layout.php` file to complete the look of this page:

```
footer();
```

Finally, you close the `case` by issuing a `break`:

```
break;
```

Shopping Cart Interface: *cart.php default case*

I will cover the `default case` out of order from the flow of the script code because you need to understand some things before I cover the rest of the script. The `default` case is the portion of the `cart.php` file that displays the contents of the shoppers' carts and allows them to modify their contents, to update quantities, to remove individual items, or to empty their carts. Figure 8.3 shows what this case looks like in the web browser.

FIGURE 8.3:
`cart.php` file,
`default` case

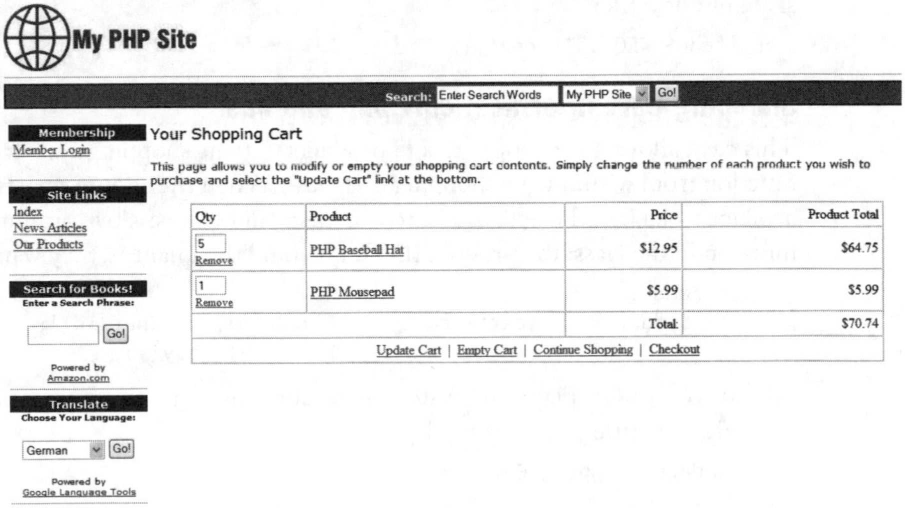

I will now break the `default case` down. You start the case by identifying it as the default value for the `switch` and include the custom `myheader` function from the `layout.php` file:

```
default:
    myheader("Your Shopping Cart");
```

Next, you need to find if the shopper has a `$cart_id` and, if they do, if their cart is empty. You do this by first checking if the `$cart_id` exists and is not a `FALSE` value. If it does exist, you will perform a query based on the `$cart_id` and return the number of products the shopper has in their cart:

```
if($cart_id){
```

```
$num_items = mysql_result(mysql_query("SELECT
                COUNT(*) as items
                FROM shopping_carts
                WHERE cart_identifier='$cart_id'"),0);
```

At this point, you have determined that the $cart_id does exist, and you have found the number of items the shopper has in the cart. If the value is 0, you display the message that their cart is empty, display the footer, and exit this script from going any further:

```
if($num_items == 0){
    echo "<center>Your Shopping Cart is Empty!</center>";
    footer();
    exit();
}
```

If the shopper does not have a $cart_id, you display a message about the cart being empty and display the custom footer and then exit the script from going any further:

```
} else {
    echo "<center>Your Shopping Cart is Empty!</center>";
    footer();
    exit;
}
```

By this point, if the script is still executing, you have determined that the shopper has a $cart_id and that they have products in their cart. So, you will format the page that displays the shopping cart contents and allows them to modify their cart.

Next, you will exit PHP so you can easily format the HTML code for the top portion of the shopping cart page that is directly below the custom myheader function from the layout.php file:

```
?>
```

The next portion of HTML code creates a page heading and a table and starts a form that will post to the update case of this script:

```
<p><font size="4" face="Verdana, Arial, Helvetica, sans-serif">
Your Shopping Cart
</font></p>
<p><font size="2" face="Verdana, Arial, Helvetica, sans-serif">
This page allows you to modify or empty your shopping cart contents.
Simply change the number of each product you wish to purchase and
select the "Update Cart" link at the bottom.</font></p>
<form name="update" method="post" action="/cart.php">
<input type="hidden" name="req" value="update">
<table width="90%" border="1" cellspacing="0" cellpadding="4" align="center">
<tr>
<td>Qty</td>
<td>Product</td>
```

```
<td align="right">Price</td>
<td align="right">Product Total</td>
</tr>
```

Next, you will fire up the PHP engine and perform a query that will utilize the MySQL SUM function. The SUM function allows you to calculate the total number values of one or more columns combined for each row in the database matching the query. You utilize the SUM function to get the total of the shopper's order by multiplying the product price and the product quantity for each row found and then adding the totals together to output a number.

You use the SUM function like this: SELECT SUM(column) AS new_value FROM table. You can use SUM on multiple columns like the next example:

```php
<?php
$total = mysql_result(mysql_query(
            "SELECT sum(product_qty * product_price) AS
             subtotal FROM shopping_carts
             WHERE cart_identifier='$cart_id'"),0);
```

PHP and MySQL have a tendency to convert numbers to decimal values to provide an exact number output. To simplify this number into an everyday use, such as dollars and cents, you use the PHP number_format function on the value. I set the precision to 2 for my preferred output. It would convert a number such as 322.5983 to 322.60.

```php
$total = number_format($total, 2);
```

Next, you will perform a query that will allow you to get the contents of your shoppers' carts, loop it through a while loop, and display the results on the page:

```php
$sql = mysql_query("SELECT * FROM shopping_carts
            WHERE cart_identifier='$cart_id'");
while($row = mysql_fetch_array($sql)){
```

In your shopping cart, you will display the product quantity, the title, the individual price for this product, and a total price for this product and the quantity the user wants to purchase. Based on this design, you will use number_format for the product_qty multiplied by the product_price and assign it to the $product_total variable to display in the cart:

```php
$product_total =
    number_format(($row[product_qty] * $row[product_price]),2);
```

Now you will complete your HTML table and form with the results of each product in the shoppers' carts. But I will break this HTML down a little because there are some new elements I have not covered yet.

The first portion is the HTML table row and the first cell that is going to contain an input box with the value of product_qty for the current product:

```php
echo "<tr>".
    "<td>".
```

The next element is important; PHP allows you to create an array from a form-posted value. For each product you have, when the user updates their cart, you will create an array named qty. This array will contain the product ID and the quantity they want to specify. So, for your input type value, you can use qty[$row[product_id]] as the name of the input field, and then you can use the value of the field when the form was posted to make the changes to the cart.

If your cart contained three items—for example, product_id 1, 2, and 3—and the quantity values were all set to 5, you would have an array that looks similar to this when the form posted, after you used the PHP function print_r() on the posted array:

```
Array([1] => 5 [2] => 5 [3] => 5)
```

Based on this concept, you can post an array of product IDs and their current or new quantities and update the database with this information. I will cover how to handle the results in the update case:

```
"<input type=\"text\" ".
"name=\"qty[$row[product_id]]\" ".
"size=\"2\" value=\"$row[product_qty]\">".
```

Next you create a hyperlink that links to the remove case to remove the product from the cart:

```
"<br /><font size=\"2\">".
"<a href=\"/cart.php?req=remove&".
"product_id=$row[product_id]\">".
"Remove</a>".
"</td>".
```

Now you display the product title and use the stripslashes function on the value, and you also link to the product page for this item:

```
"<td><a href=\"/products.php?req=view&".
"product_id=$row[product_id]\">".
stripslashes($row[product_title]).
"</a></td>".
```

The next section of code displays the individual product price for this item:

```
"<td align=\"right\">\$$row[product_price]</td>".
```

And finally, for your loop, you display the price for this product from the $product_total variable created earlier:

```
"<td align=\"right\">\$$product_total</td>".
"</tr>";
```

Close your while loop and close the PHP engine because the rest of this case is going to be HTML with embedded PHP:

```
}
?>
```

The next portion of HTML code is the table row and cells that display the total price of the shopping cart using the $total variable:

```
<tr>
<td colspan="2"> </td>
<td align="right">Total:</td>
<td align="right">$<?=$total?></td>
</tr>
```

To make your shopping cart look nicer, you will use a JavaScript function that allows you to post a form from a hyperlink based on the name of the form instead of creating a form submit button:

```
<tr>
     <td colspan="4" align="center">
<a href="javascript:void(document.update.submit())">Update Cart</a>
 | 
```

Next, you will provide a hyperlink to the empty_confirm case to present a last-chance confirmation to empty the shopping cart:

```
<a href="/cart.php?req=empty_confirm">Empty Cart</a>
 | 
```

You always want to provide a link to allow the shopper to go back to the storefront and keep shopping! The following link takes the shopper back to the products.php page:

```
<a href="/products.php">Continue Shopping</a>
 | 
```

The following link takes you to the checkout.php file that you will build in Chapter 9, "Processing Payments for Your Website":

```
<a href="/checkout.php">Checkout</a>
</td>
```

The rest of this case is cleanup. You close your table, open PHP to display your custom footer from the layout.php file, and then issue the break:

```
</tr>
</table>
</form>

<?php
footer();
break;
```

Now that you know where all of the other cases in this switch will come into play, let's take a look at the rest of them now.

Shopping Cart Interface: *cart.php update case*

The next case is interesting. It processes the information in the $_POST[qty] array that you created with the input fields that allow your shopper to change the product quantity for each product. This case will also perform some stock control to prevent overselling your stock.

First, you will define the case:

```
case "update":
```

Second, you perform a while loop and create a list of the keys and values in the $_POST[qty] array by using the each function in PHP:

```
while(list($product_id, $qty) = each($_POST[qty])){
```

After you build your list and put it in a loop, you can go through each element of the array and perform a query on the $product_id you extracted from the array in the list function:

```
$sql = mysql_query("SELECT * FROM
            shopping_products
            WHERE product_id='$product_id'");
```

Once you have performed the query, you can fetch the results into an associative array using mysql_fetch_assoc and then check the stock against the requested quantity:

```
$row = mysql_fetch_assoc($sql);
```

If the shopper tries to be tricky and enter 0 as the quantity they want to purchase, you will remove the item from their shopping cart. Believe it or not, someone will try to do this, so be prepared:

```
if($qty == 0){
    mysql_query("DELETE FROM shopping_carts
            WHERE cart_identifier='$cart_id'
            AND
            product_id='$product_id'");
}
```

If the shopper wants more than you currently have in stock, you will simply give them your maximum stock value and prevent overselling your stock. You do this by updating their quantity with the value from the $sql query that returns the maximum number of stock you have for this product:

```
if($qty > $row[product_qty]){
    mysql_query("UPDATE shopping_carts
            SET product_qty='{$row[product_qty]}'
            WHERE cart_identifier='$cart_id'
            AND
            product_id='$product_id'");
```

You want to notify the shopper that you have modified their requested quantity to match your stock, so you build an array and add the adjusted product title and product ID to this array. And then you create an `$error` Boolean variable and assign the `TRUE` value to it. You will use the `$products` array and the `$error` Boolean later in this `case`:

```
$error = TRUE;
$products[$product_id] =
    stripslashes($row[product_title]);

}
```

The next `ELSE` statement is used when you do not have to modify the requested product quantity because the shopper has not requested more than you have in stock. Here you will update the affected product in the shopper's cart with the quantity requested:

```
else {
    mysql_query("UPDATE shopping_carts
        SET product_qty='$qty'
        WHERE cart_identifier='$cart_id'
        AND
        product_id='$product_id'");
}
```

Close the `while` loop for the `$_POST[qty]` array:

```
}
```

If the script assigned the `$error` Boolean, you will create a message to display to the shopper after the script executes. This message will notify them that they have requested more than your maximum stock and you have adjusted their cart to fix this. This `IF` statement uses a `while` loop with the `list` function and the `each` function for the `$products` array that was created when the `$error` Boolean was assigned a `TRUE` value. Then each product that had a maximum value reached will be displayed with a hyperlink back to that product:

```
if($error){
    myheader("Shopping Cart");
    echo "<center>You have selected more ".
        "than our current stock for the following ".
        "product(s): <br />";

    while(list($product_id, $product_name) = each($products)){
        echo "<a href=\"/products.php?req=view&product_id=$product_id\">".
            "$product_name</a><br />";
    }

    echo "<br />";
    echo "We have updated your quantity to the maximum ".
        "value that we have in stock.</center><br />";
    echo "<center><a href=\"/cart.php\">".
        "Back to Cart</a></center>";
    footer();
}
```

To understand what happens when you reach a maximum stock value, Figure 8.4 depicts the message displayed to the user.

If the `$error` Boolean was not assigned, you will direct the shopper back to their shopping cart with the updated values by using the PHP `header` function. This usually happens as quickly as the shopper submits the button and the page can load. If they did not reach your maximum stock, the updated shopping cart should appear nearly instantly:

```
else {
    header("Location: /cart.php");
}
```

Next, you close the case by issuing a `break`:

```
break;
```

Now your shopping cart has a method of updating the stock quantities of each item! Let's move on to the portion of your cart where you can remove individual items.

FIGURE 8.4:
cart.php file, maxi-
mum stock reached
while updating quantity

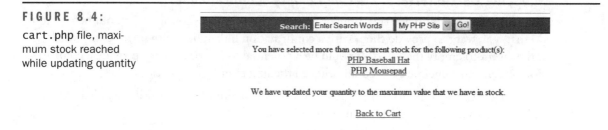

Shopping Cart Interface: *cart.php remove case*

This case allows a single product to be removed from the shopping cart. You achieve this by adding a hyperlink below the product quantity input field for each product in the shopping cart. The hyperlink contains the `case` name and the `product_id` to perform the `DELETE` query in MySQL and then immediately directs the shopper back to the shopping cart. This `case` should execute the query and immediately display the shopping cart as soon as the page reloads when the user clicks the Remove hyperlink below a product's quantity. Figure 8.5 shows the Remove hyperlink.

The following is the code for the `remove case`:

```
case "remove":
    $sql = mysql_query("DELETE FROM
                shopping_carts
                WHERE cart_identifier='$cart_id'
                AND product_id='{$_REQUEST['product_id']}'");
    header("Location: /cart.php");

break;
```

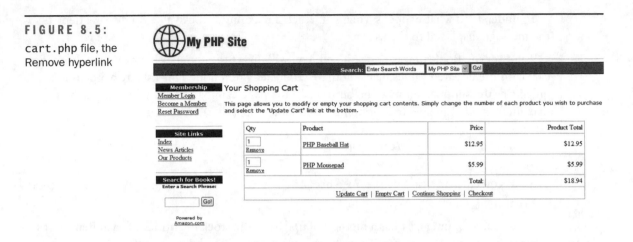

Shopping Cart Interface: *cart.php empty_confirm case*

You will offer the ability for the shopper to empty their entire shopping cart, but before you do that, you want to provide them with a confirmation link and give them a Yes or No choice if they want to empty their cart. It could be a potential loss if you do not provide a confirmation screen and someone accidentally clicked the link to empty their cart.

This case simply links to the empty case, which will empty their cart if they click the Yes link or link to the cart.php file if they choose No.

Figure 8.6 shows the confirmation screen.

The following is the code for the empty_confirm case:

```
case "empty_confirm":
   myheader("Shopping Cart");
     echo "<center>Are you sure ".
         "you want to empty your cart?<br />".
         "<a href=\"/cart.php?req=empty\">Yes</a>".
         " | ".
         "<a href=\"/cart.php\">No</a></center>";
     footer();

   break;
```

Search: Enter Search Words   My PHP Site   Go!

Are you sure you want to empty your cart?
Yes | No

Shopping Cart Interface: *cart.php empty case*

This case utilizes the empty_cart function inside your shopping cart class and deletes all of the affected rows for the shopping cart IDs this shopper has been assigned. When this case executes, the shopper will see a message on the page.

Figure 8.7 shows the message displayed after the cart has been emptied.

The following shows the code for the empty case:

```
case "empty":
    myheader("Shopping Cart");
    $cart->empty_cart();
    echo "<center>Your cart has been emptied!</center>";
    footer();
break;
```

FIGURE 8.7:
cart.php file, cart
emptied message

Search: Enter Search Words | My PHP Site | Go!

Your cart has been emptied!

Building the Shopping Cart Interface: *checkout.php*

At this point, you have your shopping cart set up to allow your customers to add products to, update, delete, and empty their shopping cart. The last step to prepare for the payment system you will build in the next chapter is to create a checkout page that performs a sanity check on your product stock and then provides users with a payment method. Listing 8.6 shows the shopping cart checkout.php script.

Listing 8.6 **Shopping Cart *checkout.php* Script**

```php
<?php
include $_SERVER['DOCUMENT_ROOT'].
    '/layout.php';

$cart = &new ShoppingCart;
$cart_id = $cart->get_cart_id();

myheader("Confirm Order");

// Sanity check!
if($cart_id){
    $num_items - mysql_result(mysql_query("SELECT
                COUNT(*) as items
                FROM shopping_carts
                WHERE cart_identifier='$cart_id'"),0);
```

```php
        if($num_items == 0){
            echo "<center>Your Shopping Cart is Empty!</center>";
            footer();
            exit();
        }
    } else {
        echo "<center>Your Shopping Cart is Empty!</center>";
        footer();
        exit;
    }

    // Get cart conents
    $sql = mysql_query("SELECT * FROM shopping_carts
                        WHERE cart_identifier='$cart_id'");

    while($row = mysql_fetch_array($sql)){
        // Get product stock
        $stock_sql = mysql_query("SELECT * FROM shopping_products
                                  WHERE product_id = '{$row['product_id']}'");

        // Determine if cart stock is higher than product
        // stock, if so, adjust cart and build error
        // message.

        while($stock = mysql_fetch_array($stock_sql)){
            if($stock['product_qty'] < $row['product_qty']){

                // stock is lower than requested
                // perform query to update cart
                mysql_query("UPDATE shopping_carts
                             SET product_qty = '{$stock['product_qty']}'
                             WHERE product_id = '{$row['product_id']}'
                             AND cart_identifier = '$cart_id'");

                // create $error and build products error array
                $error = TRUE;
                $products[$row[product_id]] = stripslashes($row[product_title]);
            }
        }
    }
    if($error){
        // $error is present, so show message
        echo "<center>You have selected more ".
             "than our current stock for the following ".
             "product(s): <br />";

        while(list($product_id, $product_name) = each($products)){
            echo "<a href=\"/products.php?req=view&product_id=$product_id\">".
                 "$product_name</a><br />";
        }
```

```
        echo "<br />";
        echo "We have updated your quantity to the maximum ".
            "value that we have in stock.</center><br />";
        echo "<center><a href=\"/cart.php\">Back to Cart</a></center>";

        // Display footer
        footer();

        // Exit script to prevent
        // the rest of the script showing
        exit();
}

// No errors present here, so show the
// order confirmation page.
?>

<p><font size="4" face="Verdana, Arial, Helvetica, sans-serif">
Please Confirm Your Order
</font></p>
<p><font size="2" face="Verdana, Arial, Helvetica, sans-serif">
Please verify your shopping cart contents before proceeding to the payment
pages.</font></p>
<table width="90%" border="1" cellspacing="0" cellpadding="4" align="center">
<tr>
<td>Qty</td>
<td>Product</td>
<td align="right">Price</td>
<td align="right">Product Total</td>
</tr>

<?php
$total = mysql_result(mysql_query("SELECT
        sum(product_qty * product_price) AS subtotal
        FROM shopping_carts
        WHERE cart_identifier='$cart_id'"),0);
$total = number_format($total, 2);

$sql = mysql_query("SELECT * FROM shopping_carts
        WHERE cart_identifier='$cart_id'") or die (mysql_error());

while($row = mysql_fetch array($sql)){
    $product_total = number_format(($row[product_qty] * $row[product_price]),2);
    echo "<tr>".
        "<td>".
        "$row[product_qty]".
        "<br /><font size=\"2\">".
        "</td>".
        "<td><a href=\"/products.php?req=view&product_id=$row[product_id]\">"
        .stripslashes($row[product_title]).
        "</a></td>".
```

```
            "<td align=\"right\">\$".number_format($row[product_price],2)."</td>".
            "<td align=\"right\">\$$product_total</td>".
            "</tr>";
}
?>
<tr>
<td colspan="2"> </td>
<td align="right">Total:</td>
<td align="right">$<?=$total?></td>
</tr>
<tr>
<td colspan="4" align="center">
<a href="/cart.php">Back to Cart</a>
 | 
<a href="/products.php">Continue Shopping</a>
 | 
<a href="/payment.php">Submit Payment</a>
</td>
</tr>
</table>
<?php
footer();
?>
```

I will break this script down into parts. The first portion of the script includes your layout, initializes the ShoppingCart class, and then includes the custom myheader function from the layout.php file:

```
<?php
include $_SERVER['DOCUMENT_ROOT'].
    '/layout.php';

$cart = &new ShoppingCart;
$cart_id = $cart->get_cart_id();

myheader("Confirm Order");
```

I call this next part of the code a "sanity check" because you will check one last time for the amount of stock you have in your inventory and compare it to the number of products this customer is requesting. This will prevent you from overselling the item. This code is almost identical to the update case in the cart.php file except you will not show the HTML forms like you did with the cart.php. Instead, you will show static values for the product quantities, and you will also not show the Remove hyperlinks and Update Cart hyperlink at the bottom of the page:

```
// Sanity check!
if($cart_id){
    $num_items = mysql_result(mysql_query("SELECT
```

```
                        COUNT(*) as items
                        FROM shopping_carts
                        WHERE cart_identifier='$cart_id'"),0);
      if($num_items == 0){
         echo "<center>Your Shopping Cart is Empty!</center>";
         footer();
         exit();
      }
   } else {
      echo "<center>Your Shopping Cart is Empty!</center>";
      footer();
      exit;
   }

   // Get cart conents
   $sql = mysql_query("SELECT * FROM shopping_carts
                       WHERE cart_identifier='$cart_id'");

   while($row = mysql_fetch_array($sql)){
      // Get product stock
      $stock_sql = mysql_query("SELECT * FROM shopping_products
                                WHERE product_id = '{$row['product_id']}'");

      // Determine if cart stock is higher than product
      // stock, if so, adjust cart and build error
      // message.

      while($stock = mysql_fetch_array($stock_sql)){
         if($stock['product_qty'] < $row['product_qty']){

            // stock is lower than requested
            // perform query to update cart
            mysql_query("UPDATE shopping_carts
                         SET product_qty = '{$stock['product_qty']}'
                         WHERE product_id = '{$row['product_id']}'
                         AND cart_identifier = '$cart_id'");

            // create $error and build products error array
            $error = TRUE;
            $products[$row[product_id]] = stripslashes($row[product_title]);
         }
      }
   }
   if($error){
      // $error is present, so show message
      echo "<center>You have selected more ".
           "than our current stock for the following ".
```

```
              "product(s): <br />";

       while(list($product_id, $product_name) = each($products)){
           echo "<a href=\"/products.php?req=view&product_id=$product_id\">".
                "$product_name</a><br />";
       }

       echo "<br />";
       echo "We have updated your quantity to the maximum ".
            "value that we have in stock.</center><br />";
       echo "<center><a href=\"/cart.php\">Back to Cart</a></center>";

       // Display footer
       footer();

       // Exit script to prevent
       // the rest of the script showing
       exit();
   }

   // No errors present here, so show the
   // order confirmation page.
   ?>
```

From this point forward, you will alter the HTML output from the way your cart.php file displays it. Remove the HTML forms that allow changes to be made to the cart:

```
<p><font size="4" face="Verdana, Arial, Helvetica, sans-serif">
Please Confirm Your Order
</font></p>
<p><font size="2" face="Verdana, Arial, Helvetica, sans-serif">
Please verify your shopping cart contents before proceeding to the payment
pages.</font></p>
<table width="90%" border="1" cellspacing="0" cellpadding="4" align="center">
<tr>
<td>Qty</td>
<td>Product</td>
<td align="right">Price</td>
<td align="right">Product Total</td>
</tr>

<?php
$total = mysql_result(mysql_query("SELECT
        sum(product_qty * product_price) AS subtotal
        FROM shopping_carts
        WHERE cart_identifier='$cart_id'"),0);
$total = number_format($total, 2);
```

```
$sql = mysql_query("SELECT * FROM shopping_carts
            WHERE cart_identifier='$cart_id'") or die (mysql_error());

while($row = mysql_fetch_array($sql)){
    $product_total = number_format(($row[product_qty] * $row[product_price]),2);
     echo "<tr>".
            "<td>".
            "$row[product_qty]".
            "<br /><font size=\"2\">".
            "</td>".
            "<td><a href=\"/products.php?req=view&product_id=$row[product_id]\">"
            .stripslashes($row[product_title]).
            "</a></td>".
            "<td align=\"right\">\$".number_format($row[product_price],2)."</td>".
            "<td align=\"right\">\$$product_total</td>".
            "</tr>";
}
?>
<tr>
<td colspan="2"> </td>
<td align="right">Total:</td>
<td align="right">$<?=$total?></td>
</tr>
```

You also want to provide a hyperlink back to the shopping cart and product pages in the event the customer changes their mind and decides to keep shopping. The other hyperlink on this page, Submit Payment, will take the customer to the payment options you will create in the next chapter:

```
<tr>
<td colspan="4" align="center">
<a href="/cart.php">Back to Cart</a>
 | 
<a href="/products.php">Continue Shopping</a>
 | 
<a href="/payment.php">Submit Payment</a>
</td>
</tr>
</table>
<?php
footer();
?>
```

Now your cart is all ready to allow your customers to populate it with the products they want to purchase, to update it, and to modify it. Furthermore, they will be able to go to the checkout confirmation pages where you will perform a sanity check on the stock for your product inventory.

Providing a Shopping Cart Side Box

You want to provide a method to notify the shopper of how many items are in their shopping cart and provide a link to the cart in the event that they get distracted by other areas of your site while shopping. You can do this by creating a box and displaying it in the right column away from your hyperlinks and features in the left column of the site.

Create a file named box_shopping_cart.php in your website document root boxes directory. Listing 8.7 shows the code.

Listing 8.7   Shopping Cart Box

```php
<?php
$cart = &new ShoppingCart;
$cart_id = $cart->get_cart_id();

if($cart_id){
    $num_items = mysql_result(mysql_query("SELECT
                        COUNT(*) as items
                        FROM shopping_carts
                        WHERE cart_identifier='$cart_id'"),0);
    if($num_items > 0){
?>

<table width="160" border="0" cellspacing="0" cellpadding="0">
<tr bgcolor="#000066">
<td width="5" height="10"><font color="#FFFFFF"> </font></td>
<td width="150">
<div align="center">
<font color="#FFFFFF" size="2" face="Verdana, Arial, Helvetica, sans-serif">
<strong>Shopping Cart</strong></font>
</div>
</td>
<td width="5"> </td>
</tr>
<tr>
<td height="5"> </td>
<td align="left" valign="top">
<center>
<font size="2" face="Verdana, Arial, Helvetica, sans-serif">
<?=$num_items?> item(s) in cart!
</font>
</center>
<center><font size="1" face="Verdana, Arial, Helvetica, sans-serif">
<font size="1" face="Verdana, Arial, Helvetica, sans-serif">
<a href="/cart.php">View Cart!</a>
</font>
</center>
</td>
```

```
<td> </td>
</tr>
</table>
<hr size="1">

<?php
}
}
?>
```

I will break this code down to the important elements. First, you start PHP, initialize the shopping cart class, and get the shopper's cart ID:

```
<?php
$cart = &new ShoppingCart;
$cart_id = $cart->get_cart_id();
```

If the $cart_id exists, you perform a query to find out how many products are in the shopper's cart:

```
if($cart_id){
    $num_items = mysql_result(mysql_query("SELECT
                        COUNT(*) as items
                        FROM shopping_carts
                        WHERE cart_identifier='$cart_id'"),0);
```

If the number of products is greater than 0, you will display this box on the right column. Otherwise, you will not display anything to the shopper or website visitor because it is irrelevant that they see this box:

```
    if($num_items > 0){
?>
```

The rest of the code, with the exception of closing the IF statements, is a simple HTML-formatted table like you have created in previous chapters of this book. This box will contain a message saying *xx item(s) in cart* and provide a hyperlink to the user's cart.

Open the layout.php file and add this box into the right column under the footer function. I have made some minor modifications to my layout.php file to accommodate the right column. Here is the footer function code for my layout.php file:

```
<?php
}
function footer(){
?>
<!-- End Content and Begin Footer -->
    </td>
    <!-- Right Column Boxes and Links -->
    <td width="130" valign="top">
    <?php
```

```
        include $_SERVER['DOCUMENT_ROOT'].
            '/boxes/box_shopping_cart.php';
    ?>
    </td>
   <!-- End Right Column Boxes and Links -->
  </tr>
  <tr>
    <td> </td>
    <td> </td>
    <td width="130" nowrap>   </td>
  </tr>
</table>
</body>
</html>
<?php
}
?>
```

Figure 8.8 shows this box example.

FIGURE 8.8:

Shopping cart box

Testing Your Shopping Cart System

After you have completed the code in this chapter, let's test your shopping cart system. Follow these steps:

1. Open your web browser and go to the products.php page. You should see a page similar to Figure 8.9. Notice the product titles and form to add the product to the cart. Also, take notice that the box_shopping_cart.php file is not displayed in the right column.

2. Under the first product on the page, enter the value **25** into the input field and click the Add to Cart button. Take notice that the box_shopping_cart.php file is now displayed in the right column of the website. When the message is displayed saying *The product has been added to your cart*, click the View Cart hyperlink. You should now see the shopping cart depicted in Figure 8.10.

    Take special notice that the quantity was automatically adjusted to the maximum number of stock you have for this product: 19. The Product Total column and Total column should read $246.05.

FIGURE 8.9:

Products page

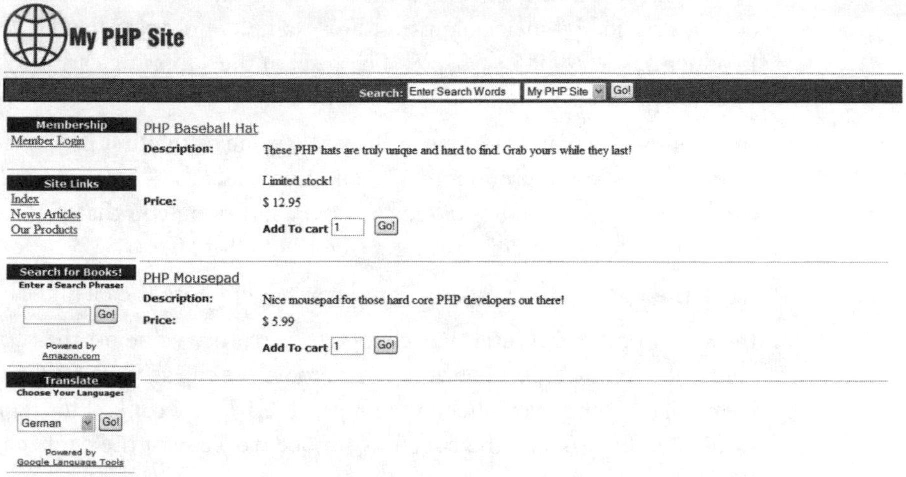

FIGURE 8.10:

Shopping cart interface

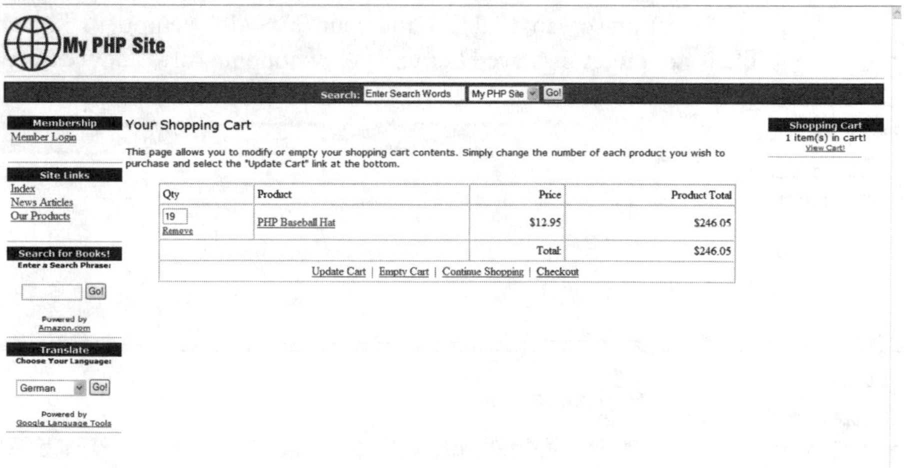

3. Click the Continue Shopping hyperlink at the bottom of the shopping cart and go back to the product page. For the same product you added earlier, add three more of this product to your cart. Once you click the View Cart link on the next page, you will see your shopping cart again. The quantity of this product should still be 19, which is the maximum number of stock you have for this product.

4. Click the Continue Shopping hyperlink at the bottom of the shopping cart and go back to the products page. Add five of the second product on the page to your cart and click the Add to Cart button. Once again, click the View Cart link on the confirmation page. Note

the Total value at the bottom of the shopping cart. It should be the sum of the two products multiplied by their quantities. For example, product 1 is $12.95 \times 19 = $246.05. Product 2 is $5.99 \times 5 = $29.95. The total of the shopping cart is $276.00, which is the total for product 1 and product 2 combined.

5. In the shopping cart interface, change the value of the first product to **5** and change the value of the second product to **110** and then click the Update Cart hyperlink at the bottom of the page. You should see a message notifying you that you have reached the maximum stock for the second product (see Figure 8.11).

6. Click the Back to Cart link on your browser and note the changes (see Figure 8.12).

7. In the shopping cart interface, change the quantity value for the second product to **0** and click the Update Cart hyperlink. You should see the second product disappear almost immediately when you clicked the Update Cart hyperlink. This happened because the value was set to 0, and the code in your `update case` of the `cart.php` file took care of this for you.

8. At the bottom of the shopping cart interface, click the Empty Cart hyperlink. On the confirmation screen, click Yes and your cart will be emptied. The `box_shopping_cart.php` file is no longer displayed because your shopping cart is now empty.

FIGURE 8.11:

Maximum stock
reached for product 2

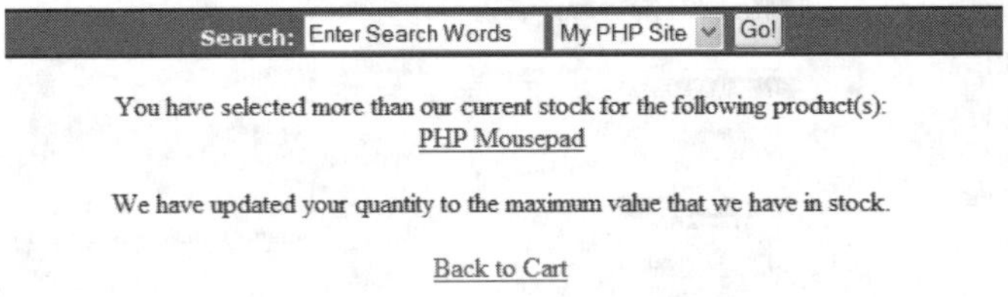

FIGURE 8.12:

Shopping cart interface
with updated values

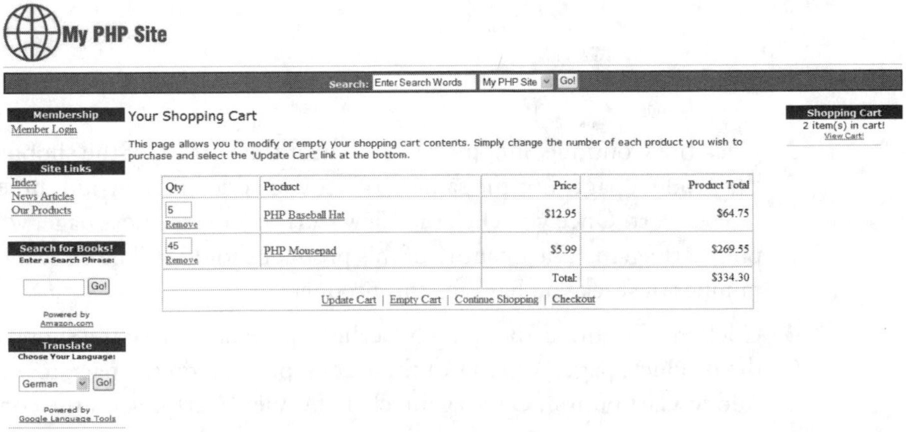

9. Go to your products page, add any quantity of a product, and then view your shopping cart. Close your web browser and then open it again to your site. If you have cookies enabled, you should see `box_shopping_cart.php` displayed. Click the View Cart link in the `box_shopping_cart.php` box and view your cart. This step will test the cookies to ensure they are working properly. If they are not working, then the shopping cart will not be linked to the shopper if they leave your site. This is a common problem for nearly all shopping carts that do not require a login system.

If everything is working as you intended, then you are on your way to making some money with your site! Every shopping cart system will need to be tailored to your own needs. By now, you should have enough knowledge of PHP to customize your cart to your requirements.

Creating a Products Catalog Hyperlink

The last task is to create the hyperlinks that will allow your shoppers to access the products catalog. In my `box_main_links.php` file, I simply added a link to `products.php`. Take a look at my `box_main_links.php` file:

```
<table width="160" border="0" cellspacing="0" cellpadding="0">
  <tr bgcolor="#000066">
    <td width="5" height="10"><font color="#FFFFFF"> </font></td>
    <td width="150">
    <div align="center">
    <font color="#FFFFFF" size="2" face="Verdana, Arial, Helvetica, sans-serif">
    <strong>Site Links</strong></font>
    </div>
    </td>
    <td width="5"> </td>
  </tr>
  <tr>
    <td height="5"> </td>
    <td align="left" valign="top">
<a href="/">Index</a><br />
<a href="/articles.php">News Articles</a><br />
<a href="/products.php">Our Products</a>
    </td>
    <td> </td>
  </tr>
  <tr>
    <td width="5" height="10"><font color="#FFFFFF"> </font></td>
    <td width="150"> </td>
    <td width="5"> </td>
  </tr>
</table>
<hr size="1">
```

When you are done modifying this file, the Our Products link should appear in the left column under the "Site Links" box.

What's Next?

In this chapter, you built a simple storefront followed by a complex shopping cart system that will keep your shoppers from getting too confused. You have controlled your stock and given your shoppers a method to store the products they want to purchase in their carts. Now it is time to actually sell the product. The shopping cart system is ready for you to check out, so you need to provide a method to perform credit card transactions on the Internet.

The next chapter covers what is required to get a merchant account and how to use merchant account gateways and APIs to send your shopper's credit card information to a gateway for processing and to receive a result for finishing the order process. The chapter also covers how to use a module for PHP to send and receive data to and from servers without being visible by the user.

CHAPTER 9

Processing Payments for Your Website

W hen it is time to move into processing payments for your website, you will find many solutions available. The Internet is constantly expanding, and e-commerce is still blooming with ways to earn money on the Internet. As a webmaster, you can take advantage of these opportunities by utilizing merchant account gateway Application Programming Interfaces (APIs) such as VeriSign or third-party payment solutions such as PayPal.

Chapter 8, "Creating a Shopping Cart System," left off at the billing pages. Your shopping cart system is ready to allow the customer to pay for their items and complete their shopping experience. It is up to you, the web developer, to determine how to obtain a customer's money and complete their order. This chapter discusses the differences between using a merchant account gateway API and using third-party payment solutions. It also shows you practical uses of each type of payment system.

Merchant Account Gateways vs. Third-Party Payment Solutions

The major goal I try to accomplish when selling products or services on the Internet is to project a professional, business-like appearance. The best method I can recommend is to utilize a merchant account gateway instead of a third-party payment solution. Why? Because the processing of the customer information remains on your website with a merchant account gateway compared to outside your site with PayPal or another third-party payment solution. There are plenty of pros and cons when trying to determine the best method to utilize. The following sections explore some of them.

What Is a Merchant Account Gateway?

A *merchant account gateway* is a service you can utilize to process billing information regarding a specific transaction with your customers. The customer information is compiled into a special format and sent through a back-end resource to the gateway. The gateway validates the information, processes it through a bank or financial institution, receives a response, and in turn generates a response to send back to the requesting site (you) while recording the transaction into your gateway account.

Merchant account gateways are growing rapidly in popularity, with more companies starting to offer them. You must have a valid merchant account through a financial institution to utilize a merchant account gateway. Some companies on the Internet offer a merchant account gateway in conjunction with a merchant account. Do not get the impression that you cannot get a merchant account because you do not have a business license, though. This myth is not true; however, you will have to dig a little when talking to the merchant account sales representatives. If you do not have a business license, ask about opening an account based on a sole proprietorship, meaning that you are opening the account in your name to do business.

Usually, when you set up a merchant account gateway, the gateway provider will list merchant accounts they partner with, and you can get special deals through them.

This chapter covers using VeriSign because it offers a free 30-day trial (demo) account that you do not need a merchant account to use. The following are some of the most popular merchant account gateway providers:

Gateway Provider	URL
VeriSign	`www.verisign.com/products/payment.html`
Authorize.Net	`www.authorize.net`
Cardservice International (LinkPoint)	`www.cardservice.com`

The previous list is a small group of the most popular gateways. You can find thousands of results by going to Google (`www.google.com`) and searching for *merchant account gateways*.

Merchant Account Gateway Pros

The following are some of the advantages of processing payments with a gateway:

- You do not have to redirect the customer to a different site to perform the billing.

- You project a more business-like appearance without losing the relationship between your business and the customer performing the transaction.

- You have more options when logging the transaction; by gathering the billing information on your site, you can log as much user input as you like.

- It is easier to set up recurring billing by altering the responses sent to the merchant account gateway for the transaction.

- The customer is not forced to create an account on a third-party site to process the payment.

- They have extremely fast processing! Usually it is quicker than three seconds from submission to retrieval of results.

Merchant Account Gateway Cons

Every solution has disadvantages; the following are some cons of a merchant account gateway:

- They are usually expensive to set up, about $300 in some cases.

- Monthly fees are not uncommon, sometimes up to $60 per month.

- An average of 2.5-percent transaction fees are deducted for the company that runs the gateway.

- It is not as easy to develop for them. Sometimes they do not offer PHP support; however, this is not a showstopper! Keep reading in this chapter to find out how to get around a lack of PHP support.

- You should utilize a Secure Sockets Layer (SSL) certificate and a Hypertext Transfer Protocol—Secure (HTTPS) website while gathering billing information from the customer. SSL certificates cost from $39 per year to $199 per year, depending on where you buy them.

TIP   You can purchase valid QuickSSL certificates from www.rackshack.net in quicker than 20 minutes for less than $50. This is extremely easy to do, and you do not have to go through the difficult process that most companies provide.

- If the gateway goes offline and your website is running, billing will fail. This causes customers to get frustrated and cancel their orders because they may think your system is not running properly and they lose trust in you.

What Is a Third-Party Payment Solution?

A third-party payment solution is a company that allows you to create virtual accounts with a company; it processes transactions on your behalf. These companies are growing in popularity since the advent of PayPal.

These companies have many different methods of allowing you to send your customers to their websites and process a transaction on your behalf. Once the transaction has cleared through their system, the company will credit the money to your virtual account, and you can transfer or spend the money how you desire from that point.

This chapter shows how to use PayPal because it is the most popular and commonly used third-party payment solution. However, the following are some of the other popular third-party payment solutions I have found (and used) on the Internet.

Third-Party Payment Solution	URL
PayPal	www.paypal.com
iBill	www.ibill.com
CCBill	www.ccbill.com
2CheckOut.com	www.2checkout.com

You can also find a complete list of these by searching the keywords *credit card processing* in the Google search engine.

Third-Party Payment Solution Pros

The following are some of the advantages of third-party payment solutions:

- They are usually easy to set up without a large fee up front.

- They usually have an easy-to-use interface.

- They allow you to transfer the money you make to your bank account at any time and allow you to pay other members with it (PayPal).

- They process the customers' billing information and provide records of the payments.

- They usually do not charge monthly fees.

Third-Party Payment Solution Cons

Even third-party payment solutions have some disadvantages:

- When your customer leaves your site to complete a purchase, they may lose a brand awareness of your site during the transaction. As a business, you should always try to eliminate the middleman, especially when dealing with money. Third-party payment solutions have a tendency to break this rule of thumb.

- They charge an average of 2.5-percent transaction fees. PayPal charges a different amount every transaction, sometimes up to 5 percent or more.

- Support staff is overloaded. Because these companies usually process multiple types of payments from a large quantity of users, you will usually get the runaround when trying to contact support.

- They could require more extensive planning on your part to determine how to properly check the customer out in your shopping cart system because the customer will depart your site while making the transaction.

What's the Major Difference?

There are many major differences between the two systems. Not only do you have to develop your systems differently, the control panels between a merchant account gateway and a third-party payment solution could differ greatly. Let's concentrate on the process of accepting customer payments through each of these solutions.

Figure 9.1 shows the processing of payments through your website with a merchant account gateway API.

The following are the steps of Figure 9.1:

1. The customer comes to your website and populates their shopping cart system with the products they want to purchase. Then they go to the checkout page, select the credit card payment method, and enter their billing information.

FIGURE 9.1:

Processing payments
through a merchant
account gateway

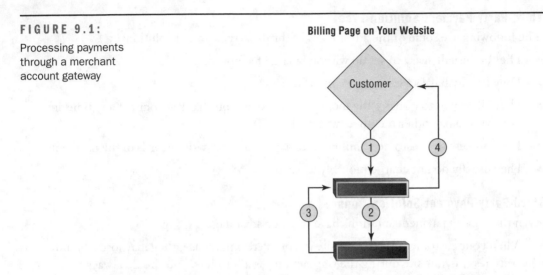

FIGURE 9.1:

Processing payments
through a merchant
account gateway

2. Your script will compile the information required and send the customer's billing information to the payment gateway for processing.

3. The payment gateway will send a response through the API to the binary that is on your server, and your script will decode the results and perform the proper checkout actions in your shopping cart system.

4. You present a custom response to the customer.

That looks pretty simple, doesn't it? The entire process takes usually less than three seconds to complete! During this entire process, your customer never leaves your website to process a payment somewhere else.

Figure 9.2 shows the third-party payment solution process.

FIGURE 9.2:

Processing payments
through a third-party
payment solution

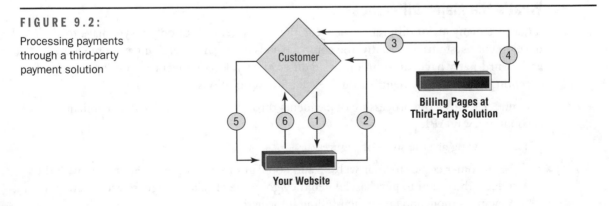

This is the process step by step:

1. The customer comes to your website and populates their shopping cart system with the products they want to purchase. When they go to the checkout page, they select a third-party payment solution for their payment method.

2. Your scripts will generate a special form and send it to the customer's web browser.

3. Upon receiving the form, the customer's web browser will be redirected to the third-party payment solution's billing pages, and the user will enter their billing information for processing.

4. The customer is still on the third-party website, and the results are displayed in the third-party payment processor.

5. The third-party payment processor provides a method for the customer to return to your website with a "token" key that you embedded into the form from step 2. Once your script receives this token, you process it immediately and check out the customer from the shopping cart.

6. You now send the final custom response to the customer's web browser.

As you may notice, the process of using a third-party payment solution is a lot more work for you as the developer and for the customer. Furthermore, this process generally takes longer to complete than a merchant account gateway takes.

Now that you have a better understanding of gateways and third-party payment solutions, you will begin developing for them.

Preparing Your Site for E-Commerce

Before you begin processing, you need to prepare your site by adding some new tables to your database. The first table you will create is for a special security measure called *tokens*, which you will create in your processing scripts. I will explain using tokens later; for now, you will just create the tables. Table 9.1 shows the structure for the shopping_cart_tokens table.

TABLE 9.1: Structure for shopping_cart_tokens Table

Field Name	Data Type	Length	Extra
cart_id	VARCHAR	255	Primary key
token	VARCHAR	100	

If you prefer the command line, you can use this query:

```
CREATE TABLE shopping_cart_tokens (
  cart_id varchar(255) NOT NULL default '',
  token varchar(100) NOT NULL default '',
  PRIMARY KEY  (cart_id)
) TYPE=MyISAM COMMENT='Tokens for Shopping Carts';
```

Next, you create another table to store the order information upon successful checkout. This table is named shopping_cart_orders (see Table 9.2).

TABLE 9.2: Structure for shopping_cart_orders Table

Field Name	Data Type	Length	Extra
orderid	MEDIUMINT	25	Primary key, auto increment
order_date	DATETIME		
token	VARCHAR	100	
products	TEXT		
total	FLOAT	0	
type	VARCHAR	25	
user_id	VARCHAR	10	

If you prefer the command line, you can use this query:

```
CREATE TABLE shopping_cart_orders (
  orderid mediumint(25) NOT NULL auto_increment,
  order_date datetime NOT NULL default '0000-00-00 00:00:00',
  token varchar(100) NOT NULL default '',
  products text NOT NULL,
  total float NOT NULL default '0',
  type varchar(25) NOT NULL default '',
  user_id varchar(10) NOT NULL default '',
  PRIMARY KEY  (orderid)
) TYPE=MyISAM COMMENT='Shopping Cart Orders';
```

That concludes the preparation for this chapter. Let's jump into processing some payments!

Creating the Payment Processing Scripts

In Chapter 8, "Creating a Shopping Cart System," you left your shopping cart system ready for the payment pages. This chapter covers two methods to process payments: VeriSign Payflow Pro payment services (with a payment gateway API) and PayPal (a third-party payment service).

The checkout page in the shopping cart performed one last sanity check, adjusted the customer's order as necessary, and gave them a link to make a payment. The link pointed to a script named `payment.php`, so you will create that script now.

Create a file in your document root named `payment.php`. This file will be a simple page that asks the customer which method of payment they would like to use. In this book, I cover two payment methods, so you will give hyperlinks to those payment methods in this script. If you are going to offer only one payment method in your shopping cart, you can bypass this page by altering the link in your shopping cart checkout page and pointing it to the relevant script you will create in this chapter.

The following is the code for the `payment.php` script:

```php
<?php
include $_SERVER['DOCUMENT_ROOT'].
    '/layout.php';

myheader("Select Payment Type");
echo "<center>Please choose your ".
    "payment method:<br />".
    "<a href=\"/creditcard.php\">".
    "Credit Card via our Secure Server</a><br />".
    "<a href=\"/paypal.php\">".
    "Pay using PayPal</a><br /></center>";
footer();
?>
```

When a user goes through your shopping cart system and confirms their order by clicking the Submit Payment hyperlink, they will see a page like Figure 9.3 depicts.

FIGURE 9.3:

Payment options page

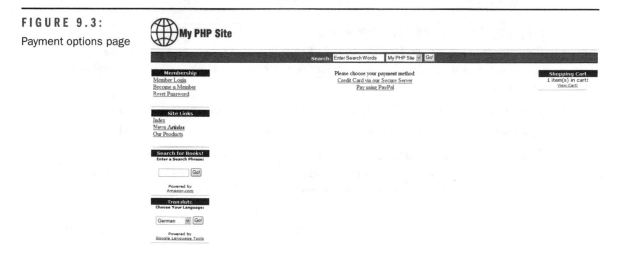

As you may notice, you will give an option to process payments via your secure server first, so the next section shows how to process credit cards with a payment gateway.

Processing Payments with VeriSign Payflow Pro

VeriSign has one of the best payment processing gateways available. VeriSign offers a gateway payment service called Payflow Pro that is fully loaded with all kinds of options including: the Payflow Pro Manager (PPM) control panel, Address Verification Service (AVS), recurring billing services, and much more. Additionally, VeriSign offers a 30-day trial account that you can enable in less than an hour. This is a perfect place for you to explore the developmental process for a payment services gateway!

WARNING   Before you begin processing any live payments on your website, you should obtain an SSL certificate for your website and run your processing scripts on your SSL website using HTTPS. If you are using virtual web hosting, contact your web hosting provider and obtain an SSL certificate. If you are using your own server, you can obtain an SSL certificate for cheap at www.rackshack.net in less than 20 minutes.

Getting Your Payflow Pro Demo Account

Begin the process of setting up your payment gateway by going to www.verisign.com/products/payflow/pro/ and signing up for a trial account. While viewing this page, you should see a Free Payment Trial Account link. Click this link, and complete the signup process. Once you have completed the signup process, you will receive an e-mail notifying you of the signup and giving you some links to the PPM control panel. The Uniform Resource Locator (URL) I received was https://manager.verisign.com/login/login.cfm?partner=VeriSign.

Preparing Your System for Payflow Pro

Before you begin coding for the Payflow Pro payment services, you need to set up your web server for its system. This is easy and does not require any compilations or restarting. Follow these steps:

1. First, log in to the PPM with the username and password you created during signup.

2. Once you have logged in, click the Downloads tab at the top of the PPM.

3. Under the Documentation section, download the developer guide to your hard drive. Click the Payflow Pro Developers Guide–Zipped PDF link. This is important because you will learn how to use a developer guide in this chapter.

4. Under the Payflow Pro Software Development Kit (SDK) section, download the appropriate SDK for your system. I will cover how to use how to install the Windows SDK in this chapter; however, the Linux installation is not much different. If you are a Linux user,

click the Linux–libc6 / glibc2 / ELF kernels 2.0.36 and Above link (or the one called something similar). If you are a Windows user, click the Windows NT 4.0 or Windows 2000 link.

5. Depending on which file you downloaded in the previous step, extract these files onto your web server. Do not put them in your website's document root because it is not secure to do so. Put them somewhere on your system that the public cannot access through their web browser. On my Windows system, I put them in `d:\sites\sybex\win32` whereas my document root is `d:\sites\sybex\public_html`.

Believe it or not, those are all of the prerequisites for configuring your system to develop your scripts to use Payflow Pro.

You need the files you downloaded in the previous steps to utilize Payflow Pro. The main files in the SDK consist of a binary file that will perform the transaction and return the results and a certificate file that is required for the binary file to authenticate to the gateway. These files really have nothing to do with PHP, but using some PHP system commands, you will call these files, pass the arguments required to them, and capture the output.

Before you go any further, you should also understand that PHP supports Payflow Pro through a special module that you can compile during installation. However, because your web hosting provider probably does not have the Payflow Pro support modules enabled, I cover how to use this payment service without them. By giving you the examples in this chapter, you should be able to figure out how to code for any payment gateway, not just VeriSign.

Understanding the Gateway and API Documentation

Each payment processing gateway has some sort of developer guide associated with its documentation. In the previous section, you downloaded the Payflow Pro developer guide from the PPM. If you have never seen this type of documentation before, it could be difficult to understand. Basically, these guides tell a developer how to determine where, how, and what information to send to the payment gateway. Additionally, a good developer guide will list the required data to send and give you a list of response codes.

After analyzing the Payflow Pro developer guide, you can determine how to develop your scripts for the results you will retrieve. Looking through the documentation, you should notice that you will have to develop your scripts to execute a binary file with arguments such as the credit card numbers, your gateway username, and your gateway password in a URL-encoded format. By executing this binary file, you will be able to retrieve a result, usually in a URL-encoded format such as this: `variable=value&variable2=value&variable3=value`.

Do not worry; I will cover this in depth when it is time to start processing the information through the gateway.

VeriSign Payflow Pro Payment Processing Scripts

The first script you will create is named `creditcard.php`. The `payment.php` page links to it when the user clicks the Credit Card via Our Secure Server hyperlink. This script will gather the required billing information from the customer, send it to the VeriSign Payflow Pro gateway for processing, retrieve a result from the gateway, and redirect the user to your `ordercomplete.php` script according to the results.

Before you begin with this script, I have created a PHP class file that takes care of the hard work involved in creating a billing information form. This class is the payment forms class, and you can download it at `www.phpfreaks.com/script/view/209.php`. Download this class file, and extract it into your website document root under the `classes` directory.

Next, you will create the Hypertext Markup Language (HTML) form that will gather the customer billing information. Create a new HTML file named `payment_form.html`, and place it in `html/payment` under your website document root.

This HTML page will utilize embedded PHP with the functions inside the payment forms class to generate drop-down menus for dates, states, and countries. Listing 9.1 shows this HTML form.

Listing 9.1   Billing Information Form

```
<div align="center">
<font size="4" face="Verdana, Arial, Helvetica, sans-serif">Please
  Enter Your Billing Information </font>
</div>
<form method="post" action="/creditcard.php">
  <table width="50%" border="1" align="center" cellpadding="4" cellspacing="0">
    <tr>
      <td width="18%">Order Total</td>
      <td width="82%">$<?=$total?>
      </td>
    </tr>
    <tr>
      <td nowrap>Name on Credit Card</td>
      <td><input name="name" type="text"></td>
    </tr>
    <tr>
      <td>Credit Card Number</td>
      <td><input name="cardnumber" type="text"></td>
    </tr>
    <tr>
      <td>CCV2 Number</td>
      <td><input name="ccv2" type="text" id="ccv2" size="6"></td>
    </tr>
    <tr>
      <td>Expiration Date</td>
```

```
        <td>
          <?=$ccform->month_select($month);?>
          /
          <?=$ccform->year_select($year);?>
        </td>
      </tr>
      <tr>
        <td>Street Address</td>
        <td><input name="street" type="text"></td>
      </tr>
      <tr>
        <td>City</td>
        <td><input name="city" type="text"></td>
      </tr>
      <tr>
        <td>State</td>
        <td>
          <?=$ccform->state_select($state);?>
        </td>
      </tr>
      <tr>
        <td>Zip Code</td>
        <td><input name="zip" type="text" size="6"></td>
      </tr>
      <tr>
        <td>Country</td>
        <td>
          <?=$ccform->country_select($country);?>
        </td>
      </tr>
      <tr>
        <td> </td>
        <td><input name="req" type="hidden" value="process">
        <input type="submit" name="Submit" value="Submit Payment!"></td>
      </tr>
    </table>
  </form>
  </body>
  </html>
```

Next, you will create the script that will utilize the previous HTML form and process your payments using the gateway. Create a new file inside your website document root, and name it creditcard.php. Listing 9.2 shows the script, which I will explain in further detail.

Listing 9.2   *creditcard.php* **Processing Script**

```
<?php
include $_SERVER['DOCUMENT_ROOT'].
    '/layout.php';
```

```php
$cart = &new ShoppingCart;
$cart_id = $cart->get_cart_id();

switch($_REQUEST['req']){
   default:
   myheader("Payment Information");

   include $_SERVER['DOCUMENT_ROOT'].
      '/classes/clsCCForms.php';

   // Get shopping cart total.
   $total = mysql_result(mysql_query("SELECT
                        sum(product_qty * product_price) AS subtotal
                        FROM shopping_carts
                        WHERE cart_identifier='$cart_id'"),0);
   $total = number_format($total, 2);

   // Credit Card Forms Class by phpfreak
   $ccform = &new CCForms;
   include $_SERVER['DOCUMENT_ROOT'].
      '/html/payment/payment_form.html';

   break;

   case "process":
      stripslashes(extract($_POST));

      $total = mysql_result(mysql_query("SELECT
                     sum(product_qty * product_price) AS subtotal
                     FROM shopping_carts
                     WHERE cart_identifier='$cart_id'"),0);
      $total = number_format($total, 2);

      $expdate = $month.substr($year, 2, 2);

      $pfpro_path = "d:\sites\sybex\win32\bin\pfpro.exe";
      $params = "TRXTYPE=S&TENDER=C".
               "&PWD=XXXXXXXX&USER=XXXXXXXX".
               "&PARTNER=VeriSign".
               "&ACCT=$cardnumber&CCV2=$ccv2".
               "&EXPDATE=$expdate&AMT=$total".
               "&NAME=$name&STREET=$street".
               "&ZIP=$zip";
      putenv("PFPRO_CERT_PATH=d:\sites\sybex\win32\certs");
      $transaction = exec($pfpro_path.'
                        test-payflow.verisign.com 443
                        "'.$params.'" 30');

      // Convert the results into an array
      $tmp_results = explode('&', $transaction);
```

```php
        foreach($tmp_results AS $tmp_result){
            $tmp = explode('=', $tmp_result);
            $result[$tmp[0]] = $tmp[1];
        }
        // Debug: Uncomment lines below
        // to see $result array

        // echo "<pre>";
        // print_r($result);
        // echo "</pre>";
        // exit();

        switch($result[RESULT]){
            case "0":
                // Generate token
                $token = md5(uniqid(rand(),1));

                // Insert token into DB
                $token_check = mysql_result(mysql_query("SELECT COUNT(*)
                                FROM shopping_cart_tokens
                                WHERE cart_id='$cart_id'"),0);

                if($token_check == 0){
                   mysql_query("INSERT INTO shopping_cart_tokens
                         (cart_id, token)
                         VALUES ('$cart_id', '$token')");
                } else {
                   mysql_query("UPDATE shopping_cart_tokens
                         SET token='$token'
                         WHERE cart_id='$cart_id'");
                }

                // Redirect user to ordercomplete.php
                header("Location: /ordercomplete.php?req=success&t=$token");
            break;

            default:
                myheader("Transaction Error");
                echo "There has been a problem with your transaction. ".
                     "You have not been charged for this order.<br />".
                     "Please see below:<br />".
                     "Results: $result[RESPMSG]<br />".
                     "Reference Number: $result[PNREF]<br />";
            break;
        }
    break;
}
footer();
?>
```

The first portion of this script should be pretty standard to you by now. You start the PHP engine, include your required files, and then initialize the switch for the script. Because this script is related to your shopping cart system, you utilize the ShoppingCart class and get the cart identifier:

```php
<?php
include $_SERVER['DOCUMENT_ROOT'].
    '/layout.php';

$cart = &new ShoppingCart;
$cart_id = $cart->get_cart_id();


switch($_REQUEST['req']){
```

The default case includes the payment forms class (clsCCForms.php) that you downloaded earlier and then performs a query to get the total price of everything in the customer's shopping cart. After you initialize the payment forms class, you include the payment_form.html file.

NOTE I show the default case in this switch first. This is to show you that even though the PHP documentation shows the default case last, you can still use it in the first position.

The following is the default case:

```php
default:
myheader("Payment Information");

include $_SERVER['DOCUMENT_ROOT'].
    '/classes/clsCCForms.php';

// Get shopping cart total.
$total = mysql_result(mysql_query("SELECT
                        sum(product_qty * product_price) AS subtotal
                        FROM shopping_carts
                        WHERE cart_identifier='$cart_id'"),0);
$total = number_format($total, 2);

// Credit Card Forms Class by phpfreak
$ccform = &new CCForms;
include $_SERVER['DOCUMENT_ROOT'].
    '/html/payment/payment_form.html';

break;
```

The form in the `default case` will post the user inputs to the `process case`. Now you get to figure out how to use that Payflow Pro gateway! Like always, I will break this `case` down into smaller portions:

```
case "process":
```

First, you extract the `$_POST` values into simple variables. Remember, when you use `extract`, the key in an array becomes the variable name, and the value is assigned to it. For example, `$_POST['myvar'] = "test"` would become `$myvar = "test"`:

```
stripslashes(extract($_POST));
```

Second, for security purposes, you never want to allow the total to be obtained by input from the HTML form. Sooner or later, someone will try to alter their form posts and even alter the prices of their shopping carts; therefore, you always recalculate after the form has been submitted:

```
$total = mysql_result(mysql_query("SELECT
                sum(product_qty * product_price) AS subtotal
                FROM shopping_carts
                WHERE cart_identifier='$cart_id'"),0);
$total = number_format($total, 2);
```

VeriSign requires the credit card expiration date to be formatted as `MMYY`, and in my payment forms class the output of the year is `YYYY`. To compensate for the requirements of Payflow Pro, you combine the `$month` and `$year` values and use the substring (`substr`) PHP function to chop off the first two numbers of the year to make a variable named `$expdate`. To simplify the explanation, the expiration date of January 2004 would be `0104` after you have corrected it with this code:

```
$expdate = $month.substr($year, 2, 2);
```

Now you will dig into the Payflow Pro processing. You will define some variables that you will pass into the PHP exec function, which will execute system commands, such as executables, with the arguments you pass into it. Using the `exec` function is similar to typing into a DOS or shell prompt.

NOTE For this example, you will assign variables to each element of the `exec` argument. If you choose, you could create one simple string and execute it with all of the variables in Table 9.3.

The first variable you will define is the path to the Payflow Pro executable (`pfpro.exe`) file:

```
$pfpro_path = "d:\sites\sybex\win32\bin\pfpro.exe";
```

The next variable you will create is the querystring of information about the user and your Payflow Pro account. Table 9.3 explains the querystring.

TABLE 9.3: Querystring Variables

Variable	Value	Purpose
TRXTYPE	S	The transaction type. Use S for sale.
PWD	XXXXXXXX	Your Payflow Pro password.
USER	XXXXXXXX	Your Payflow Pro username or store name.
Partner	VeriSign	Required! Demo accounts use VeriSign.
ACCT	$cardnumber	Credit card number. You obtained this by extracting the $_POST array from the billing information form.
CCV2	$ccv2	Credit card verification number obtained from the billing information form.
EXPDATE	$expdate	Expiration date. Previously defined in this script.
AMT	$total	Order total price. Previously obtained in this script.
NAME	$name	Name on credit card from billing information form.
STREET	$street	Street address from billing information form.
ZIP	$zip	ZIP code from billing information form.

The following shows the querystring:

```
$params = "TRXTYPE=S&TENDER=C".
          "&PWD=XXXXXXXX&USER=XXXXXXXX".
          "&PARTNER=VeriSign".
          "&ACCT=$cardnumber&CCV2=$ccv2".
          "&EXPDATE=$expdate&AMT=$total".
          "&NAME=$name&STREET=$street".
          "&ZIP=$zip";
```

Next, you have to notify your system where the Payflow Pro certificate file is located. You downloaded this file in the SDK during the "Preparing Your System for Payflow Pro" section of this chapter. When I extracted the SDK, the file was located at d:\sites\sybex\win32\certs. Using the PHP putenv function, you can put the required PFPRO_CERT into your system environment variable path:

```
putenv("PFPRO_CERT_PATH=d:\sites\sybex\win32\certs");
```

Now you will execute the Payflow Pro binary with all of the information you have gathered. Look at the usage of the following exec function. You will assign a variable $transaction to it. All of the output from the execution of the binary will be assigned to the $transaction variable, and from there you can figure out how to use it:

```
$transaction = exec($pfpro_path.'
                test-payflow.verisign.com 443
                "'.$params.'" 30');
```

This exec function is executing a command line like this:

```
d:\sites\sybex\win32\bin\pfpro.exe test-payflow.verisign.com 443 [PARAMS] 30
```

NOTE   Notice the 30 after PARAMS. This is the number of seconds to allow the binary file to wait before it times out if no response is available from the gateway. Do not set this too high or your PHP script may time out and the user may click away from the page; however, do not set this too low or the script may not receive a response from the gateway. Fifteen to thirty seconds is sufficient.

Now you have the output assigned to the $transaction string. This output is in the format of a querystring, as mentioned earlier. With this string, you can break it into an array using the explode function. The explode function accepts an argument and a string. It will search for the argument inside of the string and create a new array key each time it finds a match for the argument passed to it.

If you were to run your transaction script right now and echo the $transaction, you would see something like this:

```
RESULT=0&PNREF=V64A31660131&RESPMSG=Approved&AUTHCODE=023PNI&AVSADDR=X&AVSZIP=
X&IAVS=X
```

The previous result will do you no good until you can break it apart. Break each element into an array using the & argument:

```
// Convert the results into an array
$tmp_results = explode('&', $transaction);
```

The output of the $tmp_results array using print_r and preformatted HTML tags would be as follows:

```
Array
(
    [0] => RESULT=0
    [1] => PNREF=V64A31660131
    [2] => RESPMSG=Approved
    [3] => AUTHCODE=023PNI
    [4] => AVSADDR=X
    [5] => AVSZIP=X
    [6] => IAVS=X
)
```

Now that you have $tmp_results in an array, you still do not have exactly what you need to best determine how to handle the transaction results. Let's break this array down one more time using explode on the = argument:

```
foreach($tmp_results AS $tmp_result){
    $tmp = explode('=', $tmp_result);
    $result[$tmp[0]] = $tmp[1];
}
```

The output of the `$result` array you generated in the previous code would look like this:

```
Array
(
    [RESULT] => 0
    [PNREF] => V64A31660131
    [RESPMSG] => Approved
    [AUTHCODE] => 023PNI
    [AVSADDR] => X
    [AVSZIP] => X
    [IAVS] => X
)
```

Now you have something with which to work!

If you would like to debug your arrays at any time, you can uncomment the following code to see output similar to the previous examples:

```
// Debug: Uncomment lines below
// to see $result array

// echo "<pre>";
// print_r($result);
// echo "</pre>";
// exit();
```

After you have processed the return from `$transaction`, you can use a `switch` on the value of `$result[RESULT]` to redirect the customer to the desired results based on the success or failure of the transaction:

```
switch($result[RESULT]){
```

The first case is a successful transaction because the value of `$result[RESULT]` is 0. Check the Payflow Pro developer guide to see what other values may be assigned to the RESULT. For now, you really only care about 0 because for anything else you will display the other array values and tell the customer their transaction has failed:

```
case "0":
```

Okay, you are inside the successful transaction `case` now. Before you direct the customer to a shopping cart checkout page where you record the order and empty their cart, you will add some security to this transaction. This prevents anyone with an active shopping cart on your site to find your `ordercomplete.php` script and check out by accident.

First, you use the `md5`, `uniqid`, and `rand` functions to generate an unpredictable and difficult-to-reproduce unique ID. You assign this value to the `$token` variable:

```
// Generate token
$token = md5(uniqid(rand(),1));
```

Second, you check and see if the `$cart_id` is already in your `shopping_cart_tokens` table. If it is, you update the row with the new `$token`; if it is not, you insert a new row. This check allows your users to use the same shopping cart identifier for multiple purchases:

```
// Insert token into DB
$token_check = mysql_result(mysql_query("SELECT COUNT(*)
                    FROM shopping_cart_tokens
                            WHERE cart_id='$cart_id'"),0);

if($token_check == 0){
   mysql_query("INSERT INTO shopping_cart_tokens
        (cart_id, token)
        VALUES ('$cart_id', '$token')");
} else {
   mysql_query("UPDATE shopping_cart_tokens
            SET token='$token'
                    WHERE cart_id='$cart_id'");
}
```

After you have the `$token` generated and stored properly, you redirect the customer to the `ordercomplete.php` script, which you will develop later in this chapter:

```
// Redirect user to ordercomplete.php
header("Location: /ordercomplete.php?req=success&t=$token");
break;
```

The `default case` is for any results other than 0 on the `$result[RESULT]` values. By using the method shown here, you can eliminate long code by simply showing `$result[RESPMSG]`, which is the response message from the gateway, and giving the customer the PNREF code, which is the transaction ID stored in the PPM:

```
default:
   myheader("Transaction Error");
   echo "There has been a problem with your transaction. ".
        "You have not been charged for this order.<br />".
        "Please see below:<br />".
        "Results: $result[RESPMSG]<br />".
        "Reference Number: $result[PNREF]<br />";
break;
```

The rest of this script is cleanup from the open switches and displays the custom `footer` function:

```
   }
   break;
}
footer();
?>
```

If you are up to speed now, then congratulations! You are now processing payments with a gateway! This example is as simple as possible to describe the basics of this process. I recommend you put extra-heavy error checking in your billing pages. Furthermore, I recommend you use PHP to validate the information to the payment gateway because web browsers give your users the ability to disable JavaScript; therefore, the information may be processed without any error checking and could result in a declined transaction. When a customer gets a "declined" message from a gateway, and you could have prevented it by error checking, then you have just potentially lost money. So, be smart!

You will break apart from this script now and develop the script to use PayPal. After you are done with the PayPal script, you will pick up where you left off and develop the order-complete.php script.

Processing Payments with PayPal

PayPal offers a simple method to accept payments for orders on your website, known as the Buy Now buttons. With some creative thinking, you can utilize the Buy Now buttons and manipulate them to fit your needs.

A common thought about the Buy Now buttons is that you have to generate them from the PayPal website and then copy and paste the code into your website; however, this is not true. You will create a script that will generate the required information and automatically send the customer to the PayPal payment pages.

The methods you will use in this section will help you prevent users from altering their shopping cart total price. You will use the $token system that you utilized earlier to identify the customer when they return to your ordercomplete.php script after a successful transaction at PayPal.

Begin by creating a file named paypal.php in your website document root. This file is also linked to from the payment.php page when a customer clicks the Pay Using PayPal hyperlink. Listing 9.3 shows this script.

Listing 9.3   **PayPal Script**

```php
<?php
include $_SERVER['DOCUMENT_ROOT'].
    '/layout.php';

$cart = &new ShoppingCart;
$cart_id = $cart->get_cart_id();

$total = mysql_result(mysql_query("SELECT
                sum(product_qty * product_price) AS subtotal
                FROM shopping_carts
                WHERE cart_identifier='$cart_id'"),0);
$total = number_format($total, 2);
```

```php
// Generate token
$token = md5(uniqid(rand(),1));

// Insert token into DB
$token_check = mysql_result(mysql_query("SELECT COUNT(*)
                    FROM shopping_cart_tokens
                    WHERE cart_id='$cart_id'"),0);

if($token_check == 0){
    mysql_query("INSERT INTO shopping_cart_tokens
            (cart_id, token)
            VALUES ('$cart_id', '$token')");
} else {
    mysql_query("UPDATE shopping_cart_tokens
            SET token='$token'
            WHERE cart_id='$cart_id'");
}

// Redirect user to PayPal
?>
<html>
<head>
<body onload="document.paypal.submit();">
<form name="paypal" action="https://www.paypal.com/cgi-bin/webscr"
method="post">
<input type="hidden" name="cmd" value="_xclick">
<input type="hidden" name="business" value="you@you.com">
<input type="hidden" name="return"
value="http://<?=$_SERVER['SERVER_NAME']?>/ordercomplete.php?req=success&type=pa
ypal&t=<?=$token?>">
<input type="hidden" name="item_name" value="MyPHP Site Order">
<input type="hidden" name="item_number" value="<?=$token?>">
<input type="hidden" name="amount" value="<?=$total?>">
<input type="hidden" name="no_shipping" value="1">
<input type="hidden" name="cancel_return"
value="http://<?=$_SERVER['SERVER_NAME']?>/ordercomplete.php?req=error">
<input type="hidden" name="quantity" value="1">
<input type="hidden" name=" no_note" value="1">
</form>
</body>
</html>
```

In this script, your first tasks are to start PHP, include the shopping cart class file, and get the cart identifier of this customer:

```php
<?php
include $_SERVER['DOCUMENT_ROOT'].
    '/layout.php';

$cart = &new ShoppingCart;
$cart_id = $cart->get_cart_id();
```

Next, you determine the total amount of the order and assign it to the $total variable:

```
$total = mysql_result(mysql_query("SELECT
                sum(product_qty * product_price) AS subtotal
                FROM shopping_carts
                WHERE cart_identifier='$cart_id'"),0);
$total = number_format($total, 2);
```

Now you generate the $token key like you did for the credit card processing earlier in this chapter. This is where the $token is really going to shine because you need to figure out who this customer is when PayPal sends them back to your site. Utilizing the $token in this matter will help you:

```
// Generate token
$token = md5(uniqid(rand(),1));

// Insert token into DB
$token_check = mysql_result(mysql_query("SELECT COUNT(*)
                FROM shopping_cart_tokens
                WHERE cart_id='$cart_id'"),0);

if($token_check == 0){
   mysql_query("INSERT INTO shopping_cart_tokens
        (cart_id, token)
        VALUES ('$cart_id', '$token')");
} else {
   mysql_query("UPDATE shopping_cart_tokens
        SET token='$token'
        WHERE cart_id='$cart_id'");
}
// Redirect user to PayPal
?>
```

The next portion of the script builds the HTML form with hidden input values and automatically submits it to PayPal by using a JavaScript onload function in the BODY tag of the HTML. Table 9.4 explains the fields and values you are posting to PayPal for the payment processing.

TABLE 9.4: PayPal Data Fields

Field	Value	Purpose
Form Action	https://www.paypal.com/ cgi-bin/webscr	URL of the PayPal payment processor.
cmd	_xclick	The type of transaction for the PayPal server. Do not change this value!

Continued on next page

TABLE 9.4 CONTINUED: PayPal Data Fields

Field	Value	Purpose
business	You@you.com	This is your PayPal ID or e-mail address used to create your PayPal account.
return	http://<?=$_SERVER['SERVER_NAME'] ?>/ordercomplete.php?req= success&type=paypal&t=<?=$token?>	The URL to return the customer to after a successful transaction. Notice the usage of $token.
item_name	MyPHP Site Order	Name of the item, in your case the order. Can be anything you want.
item_number	$token	This identifies a stock number of an item. For your purposes, you use $token.
amount	$total	The total amount of the order.
no_shipping	1	Do not display shipping pages. For these purposes, I do not cover shipping, so you can alter or remove this if you want.
cancel_return	http://<?=$_SERVER['SERVER_NAME'] ?>/ordercomplete.php?req=error	This is the error page the customer will be returned to if the transaction was not successful. Do not put the $token here!
quantity	1	The quantity of the item to purchase. In your case, you use 1 and define it here. If you alter this, the total amount will be multiplied by this value. Do not alter this!
no_note	1	Displays the note box to the customer. Use 0 for yes and 1 for no.

Based on the fields in Table 9.4, build an HTML page that will automatically submit the form contained inside it when the page loads into the web browser:

```
<html>
<head>
<body onload="document.paypal.submit();">
<form name="paypal" action="https://www.paypal.com/cgi-bin/webscr"
method="post">
<input type="hidden" name="cmd" value="_xclick">
<input type="hidden" name="business" value="you@you.com">
<input type="hidden" name="return"
value="http://<?=$_SERVER['SERVER_NAME']?>/ordercomplete.php?req=success&type=pa
ypal&t=<?=$token?>">
<input type="hidden" name="item_name" value="MyPHP Site Order">
```

```
<input type="hidden" name="item_number" value="<?=$token?>">
<input type="hidden" name="amount" value="<?=$total?>">
<input type="hidden" name="no_shipping" value="1">
<input type="hidden" name="cancel_return"
value="http://<?=$_SERVER['SERVER_NAME']?>/ordercomplete.php?req=error">
<input type="hidden" name="quantity" value="1">
<input type="hidden" name="no_note" value="1">
</form>
</body>
</html>
```

Once this page loads into the web browser after the user clicks the Pay with PayPal link on the payment.php page, the user will be redirected almost immediately to PayPal, and all of the required information will be passed to the PayPal system to process the transaction with the user input for their billing information. Pretty easy, no?

You can utilize more options in the Buy Now section of the PayPal website once you log in. See the *PayPal Buy Now Buttons Manual* at https://www.paypal.com/html/single_item.pdf.

Also, PayPal is developing a new system called Instant Payment Notification (IPN), which will send special responses back to your script regarding the transactions. You can find more information about IPN at https://www.paypal.com/html/ipn.pdf.

NOTE   When testing the PayPal scripts, you need to use a different PayPal account as either the store account or the customer account. In other words, PayPal will not allow you to pay yourself for a transaction.

Now that you have your payment methods complete, it is time to build the script to accept the responses from these different payment options and record the orders.

Completing the Order: *ordercomplete.php*

This chapter has been building up to the ordercomplete.php script for some time. The previous scripts, creditcard.php and paypal.php, are sending triggers to this script that allow you to perform the final steps in the customer order if it was successful after the payment processing.

Create a script named ordercomplete.php in your website document root (see Listing 9.4).

Listing 9.4   *ordercomplete.php* Script

```
<?php
include $_SERVER['DOCUMENT_ROOT'].
    '/layout.php';

$cart = &new ShoppingCart;
```

```
$cart_id = $cart->get_cart_id();

switch($_REQUEST['req']){
    case "success":
        $sql = mysql_query("SELECT * FROM shopping_cart_tokens
                    WHERE token='{$_REQUEST['t']}'");

        // Quick $token check
        if(mysql_num_rows($sql) != 1){
            echo "<center>Error! Please contact webmaster!</center>";
            footer();
            exit();
        }

        list($cart_id, $token) = mysql_fetch_row($sql);

        // if customer came from paypal,
        // log them back in.
        if($_REQUEST['type'] == "paypal"){
           $_SESSION['cid'] = $cart_id;
           mysql_query("SELECT * FROM members
                members WHERE cart_id='$cart_id'");
           while($row = mysql_fetch_array($sql)){
               $_SESSION['login'] = true;
               $_SESSION['userid'] = $row['id'];
               $_SESSION['first_name'] = $row['first_name'];
               $_SESSION['last_name']  = $row['last_name'];
               $_SESSION['email_address'] = $row['email_address'];
               if($row['admin_access'] == 1){
                   $_SESSION['admin'] = true;
               }
           }
        } else {
         $type = "credit";
        }

        // Get shopping car total again.
        $total = mysql_result(mysql_query("SELECT
                sum(product_qty * product_price) AS subtotal
                FROM shopping_carts
                WHERE cart_identifier='$cart_id'"),0);
        $total = number_format($total, 2);

        $sql_get_cart = mysql_query("SELECT * FROM
                            shopping_carts
                            WHERE cart_identifier='$cart_id'");

        while($row = mysql_fetch_array($sql_get_cart)){
         mysql_query("UPDATE shopping_products
                SET product_qty = (product_qty - {$row['product_qty']})
                WHERE product_id ='{$row['product_id']}'");
```

```
                    $storage_array[$row['product_id']]['qty'] =
                                        $row['product_qty'];
                    $storage_array[$row['product_id']]['price'] =
                                        $row['product_price'];
                    $storage_array[$row['product_id']]['name'] =
                                        $row['product_title'];

            }

            $sproducts = serialize($storage_array);
            // record the order into the shopping cart
            mysql_query("INSERT INTO shopping_cart_orders
                    (order_date, token, products, total, type, user_id)
                    VALUES (now(), '$token', '$sproducts', '$total',
                            '$type', '{$_SESSION['userid']}')");

            // Empty the shopping cart
            $cart->empty_cart();

            // E-mail users and Store Owner a receipt


            // Display message
            myheader("Payment Success");
            echo "<center>Thank you for your payment!<br /><br />".
                    "Please check your email for your receipt.</center>";
        break;

    case "error":
            // This case used for PayPal only.
            myheader("Payment Error");
            echo "<center>We're sorry, there have been problems ".
                    "with your payment</center>";
        break;

    default:
        myheader("Access Denied");
        echo "<center>You can't access ".
                "this page directly!</center>";

    break;
    }

    footer();
    ?>
```

In this code, you start PHP, include your layout and shopping cart class files, and then grab the $cart_id:

```
<?php
include $_SERVER['DOCUMENT_ROOT'].
```

```
'/layout.php';

$cart = &new ShoppingCart;
$cart_id = $cart->get_cart_id();
```

Next, you define your switch and build the case used when you have a successful payment:

```
switch($_REQUEST['req']){
    case "success":
```

To ensure that the $token is found in your database and that it was not altered between the transaction pages, you perform a check to see if the $token passed to this script matches the one you have stored:

```
$sql = mysql_query("SELECT * FROM shopping_cart_tokens
              WHERE token='{$_REQUEST['t']}'");
```

If the value of $token found from the query is not equal to 1, you provide an error and exit the script:

```
// Quick $token check
if(mysql_num_rows($sql) != 1){
    echo "<center>Error! Please contact webmaster!</center>";
    footer();
    exit();
}
```

At this point, you have verified the $token is valid, and you extract the $cart_id from the shopping_cart_tokens table that matches the $token:

```
list($cart_id, $token) = mysql_fetch_row($sql);

// if customer came from paypal,
// log them back in.
```

Chances are that when the customer went to the PayPal site, their session was lost and you do not have a session value for the cart. Just to be sure in case the cookie did not work for some reason (browsers are picky about cookies), then you reset the session cid value to the one you found in the database:

```
if($_REQUEST['type'] == "paypal"){
    $_SESSION['cid'] = $cart_id;
```

Next, you can determine if the customer is a member on your site and give them the courtesy of logging them in based on the cart_id field in the database. If the $cart_id matches the members table's cart_id column, you assume this is the right person and register the session values for them:

```
        mysql_query("SELECT * FROM members
        members WHERE cart_id='$cart_id'");
    while($row = mysql_fetch_array($sql)){
```

```
            $_SESSION['login'] = true;
            $_SESSION['userid'] = $row['id'];
            $_SESSION['first_name'] = $row['first_name'];
            $_SESSION['last_name']  = $row['last_name'];
            $_SESSION['email_address'] = $row['email_address'];
             if($row['admin_access'] == 1){
                $_SESSION['admin'] = true;
             }
        }
      } else {
```

In your `creditcard.php` script, you did not need to define a `type` variable for this script. If `$type` is not equal to `paypal`, you set it to `credit` and use this value in the order storing process later:

```
$type = "credit";
}
```

Once again, you want to obtain the total amount of the order used to process this transaction. You do not want to retrieve this anywhere but your database for security reasons:

```
// Get shopping car total again.
$total = mysql_result(mysql_query("SELECT
        sum(product_qty * product_price) AS subtotal
        FROM shopping_carts
        WHERE cart_identifier='$cart_id'"),0);
$total = number_format($total, 2);
```

You want to ensure that you update the current stock of all of your products to subtract the number of stocks sold in this transaction, so you will perform the query, loop through it, and update the current stock deducted by the values in the shopping cart:

```
$sql_get_cart = mysql_query("SELECT * FROM
                    shopping_carts
                    WHERE cart_identifier='$cart_id'");

while($row = mysql_fetch_array($sql_get_cart)){
  mysql_query("UPDATE shopping_products
      SET product_qty = (product_qty - {$row['product_qty']})
      WHERE product_id ='{$row['product_id']}'");
```

The next task is going to grab all of the information from the customer's shopping cart and then put it into a custom built array. After the information is in the array, you will compact it by using a PHP function called `serialize`:

```
        $storage_array[$row['product_id']]['qty'] =
                            $row['product_qty'];
        $storage_array[$row['product_id']]['price'] =
                            $row['product_price'];
```

```
$storage_array[$row['product_id']]['name'] =
                    $row['product_title'];

}
```

PHP and MySQL will not allow you to save an array in the database, so you must serialize it before storage; when you want to extract it, you can use unserialize to turn the values back into an array. You use this method to allow you to store an order with multiple products in a single row in your shopping_cart_orders table. This is how you serialize the array:

```
$sproducts = serialize($storage_array);
```

Now you store the shopping cart values in the shopping_cart_orders table:

```
// record the order into the shopping cart
mysql_query("INSERT INTO shopping_cart_orders
     (order_date, token, products, total, type, user_id)
     VALUES (now(), '$token', '$sproducts', '$total',
            '$type', '{$_SESSION['userid']}')");
```

WARNING Do not store credit card numbers regarding your transactions. It is extremely dangerous, and you could potentially face severe penalties if your database is hacked and credit cards are stolen. I do not even recommend encrypting them. Usually, payment gateways will store them for you if you should need a credit card number for a recurring payment later. Let the gateways handle the credit card numbers; if they get hacked, it is not only your business that will be affected.

The next task for the successful transaction is to empty the customer's shopping cart by using the empty_cart function from the shopping cart class:

```
// Empty the shopping cart
$cart->empty_cart();
```

At this point, you can e-mail a copy of the receipt to yourself and your customer. Some merchant account gateways can send a generic receipt to both of you if you include the customer's e-mail address in the transaction. I left this part out of the code for a couple of reasons, mainly to keep this example as simple as possible and to allow you to determine which method of notification you want to perform:

```
// E-mail users and Store Owner a receipt
```

And, finally, you display a "thank you" message to the customer:

```
// Display message
myheader("Payment Success");
echo "<center>Thank you for your payment!<br /><br />".
     "Please check your email for your receipt.</center>";
break;
```

The next `case` is only used when something happens on the PayPal server and the transaction was not completed successfully. Because PayPal will not transfer any relevant information about the failure, you have to display a generic message to the customer:

```
case "error":
        // This case used for PayPal only.
        myheader("Payment Error");
        echo "<center>We're sorry, there have been problems ".
            "with your payment</center>";
break;
```

In the event that someone accesses the script and a `case` is not defined, you display an access denied error to them:

```
default:
    myheader("Access Denied");
    echo "<center>You can't access ".
        "this page directly!</center>";

break;
```

Close out the switch, display the footer, and close the script.

```
}
footer();
?>
```

That is about it for the processing script. I cover more options after you test all of these scripts.

Testing the Payment Systems

You have been working on your payment processing scripts, and you are now ready to test them.

Testing the VeriSign Scripts

The first task you will accomplish is to test the VeriSign processing scripts. The VeriSign documentation gives you a set of credit card numbers to test. Any other card numbers you use are supposed to fail, so trying your personal credit card will not work. According to the Payflow Pro developer guide, the credit cards and types shown in Table 9.5 will work with the test gateway.

VeriSign Payflow Pro has a couple more requirements. The first requirement is that the expiration date must be in the future. The second requirement is that the transaction is less than $2001 because of the maximum transaction values set up for fraud protection.

TABLE 9.5: VeriSign Payflow Pro Test Credit Card Numbers

Card Number	Card Type
4111111111111111	Visa
4012888888881881	Visa
4222222222222	Visa (This card number is valid, even though the character count is fewer than 16 digits.)
5555555555554444	MasterCard
5105105105105100	MasterCard
378282246310005	American Express
371449635398431	American Express
378734493671000	American Express Corporate
6011111111111117	Discover
6011000990139424	Discover
3530111333300000	JCB
3566002020360505	JCB
38520000023237	Diners Club
30569309025904	Diners Club

To test your scripts, follow these steps:

1. First, go to your site and add some products to your shopping cart.

2. After adding your products, go to the checkout page from the shopping cart.

3. Confirm your shopping cart order by clicking the Submit Payment hyperlink.

4. Click the payment method Credit Card via Our Secure Server.

5. Complete the payment form by using one of the valid credit card numbers from Table 9.5 and use any information you desire for the rest of the form (see Figure 9.4).

6. Click the Submit Payment button, and notice how long the process takes. Usually it is quicker than 2 seconds. The next screen you should see is the ordercomplete.php page with the "thank you" message. Also, notice that the shopping cart box on the right column is no longer there; hence, your shopping cart is now empty (see Figure 9.5).

7. Finally, log in to the PPM, click the Reports link at the top, and then click Daily Activity Report on the left column. You will see a form; just click the Submit button, and you should see your transaction in the table. My transaction was assigned a number such as V63A31666815. Click the hyperlink with your transaction number, and you can see all of the information about the transaction.

FIGURE 9.4:

Billing information page

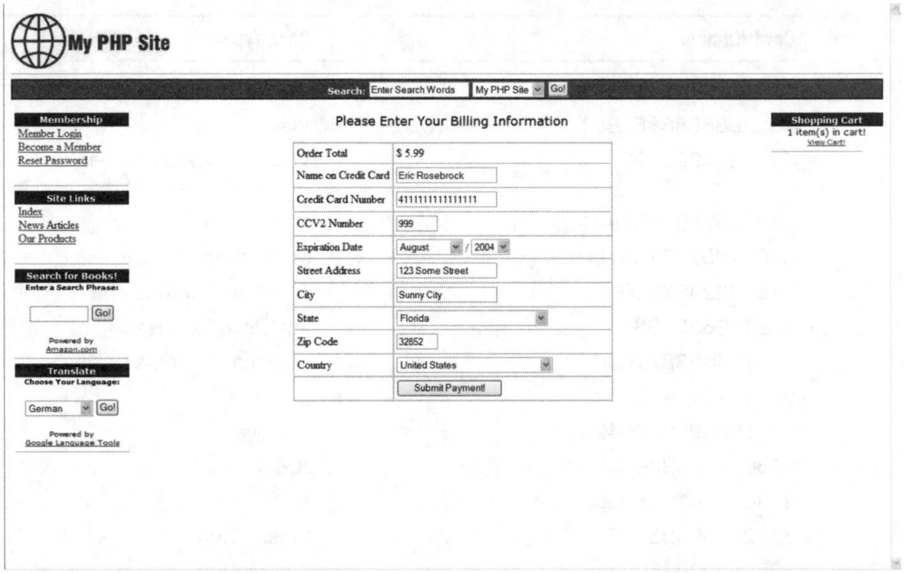

FIGURE 9.5:

The "thank you" page

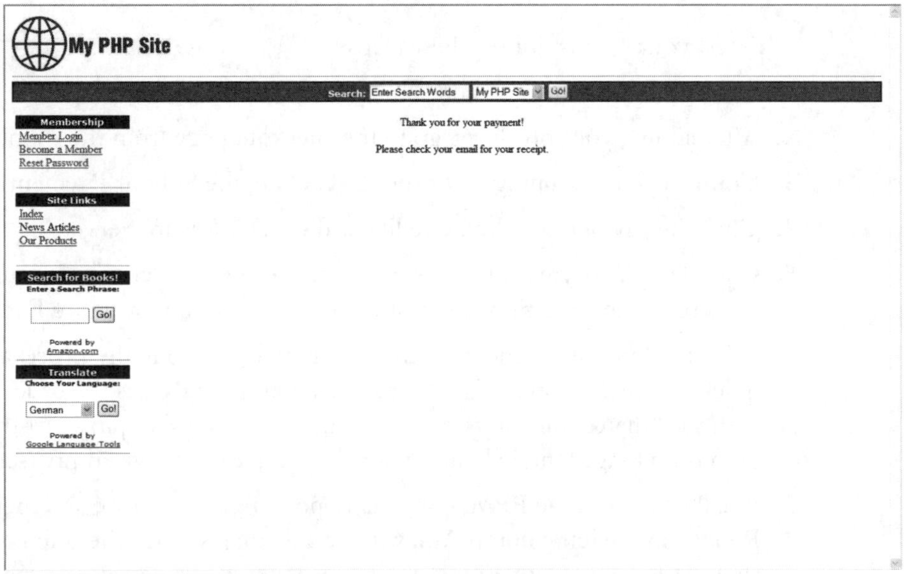

If you are interested in testing a transaction failure, repeat steps 1 through 7 again and enter a false credit card number or an invalid expiration date (one from the past) during step 5. Your transaction will still be recorded in the PPM, so you can see what happens when someone does not enter valid information.

The last step is to check your shopping_cart_orders table and see if the new row was entered for the order. If a new row was created, then everything is working properly.

Testing PayPal Payment Scripts

Next, you will test the PayPal system you have created. There is only one catch: You cannot pay yourself with PayPal, and there is no way to perform test transactions with the Buy Now button you are using. To test this, I set up my PayPal script to use a friend's PayPal account, and I also changed the price of my products to $1 so that I would not have to send my friend too much money during the transactions. ("Brad, can I have my $20 back?") Follow these steps:

1. Go to your site and add some products to your shopping cart.

2. After adding your products, go to the checkout page from the shopping cart.

3. Next, confirm your shopping cart order by clicking the Submit Payment hyperlink.

4. Click the payment method Pay via PayPal. Immediately, your browser should be redirected to the PayPal pages, and you can complete the payment process.

5. After you have successfully made a payment, you will see a Complete This Transaction link. When you click this link, you will be sent back to the ordercomplete.php page on your website. Take special notice of the URL in your browser. The URL will contain req=success&type=paypal&token=XXXXXXXXXXXXXXX. You should also notice that you will see a screen similar to Figure 9.5 in the previous section.

The last steps you need to complete are to have your friend log in to their PayPal account and view the transaction that took place. Additionally, check your shopping_cart_orders table and ensure that the order was recorded properly. If everything is working, then congratulations! You are now on your way to making money with your shopping cart system. Good work!

Utilizing Curl to Process Payments

Some payment gateway systems do not always have a binary file to use on your servers so that you can execute and receive responses from the system. Often, you will find a gateway that requires you to send information to its servers and receive a response via an HTML page. This is actually quite common with many of the basic gateways; fortunately, you have methods of making them work and appear just like the API described earlier.

Thanks to the folks over at Curl (curl.haxx.se), you can compile or enable a module in PHP that allows you to post form information and capture the results into a string.

The Curl website states, "Curl is a command line tool for transferring files with URL syntax, supporting FTP, FTPS, HTTP, HTTPS, GOPHER, TELNET, DICT, FILE, and LDAP. Curl supports HTTPS certificates, HTTP POST, HTTP PUT, FTP uploading, kerberos, HTTP form-based upload, proxies, cookies, user+password authentication, file transfer resume, HTTP proxy tunneling, and a busload of other useful tricks."

For this example, you will use a fictional processor. Let's say you have signed up for Acme Gateway payment processing, and you have downloaded the Acme Gateway developer guide. You see that the fields in Table 9.6 are required to send to the gateway to receive the responses outlined in Table 9.7.

TABLE 9.6: Acme Gateway Required Fields

Field	Purpose
NAME	Account holder name
CARDNUMBER	Credit card number
EXPDATE	Credit card expiration date
USERNAME	Username or store identifier in the Acme Gateway system

TABLE 9.7: Acme Gateway Responses

Field	Value
Response	0 = Success, 1 = Failure, 3 = Unknown
Result	Approved, Declined, Unknown
transaction_id	Transaction ID number generated by the gateway

To send these fields to the payment gateway via Curl, use the code in Listing 9.5.

Listing 9.5   **Processing Acme Gateway Payments with Curl**

```php
<?php
$urlstring = "USERNAME=wylie&NAME=Eric&CARDNUMBER=4111111111111111&EXPDATE=0905";

$ch = curl_init();
curl_setopt($ch, CURLOPT_URL,"https://mypayment.acme.com");
curl_setopt($ch, CURLOPT_POST, 1);
curl_setopt($ch, CURLOPT_POSTFIELDS, $urlstring);
ob_start();
curl_exec ($ch);
$retrieved_result = ob_get_contents();
```

```
    ob_end_clean();
    curl_close ($ch);

    // $retrieved_result of
    // response=0&result=Approved&transaction_id=92938493
    $a = explode('&', $retrieved_result);
    $i = 0;
    while ($i < count($a)) {
        $b = split('=', $a[$i]);
        $var = htmlspecialchars(urldecode($b[0]));
        $val = htmlspecialchars(urldecode($b[1]));
        $$var = $val;

        $i++;
    }

    echo "Response: $response<br />";
    echo "Result: $result<br />";
    echo "Transaction ID: $transaction_id";
    ?>
```

In this code, the first task you have to do is to build the querystring of fields to post to the gateway:

```
<?php
$urlstring = "USERNAME=wylie&NAME=Eric&CARDNUMBER=4111111111111111&EXPDATE=0905";
```

Next, you initialize Curl with the PHP function `curl_init`. You also have to assign a resource identifier $ch to this because you use this resource in the rest of the code:

```
$ch = curl_init();
curl_setopt($ch, CURLOPT_URL,"https://mypayment.acme.com");
```

Some gateways do not allow HTTP GET methods, so you must find a way to post the information using the HTTP POST method just like you would with an HTML form. Curl makes this easy for you by providing the CURLOPT_POST and CURLOPT_POSTFIELDS options:

```
curl_setopt($ch, CURLOPT_POST, 1);
curl_setopt($ch, CURLOPT_POSTFIELDS, $urlstring);
```

Output buffering is a lifesaver here! I talked about output buffering in Chapter 1, "Introducing PHP." Here you will use an output buffer to capture the response into a string for further decoding:

```
ob_start();
curl_exec ($ch);
$retrieved_result = ob_get_contents();
ob_end_clean();
curl_close ($ch);
```

At this point you have a string called `$retrieved_result` with the results of your transaction. This string looks like a querystring, such as `response=0&result=Approved&transaction_id=92938493`. I will break this string apart into individual variables. Using a more difficult method than the one you used in the VeriSign payment processing scripts, you will retrieve each element of this string in a variable with its value:

```
// $retrieved_result of
// response=0&result=Approved&transaction_id=92938493
$a = explode('&', $retrieved_result);
$i = 0;
while ($i < count($a)) {
    $b = split('=', $a[$i]);
    $var = htmlspecialchars(urldecode($b[0]));
    $val = htmlspecialchars(urldecode($b[1]));
    $$var = $val;

    $i++;
}
```

Now that you have the variables from the `$retrieved_result`, you can display them or utilize a `switch` to determine which action to take on the `$response` value:

```
echo "Response: $response<br />";
echo "Result: $result<br />";
echo "Transaction ID: $transaction_id";
?>
```

Using Curl can be a lifesaver when you need one most. With Curl, I have been able to bypass expensive gateways by using basic HTML payment processors and still maintain the appearance of using an expensive full-blown API or gateway on my website. You may find many different uses for Curl when trying to retrieve data from other sources on the Internet. To learn more about Curl, you can visit these resources:

- Curl homepage: `curl.haxx.se`
- PHP manual for Curl functions: `www.php.net/curl`
- My tutorial for other methods of using Curl: `www.phpfreaks.com/tutorials/49/0.php`

Customizing This Project

This chapter's examples were as basic as possible. With that in mind, I excluded a few elements from the payment processing system. At this point, you should feel comfortable with the common routines of PHP and MySQL; therefore, I will leave the rest of the process up to you to complete with the knowledge you have obtained from this book.

The following are some tasks you could perform next:

- Follow up in the Payflow Pro developer guide for additional fields to send to the gateway for payment processing.

- Include detailed error checking in the billing form.

- Modify the payment scripts to send invoices to the customer and store owner upon checkout.

- Create a page within the website for customers to view their orders and an extra orders page for the store owner to view all of the orders and details.

- Create a box in the right column that allows customers to view their orders, if they have any.

You may want to do something different, so be sure to carefully examine your needs and tailor your process to best suit your situation.

What's Next?

This chapter covered payment processing with payment gateways, third-party payment solutions, and Curl. It covered some nifty tricks to help secure your payment processing, and you stored customer orders into your database. You have a few more things to do to complete this system, but with a little creative thinking and the skills you have learned thus far, you should be able to make a really cool payment system.

The next chapter covers how to track website statistics with custom PHP scripts and third-party solutions.

CHAPTER 10

Tracking Website Statistics

ebsite statistics are notorious for catching a webmaster's attention. Keeping track of how your website is doing allows you to measure how valuable your efforts have been. The more traffic your website generates, the more interested you may be to improve and develop new sections for it.

On my website, I track as much information as possible. I even have a script built into my site to track the Google search engine spider and how, when, and what pages it is indexing. Why? Because I want to know how Google indexes my site. I usually use three major third-party website statistics trackers and quite a few internal mechanisms that I have created with PHP to track elements of my site.

This chapter discusses some of the different tracking techniques and creates some methods to tell how many people have been on your website in the past 15 minutes. By the time you are done with this chapter, you should be able to generate virtually any kind of custom tracking system. You will begin by coding some custom scripts to track your site visitors.

Creating Custom Tracking with PHP and MySQL

Utilizing the PHP $_SERVER superglobal array, you can obtain some important information about your users for statistical tracking. Some of this information includes a visitor's Internet Protocol (IP) address, web browser type, the referring Uniform Resource Locator (URL), and much more. This allows you to detect and analyze information about your users.

NOTE The examples in this chapter utilize the error suppression operator (@) before the MySQL queries because you do not want errors displayed if any logging fails.

Setting a PHP Sessions Counter

By tracking the number of sessions on your site, you can tell how many times a visitor has connected to your website and browsed through it. This is considered a *visit* in some website analyzing software. You can do this with easily with PHP and MySQL with minimal impact on the database size and performance with a single row in a table.

Setting Up the Database

You will start by creating a MySQL table in your database named stats_visits. Table 10.1 shows the values it will have.

TABLE 10.1: The stats_visits Table

Field Name	Data Type	Length	Extra
count	INT	15	Primary key

If you would like to dump this query into your MySQL editor, you can use the following:

```
CREATE TABLE stats_visits (
   count int(15) NOT NULL default '0',
   PRIMARY KEY (count)
) TYPE=MyISAM;
```

After you have created the table, insert a new row with a value of 0 into it using your MySQL editor or using the following command:

```
INSERT INTO stats_visits VALUES (0);
```

Creating the Logging Script

Now you have your database prepared, so you can begin coding this simple script to count how many sessions have been started on your server. Create a file in your website document root under the `includes` directory. Name this file `stats_visits.php`; it will look like the following code:

```
<?php
if(!$_SESSION['visits']){
   @mysql_query("UPDATE stats_visits
         SET count=(count + 1)");
   $_SESSION['visits'] = TRUE;
}
?>
```

This is an extremely easy portion of code to use. It starts by checking if the `$_SESSION ['visits']` session value exists. If it does, then nothing will happen in this script because it does not pass the IF statement check. If the session value does not exist, the IF statement will validate TRUE, and you will add 1 to the current value of the `stats_visits` row in the database.

All you have left to do to use this simple tracking script is to include it in your `common.php` file below where you included the `database.php` file:

```
// Include Session Counter File
include $_SERVER['DOCUMENT_ROOT'].'/includes/stats_visits.php';
```

Testing the Logging Script

To test your script, all you have to do is open your website, click a couple of pages, and close your browser. Do this a few times and then check the `stats_visits` row to verify that the value of `count` is increasing each time you open your web browser to your site.

If everything has worked properly, then congratulations! You have created your first logging script.

Displaying the Logging Results

To display the results of this script, you will perform a simple query and echo the result:

```php
<?php
// include database connection if needed
$visit_count = mysql_result(
                mysql_query("SELECT count FROM stats_visits"),0);
echo $visit_count;
?>
```

Later in this chapter, you will create a box for the left column that will show your current website statistics; you will include this query at that time.

Tracking the Number of Users and Visitors Online

Another popular tracking technique is to show how many visitors and users are visiting your website within a certan period of time. You can easily achieve this by using sessions in PHP and MySQL. The examples in the following sections show you how to utilize some of the advanced MySQL functions to extract information from your database using a specific set of limits during your queries.

Your site uses PHP sessions, so you have a unique way of identifying each user when they are on your site, their session ID. The session ID is a unique, randomly generated string of characters to identify each session on the site. It is impossible for two users to have the same session ID at one time on a site, so you do not have to worry about this factor. Let's dig in and start developing this handy script.

Setting Up the Database

You will utilize MySQL for this process, so you need to create a table in your database to store the information. Create a new table named stats_ppl_online, and use the values in Table 10.2 to set up the structure.

TABLE 10.2: The stats_ppl_online Table

Field Name	Data Type	Length	Default	Extra
session_id	VARCHAR	255		Primary key
member	ENUM('0', '1')		0	
activity	DATETIME		0000-00-00 00:00:00	
ip_address	VARCHAR	24		
refurl	VARCHAR	255		
user_agent	VARCHAR	255		

The following is the command line query for this structure:

```
CREATE TABLE stats_ppl_online (
  session_id varchar(255) NOT NULL default '',
  member enum('0','1') NOT NULL default '0',
  activity datetime NOT NULL default '0000-00-00 00:00:00',
  ip_address varchar(24) NOT NULL default '',
  refurl varchar(255) NOT NULL default '',
  user_agent varchar(255) default NULL,
  PRIMARY KEY (session_id),
  KEY session_id (session_id)
) TYPE=MyISAM;
```

Creating the Logging Script

The logging script will capture certain information about the person visiting and determine if you need to insert a new row into the database if they have not been logged yet or simply update their existing row. Because the primary key in the database is the session_id column, you can only have one entry per session ID, so this is another trick to keep from getting a false reading on the counter.

Start by creating a script in your website document root's includes directory. Name this script people_online.php. Listing 10.1 shows the full code.

Listing 10.1   People Online Logging Script

```php
<?php
if(!$_SESSION['online']){
    @mysql_query("INSERT INTO stats_ppl_online(session_id,
                                        activity,
                                        ip_address,
                                        refurl,
                                        user_agent)
                                VALUES ('".session_id()."',
                                    now(),
                                        '{$_SERVER['REMOTE_ADDR']}',
                                        '{$_SERVER['HTTP_REFERER']}',
                                        '{$_SERVER['HTTP_USER_AGENT']}'
                                        )");
    $_SESSION['online'] = TRUE;
} else {
    if($_SESSION['login']){
        @mysql_query("UPDATE stats_ppl_online
                    SET activity=now(),
                    member='1'
                    WHERE
                    session_id='".session_id()."'");
    }
}
```

```
if($_SESSION['online'] && !$_SESSION['login']){
    @mysql_query("UPDATE stats_ppl_online
            SET activity=now()
            WHERE session_id='".session_id()."'");
}

// cleanup
$cleanup_time = time() - 301;
@mysql_query("DELETE FROM stats_ppl_online
            WHERE
            UNIX_TIMESTAMP(activity) < '$cleanup_time'");
?>
```

I will now cover how this script works. The first task you want to do is open PHP and check to see if a session value named online is set. If it is not, you will perform a query and insert a new row into the database:

```
<?php
if(!$_SESSION['online']){
    @mysql_query("INSERT INTO stats_ppl_online (session_id,
                                    activity,
                                    ip_address,
                                    refurl,
                                    user_agent)
```

You use the PHP session_id function to insert into the session_id field of the new row:

```
VALUES ('".session_id()."',
```

Next, you use the MySQL now() function to set the date and time of the activity column. This column is specifically used to record the last time the user accessed a page on your site and to update the row matching the session_id with the correct time values.

While you are here, I will explain why I used a DATETIME column type instead of a TIME-STAMP column type in the database structure. A TIMESTAMP is the number of seconds from January 1, 1970, until the TIMESTAMP was made. When I am browsing the database, I do not like to perform math equations in my head to figure out the date of a TIMESTAMP, so I use a more human-readable format for storage. That way, you can see what is going on by merely browsing your database entries. You have the ability to convert any date and time into a TIMESTAMP; I will show you how to do this later in this script. For now, let's insert the current time for this field using the MySQL now() function:

```
now(),
```

The next value you insert into the ip_address field is the IP address of the person accessing your website. You utilize the $_SERVER['REMOTE_ADDR'] superglobal, which is the IP address of the visitor:

```
'{$_SERVER['REMOTE_ADDR']}',
```

The next field, `refurl` (the referring URL), is only used when browsing through the database to tell you from where the visitor came. For example, if I had a link on www.phpfreaks.com and the visitor clicked that link, the HTTP_REFERER would be http://www.phpfreaks.com. Pretty cool! Here is the code:

```
'{$_SERVER['HTTP_REFERER']}',
```

Even though the `user_agent` fields are not used in anything to display the number of visitors online, you can still log them to figure out what type of web browser the visitor is using to access your website. You obtain the web browser type by using the `$_SERVER['HTTP_USER_AGENT']` superglobal values:

```
'{$_SERVER['HTTP_USER_AGENT']}'
)");
```

The next task is to prevent any attempts to perform the previous query again. You do this by registering the `online` session value and setting it to a TRUE Boolean value. This will cause the first IF statement in your script to bypass the query because the session value is set:

```
$_SESSION['online'] = TRUE;
} else {
```

At this point, you have already inserted a row into the database for this visitor. Now you are going to check to see if the visitor is logged in as a member by validating the `login` session Boolean that you set when a user logs into the site. When this IF statement validates TRUE, you will update the row in the table for this visitor and set the member field ENUM flag to 1 to indicate that this visitor is a member. You will also update the time this script was accessed. You will utilize this ENUM flag later when you display how many visitors and members are logged into your site. Additionally, this query is only used for members who are logged in and have the `online` session value set:

```
if($_SESSION['login']){
    @mysql_query("UPDATE stats_ppl_online
            SET activity=now(),
            member='1'
            WHERE
            session_id='".session_id()."'");
}

}
```

In this portion of the script, you have already logged the visitor in the database, and you are going to determine if they are a member by using the && operator to limit the IF statement to matching two rules. Once you have determined that the `online` session value has been set and that this is a visitor and not a member, you want to update the database with the time of the last page they accessed through the site. Based on this theory, you will perform a query if the online session value has been set:

```
if($_SESSION['online'] && !$_SESSION['login']){
    @mysql_query("UPDATE stats_ppl_online
            SET activity=now()
            WHERE session_id='".session_id()."'");
}
```

After a few weeks of running this script on a high-traffic website, this database table can grow rather quickly, so you want to perform some maintenance on your tables while the script runs. You can set a time limit to clean up old entries that are no longer counted when you display the results; so, based on that factor, you set a variable called $cleanup_time. The $cleanup_time value utilizes the PHP time function that returns a TIMESTAMP, and then you subtract the equivalent of five minutes and one second from that value returned by the time function. The 301 value is equivalent to 60 seconds × 5 minutes + 1 second:

```
// cleanup
$cleanup_time = time() - 301;
```

NOTE   Using a five-minute timeout is the standard that most websites use for these types of statistics.

Now that you have determined the limit of records you want to keep, you will perform a DELETE query and utilize the MySQL UNIX_TIMESTAMP function to convert that DATETIME field into a TIMESTAMP. This query would read like the following if you were to say it aloud: "DELETE records FROM the stats_ppl_online table WHERE the UNIX_TIMESTAMP-converted value of the activity field is less than the $cleanup_time." Here is the code:

```
@mysql_query("DELETE FROM stats_ppl_online
            WHERE
            UNIX_TIMESTAMP(activity) < '$cleanup_time'");
?>
```

Go ahead and include this file in your common.php file located inside the document root. Be sure to add this below your session.php file because you need to ensure that the sessions have already been started to utilize the session array. The following is how my full common.php file looks from all of the previous chapters in this book with the new entry for the people_online.php file:

```
<?php

// Include Meta Content Class
include $_SERVER['DOCUMENT_ROOT'].'/classes/clsMetaContent.php';
```

```
// Include Database Connection File
include $_SERVER['DOCUMENT_ROOT'].'/includes/database.php';

// Include Email Class
include $_SERVER['DOCUMENT_ROOT'].'/classes/clsEmail.php';

// Include Session Start & Name File
include $_SERVER['DOCUMENT_ROOT'].'/includes/session.php';

// Include Shopping Cart Class
include $_SERVER['DOCUMENT_ROOT'].'/classes/clsShoppingCart.php';

// Include Session Counter File
include $_SERVER['DOCUMENT_ROOT'].'/includes/stats_visits.php';

// Include People Online Counter File
include $_SERVER['DOCUMENT_ROOT'].'/includes/people_online.php';
?>
```

Testing the Logging Script

After you have everything coded and included in your site, test this script by following these steps:

1. Open your website.

2. Check your database using your MySQL management tool. You should see a new row created with your relevant information. Note that the member field has an ENUM value of 0 at this point. Also, note the date and time values of the activity field.

3. Click any page in your site. Go back to the database, and refresh the results of the table. Notice that the date and time values of the activity field should be updated at this point.

4. Log in to your website as a member. Go back to the database, and refresh the results of the table. Notice that the date and time values of the activity field have updated and also notice that the member ENUM value should now be 1.

5. Close your web browser, open it again, and access your website. Check the database: You should have two rows with different session ID values at this point.

6. Leave your website open and go take about a five-minute break—go grab some caffeine (a web developer's lifeline), stretch your legs, or do whatever makes you happy.

7. After your five-minute sanity break, click another page on your website. Go back to the database, and refresh the results. You should notice that the old row is now deleted because it is older than the five minutes and one second that you configured as the $cleanup_time.

Displaying the Logging Results

You have coded your script and have determined that it is working properly at this point. So, it is time to figure out how to display the results and show off how many people have accessed your website within the past five minutes. To do this, you will perform some queries with MySQL and display the results.

If you have been analyzing the script you just created, you may be wondering how you can get an accurate reading if a visitor closes their browser and then opens it to your site within five minutes. The question may have popped into your head, "Wouldn't that create a duplicate entry?" Well, with MySQL, you can group your results by field and eliminate duplicate entries from being counted as individual entries.

Listing 10.3 shows the code required to properly display these results.

Listing 10.3   Visitors and Members Online Results Script

```php
<?php
// include database connection if necessary
$limit_time = time() - 300;
$visitors_sql = @mysql_query("SELECT COUNT(*) AS visitors FROM
            stats_ppl_online
            WHERE UNIX_TIMESTAMP(activity) >= $limit_time
            AND member='0'
            GROUP BY ip_address");
$visitors = @mysql_num_rows($visitors_sql);

$members_sql = @mysql_query("SELECT COUNT(*) AS members FROM
            stats_ppl_online
            WHERE UNIX_TIMESTAMP(activity) >= $limit_time
            AND member='1'
            GROUP BY ip_address");
$members = @mysql_num_rows($members_sql);

echo "Visitors Online: $visitors<br />";
echo "Members Online: $members<br />";
?>
```

Listing 10.3 contains some new routines that I have not explained yet, so I will do that now. First, you start PHP and include a database connection if necessary; however, you will use this code in a box included on your site, so you do not need to include one here:

```php
<?php
// include database connection if necessary
```

Second, you a set a time limit on the results to be extracted. This is similar to the DELETE query you created in the logging script:

```php
$limit_time = time() - 300;
```

For this query, you perform the query and utilize the PHP `mysql_num_rows` function to get the results. This query will select all of the rows from the `stats_ppl_online` table where the member `ENUM` value is equal to 0, and then it will return all the results in groups of IP addresses from the `ip_address` field. By utilzing the `GROUP BY` clause, you can get a more accurate number of visitors on your site:

```
$visitors_sql = @mysql_query("SELECT COUNT(*) AS visitors FROM
          stats_ppl_online
          WHERE UNIX_TIMESTAMP(activity) >= $limit_time
          AND member='0'
          GROUP BY ip_address");
```

Now you will assign the result of the `mysql_num_rows` function from the previous query to the `$visitors` variable. The value of `$visitors` is the number of rows found in the database matching your query:

```
$visitors = @mysql_num_rows($visitors_sql);
```

The next query is the same routine as the previous one, except now you are getting the number of results for the `members` `ENUM` value of 1 indicating how many members are online:

```
$members_sql = @mysql_query("SELECT COUNT(*) AS members FROM
          stats_ppl_online
          WHERE UNIX_TIMESTAMP(activity) >= $limit_time
          AND member='1'
          GROUP BY ip_address");
$members = @mysql_num_rows($members_sql);
```

Now you display the results by using the echo function:

```
echo "Visitors Online: $visitors<br />";
echo "Members Online: $members<br />";
?>
```

Everything should be working as advertised at this point; you now have a method of displaying how many users have been on your site in the past five minutes.

NOTE   If you are testing your counter by closing and opening your browser, logging in and logging out, keep in mind that some of these statistics may not be entirely accurate until a five-minute timeout period has passed. This statstics tracking mechanism was designed for normal usage of your website, so keep that in mind before you get the impression that it does not work properly.

Tracking Search Engine Spiders

I will now show you a trick for figuring out exactly what that good ol' GoogleBot (the search engine web spider) is doing on your site. Let's face it, Google is growing to be the number-one search engine on the Internet. If your site ranks well in Google, you are definitely golden—you will be getting traffic like crazy from it. In order to really understand what the GoogleBot is doing, I devised a method of tracking it and storing the results in my database. This may be considered extremely "geeky," but, hey, I like knowing what is going on!

Expanding on my original code, this section presents a better solution for you to be able track more than just the GoogleBot. The following sections show you a method of tracking the major search engine bots on the Internet and logging what they do.

Preparing the Database

Create a table named `stats_search_engines` in your database using the values in Table 10.3.

TABLE 10.2: The `stats_search_engines` Table

Field Name	Data Type	Length	Default	Extra
id	INT	25		Primary key, auto increment
bot_name	VARCHAR	255	0	
access_time	DATETIME		0000-00-00 00:00:00	
page	VARCHAR	255		
ip_address	VARCHAR	24		

The following is the command line query for this structure:

```
CREATE TABLE stats_search_engines (
   id int(25) NOT NULL auto_increment,
   bot_name varchar(255) NOT NULL default '',
   access_time datetime NOT NULL default '0000-00-00 00:00:00',
   page varchar(255) NOT NULL default '',
   ip_address varchar(24) NOT NULL default '',
   PRIMARY KEY  (id)
) TYPE=MyISAM;
```

Creating the Logging Script

This script works based on the results found from the `$_SERVER` superglobal array. You search for certain words in the `HTTP_USER_AGENT` that will identify the search engine bots. For example, by analyzing some search engine logs, I was able to determine that the GoogleBot uses the `HTTP_USER_AGENT` value of `Googlebot/2.1 (+http://www.googlebot.com/bot.html)` and the MSN search engine spider uses `MSNBOT/0.1 (http://search.msn.com/msnbot.htm)`. Even though these spiders are using versions, you can still provide a method to detect the spiders in your script. Let's jump into the code and learn how to perform the logging for this concept (see Listing 10.4).

Listing 10.4   **Search Engine Spider Logger**

```php
<?php
$spiders[] = "MSNBOT";
$spiders[] = "Google";
$spiders[] = "Inktomi";
$spiders[] = "Mozilla"; // Test Only
foreach($spiders AS $spider){
    if(@eregi($spider, $_SERVER['HTTP_USER_AGENT'])){
        @mysql_query("INSERT INTO stats_search_engines
                    (bot_name,
                     access_time,
                     page,
                     ip_address)
             VALUES ('{$_SERVER['HTTP_USER_AGENT']}',
                     now(),
                     '{$_SERVER['REQUEST_URI']}',
                     '{$_SERVER['REMOTE_ADDR']}')");
    }
}
?>
```

As always, I will break this script down for you. First, open PHP:

```php
<?php
```

Second, you need a method of identifying the spiders by searching the HTTP_USER_AGENT value with a simple word. To achieve this with a list of different words such as *MSN*, *Google*, *Inktomi*, you create an array with each word as a new entry. You do not want to use the entire value that the spider reports as its HTTP_USER_AGENT value because if the version changes, you will have to change your code:

```php
$spiders[] = "MSNBOT";
$spiders[] = "Google";
$spiders[] = "Inktomi";
```

NOTE   The following array entry is for testing only.

If your site is not live yet, it will not be in the spider queue for the search engines. Therefore, you will utilize the word *Mozilla* to test this script with your web browser:

```php
$spiders[] = "Mozilla"; // Test Only
```

Now you will use a `foreach` function to create a variable from the key for the current array element being looped through. With this variable, you can perform your check to see if you have a match and then perform a query:

```php
foreach($spiders AS $spider){
```

You use the PHP `eregi` function for a case-insensitive match based on the argument and the string. If a match is found with an `eregi` function, the result returned by it will be TRUE, and you can utilize an IF statement in conjunction with it to perform further actions. Based on these factors, you can validate if the value of `$spider` is found in the `$_SERVER['HTTP_USER_AGENT']` superglobal array value. If it is, the IF statement will validate TRUE, and you can perform your query to log the request:

```
if(@eregi($spider, $_SERVER['HTTP_USER_AGENT'])){
    @mysql_query("INSERT INTO stats_search_engines
                (bot_name,
                 access_time,
                 page,
                 ip_address)
         VALUES ('{$_SERVER['HTTP_USER_AGENT']}',
                 now(),
```

The next `$_SERVER` superglobal array value you will use is REQUEST_URI, which is the page you are requesting. For example, the REQUEST_URI for www.mysite.com/articles.php would be /articles.php:

```
'{$_SERVER['REQUEST_URI']}',
```

The `$_SERVER['REMOTE_ADDR']` superglobal array contains the IP address of the client accessing the script:

```
                 '{$_SERVER['REMOTE_ADDR']}')");
    }
}
?>
```

Save your work, and then edit your `common.php` toward the bottom to include this new file.

Testing the Logging Script

There is not really much to test with this script. However, you have included an array value that allows you to log your request for testing purposes. To test your script, you can open your web browser and browse a few pages. After you have browsed a few pages, open your database and view the rows in your `stats_search_engines` table. Figure 10.1 shows an example of my database rows.

You can determine the best method of viewing these logs to suit your needs. I scan my database tables using phpMyAdmin when I want to see what is happening. There is really no use for me to display this information on my websites, so I do not create a front-end script for them.

FIGURE 10.1:

Database entries for
the search engine log-
ging script

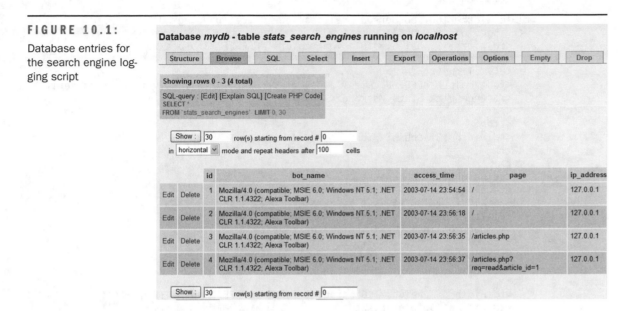

Creating a Quick Stats Box

You have the ability to log your statistics, so now it is time to show off your skills, features,
and statistics by creating a new box in your left column. Create a box in your website document root under the boxes directory. Name the file box_quick_stats.php and use the display
code from previous examples in this chapter (see Listing 10.5).

Listing 10.5   **Quick Stats Box**

```php
<?php

$visit_count = mysql_result(mysql_query("SELECT count FROM
                                    stats_visits"),0);
$limit_time = time() - 300;
$visitors_sql = mysql_query("SELECT COUNT(*) AS visitors FROM stats_ppl_online
            WHERE UNIX_TIMESTAMP(activity) >= $limit_time
            AND member='0'
            GROUP BY ip_address");
$visitors = mysql_num_rows($visitors_sql);

$members_sql = mysql_query("SELECT COUNT(*) AS members FROM stats_ppl_online
            WHERE UNIX_TIMESTAMP(activity) >= $limit_time
            AND member='1'
            GROUP BY ip_address");
$members = mysql_num_rows($members_sql);
?>
```

```
<table width="160" border="0" cellspacing="0" cellpadding="0">
  <tr bgcolor="#000066">
    <td width="5" height="10"><font color="#FFFFFF"> </font></td>
    <td width="150">
    <div align="center">
    <font color="#FFFFFF" size="2" face="Verdana, Arial, Helvetica, sans-serif">
    <strong>Quick Stats</strong></font>
    </div>
    </td>
    <td width="5"> </td>
  </tr>
  <tr>
    <td height="5"> </td>
    <td align="left" valign="top">
    Total Visits: <?=$visit_count?><br />
    Visitors Online: <?=$visitors?><br />
    Members Online: <?=$members?><br />
   </td>
    <td> </td>
  </tr>
  <tr>
    <td width="5" height="10"><font color="#FFFFFF"> </font></td>
    <td width="150"> </td>
    <td width="5"> </td>
  </tr>
</table>
<hr size="1">
```

Listing 10.5 is pretty basic to understand, and most of it was described previously. I modified my layout.php file and included this new file at the bottom of my left column. Figure 10.2 (on the following page) shows what this box looks like in action.

Using Web Analyzing Software

There are many methods to analyze your website statistics through your web server log files. Most web servers will log extensive information that it sends to the client by request. Based on this concept, you can install web statistic analyzing software on your server and generate HTML reports telling you in detail what is happening on your site. Do not worry too much if you do not have control over the web server your site is hosted on; most web hosting companies should provide these statistics for you using some of the popular analyzing software available.

The following sections show some of the web statistics analyzing software you can use to generate your reports.

FIGURE 10.2:

Quick stats box

Using Webalizer

Webalizer is a free web server log file analyzer. It can generate custom reports for multiple websites on a server. You can configure the way the reports are generated from the configuration files if you want to customize the output. Additionally, Webalizer utilizes a history feature that allows you to delete old log files after it has generated the reports.

Webalizer is available for the most popular operating systems; you can download it and learn more about it at www.webalizer.com.

If you would like to see a statistics page generated by Webalizer, you can take a look at my site's statistics at www.phpfreaks.com/webalizer.

Using Urchin

Urchin is commercial web analyzing software based on similar principles as Webalizer. Urchin, however, is rather expensive to use; you have to purchase licenses for different levels of usage. An Urchin license starts at $695 to purchase; however, you may find that your web hosting provider is a reseller, and you can purchase your licenses fairly cheaply. I was able to purchase a single-configuration Urchin license for less than $100 from my hosting provider.

You can learn more about Urchin at www.urchin.com.

Monitoring Your Website with Alexa

Amazon.com has caught the attention of many webmasters with its Alexa service. Alexa utilizes a toolbar add-on for web browsers to determine how websites rank against each other. This toolbar sends information to the Alexa server about the websites the toolbar user is browsing. According to the Alexa website, their toolbar has been downloaded more than 10 million times since 1997 when it was first introduced.

The Alexa monitoring service is packed with features for you to use when comparing your site to millions of other websites. You can view daily graphs that are generated by Alexa to see how your site was ranked each day for as long as the past year.

Alexa has its own ways of ranking websites in its system. The basic principle is that the lower the overall ranking, the better your site is. You can learn more about how Alexa ranks websites at pages.alexa.com/prod_serv/traffic_learn_more.html.

Alexa also offers webmasters services to display their traffic rankings directly on their websites using graphical images. These images may consist of a simple traffic ranking, or you can display the traffic graphs on your site, as well. To learn more about these services, visit the Alexa webmaster services at pages.alexa.com/prod_serv/webmasters.html.

What's Next?

This chapter covered how to create statistical logging scripts for your website. It covered how to log the number of visits your site has obtained, how to log and display the number of visitors and members on your website within the past five minutes, and how to track search engine spiders as they crawl through your site. Additionally, I discussed some web analyzing software that can examine your web server log files and generate reports for you to track how your site is doing.

The next chapter discusses some of the best third-party PHP scripts that you can utilize in your website.

Chapter 11

Using Third-Party PHP Scripts

PHP has a large supporting community. Within this community, developers have created scripts for many uses that are available for you to download or purchase via the Internet. This is great for most developers because it means someone else has already taken care of doing all of the hard work; all you have to do is download, install, and configure the scripts. You can usually find a solution on the Internet that has already been researched, developed, and tested for just about anything related to PHP. For example, I talked about phpMyAdmin in Chapter 3, "Building a Database Schema with MySQL." phpMyAdmin is a set of scripts that allow you to manage your MySQL databases and servers. This is just one example of a third-party script; many more are available for different types of solutions.

This chapter covers some of my favorite third-party scripts that I use on a daily basis. I will also cover where to find other third-party scripts via the Internet.

Exploring Some Great Third-Party PHP Scripts

I have been using third-party PHP scripts for quite a while now. I primarily use them as additions to sites I have developed; with them, I enhance the site's capabilities and avoid spending too much time on developing something that someone else has already developed. Like they say, why reinvent the wheel? The following sections introduce you to a few of my favorite third-party scripts.

Using the phpAdsNew Advertisement System

A superior set of PHP scripts that allows you to display advertisements on websites is phpAdsNew. phpAdsNew is loaded with features that allow you to display nearly every kind of web-based advertisement. In addition to displaying the advertisements, phpAdsNew has an extremely advanced tracking solution.

You can download phpAdsNew at www.phpadsnew.com. phpAdsNew is fairly easy to install. The scripts provide an installation wizard that is as easy as setting up an application on a Windows platform. Figure 11.1 shows the beginning of the installation process, and Figure 11.2 shows a successful installation screen.

After you have phpAdsNew installed and configured, you can log in to start working with the administrator control panel (see Figure 11.3).

One of the features of phpAdsNew is its inventory control. The Inventory tab allows you to add new advertisers, create advertiser campaigns, and add banners for advertisers. Figure 11.4 shows the Inventory tab, Figure 11.5 shows the Add New Campaign screen, and Figure 11.6 shows the Campaign Overview screen.

FIGURE 11.1:

Setting up a phpAdsNew account

FIGURE 11.2:

Completing the installation

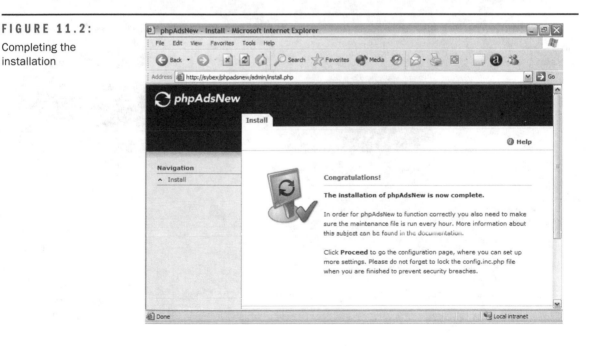

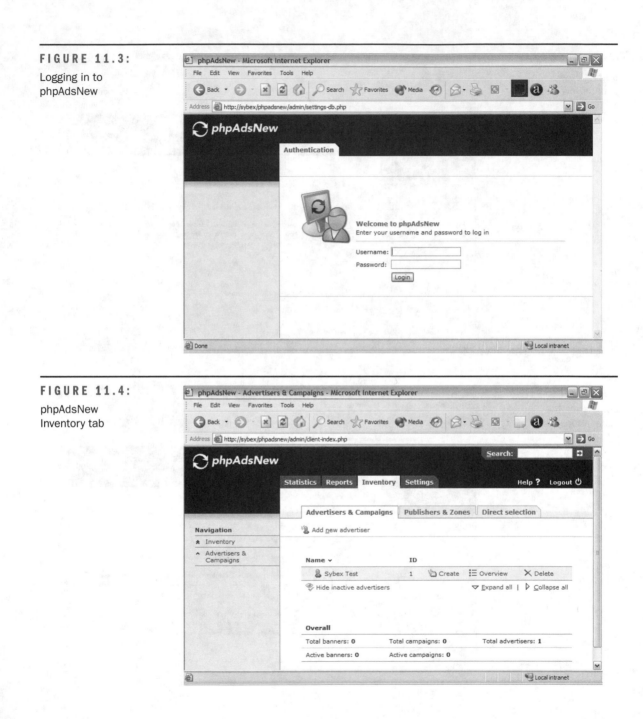

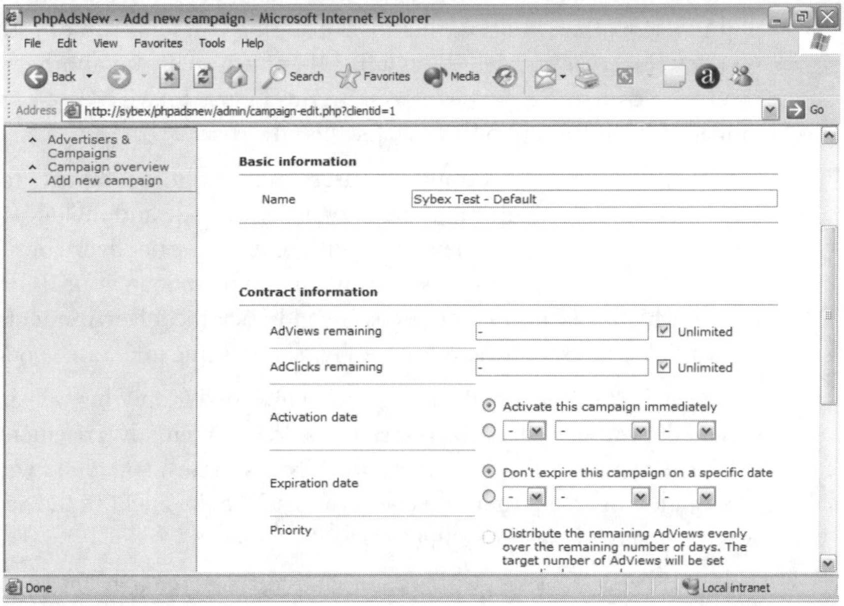

FIGURE 11.5:

phpAdsNew Add New
Campaign screen

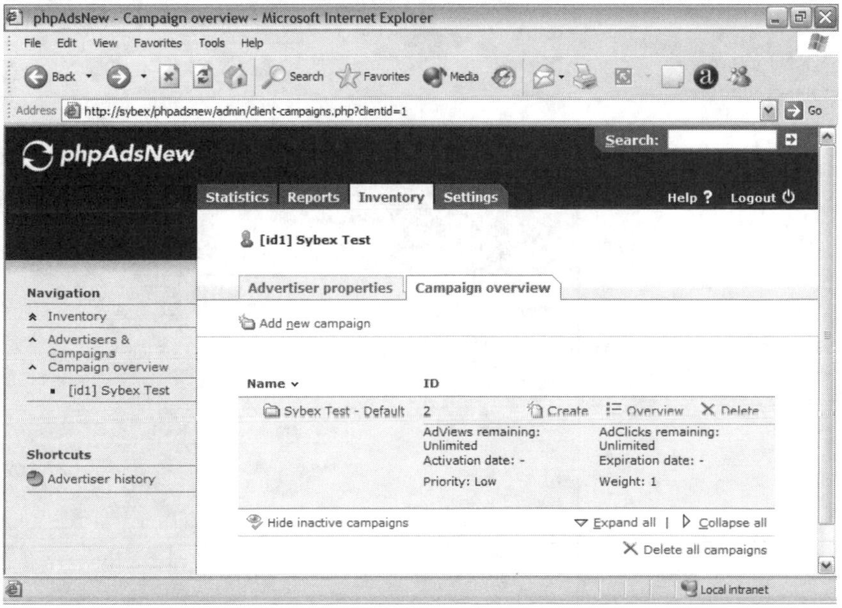

FIGURE 11.6:

phpAdsNew Campaign
Overview screen

After you have created an advertiser campaign, you can add banners to that campaign. phpAdsNew offers multiple methods of storing banners. You can store your banners locally on the web server, in MySQL as a BLOB, or externally on another website. Figure 11.7 shows the Banner Properties screen. In this figure, I have created a simple JPEG banner and uploaded it through phpAdsNew for this advertiser.

After you have created your advertisers and configured banners for them, you can use the phpAdsNew Direct Selection screen to generate code and include it on your website to display the banners. phpAdsNew offers different types of delivery options, including a local mode, which is a set of PHP code that you can include in your PHP scripts, or remote invocation, which uses JavaScript to display and track the advertisements. Figure 11.8 shows the Direct Selection screen, and Figure 11.9 shows some generated code.

Once you have obtained your code and included it on your website, your advertisements should display according to your settings. While your advertisements are displayed, phpAdsNew keeps track of how many impressions (times) and clicks you get for your banners. You can log in at any time and check the statistics by clicking the Statistics tab of the phpAdsNew control panel (see Figure 11.10).

phpAdsNew is packed with options and features you may find handy. To learn more about this awesome advertisement script, refer to the website at www.phpadsnew.com.

FIGURE 11.7:

phpAdsNew Banner Properties screen

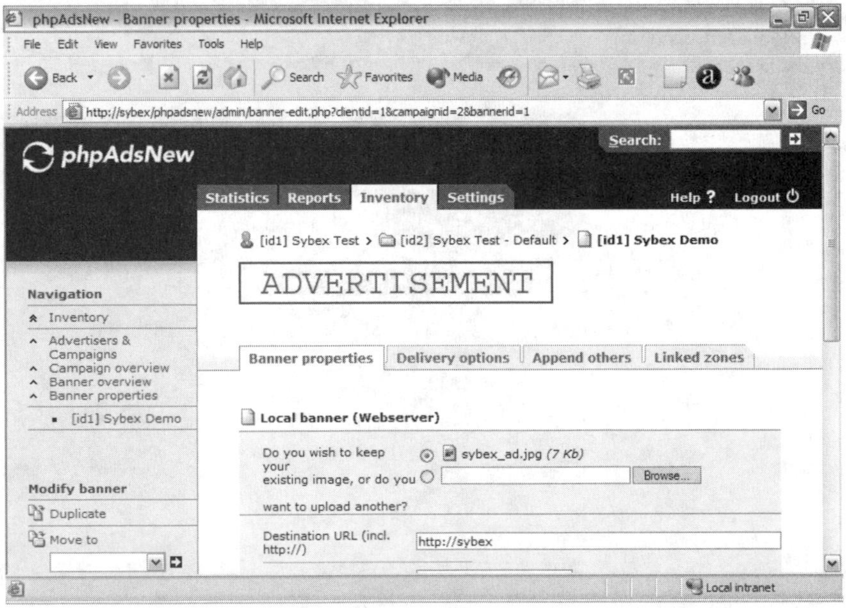

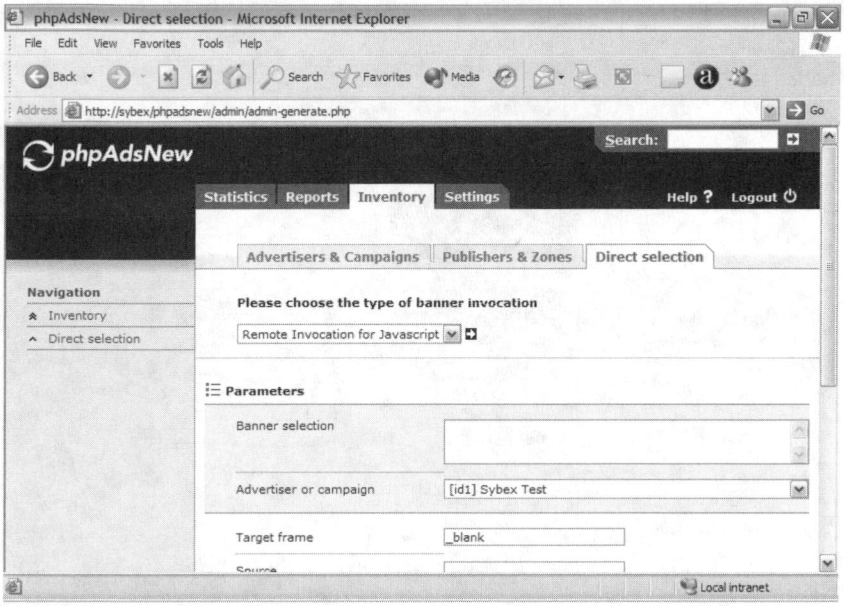

FIGURE 11.8: phpAdsNew Direct Selection screen

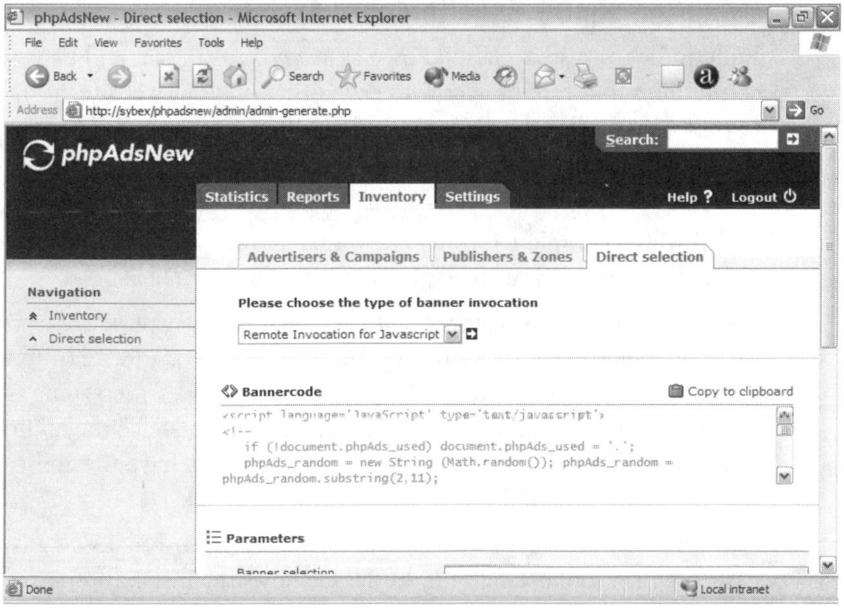

FIGURE 11.9: phpAdsNew-generated code

FIGURE 11.10:

phpAdsNew
Statistics tab

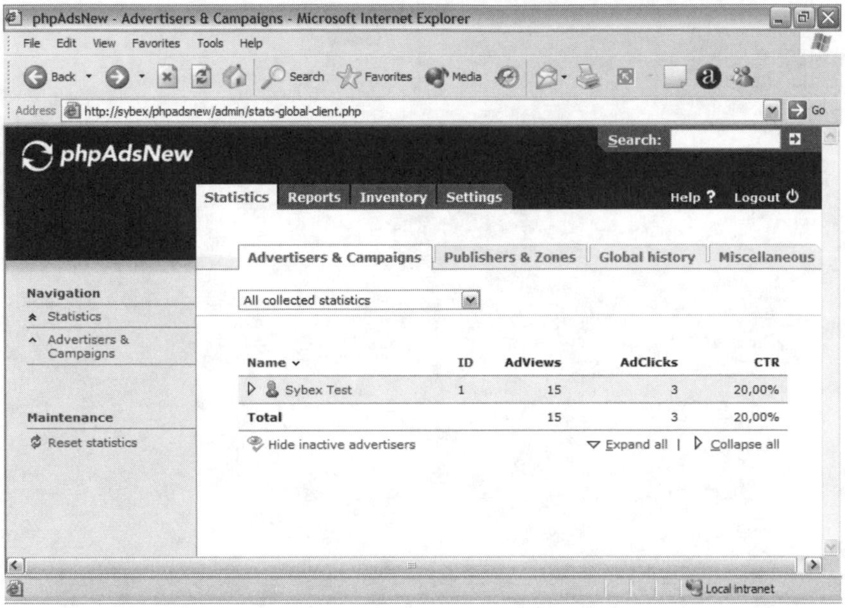

Using the phpBB Bulletin Board System

Bulletin board systems, also known as *forums*, are a great and easy way to build an online community that can interact with each other on your website. You can allow your members to post questions and get answers utilizing these systems. The great thing about the PHP community is that there are more than 20 different types of bulletin board systems you can use for free! This section covers my favorite bulletin board system.

phpBB is a complete forum system that allows online collaboration between community members. You can download phpBB for free at www.phpbb.com.

phpBB offers many features that will enhance the experience of your members. Some of these include topic watches (e-mail notifications), code formatting within the topics, smart Uniform Resource Locator (URL) conversion, private messaging, search engines, cookie features, and much more. For the administrator, you have the ability to administer forums, categories, users, posts, and more. Additionally, you have the ability to back up and restore the database through the swift administration panel.

phpBB also provides an excellent installation wizard that is as easy to use as a Windows-based application installer. Figure 11.11 shows the installation's welcome screen, and Figure 11.12 shows what it looks like after you have created a username.

After you complete your installation of phpBB, you will be taken to the administration panel where you can add forum categories, add forums, change your settings, back up and restore your database, and much more. Figure 11.13 shows the administrative panel.

The public side of phpBB displays a forum category index and statistics about the current database (see Figure 11.14).

When you are on the main forum page of phpBB, you can select a forum and post a topic inside (see Figure 11.15). Notice how I use the special formatting options inside the text box when posting a message.

After your message has been posted, it will appear in the forum to which you posted it (see Figure 11.16).

When you click your topic inside the forum, you will see a screen that shows you the topic text (see Figure 11.17). Notice the special formatting inside the text.

Figure 11.18 shows a customized and populated version of phpBB.

FIGURE 11.13:

phpBB administration panel

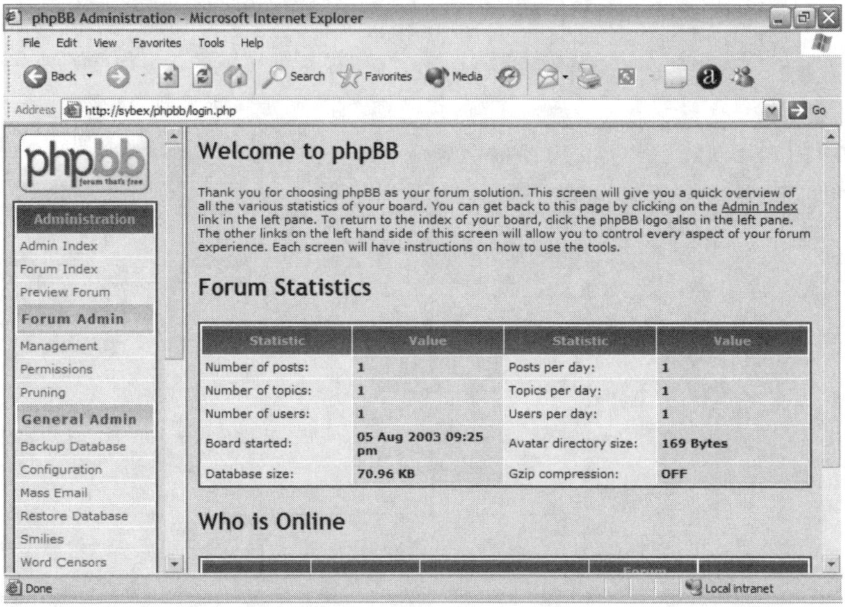

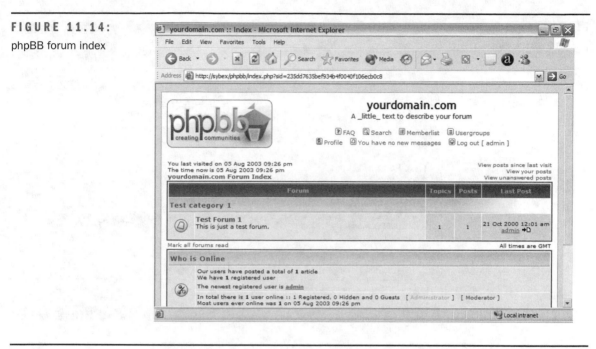

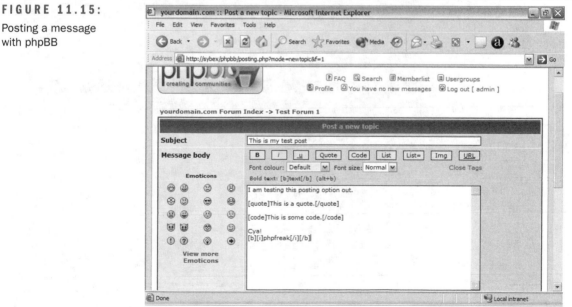

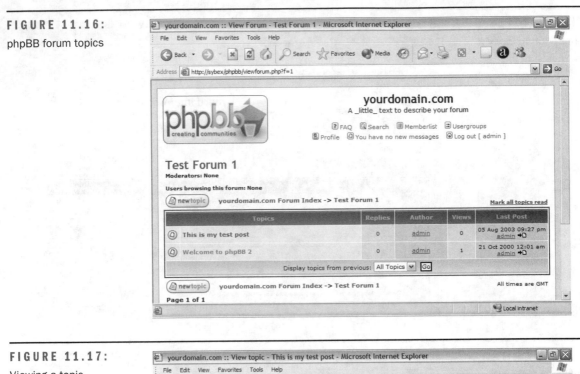

FIGURE 11.18:

Populated and customized version of phpBB

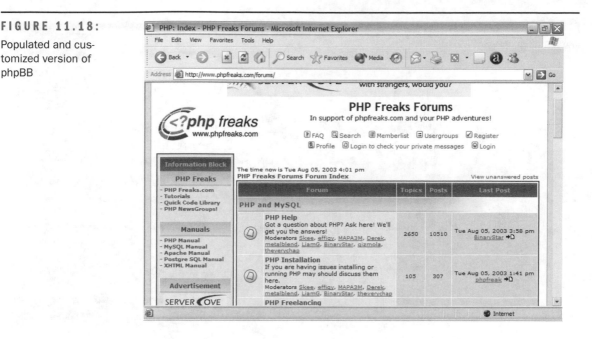

Using the PowerPhlogger Statistics Tracking Script

When keeping track of statistics is your game, PowerPhlogger could help you out. Power-Phlogger is a set of scripts designed to track your website's visits, clicks, referrers, keywords, and more. PowerPhlogger was also written to allow webmasters to run a hit counter service for other websites. It has a complete control panel for administrators and users to manage statistics. You can download PowerPhlogger at www.phpee.com.

PowerPhlogger tracks your website statistics by embedding a JavaScript code into your website's Hypertext Markup Language (HTML). The JavaScript code sends information to a receiving PHP script and stores that information in your database. Figure 11.19 shows the logs, Figure 11.20 shows the statistics, and Figure 11.21 shows the calendar and charts that you can generate.

FIGURE 11.19:

PowerPhlogger logs

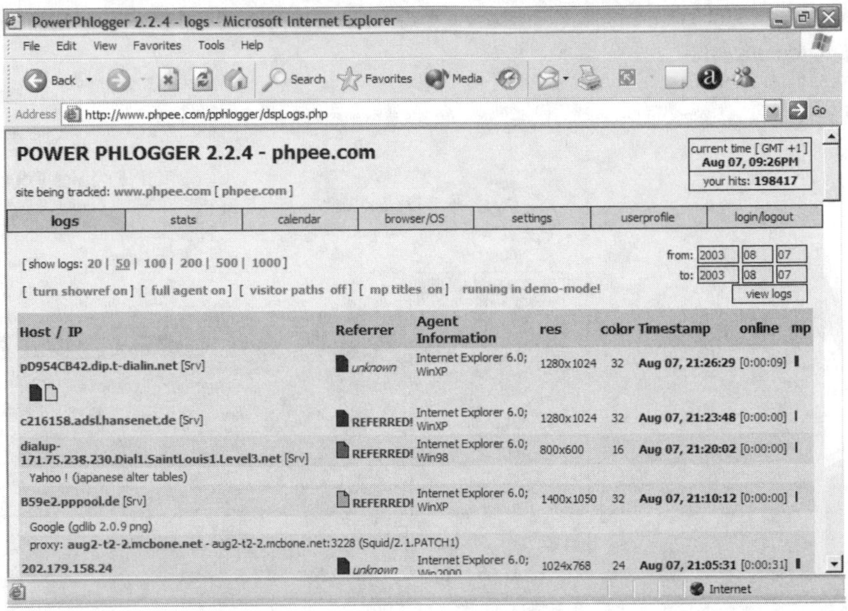

FIGURE 11.20:

PowerPhlogger statistics

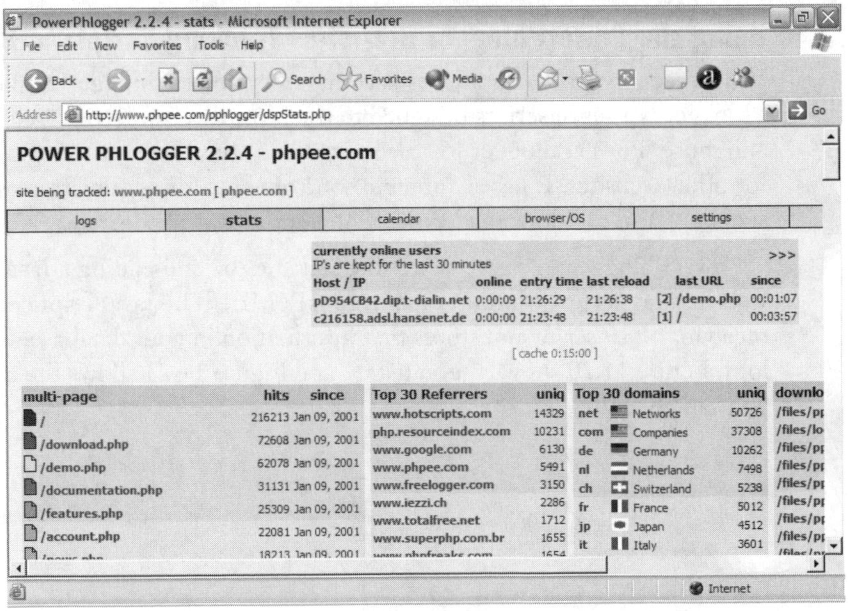

FIGURE 11.21:

PowerPhlogger calendar and charts

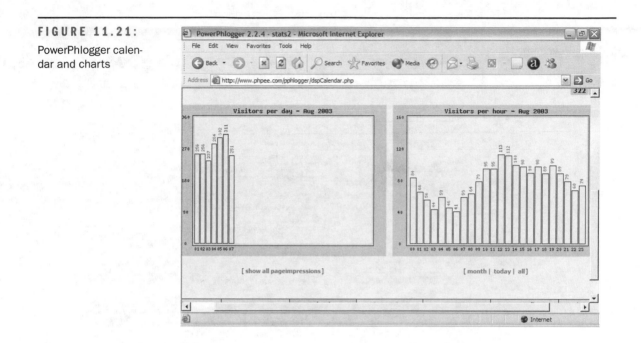

Using the MyNewsGroups News Client

If you have ever used a newsgroup before, you probably know that they contain a lot of information that is posted much like sending an e-mail. The information is stored on a server, and newsgroup users from around the world are able to respond to topics and communicate through the newsgroups. Well, there is a set of PHP scripts called MyNewsGroups for your website that allows you to retrieve and store these messages in your MySQL database. Once you have retrieved the messages, you can view, respond, and subscribe to them with the smooth web-based interface.

You can download MyNewsGroups at mynewsgroups.sourceforge.net for free.

Figure 11.22 shows the MyNewsGroups welcome screen, Figure 11.23 shows the newsgroup index screen, Figure 11.24 shows the topic list, and Figure 11.25 shows an individual post.

If you would like to view a customized and populated version of MyNewsGroups, visit www.phpfreaks.com/newsgroups.

FIGURE 11.22:

MyNewsGroups welcome screen

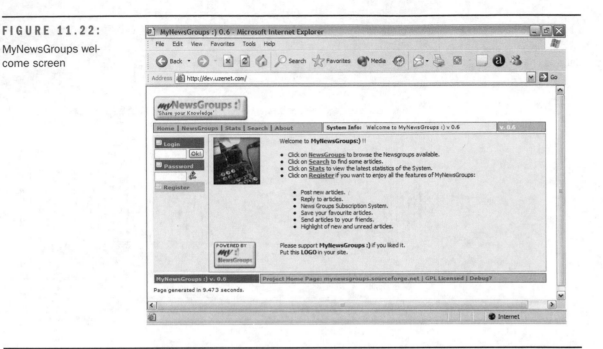

FIGURE 11.23:

MyNewsGroups newsgroup index screen

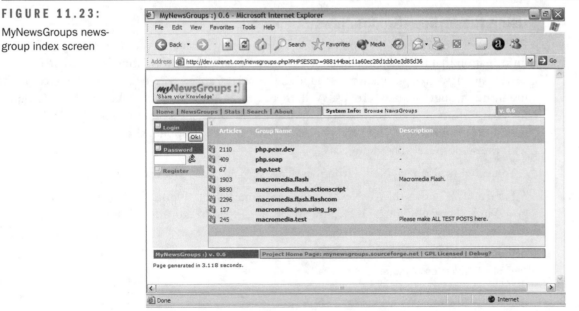

FIGURE 11.24:

MyNewsGroups news-group topic list

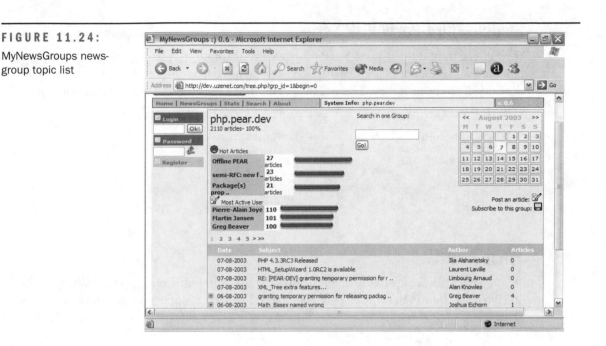

FIGURE 11.25:

MyNewsGroups post

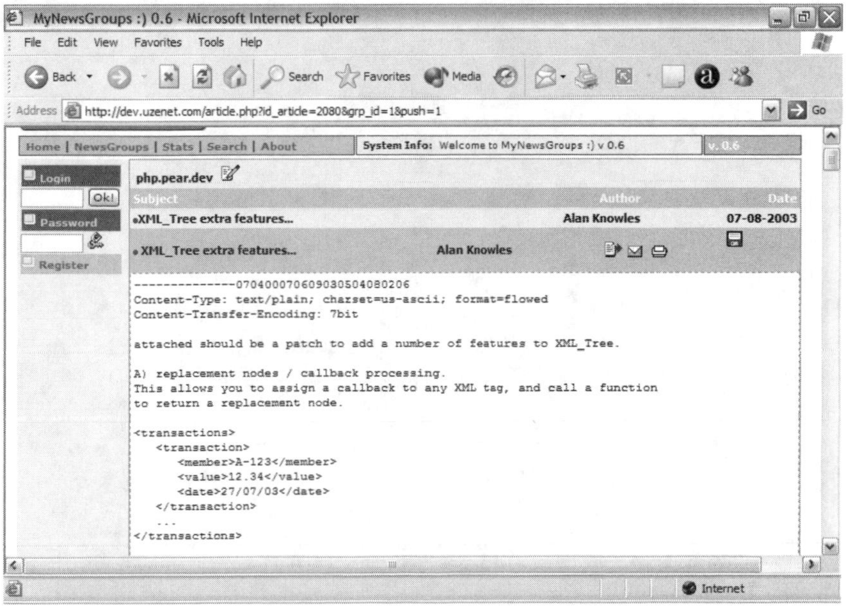

Finding Third-Party PHP Scripts

If you need to find third-party PHP scripts for your solutions, you can search for them in quite a few places. Script archive websites contain directories of scripts for you to browse, download, rate, and review. The following are a few I use when trying to find a solution:

PHP Freaks script archive	`www.phpfreaks.com/scripts.php`
HotScripts.com	`www.hotscripts.com`
freshmeat.net	`www.freshmeat.net`
SourceForge	`www.sourceforge.com`
Zend.com	`www.zend.com`

What's Next?

If you have made it this far through the book, you are probably ready to take advantage of all PHP has to offer. Where do you go from here? The next chapter presents some additional resources so you can jump in with both feet!

CHAPTER 12

Closing Statements

This book has presented practical examples of PHP and has discussed the major issues of working with PHP every day. Even though the book went into depth on some topics, it kept the topics as simple as possible, logical in nature, and practical to use. At the same time, you were able to get your hands dirty by digging in and developing the real-world examples.

This chapter provides resources where you can find more information about PHP.

It Gets in Your Blood

If you have enjoyed what you have learned so far, which I hope you have, you will find that PHP is an addictive language. It is easy to learn, forgiving, and constantly expanding. Most important, it provides you with excellent results when you do it right. With all of these factors, once you have tackled and achieved your first objective with PHP, you will find that it will get into your blood, and you will want to find something new to do with it next.

I work with PHP on a daily basis; in fact, it has become part of my thought process. I cannot tell you how many times I have looked at a problem related to website development and thought about how I could conquer it using PHP. I will be honest: There are not too many problems related to web development that I have not been able to solve with some quick research, development, and basic testing of how things flow together.

If you want to become a serious PHP developer, naturally you will have to constantly push yourself to learn everything you can about PHP. I found myself learning just enough to get myself by when I first started, and then I later found more efficient methods of reducing the amount of code and optimizing it at the same time. Now I look for the more complicated yet proper methods to create my scripts.

Regardless of how you approach developing with PHP, you should keep an open mind about the right ways to develop your project. In Chapter 2, "Planning Your Project," I gave you the methods I use to plan and implement a project. With these examples, you should have no problem making your real-life "Acme.com" websites.

Getting Support

Getting support for PHP is becoming easier every day. In fact, the communities that support PHP are growing as you read this book. You do not have to pay for support, and you will more than likely not have to wait long to get an answer to your question within these realms of information. The following sections provide some of the great support channels you can use if you get stumped when working with PHP.

PHP Support Sites

PHP support sites are spawning all over the place because of the rapidly growing popularity of this awesome language. I receive e-mails nearly every day from a new PHP help site webmaster who asks me to help publicize a new site, and I try to help the best I can. The following sites are the ones that I found most useful.

PHP Freaks.com

During the writing of this book, I have watched the community of members at PHP Freaks (www.phpfreaks.com) nearly double. Even though this is not the only source of help related to PHP on the Internet and although it is my personal site, a growing community of developers—of all levels—use the site to provide support for each other.

You can find the following resources on PHP Freaks to help you solve your problems:

Online manuals   The online manuals offer a plethora of official information for you to learn from:

- PHP manual: www.phpfreaks.com/phpmanual.php
- MySQL manual: www.phpfreaks.com/mysqlmanual.php
- Smarty manual: www.phpfreaks.com/smartymanual.php
- Apache manual: www.phpfreaks.com/apachemanual.php

More manuals are available; please see the site's Documentation section.

Quick code libraries   These libraries are examples of real scripts you can download to your hard drive from PHP users who have contributed their work. The code libraries are available at www.phpfreaks.com/quickcode.php.

Tutorials   I have a selective writing staff that writes tutorials on a regular basis. These tutorials walk you through the planning and developing process for PHP tasks. More than 100 tutorials are available at www.phpfreaks.com/tutorials.php.

Forums   This site offers an extremely active community of forums members that answer questions quickly and efficiently. Usually, if you post a sensible question, you will get an answer within a couple of hours. You can find the forums at www.phpfreaks.com/forums.

PHP newsgroups   More than 250,000 questions, answers, and announcements about PHP are available in this section. If you can't find your answer, try digging through this archive, and you'll probably find something of use. You can find the newsgroups at www.phpfreaks.com/newsgroups.

PHP reference library   This is a growing library of the most commonly used elements in PHP. Each reference should have a practical example of how to use the reference in a real PHP script. This is a great section for browsing and picking up tidbits. Browse the library at `www.phpfreaks.com/phpref.php`.

Much more is available on PHP Freaks.com. Stop by if you need help or if you come to the point where you can assist a struggling newbie.

PHP.net

PHP.net (not PHP.com) is the official resource for PHP. You can find support in the online manual and mailing lists. Additionally, the site has downloadable documentation and source files for PHP. You can find PHP.net at `www.php.net`.

PHP-Editors.com

PHP-Editors.com is a quickly growing website that has many similar topics as PHP Freaks.com. If you are looking for other resources to get support, give this site a shot. It has tutorials, code examples, forums, contests, and more. You can find PHP-Editors.com at `www.php-editors.com`.

SitePoint

SitePoint is another great resource for PHP and other web-related topics. SitePoint has an active community and offers some excellent affiliate programs for webmasters to earn money. Find it at `www.sitepoint.com`.

WeberDev.com

This is a large webmaster-related site that caters to PHP. There is a lot of information on this site; however, you just have to dig for it. Visit `www.weberdev.com`.

Zend Technologies

Zend Technologies provides the Zend engine that runs inside the core of PHP. Zend has advanced tutorials and even add-ons for PHP. Find the site at `www.zend.com`.

This list is a small portion of the sites where you will find PHP support. If you want to look for additional sites, just jump onto Google and search for *PHP Help*; you will definitely find some help.

PHP Manual

Regardless of the numerous websites available for getting PHP help, I can tell you the major source that helps me out the most: the PHP manual. The PHP manual is written very well, and you can learn practically everything you need to know. However, the PHP manual is not exactly written for everyone to understand, but once you have worked with it for a short period of time, you will be able to decipher the language in it and make it work to your advantage.

You have your choice when it comes to reading the PHP manual. You can either read it online or download it for offline reading. Additionally, you can print it and take it on the road with you. The copyrights within the manual allow you to reproduce it for your personal needs.

To obtain the official PHP manual, go to `www.php.net/download-docs.php`.

Live Support

Believe it or not, there is actually live support throughout the Internet for PHP. For example, I run a live Internet Relay Chat (IRC) channel that is usually staffed 24 hours a day by enthusiasts who love to help for free. To find my IRC channels, please visit `www.phpfreaks.com/ircchan.php`.

Additionally, you can usually access a channel by the identifier "#php" on most popular IRC servers.

If you need to learn more about IRC, go to `www.irc.org` and learn how to use it to get online with your preferred network.

WARNING   Beware of IRC channels. They are not the friendliest places to get help. Be sure you have done your research before asking questions on any IRC channel, or you may be treated with less than respect when receiving your answers. However, if you approach your question in a mature way and present yourself as having done your research, you should have no problems retrieving answers for your problems.

PHP Frequently Asked Questions (FAQ)

When a language gets as popular as PHP is, the same questions get asked repeatedly. Many resources are available that have documented these FAQs and the answers to them. The following are some sites that may help you along your journeys into PHP development:

Official PHP.net FAQ	`www.php.net/FAQ.php`
PHP Freaks.com PHP FAQ	`www.phpfreaks.com/faq.php`
ALT-PHP-FAQ	`www.alt-php-faq.org`
PHP.Faqts	`php.faqts.com`

Contributing to PHP

If you are one of the more skillful people who know how to develop the inner workings of something such as PHP, you can join the open-source development community and contribute to future releases of PHP. To learn more about contributing, see `www.php.net/cvs-php.php`.

Keep On Truckin'

Well, my fellow PHP developers, I hope I have shown you the light about PHP. Keep your head up, keep the wheels turning, and hone your skills to help spread PHP throughout the Internet. You and I both know it is a powerful language, but how powerful is it really? This is a question I will leave to you because my answer keeps getting reconfirmed every day I use it. I have no reason to switch to another language to make a dynamic website, and I hope you will feel the same way soon. So, keep on truckin' your way through as you learn the tricks to hone your skills as a powerful PHP developer. I will see you on the other side!

APPENDIX A

PHP Reference

Throughout this book, you have been utilizing numerous PHP features and functions. This appendix emphasizes the most common features of PHP; you can use it as a quick reference on a daily basis. This is not a complete reference to PHP, however. Please refer to the PHP manual for more in-depth PHP information.

Popular PHP Functions

To make the following sections easier to use, I list only the most popular PHP functions that I use in my PHP applications.

Array Functions

The following are array functions:

array_chunk (array input, int size [, bool preserve_keys])   Splits an array into chunks

array_count_values (array input)   Counts all the values of an array

array_diff (array array1, array array2 [, array ...])   Computes the difference of arrays

array_fill (int start_index, int num, mixed value)   Fills an array with values

array_flip (array trans)   Flips all the values of an array

array_key_exists (mixed key, array search)   Checks if the given key or index exists in the array

array_keys (array input [, mixed search_value])   Returns all the keys of an array

array_merge_recursive (array array1, array array2 [, array ...])   Merges two or more arrays recursively

array_merge (array array1, array array2 [, array ...])   Merges two or more arrays

array_pad (array input, int pad_size, mixed pad_value)   Pads array to the specified length with a value

array_pop (array array)   Pops the element off the end of array

array_push (array array, mixed var [, mixed ...])   Pushes one or more elements onto the end of array

array_rand (array input [, int num_req])   Picks one or more random entries out of an array

array_reverse (array array [, bool preserve_keys])   Returns an array with elements in reverse order

array_search (mixed needle, array haystack [, bool strict])   Searches the array for a given value and returns the corresponding key if successful

array_shift (array array)   Shifts an element off the beginning of array

array_slice (array array, int offset [, int length])   Extracts a slice of the array

array_splice (array input, int offset [, int length [, array replacement]])   Removes a portion of the array and replaces it with something else

array_sum (array array)   Calculates the sum of values in an array

array_unique (array array)   Removes duplicate values from an array

array_unshift (array array, mixed var [, mixed ...])   Prepends one or more elements to the beginning of array

array_values (array input)   Returns all the values of an array

array_walk (array array, string func [, mixed userdata])   Applies a user-defined function to each member of an array

array ([mixed ...])   Creates an array

arsort (array array [, int sort_flags])   Sorts an array in reverse order and maintains index association

asort (array array [, int sort_flags])   Sorts an array and maintains index association

compact (mixed varname [, mixed ...])   Creates array containing variables and their values

count (mixed var)   Counts elements in a variable

current (array array)   Returns the current element in an array

each (array array)   Returns the current key and value pair from an array and advances the array cursor

end (array array)   Sets the internal pointer of an array to its last element

extract (array var_array [, int extract_type [, string prefix]])   Imports variables into the current symbol table from an array

in_array (mixed needle, array haystack [, bool strict])   Returns TRUE if a value exists in an array

key (array array)   Fetches a key from an associative array

krsort (array array [, int sort_flags])   Sorts an array by key in reverse order

ksort (array array [, int sort_flags])   Sorts an array by key

list (mixed ...)   Assigns variables as if they were arrays

next (array array)   Advances the internal array pointer of an array

pos (array array)   Gets the current element from an array

prev (array array)   Rewinds the internal array pointer

range (mixed low, mixed high)   Creates an array containing a range of elements

reset (array array)   Sets the internal pointer of an array to its first element

rsort (array array [, int sort_flags])   Sorts an array in reverse order

shuffle (array array)   Shuffles an array

sizeof (mixed var)   Gets the number of elements in variable

sort (array array [, int sort_flags])   Sorts an array

uasort (array array, function cmp_function)   Sorts an array with a user-defined comparison function and maintains index association

uksort (array array, function cmp_function)   Sorts an array by keys using a user-defined comparison function

usort (array array, function cmp_function)   Sorts an array by values using a user-defined comparison function

Date and Time Functions

The following are date and time functions:

checkdate (int month, int day, int year)   Validates a Gregorian date

date (string format [, int timestamp])   Formats a local time/date (with the format rules in Table A.1):

```
echo date('H:j');
```

TABLE A.1: Date Function Format Rules and Output

Format Rule	Output
a	am or pm
A	AM or PM
B	Swatch Internet time
d	Day of the month, two digits with leading zeros; in other words, 01 to 31
D	Day of the week, textual, three letters; for example, Fri
F	Month, textual, long; for example, January
g	Hour, 12-hour format without leading zeros; in other words, 1 to 12
G	Hour, 24-hour format without leading zeros; in other words, 0 to 23
h	Hour, 12-hour format; in other words, 01 to 12
H	Hour, 24-hour format; in other words, 00 to 23
i	Minutes; in other words, 00 to 59
I	1 if Daylight Savings Time; 0 otherwise
j	Day of the month without leading zeros; in other words, 1 to 31
l	Boolean for whether it is a leap year; in other words, 0 or 1
m	Month; in other words, 01 to 12
M	Month, textual, three letters; for example, Jan
n	Month without leading zeros; in other words, 1 to 12
O	Difference to GMT in hours; for example, +0200
r	RFC 822 formatted date; for example, Thu, 21 Dec 2000 16:01:07 +0200
s	Seconds; in other words, 00 to 59
S	English ordinal suffix for the day of the month, two characters; in other words, st, nd, rd, or th
t	Number of days in the given month; in other words, 28 to 31
T	Time zone setting of this machine; for example, EST or MDT
U	Seconds since the Unix epoch (January 1 1970 00:00:00 GMT)
w	Day of the week, numeric; in other words, 0 (Sunday) to 6 (Saturday)
W	ISO-8601 week number of year, weeks starting on Monday
Y	Year, four digits; for example, 1999
y	Year, two digits; for example, 99
z	Day of the year; in other words, 0 to 365
Z	Time zone offset in seconds (in other words, -43200 to 43200). The offset for time zones west of UTC (which is Coordinated Universal Time) is always negative; for those east of UTC, it is always positive.

getdate ([int timestamp])   Gets date/time information

gettimeofday ( )   Gets the current time

gmdate (string format [, int timestamp])   Formats a Greenwich Mean Time (GMT)/UTC date/time

gmmktime (int hour, int minute, int second, int month, int day, int year [, int is_dst]) Gets a Unix timestamp for a GMT date

gmstrftime (string format [, int timestamp])   Formats a GMT/UTC time/date according to locale settings

localtime ([int timestamp [, bool is_associative]])   Gets the local time

microtime ( )   Returns current Unix timestamp with microseconds

mktime (int hour, int minute, int second, int month, int day, int year [, int is_dst]) Gets Unix timestamp for a date

strftime (string format [, int timestamp])   Formats a local time/date according to locale settings

strtotime (string time [, int now])   Parses just about any English textual date/time description into a Unix timestamp

time ( )   Returns current Unix timestamp

File Handling Functions

The following are file handling functions:

chgrp (string filename, mixed group)   Changes file group

chmod (string filename, int mode)   Changes file mode

chown (string filename, mixed user)   Changes file owner

copy (string source, string dest)   Copies file to a destination

delete (string file)   Deletes a file (an alias for unlink or unset)

fclose (int fp)   Closes an open file pointer

feof (int fp)   Tests for end of file on a file pointer

file (string filename [, int use_include_path])   Reads entire file into an array

filesize (string filename)   Gets file size

filetype (string filename)   Gets file type

fopen (string filename, string mode [, int use_include_path [, resource zcontext]])
Opens file or Uniform Resource Locator (URL)

fputs (int fp, string str [, int length])   Writes to a file pointer (also an alias to fwrite)

fread (int fp, int length)   Performs a binary-safe file read

fwrite (int fp, string string [, int length])   Performs a binary-safe file write

readfile (string filename [, int use_include_path])   Outputs a file

touch (string filename [, int time [, int atime]])   Sets access and modification time of file

unlink (string filename)   Deletes a file

MySQL Database Functions

For this appendix, I will show all example code with the resource identifier `$sql_result` for the query, and I will reference all MySQL connection identifiers as `$connection`. The following are MySQL database functions:

mysql_affected_rows ([resource link_identifier])   Returns the number of affected rows from the previous MySQL query:

```
print mysql_affected_rows($sql_result);
```

mysql_close ([resource link_identifier])   Closes a connection identified by the resource link identifier to a MySQL database:

```
mysql_close($connection);
```

NOTE   `mysql_close` will not close persistent connections from `mysql_pconnect`.

mysql_connect ([string server [, string username [, string password [, bool new_link [, int client_flags]]]]])   Creates a resource connection to the MySQL server to be used with MySQL queries in your PHP scripts. See also `mysql_pconnect`:

```
$connection = mysql_connect('localhost', 'usrename', 'password');
```

mysql_error ([resource link_identifier])   Returns an error message from the MySQL server if an error occurs:

```
print mysql_error();
```

mysql_escape_string (string unescaped_string)   Escapes a string for use with a
`mysql_query`. This function is useful for preventing SQL commands to be executed from
user input:

```
$string = mysql_escape_string($string);
// perform MySQL query with $string
```

mysql_fetch_array (resource result [, int result_type])   Creates an associative or
numeric array with the results from a MySQL query:

```
$sql_result = mysql_query("….");
while($row = mysql_fetch_array($sql_result)){
    echo $row['column_name'].'<br />';
}
```

mysql_fetch_assoc (resource result)   Equivalent to `mysql_fetch_array` when the
`MYSQL_ASSOC` argument is passed as to the `result_type`:

```
$sql_result = mysql_query("….");
while($row = mysql_fetch_assoc($sql_result)){
    echo $row['column_name'].'<br />';
}
```

mysql_fetch_row (resource result)   Returns an array that corresponds to the fetched
row or `FALSE` if there are no more rows.

mysql_fetch_object (resource result)   Returns the result of a MySQL query into an
object:

```
$sql_result = mysql_query("….");
while($row = mysql_fetch_object($sql_result)){
    echo $row->column_name.'<br />';
}
```

mysql_free_result (resource result)   Frees the memory associated with a resource:

```
$sql_result = mysql_query("….");
mysql_free_result($sql_result);
```

mysql_info ([resource link_identifier])   Returns detailed information about the last
MySQL query:

```
$sql_result = mysql_query("….");
print mysql_info($sql_result);
```

mysql_insert_id ([resource link_identifier])   Returns the ID of a row inserted with
an `AUTO_INCREMENT` column present:

```
$sql_result = mysql_query("INSERT INTO…");
print mysql_insert_id();
```

mysql_num_rows (resource result)   Returns the number of rows found in a query:

```
$sql_result = mysql_query("SELECT …");
print mysql_num_rows($sql_result);
```

mysql_pconnect ([string server [, string username [, string password [, int client_flags]]]])   Creates a persistent connection to a MySQL server:

```
$connection = mysql_pconnect('localhost', 'username', 'password');
```

mysql_query (string query [, resource link_identifier [, int result_mode]])
Performs a MySQL query based upon the arguments passed to the function:

```
$sql_result = mysql_query("SELECT * FROM mytable WHERE
something='some_value'");
```

mysql_result (resource result, int row [, mixed field])   Retrieves data from a MySQL query:

mysql_select_db (string database_name [, resource link_identifier])   Selects a database to be used by default in a mysql_query:

```
mysql_select_db($connection);
$sql_result = mysql_query("SELECT * FROM table…");
```

String Manipulation Functions

The following are string manipulation functions:

addslashes (string str)   Returns slashes before characters that need to be escaped in a string

ltrim (string str [, string charlist])   Removes white space from the beginning of a string

md5 (string str)   Calculates the md5 hash of a string

rtrim (string str [, string charlist])   Removes white space from the end of a string:

```
$string = rtrim($string);
```

trim (string str [, string charlist])   Removes white space from the beginning and the end of a string

stripslashes (string str [, string charlist])   Strips backslashes used to escape special characters in a string

str_replace (mixed search, mixed replace, mixed subject)   Replaces all occurrences of the search string with the replacement string

substr (string string, int start [, int length])   Returns a portion of a string defined by the starting point and length arguments passed to the function:

```
$string = substr($string, 3, 5);
```

System Configuration Functions

The following are system configuration functions:

error_reporting ([int level])   Sets which PHP errors are reported. The higher the integer you use for the range, the more verbose the error reporting output will be. For example, 0 turns error reporting off, and 2047 is full error reporting with warnings, notes, and so on.

getenv (string varname)   Gets the value of a system environment variable.

ini_set (string varname, string new_value)   Sets the value of a PHP configuration option.

phpinfo ([int what])   Outputs a lot of PHP information.

phpversion ( )   Gets the current PHP version.

putenv (string setting)   Sets the value of an environment variable.

set_time_limit (int seconds)   Limits the maximum execution time.

System Execution Functions

The following are system execution functions:

exec (string command [, array output [, int return_var]])   Executes an external program

passthru (string command [, int return_var])   Executes an external program and displays raw output

shell_exec (string cmd)   Executes commands via shell and returns complete output as string

system (string command [, int return_var])   Executes an external program and displays output

Text Formatting Functions

The following are text formatting functions:

htmlentities (string string [, int quote_styrrle [, string charset]])   Converts all applicable characters to Hypertext Markup Language (HTML) entities

htmlspecialchars (string string [, int quote_style [, string charset]])   Converts HTML entities to special characters

nl2br (string string)   Inserts HTML line breaks (<br />) before all new lines in a string

strtolower (string str)   Converts *all* characters in a string to lowercase

strtoupper (string str);   Converts *all* characters in a string to uppercase

ucwords (string str)   Converts the *first letter of each word* in a string to uppercase

ucfirst (string str)   Converts the *first letter of the string* to uppercase

Control Structures

Control structures allow you to compare values, perform loops, include files, and more. The following are control structures and simple examples:

if   Executes fragments of code if an expression returns TRUE:

```
$val1 = 1;
$val2 = 1;
if($val1 ==  $val2){
   // execute code
}
```

else   Used in conjunction with the IF control structure. ELSE will execute the code fragments within its control structure if the expression in the IF control structure returned FALSE:

```
$val1 = 1;
$val2 = 2;
if($val1 == $val2){
   // execute code
} else {
   // execute this code
}
```

elseif   Used in conjunction with the IF control structure. ELSEIF will execute the code fragments within its control structure if the expression in the IF control structure returned FALSE and the expression defined in the ELSEIF control structure returns TRUE:

```
$val1 = 1;
$val2 = 2;
if($val1 ==  $val2){
   // execute code
} elseif($val2 = 2) {
   // execute this code
}
```

for   This is a loop structure that accepts three expressions. The first expression is executed at the beginning of the loop, and the second expression is evaluated each time the loop is performed, which will cause the loop to occur again as long as this expression returns TRUE. The third expression is executed each time the loop occurs:

```
for($i = 0; $i < 50; $i++){
    echo "$i<br />";
}
```

foreach   A foreach is used on arrays. They are useful for extracting array elements one at a time and executing code each time the loop iterates:

```
$myarray = array("Dog", "Cat", "Cow");
foreach($myarray AS $animal){
    echo "$animal<br />";
}
```

break   Using break will stop a loop or a switch from going any further:

```
foreach($myarray AS $animal){
  echo "$animal<br />";
  if($animal == "Cat"){
    break;
  }
}
```

continue   Using continue allows you to skip over the current iteration in a loop structure and continue executing the loop:

```
foreach($myarray AS $animal){
  echo "$animal<br />";
  if($animal == "Cat"){
    continue;
  }
}
```

switch   A switch is similar to a series of IF statements made easy. However, you must evaluate the same variable or expression:

```
$val = "Dog";
switch($val){
  case "Cat":
    // this will not execute.
  break;
  case "Dog":
    echo "Woof Woof!";
  break;
  case "cow":
    // this will not execute.
  break;
}
```

return   Returns a value to the script:

```
if($val == "Dog"){
    return TRUE;
}
```

require   Includes and evaluates a specified file. Returns a fatal error and halts the script if the file is not found:

```
require("/path/to/file");
```

require_once   Same as `require`; however, if the resulting file has already been included, it will not be included again.

include   Includes and evaluates specified file. Returns a warning and allows the script to continue to execute if the specified file is not found:

```
include("/path/to/file");
```

include_once   Same as `include`; however, if the resulting file has already been included, it will not be included again.

PHP Superglobals

PHP superglobals are arrays of information that are available in all of your PHP scripts. They are used to store information about the type of request performed, about user sessions and cookies, and about global scope.

Superglobal: *$_SERVER*

PHP contains an array that contains headers, paths, script locations, remote IP addresses, and much more. This array is called $_SERVER, and it is a superglobal. In Table A.2, you will find a list of array keys that may be available on your server.

TABLE A.2: PHP $_SERVER Superglobal

Key	Output
PHP_SELF	The filename of the currently executing script, relative to the document root.
ARGV	Array of arguments passed to the script. When the script is run on the command line, this gives C-style access to the command line parameters. When called via the GET method, this will contain the query string.
ARGC	Contains the number of command line parameters passed to the script (if run on the command line).

Continued on next page

TABLE A.2 CONTINUED: PHP $_SERVER Superglobal

Key	Output
GATEWAY_INTERFACE	What revision of the CGI specification the server is using; in other words CGI/1.1.
SERVER_NAME	The name of the server host under which the current script is executing. If the script is running on a virtual host, this will be the value defined for that virtual host.
SERVER_SOFTWARE	Server identification string, given in the headers when responding to requests.
SERVER_PROTOCOL	Name and revision of the information protocol via which the page was requested; in other words, HTTP/1.0.
REQUEST_METHOD	Which request method was used to access the page; in other words, GET, HEAD, POST, or PUT.
QUERY_STRING	The query string, if any, via which the page was accessed.
DOCUMENT_ROOT	The document root directory under which the current script is executing, as defined in the servers configuration file.
HTTP_ACCEPT	Contents of the Accept: header from the current request, if there is one.
HTTP_ACCEPT_CHARSET	Contents of the Accept-Charset: header from the current request, if there is one. For example: iso-8859-1,*,utf-8.
HTTP_ACCEPT_ENCODING	Contents of the Accept-Encoding: header from the current request, if there is one. For example: gzip.
HTTP_ACCEPT_LANGUAGE	Contents of the Accept-Language: header from the current request, if there is one. For example: en.
HTTP_CONNECTION	Contents of the Connection: header from the current request, if there is one. For example: Keep-Alive.
HTTP_HOST	Contents of the Host: header from the current request, if there is one.
HTTP_REFERER	The address of the page (if any) that referred the user agent to the current page. This is set by the user agent. Not all user agents will set this, and some provide the ability to modify HTTP_REFERER as a feature. In short, it cannot really be trusted.
HTTP_USER_AGENT	Contents of the User_Agent: header from the current request, if there is one. This is a string denoting the user agent that is accessing the page. A typical example is Mozilla/4.5 [en] (X11; U; Linux 2.2.9 i586). Among other things, you can use this value with get_browser() to tailor your page's output to the capabilities of the user agent.
REMOTE_ADDR	The Internet Protocol (IP) address from which the user is viewing the current page.
REMOTE_PORT	The port being used on the user's machine to communicate with the web server.
SCRIPT_FILENAME	The absolute pathname of the currently executing script
SERVER_ADMIN	The value given to the SERVER_ADMIN (for Apache) directive in the web server configuration file. If the script is running on a virtual host, this will be the value defined for that virtual host.

Continued on next page

TABLE A.2 CONTINUED: PHP $_SERVER Superglobal

Key	Output
SERVER_PORT	The port on the server machine being used by the web server for communication. For default setups, this will be 80; using Secure Sockets Layer (SSL), for instance, will change this to whatever your defined secure HTTP port is, which is 443 by default.
SERVER_SIGNATURE	String containing the server version and virtual host name that are added to server-generated pages, if enabled.
PATH_TRANSLATED	File system–based path (not document root–based) to the current script, after the server has done any virtual-to-real mapping.
SCRIPT_NAME	Contains the current script's path. This is useful for pages that need to point to themselves.
REQUEST_URI	The Uniform Resource Indicator (URI) that was given in order to access this page; for instance, /index.html.
PHP_AUTH_USER	When running under Apache as module doing HTTP authentication, this variable is set to the username provided by the user.
PHP_AUTH_PW	When running under Apache as a module doing HTTP authentication, this variable is set to the password provided by the user.
PHP_AUTH_TYPE	When running under Apache as a module doing HTTP authentication, this variable is set to the authentication type.

Other Superglobals

Table A.3 lists PHP superglobals that contain arrays of information relative to the naming of the superglobal.

TABLE A.3: Other Superglobals

Superglobal	Description
$_COOKIE	Contains an array of HTTP cookie values
$_ENV	Contains variables imported into PHP's global namespace from the environment under which PHP is running
$_FILES	Contains an array of file information from files uploaded via the HTTP POST method
$_GET	Contains an array of HTTP GET values
$GLOBALS	Contains an array of information containing references to all variables that are currently defined in the global scope of the script
$_POST	Contains an array of HTTP POST values
$_REQUEST	Contains an array of $_GET, $_POST, $_COOKIE, and $_FILES information
$_SESSION	Session information is stored inside this superglobal array

Operators

Operators are used in nearly every application of PHP. They allow you to alter, assign, compare, and modify values of variables and strings.

Arithmetic Operators

Arithmetic operators allow you to perform calculations on variables. A simple usage is $var1 + $var2 = $var3. As such, $var3 would contain the sum values of $var1 and $var2. See Table A.4 for more arithmetic operators.

TABLE A.4: Arithmetic Operators

Operator	Purpose
+	Addition
-	Subtraction
*	Multiplication
/	Division
%	Modulus

Assignment Operators

Assignment operators allow you to set values to variables. A common example is $var = "my value". See Table A.5 for more assignment operators.

TABLE A.5: Assignment Operators

Operator	Purpose
=	Sets value
+=	Adds the current value of a variable to this value and makes the variable the sum of both
.=	Appends this value to the current string.

Comparison Operators

Comparison operators allow you to compare values together and will return a TRUE or FALSE Boolean depending on the result. A common example is to compare dog and cat together by using the == operator. The result would be FALSE because dog and cat are not the same. See Table A.6 for a list of comparison operators.

TABLE A.6: Comparison Operators

Operator	Purpose
==	Equal
===	Identical
!=	Not equal
<>	Not equal
<	Less than
>	Greater than
<=	Less than or equal to
>=	Greater than or equal to

Error Control Operator

By using an at (@) symbol before an expression, you can easily suppress any errors from being output by the script. A common example is `$fp =` `@fopen('/incorrect/path/to/file.txt', 'r');` If the `fopen` function fails, no error output will be displayed.

NOTE The @ operator works only on expressions. A simple rule of thumb is if you can take the value of something, you can prepend the @ operator to it. For instance, you can prepend it to variables, function and `include()` calls, constants, and so forth. You cannot prepend it to function or class definitions, conditional structures such as IF and `foreach`, and so forth.

Incrementing Operators

If you need to increment a value, you can use incrementing operators. A common example of how to increment the value of $var1 by 1 is `$var1 = 1; $var1++;`. Incrementing operators are commonly used in loops. See Table A.7 for a list of incrementing operators.

TABLE A.7: Incrementing Operators

Operator	Purpose
++$var	Pre-increment the value of $var by 1
$var++	Post-increment the value of $var by 1
--$var	Pre-decrement the value of $var by 1
$var--	Post-decrement the value of $var by 1

Logical Operators

Logical operators compare whether variables hold TRUE or FALSE values. A common example is if(!$val) { echo "$val is FALSE."; } See Table A.8 for a list of logical operators.

TABLE A.8: Logical Operators

Operator	Purpose
and	Returns TRUE if both values compared are TRUE
or	Returns TRUE if either one of the values compared are TRUE
xor	Returns TRUE if one of the values compared are TRUE, but not both
!	Returns TRUE if value compared is not TRUE
&&	Alias for and
||	Alias for or

String Operators

String operators assign values to and manipulate strings. A common example is $val = "mystring";. See Table A.9 for the string operators.

TABLE A.9: String Operators

Operator	Purpose
=	Assigns a string to a variable
.=	Appends a string to an existing variable
.	Appends a string to a string

APPENDIX B

MySQL Syntax Reference

This appendix contains the SQL statements and syntax used by MySQL version 4.0. For newer versions, you should see the documentation that comes with your distribution, or visit the MySQL site (www.mysql.com).

NOTE   Adapted from *Mastering MySQL 4* by Ian Gilfillan, ISBN 0-7821-4162-5

The convention used throughout the appendixes is as follows:

- Square brackets ([]) denote something optional. For example:

```
SELECT expression [FROM table_name [WHERE where_clause]]
```

indicates that the expression is compulsory (for example SELECT 42/10) and that the WHERE clause is optional but can only exist if the optional FROM table_name clause exists. (You can have SELECT * FROM t1, but not SELECT * WHERE f1>10, because the table_name clause is then missing.)

- A vertical bar (|) separates alternatives. For example:

```
CREATE [UNIQUE | FULLTEXT] INDEX
```

indicates that UNIQUE and FULLTEXT are separate options.

- Curly brackets ({}) indicate that one of the options must be chosen. For example:

```
CREATE TABLE ... [TYPE = {BDB | HEAP | ISAM | InnoDB | MERGE |
MRG_MYISAM | MYISAM }]
```

If the optional TYPE clause is specified, one of BDB, HEAP, ISAM, InnoDB, MERGE, MRG_MYISAM or MYISAM must be specified.

- Three dots (...) indicate that the option can be repeated. For example:

```
SELECT expression,...
```

indicates that the expression can be repeated (separated by a comma), as follows: SELECT f1,f2,f3.

ALTER

The ALTER syntax is as follows:

```
ALTER [IGNORE] TABLE table_name alter_specification [, alter_specification ...]
```

The alter_specification syntax can be any of the following:

```
ADD [COLUMN] create_definition [FIRST | AFTER field_name ]
ADD [COLUMN] (create_definition, create_definition,...)
ADD INDEX [index_name] (index_field_name,...)
ADD PRIMARY KEY (index_field_name,...)
ADD UNIQUE [index_name] (index_field_name,...)
```

```
ADD FULLTEXT [index_name] (index_field_name,...)
ADD [CONSTRAINT symbol] FOREIGN KEY index_name
 (index_field_name,...)[reference_definition]
ALTER [COLUMN] field_name {SET DEFAULT literal | DROP DEFAULT}
CHANGE [COLUMN] old_field_name create_definition [FIRST | AFTER field_name]
MODIFY [COLUMN] create_definition [FIRST | AFTER field_name]
DROP [COLUMN] field_name
DROP PRIMARY KEY
DROP INDEX index_name
DISABLE KEYS
ENABLE KEYS
RENAME [TO] new_table_name
ORDER BY field_name
    table_options
```

ALTER TABLE allows you to change the structure of an existing table. You can ADD columns, CHANGE column names and definitions, MODIFY (non-ANSI Oracle extension) column definitions without changing the name, DROP columns or indexes, RENAME tables, ORDER data, and DISABLE or ENABLE indexes.

A non-ANSI MySQL extension is that ALTER TABLE can contain multiple components (CHANGE, ADD, and so on) in one statement.

You need ALTER, INSERT, and CREATE permission on the table to use ALTER TABLE.

IGNORE (non-ANSI MySQL extension) causes MySQL to delete records that would result in a duplicate primary or unique key. Usually MySQL would simply abort and the ALTER would fail.

FIRST and ADD...AFTER allow you to specify where a field is to be added in the definition.

ANALYZE TABLE

```
ANALYZE TABLE table_name [,table_name...]
```

For MyISAM and BDB tables, this analyzes and stores the key distribution for the specified tables. It locks the table with a read lock for the operation's duration.

BACKUP TABLE

```
BACKUP TABLE table_name [,table_name...] TO 'path_name'
```

For MyISAM tables, this copies the data and data definition files to the backup directory.

BEGIN

```
BEGIN
```

The BEGIN statement begins a transaction, or set of statements. The transaction remains open until the next COMMIT or ROLLBACK statement.

CHECK TABLE

```
CHECK TABLE tbl_name[,tbl_name...] [option [option...]]
```

The option can be one of the following:

```
CHANGED
EXTENDED
FAST
MEDIUM
QUICK
```

This checks a MyISAM or InnoDB table for errors and, for MyISAM tables, updates the index statistics. The QUICK option doesn't scan the rows to check links. The FAST option only checks tables that weren't closed properly. The CHANGED option is the same as FAST, except that it also checks tables that have changed since the last check. The MEDIUM option verifies that deleted links are correct, and the EXTENDED option does a full index lookup for each key in each row.

COMMIT

```
COMMIT
```

The COMMIT statement ends a transaction, or set of statements, and flushes the results to disk.

CREATE

The CREATE syntax can be one of the following:

```
CREATE DATABASE [IF NOT EXISTS] database_name
CREATE [UNIQUE|FULLTEXT] INDEX index_name ON table_name
(field_name[(length)],... )
CREATE [TEMPORARY] TABLE [IF NOT EXISTS] table_name [(create_definition,...)]
 [table_options] [select_statement]
```

The create_definition syntax can be any of the following:

```
field_name type [NOT NULL | NULL] [DEFAULT default_value]
   [AUTO_INCREMENT] [PRIMARY KEY] [reference_definition]
```

```
PRIMARY KEY (index_field_name,...)
KEY [index_name] (index_field_name,...)
INDEX [index_name] (index_field_name,...)
UNIQUE [INDEX] [index_name] (index_field_name,...)
FULLTEXT [INDEX] [index_name] (index_field_name,...)
[CONSTRAINT symbol] FOREIGN KEY [index_name] (index_field_name,...)
 [reference_definition]
CHECK (expr)
```

The type syntax can be any of the following:

```
TINYINT[(length)] [UNSIGNED] [ZEROFILL]
SMALLINT[(length)] [UNSIGNED] [ZEROFILL]
MEDIUMINT[(length)] [UNSIGNED] [ZEROFILL]
INT[(length)] [UNSIGNED] [ZEROFILL]
INTEGER[(length)] [UNSIGNED] [ZEROFILL]
BIGINT[(length)] [UNSIGNED] [ZEROFILL]
REAL[(length,decimals)] [UNSIGNED] [ZEROFILL]
DOUBLE[(length,decimals)] [UNSIGNED] [ZEROFILL]
FLOAT[(length,decimals)] [UNSIGNED] [ZEROFILL]
DECIMAL(length,decimals) [UNSIGNED] [ZEROFILL]
NUMERIC(length,decimals) [UNSIGNED] [ZEROFILL]
CHAR(length) [BINARY]
VARCHAR(length) [BINARY]
DATE
TIME
TIMESTAMP
DATETIME
TINYBLOB
BLOB
MEDIUMBLOB
LONGBLOB
TINYTEXT
TEXT
MEDIUMTEXT
LONGTEXT
ENUM(value1,value2,value3,...)
SET(value1,value2,value3,...)
```

The index_field_name syntax is as follows:

```
field_name [(length)]
```

The reference_definition syntax is as follows:

```
REFERENCES table_name [(index_field_name,...)] [MATCH FULL
    | MATCH PARTIAL] [ON DELETE reference_option] [ON UPDATE reference_option]
```

The reference_option syntax is as follows:

```
RESTRICT | CASCADE | SET NULL | NO ACTION | SET DEFAULT
```

The `table_options` syntax can be any of the following:

```
TYPE = {BDB | HEAP | ISAM | InnoDB | MERGE | MRG_MYISAM | MYISAM }
AUTO_INCREMENT = #
AVG_ROW_LENGTH = #
CHECKSUM = {0 | 1}
COMMENT = "string"
MAX_ROWS = #
MIN_ROWS = #
PACK_KEYS = {0 | 1 | DEFAULT}
PASSWORD = "string"
DELAY_KEY_WRITE = {0 | 1}
ROW_FORMAT= { default | dynamic | fixed | compressed }
RAID_TYPE= {1 | STRIPED | RAID0 } RAID_CHUNKS=#  RAID_CHUNKSIZE=#
UNION = (table_name,[table_name...])
INSERT_METHOD= {NO | FIRST | LAST }
DATA DIRECTORY="absolute_path_to_directory"
INDEX DIRECTORY="absolute_path_to_directory"
```

The `select_statement` syntax can be as follows:

```
[IGNORE | REPLACE] SELECT ...  (select statement)
```

The CREATE statement creates a database, table, or index.

MySQL returns an error if the database or table already exists unless the IF NOT EXISTS clause is used.

TEMPORARY tables exist only for as long as the connection is active. You need to have CREATE TEMPORARY TABLES permission to do this.

Fields definitions default to NULL. Numeric fields default to 0 (except with AUTO_INCRE-MENT), and string fields default to an empty string (except for ENUM fields, which default to the first option). Date and time fields by default fill the field with zeros.

AUTO_INCREMENT fields begin counting at 1 by default and increment by one each time a new record is added.

KEY and INDEX are synonyms in this context.

A PRIMARY KEY specifies that the index cannot contain duplicates, and the field (or combination of fields) must be specified as NOT NULL.

UNIQUE specifies that the index cannot contain duplicates.

The RAID_TYPE option helps operating systems that cannot support large files to overcome the file size limit. The STRIPED option is the only one currently used. For MyISAM tables, this creates subdirectories inside the database directory, each containing a portion of the data file. The first 1024 * RAID_CHUNKSIZE bytes go into the first portion, the next 1024 * RAID_CHUNKSIZE bytes go into the next portion, and so on.

The DATA DIRECTORY="directory" and INDEX DIRECTORY="directory" options specify absolute paths to where the data or index file is stored.

The PACK_KEYS=1 option packs numeric fields in the index for MyISAM tables (as well as strings, which it does by default). This is only useful if you have indexes with many duplicate numbers.

Use AVG_ROW_LENGTH to give MySQL an idea of the average row length for the table. This is only useful where the table is large and has variable size records.

CHECKSUM can be set to 1 for MyISAM tables if you want to keep a checksum for all rows, which makes it easier to repair the table if it becomes corrupted but does slow down the table.

COMMENT is a comment of up to 60 characters for the table.

MAX_ROWS and MIN_ROWS specify the maximum and minimum rows, respectively, that you plan to store in the table.

PASSWORD encrypts the data definition file (.frm) with a password.

DELAY_KEY_WRITE causes MySQL to wait until a MyISAM table is closed before updating the index, which speeds up mass UPDATEs and INSERTs.

ROW_FORMAT specifies whether a MyISAM table should be FIXED or DYNAMIC.

DELETE

The DELETE syntax can be any of the following:

```
DELETE [LOW_PRIORITY | QUICK] FROM table_name [WHERE
    where_clause] [ORDER BY ...] [LIMIT rows]
DELETE [LOW_PRIORITY | QUICK] table_name[.*]
    [,table_name[.*] ...] FROM table-references [WHERE where_clause]
DELETE [LOW_PRIORITY | QUICK] FROM table[.*], [table[.*]
    ...] USING table-references [WHERE where_clause]
```

The DELETE statement deletes records from the table (or tables) that adhere to the where_clause (or all records if there is no clause).

The LOW PRIORITY keyword causes the DELETE to wait until no other clients are reading the table before processing it.

The QUICK keyword causes MySQL not to merge index leaves during the DELETE, which is sometimes quicker.

LIMIT determines the maximum number of records to be deleted.

The ORDER BY clause causes MySQL to remove records in a certain order (which is useful with a LIMIT clause).

DESC

DESC is a synonym for DESCRIBE.

DESCRIBE

```
DESCRIBE table_name {field_name | wildcard}
```

DESCRIBE returns the definition of the specified table and fields (the same as SHOW COLUMNS FROM table_name).

The wildcard can be part of the fieldname and can be a percentage sign (%), meaning a number of characters, or an underscore (_), meaning one character.

DO

The DO syntax is as follows:

```
DO expression, [expression, ...]
```

DO has the same effect as a SELECT, except that it does not return results (making it slightly faster).

DROP

The DROP syntax is as follows:

```
DROP DATABASE [IF EXISTS] database_name
DROP TABLE [IF EXISTS] table_name [, table_name,...] [RESTRICT | CASCADE]
DROP INDEX index_name ON table_name
```

DROP DATABASE removes the database and all its tables.

DROP TABLE removes the specified table.

DROP INDEX removes the specified index.

MySQL returns an error if the database doesn't exist, unless the IF EXISTS clause is used.

DROP TABLE automatically commits active transactions.

RESTRICT and CASCADE are not currently implemented.

EXPLAIN

```
EXPLAIN table_name
EXPLAIN select_query
```

The select_query is the same as specified in the SELECT description.

Using EXPLAIN with a table name is a synonym for DESCRIBE table_name. Using EXPLAIN with a query provides feedback about how the query will be executed, which is useful for optimizing the query and making the best use of the associated indexes.

FLUSH

```
FLUSH flush_option [,flush_option] ...
```

The flush_option can be any of the following:

```
DES_KEY_FILE
HOSTS
LOGS
QUERY CACHE
PRIVILEGES
STATUS
TABLES
[TABLE | TABLES] table_name [,table_name...]
TABLES WITH READ LOCK
USER_RESOURCES
```

Flushing the DES_KEY_FILE reloads the DES keys. With the HOSTS option, the host's cache is emptied (which you use after changing IP addresses, for example). Flushing the LOGS closes and reopens log files and increments the binary log. Flushing the QUERY CACHE defragments the query cache. Flushing the PRIVILEGES reloads the permission tables from the *mysql* database. Flushing the STATUS resets the status variables. Flushing the TABLES is the same as flushing the QUERY CACHE, but it also closes all open tables. You can specify only certain tables to flush. You can place a READ LOCK on the tables, which is useful for locking a group of tables for backup purposes. Flushing the USER_RESOURCES resets user resources (used for limiting queries, connections, and updates per hour).

GRANT

```
GRANT privilege_type [(field_list)] [, privilege_type [(field_list)]
...] ON {table_name | * | *.* | database_name.*} TO user_name
[IDENTIFIED BY [PASSWORD] 'password'] [, user_name [IDENTIFIED BY
'password'] ...] [REQUIRE NONE | [{SSL| X509}] [CIPHER cipher [AND]]
[ISSUER issuer [AND]] [SUBJECT subject]] [WITH [GRANT OPTION |
MAX_QUERIES_PER_HOUR # | MAX_UPDATES_PER_HOUR # |
MAX_CONNECTIONS_PER_HOUR #]]
```

GRANT gives a privilege of a particular kind of permission to a user. Table A.1 describes the available privileges.

TABLE A.1: Privileges

Privilege	Description
ALL	Grants all the basic permissions.
ALL PRIVILEGES	Same as ALL.
ALTER	Permission to change the structure of a table (an ALTER statement), excluding indexes.
CREATE	Permission to create databases and tables, excluding indexes.
CREATE TEMPORARY TABLES	Permission to create a temporary table.
DELETE	Permission to remove records from a table (a DELETE statement).
DROP	Permission to drop databases or tables, excluding indexes.
EXECUTE	Permission to run stored procedures (scheduled for MySQL 5).
FILE	Permission to read and write files on the server (for LOAD DATA INFILE or SELECT INTO OUTFILE statements). Any files that the mysql user can read are readable.
INDEX	Permission to create, modify, or drop indexes.
INSERT	Permission to add new records to the table (an INSERT statement).
LOCK TABLES	Permission to lock a table for which the user has SELECT permission.
PROCESS	Permission to view the current MySQL processes or kill MySQL processes (for SHOW PROCESSLIST or KILL SQL statements).
REFERENCES	Not currently used by MySQL and provided for ANSI SQL compatibility (it applies to the use of foreign keys).
RELOAD	Permission to reload the database (a FLUSH statement or a reload, refresh, or flush issued from mysqladmin).
REPLICATION CLIENT	Permission to ask about the replication slaves and masters.
SHOW DATABASES	Permission to see all databases.
SELECT	Permission to return data from a table (a SELECT statement).
SHUTDOWN	Permission to shut down the server.
SUPER	Permission to connect even if the maximum number of connections is reached and perform the CHANGE MASTER, KILL thread, mysqladmin debug, PURGE MASTER LOGS, and SET GLOBAL commands.
UPDATE	Permission to modify data in a table (an UPDATE statement).
USAGE	Permission to connect to the server and perform statements available to all (for early versions of MySQL 4 this included SHOW DATABASES).

INSERT

The INSERT syntax can be any of the following:

```
INSERT [LOW_PRIORITY | DELAYED] [IGNORE] [INTO] table_name
    [(field_name,...)] VALUES ((expression | DEFAULT),...),(...),...
```

```
INSERT [LOW_PRIORITY | DELAYED] [IGNORE] [INTO] table_name
    [(field_name,...)] SELECT ...
INSERT [LOW_PRIORITY | DELAYED] [IGNORE] [INTO] table_name
    SET field_name=(expression | DEFAULT), ...
INSERT [LOW_PRIORITY] [IGNORE] [INTO] table_name [(field list)] SELECT ...
```

INSERT adds new rows into a table. Without the initial field list, fields are assumed to be in the same order as they were defined, and a value must exist for each field. Any columns not explicitly set are set to their default value.

The LOW PRIORITY keyword causes the INSERT to wait until no other clients are reading the table before processing it. With the DELAYED keyword, MySQL frees the client but waits to perform the INSERT.

IGNORE causes MySQL to ignore INSERTs that would causes a duplicate primary key or unique key, instead of aborting the INSERT.

INSERT...SELECT allows you to INSERT into a table from existing rows in one or more tables.

JOIN

MySQL accepts any of the following join syntaxes:

```
table_name, table_name
table_name [CROSS] JOIN table_name
table_name INNER JOIN table_name condition
table_name STRAIGHT_JOIN table_name
table_name LEFT [OUTER] JOIN table_name condition
table_name LEFT [OUTER] JOIN table_name
table_name NATURAL [LEFT [OUTER]] JOIN table_name
table_name LEFT OUTER JOIN table_name ON conditional_expr
table_name RIGHT [OUTER] JOIN table_name condition
table_name RIGHT [OUTER] JOIN table_name
table_name NATURAL [RIGHT [OUTER]] JOIN table_name
```

The table can simply be a table_name, use an alias (with AS), or specify or ignore indexes (with USE/IGNORE index).

The condition syntax is as follows:

```
ON conditional_expr | USING (field_names)
```

The conditional_expr is the same as what can exist in a WHERE clause.

KILL

```
KILL thread_id
```

Kills the specified thread. You can use SHOW PROCESSLIST to identify thread IDs. The SUPER privilege is required to kill processes not owned by the current connection.

LOAD DATA INFILE

The LOAD DATA INFILE syntax is as follows:

```
LOAD DATA [LOW_PRIORITY | CONCURRENT] [LOCAL] INFILE
    'file.txt' [REPLACE | IGNORE] INTO TABLE table_name
    [FIELDS [TERMINATED BY '\t'] [[OPTIONALLY] ENCLOSED BY
    ''] [ESCAPED BY '\\' ]] [LINES TERMINATED BY '\n']
    [IGNORE number LINES] [(field_name,...)]
```

LOAD DATA reads data from a text file and adds it to a table. This is a quicker way of adding high volumes of data than using INSERT.

The LOCAL keyword indicates that the file is on the client machine; otherwise the file is assumed to be on the database server. LOCAL will not work if the server was started with the --local-infile=0 option, or the client has not been enabled to support it.

Files on the server must be readable by all or be in the database directory, and you need the FILE permission to use LOAD DATA for a file on the server.

On the server, the file is assumed to be in the database directory of the current database if no path is given. If the path is relative, it is assumed to be from the data directory. Absolute paths can also be used.

The LOW PRIORITY keyword causes the LOAD DATA to wait until no other clients are reading the table before processing it.

The CONCURRENT keyword allows other threads to access a MyISAM table at the same time as the LOAD DATA is executing (which will slow down the LOAD DATA).

The REPLACE keyword causes MySQL to delete and replace an existing record if it has the same primary or unique key as the record being added. IGNORE causes MySQL to continue with the next record.

If a FIELDS clause is specified, at least one of TERMINATED BY, [OPTIONALLY] ENCLOSED BY, and ESCAPED BY is required. If no FIELDS clause is specified, the defaults are assumed to be FIELDS TERMINATED BY '\t' ENCLOSED BY '' ESCAPED BY '\\'. These clauses specify the character at the end of a field (default tab), surrounding a field (default nothing), and the escape character (default backslash). Be careful when using Windows paths to escape the path correctly.

Without a LINES clause, the default is assumed to be LINES TERMINATED BY '\n'. This specifies the character at the end of a record (default newline).

The IGNORE number LINES option ignores a number of lines at the top of the file (which is useful when the file contains a header).

LOAD DATA INFILE is the complement of SELECT...INTO INFILE.

LOCK TABLES

```
LOCK TABLES table_name [AS alias] {READ | [READ LOCAL] | [LOW_PRIORITY]
WRITE} [,table_name {READ | [LOW_PRIORITY] WRITE} ...]
```

LOCK TABLES places a lock on the specified tables. The lock can be READ (other connections cannot write, only read), READ LOCAL (same as READ except that writes from other connections that do not conflict are allowed), or WRITE (which blocks reading or writing from other connections). If the WRITE lock is LOW PRIORITY, READ locks are placed first. Usually WRITE locks have higher priority.

OPTIMIZE

```
OPTIMIZE TABLE table_name [,table_name]...
```

For MyISAM tables, this sorts the index, updates the statistics, and defragments the data file.

For BDB tables, this is the same as ANALYZE TABLE.

This locks the table for the duration of the operation (which can take some time).

RENAME

The RENAME syntax is as follows:

```
RENAME TABLE table_name TO new_table_name[, table_name2 TO new_table_name2,...]
```

RENAME allows you to give a table (or list of tables) a new name. You can also move a table to a new database by specifying database_name.table_name, as long as the database is on the same disk.

You need the ALTER and DROP permissions on the old table, and the CREATE and INSERT permissions on the new table.

REPAIR TABLE

```
REPAIR TABLE table_name [,table_name...] [EXTENDED] [QUICK] [USE_FRM]
```

Repairs a corrupted MyISAM table. With the QUICK option, only the index tree is repaired. With EXTENDED, the index is re-created row by row. With USE_FRM, the index is repaired based upon the data definition file (for when the index is missing or totally corrupted).

REPLACE

The REPLACE syntax can be one of the following:

```
REPLACE [LOW_PRIORITY | DELAYED] [INTO] table_name
    [(field_name,...)] VALUES (expression,...),(...),...
REPLACE [LOW_PRIORITY | DELAYED] [INTO] table_name [(field_name,...)] SELECT ...
REPLACE [LOW_PRIORITY | DELAYED] [INTO] table_name SET
    field_name=expression, field_name=expression, ...
```

REPLACE is exactly like INSERT, except that when MySQL encounters a record with a primary or unique key that already exists, it will be deleted and replaced.

RESET

```
RESET reset_option [,reset_option] ...
```

The reset_option can be any of the following:

```
MASTER
QUERY CACHE
SLAVE
```

RESET MASTER deletes all binary logs and empties the binary log index. RESET SLAVE resets a slave's position for replicating with a master. RESET QUERY CACHE empties the query cache.

RESTORE TABLE

```
RESTORE TABLE table_name [,table_name...] FROM 'path'
```

Restores a table backed up with BACKUP TABLE. It will not overwrite existing tables.

REVOKE

```
REVOKE privilege_type [(field_list)] [,privilege_type [(field_list)]
    ...] ON {table_name | * | *.* | database_name.*} FROM user_name
    [, user_name ...]
```

Removes previously granted privileges from the specified users. The privilege_type can be one of the privileges listed for GRANT.

ROLLBACK

```
ROLLBACK
```

The ROLLBACK statement ends a transaction, or set of statements, and undoes any statements in that transaction.

SELECT

The SELECT syntax is as follows:

```
SELECT [STRAIGHT_JOIN] [SQL_SMALL_RESULT] [SQL_BIG_RESULT]
    [SQL_BUFFER_RESULT] [SQL_CACHE | SQL_NO_CACHE]
    [SQL_CALC_FOUND_ROWS] [HIGH_PRIORITY] [DISTINCT |
    DISTINCTROW | ALL] expression, ... [INTO {OUTFILE |
    DUMPFILE} 'file_name' export_options]
[FROM table_names
[WHERE where_clause] [GROUP BY {unsigned_integer |
    field_name | formula} [ASC | DESC], ... [HAVING
    where_definition] [ORDER BY {unsigned_integer |
    field_name | formula} [ASC | DESC], ...] [LIMIT
    [offset,] rows] [PROCEDURE procedure_name] [FOR UPDATE | LOCK IN SHARE MODE]]
```

SELECT statements return data from tables. The `expression` is usually a list of fields (with a function if required), but it can also be a computation or function that has nothing to do with the table fields. For example:

```
SELECT VERSION();
```

or as follows:

```
SELECT 42/10;
```

Fields can be specified as `field_name`, `table_name.field_name`, or `database_name.table_name.field_name`. The longer forms are required if there's any ambiguity.

The expression can also be given an alias with the keyword AS. For example:

```
SELECT 22/7 AS about_pi
```

The expression can be used elsewhere in the statement (but not in the WHERE clause, which is usually determined first).

The `table_names` clause is a comma-separated list of tables used in the query. You can also use an alias for a table name. For example:

```
SELECT watts FROM wind_water_solar_power AS n;
```

You can also control MySQL's index usage if you're unhappy with MySQL's choice (which you can view by using EXPLAIN) with the USE INDEX and IGNORE INDEX clauses after the table name. The syntax is as follows:

```
table_name [[AS] alias] [USE INDEX (indexlist)] [IGNORE INDEX (indexlist)]
```

The ORDER BY clause orders the returned results in ascending (default, or using the ASC keyword) or descending (DESC) order. It does not have to use items explicitly returned in the expression. For example:

```
SELECT team_name FROM results ORDER BY points DESC
```

The WHERE clause consists of conditions (which can contain functions) that a row needs to adhere to in order to be returned:

```
SELECT team_name FROM results WHERE points > 10
```

GROUP BY groups output rows, which are useful when you use an aggregate function. Two non-ANSI MySQL extensions that you can use are ASC or DESC with GROUP BY, and you can also use fields in the expression that are not mentioned in the GROUP BY clauses. For example:

```
SELECT team_name, team_address, SUM(points) FROM teams GROUP BY team_name DESC
```

The HAVING clause is also a condition, but it is applied last so it can apply to items you group by. For example:

```
SELECT team_name, SUM(points) FROM teams GROUP BY team_name HAVING SUM(points) > 20
```

Do not use it to replace the WHERE clause, as it will slow down queries.

DISTINCT and its synonym, DISTINCTROW, indicate that the returned row should be unique. ALL (the default) returns all rows, unique or not.

HIGH_PRIORITY (non-ANSI MySQL extension) gives the SELECT a higher priority than any updates.

SQL_BIG_RESULT and SQL_SMALL_RESULT (non-ANSI MySQL extensions) assist the MySQL optimizer by letting it know whether the results returned will be large or small before it begins processing. Both are used with GROUP BY and DISTINCT clauses and usually result in MySQL using a temporary table for greater speed.

SQL_BUFFER_RESULT (non-ANSI MySQL extension) causes MySQL to place the result in a temporary table.

LIMIT takes one or two arguments to limit the number of rows returned. If one argument, it's the maximum number of rows to return; if two, the first is the offset and the second the maximum number of rows to return. If the second argument is –1, MySQL will return all rows from the specified offset until the end. For example, to return from row 2 to the end, use this:

```
SELECT f1 FROM t1 LIMIT 1,-1
```

SQL_CALC_FOUND_ROWS causes MySQL to calculate the number of rows that would have been returned if no LIMIT clause existed. This figure can be returned with the SELECT FOUND_ROWS() function.

SQL_CACHE gets MySQL to store the result in the query cache, and SQL_NO_CACHE causes the result not to be cached. Both are non-ANSI MySQL extensions.

STRAIGHT_JOIN (non-ANSI MySQL extension) causes the optimizer to join the tables in the order in they are listed in the FROM clause, which can speed up queries if tables are joined non-optimally (use EXPLAIN to check this).

SELECT...INTO OUTFILE 'file_name' writes the results into a new file (readable by everyone) on the server. You need to FILE permission to use this. It is the complement of LOAD DATA INFILE, and it uses the same options.

Using INTO DUMPFILE causes MySQL to write one row into the file, without any column or line terminations and without any escaping.

With InnoDB and BDB tables, the FOR UPDATE clause write locks the rows.

SET

```
SET [GLOBAL | SESSION] variable_name=expression, [[GLOBAL | SESSION |
  LOCAL ] variable_name=expression...]
```

SET allows you to set variable values. SESSION (or LOCAL, a synonym) is the default, and it sets the value for the duration of the current connection. GLOBAL requires the SUPER privilege, and it sets the variable for all new connections until the server restarts. You still need to set it in the configuration file for an option to remain active after the server restarts. You can find the full list of variable names using SHOW VARIABLES. Table A.2 describes the variables that you set in a nonstandard way.

TABLE A.2: Variables You Set in a Nonstandard Way

Syntax	Description
AUTOCOMMIT= 0 | 1	When set (1), MySQL automatically COMMITs statements unless you wrap them in BEGIN and COMMIT statements. MySQL also automatically COMMITs all open transactions when you set AUTOCOMMIT.
BIG_TABLES = 0 | 1	When set (1), all temporary tables are stored on disk instead of in memory. This makes temporary tables slower, but it prevents the problem of running out of memory. The default is 0.
INSERT_ID = #	Sets the AUTO_INCREMENT value (so the next INSERT statement that uses an AUTO_INCREMENT field will use this value).
LAST_INSERT_ID = #	Sets the value returned from the next LAST_INSERT_ID( ) function.
LOW_PRIORITY_UPDATES = 0 | 1	When set (1), all update statements (INSERT, UPDATE, DELETE, LOCK TABLE WRITE) wait for there to be no pending reads (SELECT, LOCK TABLE READ) on the table they're accessing.

Continued on next page

TABLE A.2 CONTINUED: Variables You Set in a Nonstandard Way

Syntax	Description
MAX_JOIN_SIZE = value | DEFAULT	By setting a maximum size in rows, you can prevent MySQL from running queries that may not be making proper use of indexes or that may have the potential to slow the server down when run in bulk or at peak times. Setting this to anything but DEFAULT resets SQL_BIG_SELECTS. If SQL_BIG_SELECTS is set, then MAX_JOIN_SIZE is ignored. If the query is already cached, MySQL will ignore this limit and return the results.
QUERY_CACHE_TYPE = OFF | ON | DEMAND	Sets the query cache setting for the thread.
QUERY_CACHE_TYPE = 0 | 1 | 2	Sets the query cache setting for the thread.
SQL_AUTO_IS_NULL = 0 | 1	If set (1, the default), then the last inserted row for an AUTO_INCREMENT can be found with WHERE auto_increment_column IS NULL. This is used by Microsoft Access and other programs connecting through ODBC.
SQL_BIG_SELECTS = 0 | 1	If set (1, the default), then MySQL allows large queries. If not set (0), then MySQL will not allow queries where it will have to examine more than max_join_size rows. This is useful to avoid running accidental or malicious queries that could bring the server down.
SQL_BUFFER_RESULT = 0 | 1	If set (1), MySQL places query results into a temporary table (in some cases speeding up performance by releasing table locks earlier).
SQL_LOG_OFF = 0 | 1	If set (1), MySQL will not log for the client (this is not the update log). The SUPER permission is required.
SQL_LOG_UPDATE = 0 | 1	If not set (0), MySQL will not use the update log for the client. This requires the SUPER permission.
SQL_QUOTE_SHOW_CREATE = 0 | 1	If set (1, the default), MySQL will quote table and column names.
SQL_SAFE_UPDATES = 0 | 1	If set (1), MySQL will not perform UPDATE or DELETE statements that don't use either an index or a LIMIT clause, which helps prevent unpleasant accidents.
SQL_SELECT_LIMIT = value | DEFAULT	Sets the maximum number of records (default unlimited) that can be returned with a SELECT statement. LIMIT takes precedence over this.
TIMESTAMP = timestamp_value | DEFAULT	Sets the time for the client. This can be used to get the original timestamp when using the update log to restore rows. The timestamp_value is a Unix epoch timestamp.

The old SET OPTION syntax is now deprecated, so you should not use it anymore.

SET TRANSACTION

```
SET [GLOBAL | SESSION] TRANSACTION ISOLATION LEVEL { READ UNCOMMITTED
  | READ COMMITTED | REPEATABLE READ | SERIALIZABLE }
```

Sets the transaction isolation level. By default it will be for the next transaction only, unless the SESSION or GLOBAL keywords are used (which set the level for all transactions on the current connection or for all transactions on all new connections, respectively).

SHOW

The SHOW syntax can be any of the following:

```
SHOW DATABASES [LIKE expression]
SHOW [OPEN] TABLES [FROM database_name] [LIKE expression]
SHOW [FULL] COLUMNS FROM table_name [FROM database_name] [LIKE expression]
SHOW INDEX FROM table_name [FROM database_name]
SHOW TABLE STATUS [FROM database_name] [LIKE expression]
SHOW STATUS [LIKE expression]
SHOW VARIABLES [LIKE expression]
SHOW LOGS
SHOW [FULL] PROCESSLIST
SHOW GRANTS FOR user
SHOW CREATE TABLE table_name
SHOW MASTER STATUS
SHOW MASTER LOGS
SHOW SLAVE STATUS
```

SHOW lists the databases, tables, or columns, or it provides status information about the server.

The wildcard can be part of the database, table, or fieldname, and it can be a percentage sign (%), meaning a number of characters, or an underscore (_), meaning one character.

TRUNCATE

```
TRUNCATE TABLE table_name
```

The TRUNCATE statement deletes all records from a table. It is quicker than the equivalent DELETE statement as it DROPs and CREATEs the table. It is not transaction safe (so will return an error if there are any active transactions or locks).

UNION

```
SELECT ... UNION [ALL] SELECT ... [UNION SELECT ...]
```

Union combines many results into one.

Without the ALL keyword, rows are unique.

UNLOCK TABLES

```
UNLOCK TABLES
```

Releases all locks held by the current connection.

UPDATE

```
UPDATE [LOW_PRIORITY] [IGNORE] table_name SET field_name1=expression1 [,
field_name2=expression2, ...] [WHERE where_clause] [LIMIT #]
```

The UPDATE statement updates the contents of existing rows in the database.

The SET clause specifies which fields to update and what the new values are to be.

The where_clause gives conditions the row must adhere to in order to be updated.

IGNORE causes MySQL to ignore UPDATEs that would cause a duplicate primary key or unique key, instead of aborting the UPDATE.

The LOW PRIORITY keyword causes the UPDATE to wait until no other clients are reading the table before processing it.

The expression can take the current value of a field; for example, to add 5 to all employees' commissions, you could use the following:

```
UPDATE employee SET commission=commission+5;
```

LIMIT determines the maximum number of records to be updated.

USE

```
USE database_name
```

Changes the current active database to the specified database.

Index

Note to the Reader: Page numbers in **bold** indicate the principle discussion of a topic or the definition of a term. Page numbers in *italic* indicate illustrations.

TELL US WHAT YOU THINK!

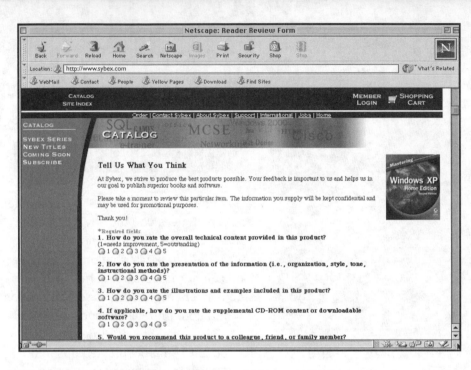

Your feedback is critical to our efforts to provide you with the best books and software on the market. Tell us what you think about the products you've purchased. It's simple:

1. Go to the Sybex website.
2. Find your book by typing the ISBN or title into the Search field.
3. Click on the book title when it appears.
4. Click **Submit a Review.**
5. Fill out the questionnaire and comments.
6. Click **Submit.**

With your feedback, we can continue to publish the highest quality computer books and software products that today's busy IT professionals deserve.

www.sybex.com

SYBEX Inc. • 1151 Marina Village Parkway, Alameda, CA 94501 • 510-523-8233

SYBEX®